Andrew Newcombe

The Advancement of International Law

Any talk of the advancement of international law presupposes that two objections are met. The first is the 'realist' objection which, observing the state of international relations today, claims that when it comes down to the important things in international life—war and peace, and more generally power politics among states—no real advancement has been made: international society remains a society of sovereign states deciding matters with regard solely to their own best interests and with international law all too often being no more than a thin cloak cast over the precept that 'might is right'. Against this excessive scepticism stands excessive optimism: international law is supposedly making giant strides forward thanks especially to the tremendous mass of soft law generated by international organisations over the past 60 years and more. By incautiously mixing all manner of customs, treaties, resolutions and recommendations, a picture of international law is painted that has little to do with the 'real world'.

The essays collected in this book are arranged into three sections. The first purports to show from the specific example of international investment law that the past half century has seen the invention of two genuinely new techniques in positive law: state contracts and transnational arbitration without privity. This is 'advancement' in international law not because the techniques are 'good' in themselves (one may well think them 'bad') but because they have introduced legal possibilities into international law that did not exist heretofore. The second section examines the theoretical consequences of those new legal techniques and especially the way they affect the theory of the state. The third widens the field of view and asks whether European law has surpassed international law in a move towards federalism or whether it represents a step forward for international law.

These reflections make for a clearer theoretical understanding of what constitutes true advancement in international law. Such an understanding should give pause both to those who argue that hardly any progress has been made, and to those who are overly fanciful about progress.

Volume 3 in the series French Studies in International Law

French Studies in International Law

General Editor: Emmanuelle Jouannet (Sorbonne Law School)

French Studies in International Law is a unique new series which aims to bring to the attention of an English-speaking audience the most important modern works by leading French and French-speaking scholars of international law. The books which appear in this series were selected by Professor Emmanuelle Jouannet of the University of Paris 1 (Sorbonne Law School). French Studies in International Law is a books collection of the CERDIN Paris 1 Sorbonne Law School (The Centre of Studies and Research on International Law). The CERDIN is the largest French research centre in international law comprising 11 professors, 3 lecturers, 21 research professors and researchers and 188 PhD students. CERDIN follows an active policy of collective work around several fields of key research, including: general international law, law of the United Nations, international dispute, international economic and finance law (in particular WTO), international human rights law, theory, philosophy and history of international law and foreign doctrines, international air space law and the law of the sea.

Volume 1: Ordering Pluralism: A Conceptual Framework for Understanding the Transnational Legal World   *Mireille Delmas-Marty translated by Naomi Norberg*

Volume 2: International Law, Power, Security and Justice: Essays on International Law and Relations   *Serge Sur*

Volume 3: The Advancement of International Law   *Charles Leben*

The Advancement
of International Law

Charles Leben

·HART·
PUBLISHING

OXFORD AND PORTLAND, OREGON
2010

Published in the United Kingdom by Hart Publishing Ltd
16C Worcester Place, Oxford, OX1 2JW
Telephone: +44 (0)1865 517530
Fax: +44 (0)1865 510710
E-mail: mail@hartpub.co.uk
Website: http://www.hartpub.co.uk

Published in North America (US and Canada) by
Hart Publishing
c/o International Specialized Book Services
920 NE 58th Avenue, Suite 300
Portland, OR 97213-3786
USA
Tel: +1 503 287 3093 or toll-free: (1) 800 944 6190
Fax: +1 503 280 8832
E-mail: orders@isbs.com
Website: http://www.isbs.com

British Library Cataloguing in Publication Data
Data Available

ISBN: 978-1-84113-278-5

Typeset by Hope Services, Abingdon
Printed and bound in Great Britain by
TJ International Ltd, Padstow, Cornwall

Series Editor's Preface

This series aims to contribute to the dissemination in English of the works of the most eminent international law scholars writing in French. Because these works have not yet been published in English, this scholarship is inaccessible to a great number of potential readers who, due to the language barrier, cannot become acquainted with or discuss it. This is highly regrettable, as it limits the debate on international law to works in English—the *lingua franca* of our contemporary world—and thus primarily to Anglophone scholars.

The publication of these works in English, therefore, seeks to create the conditions for genuine debate among Francophone and Anglophone international law scholars across the globe, a debate that should ideally be based on the work of both. *Learning* of the others' theories through translation is in fact the first essential step towards *acknowledging* the contributions and differences of each. Knowledge and acknowledgement lead to understanding the core of irreducibility, as well as truth, in each legal culture's international law doctrine, its traditions and distinct ideas, as well as each author's way of thinking. They should make it possible to avoid the all-too-frequent misunderstanding of each other's position on international law that results from simple ignorance of each other's work. Between the Francophone and Anglophone worlds, the rule is still too often mutual, even courteous indifference or ignorance, dialogue the exception.

Emmanuelle Jouannet
Professor, University of Paris I (Sorbonne Law School)

Contents

Part 1

Advances in the Techniques of International Law

1

State Contracts and their Governing Law: A Reappraisal*

O F ALL THE areas in which the advancement of international law has been implicated in the second half of the
twentieth century, that of contracts made by states with private persons is probably among those where the stakes have been
highest and the controversies keenest. This type of legal relation has
raised at least two separate but not unrelated categories of question:
that of sovereign immunities of states and that of what are called
'state contracts'. As regards the former, the substantial change undergone by international law with the abandonment of the theory of
absolute immunity and the adoption of the theory of restrictive
immunity is barely contested any longer and questions arise only over
quite how to determine restrictive immunity.[1] As regards state contracts, however, and despite considerable doctrine on the matter, no
general consensus seems to have arisen yet, as evidenced by the
polemics that very regularly recur.[2] These polemics are invariably

* First published as 'Retour sur la notion de contrat d'Etat et sur le droit applicable à celui-ci' in *Mélanges offerts au Professeur H Thierry: l'évolution du droit international* (Paris, Pedone, 1998) 247. For a more detailed study of my position see
C Leben, 'La théorie du contrat d'Etat et l'évolution du droit international des
investissements' (2003) 302 *Recueil des Cours de l'Académie de Droit International de
La Haye* 197.

[1] For a recent review see M Cosnard, *La soumission des Etats aux tribunaux internes
face à la théorie des immunités de l'Etat* (Paris, Pedone, 1996); I Pingel-Lenuzza, *Les
immunités des Etats en droit international* (Brussels, Bruylant, 1998); G Hafner,
M Kohen and S Breau (eds), *La pratique des Etats concernant les immunités* (Leiden,
Martinus Nijhoff, 2006); H Fox, *The Law of State Immunity* 2nd edn (Oxford, Oxford
University Press, 2008).
[2] See one of the last papers of RB Lillich, 'The Law Governing Disputes under
Economic Development Agreements: Reexamining the Concept of Internationalization'
in RB Lillich and CN Brower (eds), *International Arbitration in the 21st Century: Towards
'Judicialization' and Uniformity?* (New York, Transnational Publishers, 1994). Lillich
discusses Bowett's refusal to accept that international law and the general principles of
law apply to economic development agreements. See DW Bowett, 'State Contracts with

about the relevance of public international law for governing this type of contract. It appears obvious that the divergences arise essentially from contemporary conceptions of public international law, of its subjects, of the relations it may govern and of its possible advancement compared—on all these points—with a 'classical' scheme of things that prevailed at least until about 1945. It is a distinctly 'evolutionist' view that is to be defended here, both because my basic postulate is that international law, like all law, is liable to evolve with the 'society' of which it is an expression, and because it can be shown that observation of international practice confirms this position.

This study, as said, does not concern a new domain but on the contrary a domain that has been very largely explored by legal scholarship and especially French-language doctrine.[3] Within this doctrine, studies by Prosper Weil and Pierre Mayer stand as major mileposts in understanding state contracts.[4] But far from being convergent, their work is contradictory. And yet, without engaging here in any scholastic endeavour to harmonise the opinions of

Aliens: Contemporary Developments on Compensation for Termination or Breach' (1998) 59 *British Yearbook of International Law* 49, 51; AFM Maniruzzaman, 'State Contracts in Contemporary International Law: Monist versus Dualist Theories' (2001) 12(2) *European Journal of International Law* 309; M Kamto, 'La notion de contrat d'Etat: une contribution au débat' (2003) 3 *Revue de l'Arbitrage* 719. At the time of writing I was unaware of L Lankarani El-Zein, *Les contrats d'Etat à l'épreuve du droit international* (Brussels, Bruylant, éd de l'Université de Bruxelles, 2001). It contains pointed criticism of doctrinal positions seeking to connect state contracts with the international legal order.

[3] For a general bibliography on state contracts see NG Ziadé, 'References on State Contracts' (1988) 1 *ICSID Review* 212; E Paasivirta, *Participation of States in International Contracts and Arbitral Disputes* (Helsinki, Lakimiesliiton Kustannus, 1990); C Leben, 'La théorie du contrat d'Etat et l'évolution du droit international des investissements' (2003) 302 *Recueil des Cours de l'Académie de Droit International de La Haye* 197.

[4] See especially P Weil, 'Problèmes relatifs aux contrats passés entre un Etat et un particulier' (1969-III) 128 *Recueil des Cours de l'Académie de Droit International de La Haye* 101; 'Droit international et contrats d'Etat' in *Mélanges offerts à Paul Reuter* (Paris, Pedone, 1981) 549; 'Les clauses de stabilisation ou d'intangibilité insérées dans les accords de développement économique' in *Mélanges offerts à Charles Rousseau* (Paris, Pedone, 1974) 301; 'Principes généraux de droit et contrats d'Etat' in *Le droit des relations économiques internationales. Etudes offertes à B Goldman* (Paris, Litec, 1982) 387 and his general lectures at The Hague, 'Le droit international en quête de son identité' (1992-VI) 237 *Recueil des Cours de l'Académie de Droit International de La Haye* 95. Weil's writings on state contracts, except for his 1969 Hague lectures, are now collected in *Ecrits de droit international* (Paris, PUF, 2000) 303. For P Mayer see 'Le mythe de "l'ordre juridique de base" (ou *Grundlegung)*' in *Le droit des relations économiques internationales. Etudes offertes à Berthold Goldman* (Paris, Litec, 1982) 199 and 'La neutralisation du pouvoir normatif de l'Etat' (1986) *Journal du Droit International* 5.

'authorities', it does seem possible to defend the idea that while Mayer's definition of state contracts provides the sound conceptual basis the theory was lacking, it does not exclude but on the contrary supports Weil's major insight that such contracts are subject to public international law. State contracts can be conceived of as new acts of international law. Such a claim encounters strong objections that will require close examination.

State Contracts As New International Legal Acts

State Contracts as Contracts entered into by States as Subjects of Public International Law

Growing Awareness of a New Category of Contracts made by States

The first observation to be made concerns the historical dimension of the subject. One cannot understand the hesitations of arbitration tribunals and the diversity of scholarly opinion unless one allows for the fact that what was to be apprehended was a phenomenon that had appeared in a recent period and that was evolving at the same time as the first attempts were being made to systematise it. The main arbitration awards that commentators were to reason on in diagnosing the emergence of a new category of contracts related to petroleum concessions in the Middle East in the 1950s and 1960s.[5] The Libyan awards (*Texaco, Liamco, BP*) and the *Aminoil* award, not to mention the expansion of ICSID (International Centre for Settlement of Investment Disputes) case law, came after the first major studies by Mann, Verdross, Wengler and Weil, to name but a few.[6] Those commentators, then, were working on a still unestablished practice and with minimum historical hindsight relative to a phenomenon that was only just emerging.

[5] See G Cohen-Jonathan, *Les concessions en droit international public* (Thèse, University of Paris, 1966).

[6] FA Mann, *Studies in International Law* (Oxford, Clarendon Press, 1973); A Verdross, 'Quasi-international Agreements and International Economic Transactions' (1964) 18 *Yearbook of World Affairs* 230; W Wengler, 'Les accords entre Etats et entreprises étrangères sont-ils des traités de droit international?' (1972) *Revue Générale de Droit International Public* 313. On the Libyan awards see B Stern, 'Trois arbitrages, un même problème, trois solutions: les nationalisations pétrolières libyennes devant l'arbitrage international' (1980) *Revue de l'Arbitrage* 3. On the Aminoil award see P Kahn, 'Contrats d'Etat et nationalisation. Les apports de la sentence arbitrale du 24 mars 1982' (1982) 109 *Journal du Droit International* 844; G Burdeau, 'Droit international et contrats d'Etats. La sentence *Aminoil c. Koweit* du 24 mars 1982' (1982) *Annuaire Français de Droit International* 454.

While almost all of these scholars agreed that the practice seemed to produce contracts that were neither municipal law contracts nor international contracts such as are made between private persons, just as they acknowledged that not all contracts between a state and a private person are 'state contracts', they were hard pressed to come up with a purely legal criterion by which to differentiate 'state contracts' and ordinary contracts entered into by states.

State contracts are generally investment contracts, but that does not mean that all investment contracts are state contracts nor that there cannot be any state contracts outside the domain of investments (Mann's paper, which seems to have coined the expression 'state contracts' was about international borrowing).[7] These contracts contain references, in various forms, to public international law. But Mann had defended the idea as early as 1944 that the principle of freedom of contract allowed a state and a private person to adopt public international law as the law applicable to a contract between them on the basis of private international law techniques.[8]

State contracts have also been spoken of as economic development agreements,[9] without there being any objective criterion to say when and under what circumstances an investment contract could be so characterised. Even the most elaborate conception of the notion, that provided by Weil, does not escape this criticism. In distinguishing *internationalised contracts*—whose basic legal order is municipal law and whose proper law is international law—from *contracts in international law*—whose basic legal order and proper law are both international law—he characterises state contracts as having 'their centre of gravity . . . in the international orbit'. He adds 'that it is not all state contracts that should be considered thus to appertain to the international legal order but only those of them that are actually integrated by objective legal or politico-economic ties into relations

---

[7] FA Mann, 'The Law Governing State Contracts' (1944) 21 *British Yearbook of International Law* 11 reprinted in *Studies in International Law* (Oxford, Clarendon Press, 1973). In the same area see also G Delaume, 'Des stipulations de droit applicable dans les accords de prêt et de développement économique' (1968) *Journal du Droit International* 336.

[8] Mann, 'State Contracts', *ibid*, 190–91. He added though: 'In absence of an express reference a State contract should be regarded as internationalized, if it is so rooted in international law as to render it impossible to assume that the parties intended to be governed by a national system of law' (at 194). He cited the example of the obligations subscribed by Germany on the basis of the Young Plan for payment of reparations provided for by the Treaty of Versailles.

[9] See JN Hyde, 'Economic Development Agreements' (1962) 105 *Recueil des Cours de l'Académie de Droit International de La Haye* 266; SI Pogany, 'Economic Development Agreements' (1992) 7 *ICSID Review* 1.

between states, that is essentially—but not exclusively—economic development agreements or investment contracts'.[10]

But Weil himself recognised that 'this distinction between ordinary state contracts and state contracts with an international basis defies any objective and readily understandable criterion'.[11] Moreover, it rests on a further distinction between the basic legal order of the contract (*Grundlegung*) and the law governing the contract—a distinction that was to come in for some radical criticism.[12]

State Contracts as presented by Mayer

Mayer's essential contribution was to provide a purely legal criterion for distinguishing contracts entered into by states from *state contracts* in the strict sense of the term. The former are made *within the state's*

[10] Weil, 'Droit international et contrats d'Etat' (n 4) 580. It would have been hard to find an example corresponding more closely to the criterion of a contract that, through objective ties, was part and parcel of relations between states than the various contracts in the Eurodif affair: in February 1974 the Finance Ministers of France (V Giscard d'Estaing) and Iran signed a framework agreement in Paris on Franco-Iranian cooperation. France was to construct five of Iran's 25 nuclear power stations, supply enriched uranium, build a gas liquefaction plant, a steel-making complex, etc. In June 1974 during an official visit to France, the Shah of Iran signed a cooperation agreement with the French Government for the peaceful use of nuclear power. In December 1974 French Prime Minister Chirac signed a new agreement in Teheran specifying the scope of cooperation of the two countries in nuclear matters. The agreement provided, among many other things, for the formation of a French company, Sofidif, 60% owned by France's Commissariat à l'énergie atomique (CEA) and 40% owned by Iran's Atomic Energy Organisation. Subsequently the CEA was to transfer 25% of its shareholding in Eurodif (a company producing enriched uranium) to Sofidif, so indirectly allowing Iran a stake in the company. Various conventions were entered into between Sofidif and Eurodif that were governed by French law with an ICC arbitration clause. The agreement also provided for a $1 million loan from the Iranian government to France's CEA, the agreement being governed by Iranian law with an ICC arbitration clause. Besides the loan to the CEA, Iran made another $943 million loan to Eurodif in an agreement of July 1977. The agreement was governed by Iranian law with an ICC arbitration clause. Out of the mass of litigation that was to follow the Iranian revolution and last 12 years nothing need be said other than that when one aspect of the affair came before France's Cour de cassation, Advocate-General Gulphe noted: 'we are on the borderline between private international law and public international law and one may wonder whether these agreements should come under one or the other' (Cas. civ. 14 mars 1984, JCP 1984, II, 20205, concl. Gulphe, note Synvet); see also B Ancel and Y Lequette, *Grands arrêts de la jurisprudence française de droit international privé* 2nd edn (Paris, Sirey, 1992) 514. And yet the entire dispute, both in the arbitration tribunals and in the French courts, was treated as a private law matter with municipal law applying. This clearly shows that it is not being a part of relations between states through objective ties of a politico-economic order that transforms a contract made by a state with foreign persons into a state contract but solely legal criteria by which it can be recognised that the contract was made by the state as a subject of international law.

[11] Weil, 'Droit international et contrats d'Etat' (n 4) 581.

[12] Mayer, 'L'ordre juridique de base' (n 4).

legal order and with the state as it stands in its legal order, that is the state as administration, while the latter are made by the state as a subject of public international law *within a legal order external to the state*. The recognition of state contracts *stricto sensu* involves purely legal criteria: the inclusion of an arbitration clause, neutralisation of the state's normative power by the addition of clauses stabilising the law of the state, if applicable, possible inclusion of the contract in a treaty of international law and under certain circumstances, internationalisation of the governing law.[13]

However, for reasons we shall return to, Mayer refuses to consider that this external order governing contracts entered into by states as subjects of international law with private persons might be the legal order of public international law. Instead, he presents a sophisticated revamped version of the theory of the *contrat sans loi*. This second part of Mayer's theoretical construction is highly paradoxical and not very convincing. However, it seems more logical to infer from the fact that in a state contract it is the state as a subject of international law that is contracting, that the legal order within which the contract is made is indeed that of public international law. But this means admitting that international law may have evolved to allow a new category of legal acts—state contracts—to arise. This did not occur overnight but is the result of a historical process that led certain contracts made by states with private persons to be shifted from the orbit of municipal law (including its rules on conflict of laws) to the orbit of international law.

State Contracts as Contracts governed by the International Legal Order

The paradoxical character of what is announced here is obvious enough: the contracts generally in question (mostly investment contracts) are international contracts in the sense of private international law with a governing law clause that may refer to international law or to its general principles but that very often designates the contracting state's national law as the governing law and sometimes contains no *electio juris* clause. Under such circumstances it is difficult to escape the reasoning of private international law even if it is complicated by introducing the distinction between basic legal order and governing law.

---

[13] Mayer, 'La neutralisation' (n 4) 29–39. See also the development of his thinking on this point (the analysis of what an international court is) that reinforces his general analysis of state contracts in 'Contract claims et clauses juridictionnelles des traités relatifs à la protection des investissements' (2009) *Journal du Droit International* 71, 86 and see below fn 60 and ch 4 (at 111).

It is clear too that in signing such contracts the parties were unaware they were involved in creating a new category of acts of international law. The phenomenon occurred empirically over several decades: the private party seeking legal guarantees principally against the legislative hazard of its state partner, and the state granting greater or lesser guarantees depending on its bargaining power.

But now hindsight can lead us to argue that where contracts were made between states as subjects of international law and private persons, they were paving the way for a contract law governed by public international law, ie, an *international contract law*. The analysis will become clearer with input from the development of ICSID case law. An illustration shall be given in a domain relating not to a state but an international organisation with a private person.

Interpreting Choice-of-Law Clauses in Contracts between States and Private-Law Entities

We shall reason first on the clauses that make no reference to international law or its general principles of law. If they provide for the governing law to be the law of the contracting state, with no further clarification, the contract is governed in principle by municipal law even if, in some old arbitration decisions, international arbitrators being unhappy with this solution appealed to legal principles from outside to achieve what they saw as more satisfactory solutions.[14]

But in practice, examination of investment contracts of which we can have knowledge—either through their publication in specialised journals in the petroleum and mining domains above all,[15] or through the disputes to which they give rise—shows that the law of

[14] See for instance the arbitration between Saudi Arabia and Aramco of 23 August 1958 where art IV of the arbitration agreement provided for the application of Saudi Arabian law for some issues but where the arbitrator considered that in the case of gaps in the law of Saudi Arabia, of which the Concession Agreement is a part, the tribunal will ascertain the applicable principle by resorting to the world-wide custom and practice in the oil business and industry. Failing such custom and practice, the tribunal will be influenced by the solutions recognised by world case law and doctrine and by pure jurisprudence (1963) *Revue Critique de Droit International Privé* 272. See text of award in (1963) 27 *ILR* 117 at 171. In the absence of any choice of law, the arbitrator in the *Abu Dhabi* award, having sought the proper law of the contract, found it to be the law of Abu Dhabi but dismissed it arguing that '[it] would be fanciful to suggest that in this very primitive region there is any settled body of legal principles applicable to the construction of modern commercial instruments', award of 28 August 1951, (1952) *International and Comparative Law Quarterly* 247, 251.

[15] See the publications of The Barrows Company (New York) *Basic Oil Laws & Concession Contracts*. For a collection of earlier contracts see P Fischer and T Wälde, *A Collection of International Concessions and Related Instruments, Contemporary Series* (Dobbs Ferry, Oceana Publications, 4 vols 1984–86).

the contracting state is almost never opted for as it stands but is accompanied by stabilisation and intangibility clauses or is combined in various ways with general principles of law or with principles of international law. Whichever solution is chosen, it can be construed in the context of a theory that conceives of state contracts as legal acts of international law.

The Choice of a Stabilised Municipal Law

As shown in a recent study of the history of bauxite mining contracts, large European mining companies in the 1950s were looking for legal recipes to minimise the political risk in contracts made with states awaiting independence.[16] These recipes were to result in the delocalisation of the contract, firstly as regards the settlement of disputes with the host state, which was to be entrusted to arbitration tribunals. This point was obvious to everyone. However, it was not immediately obvious to the protagonists that the choice of the national law of the state, albeit stabilised, contributed to delocalisation in equal measure by neutralising the state's normative power, as Mayer showed. Under the circumstances, it is not truly the law of the state that is the *lex contractus* but a set of rules coinciding with the law of the state at a given point in time and incorporated into the contract. The contract is, then, from the legal standpoint that the arbitrator adopts, shielded from policy changes by the contracting state. Not that the state will be unable to change its legislation, but if it applies any such change to the contract containing the freezing clause, it will be answerable for it before the arbitration tribunal and may have to compensate the other contracting party.[17]

---

[16] See PH Ganem, *Sécurisation contractuelle des investissements internationaux. Grands projets, mines, énergie, métallurgie, infrastructures* (Bruxelles, Paris, Bruylant, Forum européen de la communication, 1998). The book contains a consultation by P Reuter for Pechiney on the legal guarantees a company could secure from an African state to ensure its business conditions were maintained profitable, see 115–34. The eminent French public law scholar was very reserved in his conclusions, as was G Vedel in a 1961 report on arbitration between governments and private persons, see 'Le probléme de l'arbitrage eutre gouvernements ou personnes de droit public er personnes de droit prive'(1961) *Revue de l'Arbitrage* 117. The evolution of opinions can be gauged by comparing these with the *Aminoil* award where the arbitration tribunal was presided by the same P Reuter.

[17] On this issue I concur with Mayer 'La neutralisation' (n 4) 34–36. For a general study see P Weil 'Les clauses de stabilisation' (n 4); N David, 'Les clauses de stabilité dans les contrats pétroliers. Questions d'un praticien' (1986) *Journal du Droit International* 79; Paasivirta, *Participation of States* (n 3) 51–196. See also FV Garcia Amador, 'State Responsibility in the Case of "Stabilization" Clauses' (1993) 2 *Florida State University Journal of Transnational Law and Policy* 23.

Such a situation of exteriority of the contract from the state's legal order is characteristic of the state contract *stricto sensu*. But in which legal order is the agreement made? It can easily be argued, from now on, that it may be the legal order of public international law. If it is assumed there is an international contract law, its first rule will be the principle of parties free choice of law. With the reservation, though, that this *clearly does not deliver the contract from the international legal order*. This would be the case were the parties *unreservedly* to choose some municipal law as the governing law.[18] But if they choose some municipal law as a stabilised system of reference and so as incorporated into the agreement, this is compatible with the first rule of international contract law.

The Choice of a Governing Law referring to the General Principles of Law or to International Law

Likewise, what is important here for our reasoning is not the exact sense of any such combination of municipal law with the general principles of law or with the principles of international law. What counts is that such an arrangement combined with an arbitration clause may allow the contract between the parties to be characterised as a state contract. The main consequence of such a combination is to neutralise the state's normative power. The state will be unable to interfere with the contract in a manner contrary to the general principles that are beyond its control and breach of which would be sanctioned by arbitrators in the event of dispute. It is even easier in this case to entertain the idea that the legal order of the state contract is the order of public international law that contains these principles as and when formulated by arbitrators. Admittedly it is conceivable that some other order, say a transnational order, is involved, but the arguments in favour of the international legal order shall be explained below.

The question has arisen on several occasions whether the mention of international law and/or the general principles of law was not a thing of the past and if contracts were not currently being 'relocalised'. As no one has knowledge of all the contracts entered into by states, we can have only a partial view of reality. The very restricted examination of a large collection of petroleum contracts from the late 1980s to the early 1990s has led to the following observations.[19] It is

---

[18] Even in this case, though, international law could control the application of internal law if under the Washington Convention setting up the ICSID, see ch 4.

[19] This is the collection of Basic Oil Laws & Concession Contracts published by The Barrow's Company of New York.

clear enough some states do not waive the application of their national law even if they consent to arbitration procedures. This is true of most Latin American states (at least over the period under observation), of India, Yemen, North African . . . and western European countries (Norway, UK).[20] From this standpoint there is no denying that the reference to international law and to its general principles is the sign of a balance of power in favour of the petroleum companies. This should not be thought of a priori as an immoral situation of abuse of right. As in any economic relation, whether among domestic companies or in international society, co-contractors are not always on an equal footing and some will be asked for guarantees that will not be asked of others.

Care must also be taken with the fact that certain references to municipal law must be subject to a specific reading because they are accompanied by stabilisation clauses (see above). That said, it is hardly difficult to find references to international law in recent petroleum contracts (but a similar enquiry is required for other types of investment contract). Here are a few examples.

In a contract between Ghana and a group of oil companies including Shell, entered into on 26 July 1988, article 26(1) states:

> This Agreement . . . shall be governed by and construed in accordance with the laws of the Republic of Ghana consistent with such rules of international law as may be applicable including rules and principles as have been applied by international tribunals.[21]

---

[20] One should appreciate at its true value in comparative law the *Norwegian Standard (Model) Petroleum Production Licence* (Royal Decree of 1 March 1991, 13th Round) whose art 25 (Rights and obligations according to legislation) provides: 'This licence is also subject to those provisions that are stipulated according to legislation in effect at any time. The rights granted under this licence and the agreement to be entered into in accordance with section 4, shall not restrict the State's general legislation or taxation authority'.

[21] In the 1985 revision of the Valco Master Agreement (an aluminium plant built in Ghana by an international consortium of companies for mining Ghanian bauxite) cl 47 states: 'This Agreement shall be governed by and construed in accordance with the law of Ghana and such rules of International Law as may be applicable. The parties hereto acknowledge and agree that the legislative competence of Ghana as a sovereign state is defined by its applicable constitutional instruments and can be exercised only within the limits ordained by established rules of International Law. The term, International Law, as used in this Article should be understood in the sense given to it by Article 38 (1) of the Statute of the International Court of Justice, allowance being made for the fact the Article 38 aforesaid was designed to apply to inter-state disputes'. The initial 1962 agreement provided for the governing law to be Ghanean law frozen at the date the contract was signed. My thanks to PH Ganem for providing the text of art 47 of the new agreement.

Clauses of the same kind are found in a concession contract between the Somalian Government and Comoco of 17 June 1986 (article 27) and in a hydrocarbon exploration and drilling contract between the Republic of Zaire and Amoco Zaire of 30 May 1987 (article 20).

Article 31 of a concession contract of 4 December 1990 between Paraguay and Phillips Petroleum Company Paraguay provides:

31.1 The rights and obligations of the Government and of the Concessionnaire shall be governed by the provisions of this contract and the law approving this contract and by provisions contained in Law (no. X) and regulatory decrees (no.Y) to the extent to which the aforesaid Laws and decrees have not been amended by this contract and by the Law approving this contract and supplemented by the general principles of law as internationally recognised.

31.2 Amendments to such laws and decrees or the enactment of future laws and decrees shall not be applicable to the rights and obligations of the Concessionnaire established in this contract, unless the Government and the Concessionnaire should otherwise determine by mutual agreement in writing.

Article 29(5) of a concession agreement between Texaco and Pakistan of 6 November 1990 stated:

This Agreement shall be governed by and interpreted in accordance with and shall be given effect under the laws of Pakistan to the extent such laws and interpretations are consistent with generally accepted standards of International Law including Principles as may have been applied by inter-national tribunals.

In a petroleum agreement of 4 May 1986 between Nepal and Shell, article 69 read:

This Agreement shall be interpreted according to the law of Nepal and such principles of International Law as may be applicable.

Article 34(3) of an offshore oil prospecting and drilling agreement of 24 October 1991 between Bulgaria and various companies including Texaco provided:

This Agreement and any licence shall be governed by Bulgarian laws and international conventions to which Bulgaria is a party and generally accepted principles of International Law.

Similarly in the Polish 1991 standard contract for oil exploration and drilling, article 29(1) stated:

This contract shall be interpreted in accordance with the laws of Poland and in accordance with the principles of International law and decisions of international tribunals.

All of these clauses about governing law are accompanied by arbitration clauses referring either to the ICSID or, quite often, to *ad hoc* arbitration panels formed under the UNCITRAL (United Nations Commission on International Trade Law) regulations. It can be noted, without labouring the point, that what are called 'stabilisation' clauses, instead of providing for the non-application to the contract of changes in legislation, quite frequently provide that under such circumstances parties must negotiate to restore the financial equilibrium of the contract. If they fail to reach agreement the dispute goes to arbitration.

Interpreting Article 42 of the Washington Convention Creating the ICSID

It is no overstatement to say that the creation of the ICSID by the Washington Convention of 18 March 1965 and the institution's success—in terms of the number of states having ratified the Convention (137 signatory states and 123 ratifications by October 1995; 156 and 144, respectively, by July 2009), in terms of the disputes the ICSID has already handled, and, more importantly perhaps, in terms of the disputes that will be submitted to it in future—has brought about a revolution in the whole issue of state contracts. For the first time in an international treaty, states accepted that, under certain circumstances, contracts they entered into could be governed by the principles of international law, and the preparatory works leave no doubt that the expression 'international law' here has the same meaning as in article 38(1) of the statute of the International Court of Justice.[22]

---

[22] The report by the Executive Directors of the IBRD states more clearly that 'the term "international law" as used in this context should be understood in the sense given to it by Article 38(1) of the Statute of the International Court of Justice, allowance being made for the fact that Article 38 was designed to apply to inter-States disputes' (para 40 of the report); see also GR Delaume, 'La Convention pour le règlement des différends relatifs aux investissement entre Etats et ressortissants d'autres Etats' (1966) *Journal du Droit International* 26, 47 fn 82; A Broches, 'The Convention on the Settlement of Investment Disputes between States and Nationals of Other States' (1972) 136 *Recueil des Cours de l'Académie de Droit International de La Haye* 333, 391; I Shihata and A Parra, 'Applicable Substantive Law in Disputes between States and Private Foreign Parties: The Case of Arbitration under the ICSID Convention' (1995) *ICSID Review* 183, 193; M Hirsch, *The Arbitration Mechanism of the International Centre for the Settlement of Investment Disputes* (Dordrecht, Martinus

However, article 42(1) of the Convention, which provides for the law applicable by the tribunal established under the aegis of the Washington Convention, does not refer to international law alone. It states in a first sentence that 'The Tribunal shall decide a dispute in accordance with such rules of law as may be agreed by the parties'. And in a second sentence that 'In the absence of such agreement, the Tribunal shall apply the law of the Contracting State party to the dispute (including its rules on the conflict of laws) and such rules of international law as may be applicable'.

The Choice of the Law of the State Alone

From our perspective this article may be construed as follows. The first sentence of article 42(1) allows the parties the option of purely and simply choosing a national law to govern their contract. In this case it is clear that this is not a state contract but a municipal law contract for which the contracting parties have accepted ICSID arbitration to settle their disputes, just as they could have accepted some other arbitration mechanism (such as that of the UNCITRAL). Notice that this choice has so far been made in a very limited number of cases only: *Mobil Oil v New Zealand* (ARB/87/2) where a clause in the contract provided for the application of the host country's law and in *Colt Industries v Government of the Republic of Korea* (ARB/84/2), where it was the investor's national law that was chosen.[23] It may be added that even when the parties have made no provision for the applicable law in the contract but when in proceedings they manifest their common acceptance of some municipal law, the arbitration tribunal will abide by their choice. This is what happened in *SOABI v Senegal* (ARB/82/1) where both parties considered the contract should be governed by Senegalese administrative law.[24]

Nijhoff, 1993) 109. For two recent general studies, see W Ben Hamida, *L'arbitrage transnational unilatéral* (Thesis, University of Paris 2, 2003) 514; S Manciaux, *Investissements étrangers et arbitrage entre Etats et ressortissants d'autres Etats. Trente années d'activités du CIRDI* (Dijon, CREDIMI, Paris, Litec, 2004) 301.

[23] Both these cases were settled out of court.

[24] See 2 *ICSID Reports* 190 and E Gaillard, 'Chronique' (1990) *Journal du Droit International* 193. Shihata and Parra, 'Applicable Substantive Law' (n 22) observe that in the *Klöckner* case, it was the Cameroon Government that claimed, in the first judgment in 1983, that the arbitrators should not consider its law alone and note: 'Although the argument failed in that case, it suggests that the reference to international law in the second sentence of the first paragraph of Article 42 of the ICSID Convention, although originally conceived to protect the interests of investors may equally serve the interests of host States' (at 206).

However, a correction must be made immediately to the interplay of the co-contractors' free will, and one which flows from the very existence of the Washington Convention. Even if both parties opt for the law of the contracting state, it must be considered that the arbitrator cannot accept that law if it includes provisions that are contrary to international law. To accept such provisions would come down to denying the investor the protection of international law. ICSID arbitration would then afford less protection than diplomatic protection would; an outcome that would be inconsistent, to say the least, with the Washington Convention. This was clearly stated by the first arbitration tribunal in the *Amco* case, which indicated that:

> . . . [t]he national State of the investor is precluded from exercising its normal right of diplomatic protection during the pendency of the ICSID proceedings and even after such proceedings, in respect of a Contracting State which complies with the ICSID award (Art. 27, Convention). The thrust of Article 54(1) and of Article 27 of the Convention makes sense only under the supposition that the award involved is not violative of applicable principles and rules of international law.[25]

The Choice of the Stabilised Law of the State

A distinction must be made between this first hypothesis and the case where parties choose a national law but together with stabilisation clauses, as it has been seen that in this case the frozen national law acts as a system of reference only. This occurred in *MINE v Guinea* (ARB/84/4, Guinean law frozen at the date of the investment contract)[26] and *Atlantic Triton v Guinea* (ARB/84/1, Guinean law frozen but with the possibility for the arbitrators to rule *ex aequo et bono* on the basis of article 42(3)).[27] These contracts are no longer municipal law contracts but state contracts and as such the arbitrators may, in my opinion, resort to the principles of international law.[28]

---

[25] *Amco Asia v Indonesia*, ARB/81/1, decision on the application for annulment, 16 May 1986, 1 *ICSID Reports* 509 at 515 para 21; E Gaillard, *Jurisprudence*, 178. See also CH Schreuer, *The ICSID Convention: A Commentary* (Cambridge, Cambridge University Press, 2001) 590, and *SPP v Egypt*, 20 May 1992, 84; *Wena Hotels Ltd v Arab Republic of Egypt*, decision of the ad hoc committee, 5 February 2002, 40. This point is developed below, ch 4.

[26] See (1990) 4 *ICSID Reports* 76; (1995) *ICSID Review* 95; E Gaillard, 'Chronique' (1991) *Journal du Droit International* 166.

[27] See E Gaillard, 'Chronique' (1988) *Journal du Droit International* 181. English translation of French original in (1995) 3 *ICSID Reports* 13.

[28] Notice that the 1962 Valco Master Agreement provided in its art 46 for Ghanean law frozen at the date the contract was signed as its governing law. The 1985 amended contract provides in its art 47 for Ghanean law and the rules of international

The Choice of the Law of the State and the Principles of International Law

Still in the context of the first sentence of article 42(1), ICSID case law provides hypotheses where the parties have opted for combinations of municipal law and such principles of international law as may be applicable. This was so in *Kaiser Bauxite v Jamaica* (ARB/74/2, 3 and 4 with in addition the freezing of Jamaican law)[29] and in *AGIP v Congo* (ARB/77/1).[30] This is a similar situation to that envisaged in the second sentence of article 42(1), the meaning of which must now be examined.

Leaving aside the reference to conflict of laws that so far has played virtually no part and which is probably just a relict of an old dictum of the Permanent Court of International Justice,[31] the issue that has been most discussed is that of the ways of combining municipal law and 'such principles of international law as may be applicable'. These principles have been considered by arbitrators as playing either a supplementary and/or corrective role relative to international law (*Klöckner* ARB/81/2 first annulment decision of 3 May 1985,[32] *Amco* ARB/81/1, first annulment decision of 16 May 1986)[33] or a primary role, with municipal law always having to be compared and contrasted with the requirements of international law (award of 31 May 1990).[34]

---

law that may be applicable. See above, n 21. These two provisions are in fact equivalent except that in 1985 a clear reference is made to international law, which was less common in 1962. See Ganem, *Sécurisation contractuelle* (n 16), app 5.

[29] 1 *ICSID* Reports 296.

[30] 1 *ICSID Reports* 30; H Batiffol, 'Note' (1982) *Revue Critique de Droit International Privé* 92.

[31] See *Serbian Loans*, no 14, [1929] PCIJ Series A No 20, at 41 and *Brazilian Loans* decision no 15, [1929] PCIJ Series A No 21, at 41. The first tribunal in the *Amco v Indonesia* case (award of 20 November 1984), having observed the parties had not chosen a governing law, decided to rule on the basis of art 42(1), second sentence (the law of the Contracting State—including its rules on the conflict of laws—and such rules of international law as may be applicable). But it observed that, for Indonesian law, there was no need to go into a discussion of its rules about conflicts of law as there was no doubt that it was Indonesian substantive law that applied. (See (1985) *International Legal Materials*, 1023 [148]; excerpts from the award in E Gaillard, 'Chronique' (1987) *Journal du Droit International* 145). However, commentators on the Convention envisaged that the use of rules of conflict of laws might be helpful in matters involving international borrowing and leading to the application of the law of the lender's country: see Delaume, 'La Convention' (n 22) 46; Shihata and Para, 'Applicable Substantive Law' (n 22) 191 fn 34. Such a case has not yet arisen.

[32] See E Gaillard, 'Chronique' (1987) *Journal du Droit International* 163 and 2 *ICSID Reports* 95.

[33] 1 *ICSID Reports* 509; (1986) *International Legal Materials* 1439.

[34] See 1 *ICSID Reports* 569 and E Gaillard, 'Chronique' (1991) *Journal du Droit International* 173.

These two interpretations are compatible with the analysis of state contracts defended here. It is clear that the investment host state, in accepting the intervention of international law—whether directly in the governing law clause (article 42(1), sentence 1) or indirectly by its adhesion to the Washington Convention without indicating a governing law (so resort to article 42(1), sentence 2)—at the same time accepts a special regime for some of its contracts. For these contracts, the rules of municipal law apply only on the condition that they comply with the principles of international investment law as recognised by ICSID arbitrators. As ICSID Secretary-General Shihata wrote, the preparatory works show that the second sentence of article 42(1) was introduced to authorise arbitrators to set aside applicable municipal law should any action by the host state by virtue of that law run counter to international law.[35]

We have also seen that it would be entirely contrary to the very logic of the Washington Convention to allow a state to resort to its own law and so thwart international protection, which is the Convention's reason for being, as the first arbitration tribunal in the *Amco* case stated (above).

Contracts made by the state and that fall directly or indirectly within the ambit of the second sentence are therefore contracts where the state's commitment to the investor is, in the final resort, governed by the rules of international law that prevail over any rule to the contrary. It is consistent, then, to consider that the commitment so given by the state is that of the state as a subject of international law within the international legal order.

The clearest statement to this effect was made by the second arbitration tribunal (presided by Rosalyn Higgins) in *Amco Asia v Indonesia* (ARB/81/1), award of 5 June 1990:

> Article 42 (1) refers to the application of the law of a host state and of international law. If there is no relevant provision of the host state's law on an issue, the relevant dispositions of international law must be sought. If there are applicable provisions of the host state's law, they must be appre-

---

[35] Shihata and Parra, 'Applicable Substantive Law' (n 22) 192; Broches, 'The Convention' (n 22) considers that the relationship between the law of the state and international law is as follows: 'The Tribunal will first look at the law of the host State and that law will in the first instance be applied to the merits of the dispute. Then the result will be tested against international law. That process will not involve the confirmation or denial of the validity of the host State's law, but may result in not applying it where that law, or action taken under that law, violates international law. In that sense . . . international law is hierarchically superior to national law under article 42(1)' (at 392).

ciated in respect of international law which prevails in the event of conflict. So international law is fully applicable and to characterise its role as 'merely supplementary and corrective' is a vain distinction. In any event, the Tribunal considers that its task is to assess any legal claim in this matter first in respect of Indonesian law and then in respect of international law.[36]

It is true that with *SPP v Egypt* (ARB/84/3, award of 20 May 1992),[37] the internationalist 'inclination' of the arbitral tribunal meant it considered that all national law had loopholes and that it was for international law to fill them.[38] Whatever one might think of this argument,[39] it must be acknowledged that in actual fact the first sentence of article 41(1) in no way allows provisions of internal law to be objected to international law, even if in their agreement the parties have expressly opted for the law of the contracting state as the law applicable to their dispute. That might seem surprising, but it is merely the revelation over the course of time and cases of the operating logic of the Washington Convention. It is plain that in the event of incompatibilty between the chosen national law and international law, ICSID arbitrators should always make the latter prevail. If this possibility were not recognised, the whole point of the Washington Convention for investors would come into question. But can it be imagined that an ICSID tribunal might confirm a solution that was clearly contrary to international law?

The arbitrators may decide, as in *Letco v Liberia* (ARB/83/2, award of 14 April 1986),[40] to apply the host state's law because it is consistent with international law. But in this case too the contract must be held to be governed by international law, the rules of

---

[36] 1 *ICSID Reports* 569 at 580 para 40, E Gaillard, *Jurisprudence*, 302. This award was also annulled by a decision of 3 December 1992, 9 *ICSID Reports* 9.

[37] See E Gaillard, 'Chronique' (1994) *Journal du Droit International* 229; G Delaume 'L'affaire du plateau des pyramides et le CIRDI. Considérations sur le droit applicable' (1994) *Revue de l'Arbitrage* 39; P Rambaud, 'L'affaire des Pyramides: suite et fin' (1993) *Annuaire Français de Droit International* 567.

[38] See paras 80 and 84 of the award: 'When a domestic legal system contains a loophole or when international law is breached by the application of domestic law alone, the tribunal is bound, by application of art 42 of the Washington Convention, to directly apply the relevant rules and principles of international law' *8 ICSID Review* 352 (1993); ((1994) *Journal du Droit International* 231).

[39] I accept with E Gaillard that the reasoning of the arbitration tribunal in the *SPP* case is open to criticism when it asserts [78] that 'the parties' disagreement over the question of application of article 42 is of very little if any practical interest'.

[40] See E Gaillard, 'Chronique' (1988) *Journal du Droit International* 166 and 2 *ICSID Reports* 343.

national law having been accommodated and approved beforehand by international law.

External Confirmation: Governing Law for IBRD and EBRD Contracts

A recent study shows that the advancement observed with the formation of the concept of state contracts liable to be governed by international law has occurred also in relations between banks having an international legal character—and so being international organisations—and their private borrowers.[41] In the case of the International Bank for Reconstruction and Development (IBRD), whose General Conditions were drafted in 1947, article 7.01 (now 10.01) provides that:

> The rights and obligations of the Bank and the Loan Parties under the Legal Agreements shall be valid and enforceable in accordance with their terms notwithstanding the law of any state or political subdivision thereof to the contrary.

In a 1959 commentary, the World Bank's legal counsel Aron Broches (who played a primordial role in drafting the Washington Convention) provided the following clarifications:

> [T]he loan agreement is only one element . . . in the dealings on the international level between the Bank and its member, and partakes of the international character of these dealings. This is not the same as saying that the loan agreement itself thereby becomes an international agreement and that it is governed by international law. But it does justify the internationalization of the loan agreement to the extent of insulating it from the effect of municipal law.[42]

These contracts are therefore 'delocalised' relative to the law of the state whose subjects enter into the loan agreement with the Bank. They cannot be amended by the state's unilateral action. But which law governs the contracts? Nothing is stated explicitly and this silence, for Broches, reflects the uncertainties of lawyers in 1947 about the legal capacities of the Bank as an international organisation

---

[41] JW Head, 'Evolution of the Governing Law for Loan Agreements of the World Bank and Other Multilateral Development Banks' (1996) *American Journal of International Law* 214; IBRD, *General Conditions Applicable to Loan and Guarantee Agreements* (Washington, 1985).

[42] A Broches, 'International Legal Aspects of the Operations of the World Bank' (1959) 97 *Recueil des Cours de l'Académie de Droit International de La Haye* 352. One cannot but notice how awkward the explanation is.

but also, one might think, about the nature of the contracts made with non-state persons. As these IBRD contracts have apparently given rise to no litigation the question has remained unanswered.[43]

In the decades following the drawing up of the IBRD's General Conditions came the evolution just described for state contracts; an evolution in which the World Bank and its legal counsel, as said, played an essential part. The IBRD General Conditions, never having caused problems, have not been altered. But when in 1994 a new generation of lawyers was called on to draft the Standard Terms and Conditions of the new European Bank for Reconstruction and Development, they naturally included the developments that had occurred in state contracts.[44] For one thing, article 8.04(a) of the Standard Terms and Conditions provides that disputes over loan agreements shall be submitted to arbitration organised in accordance with the UNCITRAL rules.

In addition, article 8.04(b)(v) expressly provides that the law applicable by the tribunal shall be 'public international law' regardless of whether the contract has been made with a state or a non-state person. As Head wrote, this choice of governing law was first made because 'it is now well accepted that international law can be chosen as the governing law in contracts involving one or more parties that are not subjects of international law that is, entities that are not states or international organisations'. And he added 'the body of "public international law" is now substantial and extensive enough'.[45]

And the fact is that these EBRD contracts are contracts entered into by a subject of international law as such with an individual, contracts

---

[43] Broches, 'The World Bank', *ibid*, evokes the analogy that might be made with state contracts and their internationalisation. But he specifies these contracts must not be confused with 'ageements entered into between subjects of international law, which are governed directly, *and in all respects*, by international law' (at 345) (emphasis added). Which implicitly leaves the path open for these contracts to be governed, at least in some respects, by international law. See also the report by N Valticos on 'Les contrats conclus par les organisations internationales avec des personnes privées' (1977) 57(1) *Annuaire de l'Institut de Droit International* 1–109. Valticos shows that on the whole international organisations are loath to specify the governing law in their contract but refer rather to a state law in exceptional cases where an *electio juris* is made (56). In the IDI draft resolution, art 1 asks international organisations to examine whether it is opportune to provide in the contract for the applicable system of law, namely, given the circumstances and the object of the contract, international law, the general principles of law, a state law or a combination of these systems (107–08).

[44] Head, 'Evolution of the Governing Law' (n 41) 226.

[45] Head, 'Evolution of the Governing Law' (n 41) 228–29. The full text of art 8.04 (b) (v) is at 227. It refers expressly to obligations deriving from treaties, custom and general principles of law.

governed *expressis verbis* by public international law in its three manifestations of treaty law, customary law and the general principles of law.

Responses To Some Objections

The aforementioned presentation of state contracts as new legal acts in international law raises many objections. Not all of them can be examined here. Two that seem particularly important shall be dealt with.

On it being Impossible for Contracts between States and Individuals to come within the International Legal Order

The Strictly Interstate Character of International Law

This is an argument of principle that has been reiterated many times by the opponents of any theory of internationalisation of state contracts. Mayer justifies the refusal to apply international law to state contracts, although he conceives of these as agreements between states as subjects of international law and foreign companies, by the fact that international law 'has as its subject matter only relations between the component parts of that society; states and the legal persons they create (international organisations)'.[46]

Similarly Rigaux, in his famous criticism of the Texaco award, writes:

> In the event of a mixed legal relation such as a contract between a state, subject of international law, and a private company subjected to domestic law, the status of the private person draws the settlement of the situation into its own order [so the domestic order].

But, grasping immediately that this solution is not entirely logical, Rigaux adds in a note:

> One might be surprised that the opposite does not occur, precisely because of the almost natural preponderance of the role of the state. First [because] drawing the private company into the international legal order proper involves for the private party a real privilege, an exorbitant guarantee given its own status, and because there is no reason to presume the state wished to consent thereto, supposing it had the power to do so . . .[47]

---

[46] Mayer, 'La neutralisation' (n 4) 21.
[47] F Rigaux, 'Des dieux et des héros—Réflexions sur une sentence arbitrale' (1978) *Revue Critique de Droit International Privé* 435, 446.

The final part of this sentence takes up another argument presented by Rigaux objecting on various grounds to any recognition that private persons might have the capacity of international subjects, even with limited legal capacity. One of those grounds for objection is that the international community alone can admit a new category of subject. He adds:

> There is anarchy enough already without envisaging that a single state might give to one of its partners, a private company, a club member card allowing it later to claim a would-be limitation of sovereignty.[48]

One may well wonder under what personification the 'international community' might act to accept a new category of subject of international law: a solemn resolution of the United Nations General Assembly? Hardly likely. A multilateral treaty having this aim and collecting sufficient support to supposedly express the will of the international community? Hardly likely either, presented in this way. But the issue can be taken differently; we can ask what is it, at root, that is specific about subjects of international law and so ascertain whether or not individuals truly are barred for good from international law.

Who are the Subjects of International Law?

One might consider, like Weil, that the subjects of international law are those empowered by international law to produce norms of international law. And so one will consider that states alone, and to a lesser extent intergovernmental organisations, fit the bill.[49] But to reason like this is to lose sight of the general understanding of what

---

[48] Rigaux, *ibid*, 445. To this is added the argument raised in several affairs that the principle of the permanent sovereignty of states over their natural resources would prevent them from granting 'by contract or by treaty guarantees of any kind whatsoever against the exercice of public authority in respect of natural wealth' (see *Aminoil* award of 24 March (1982) (1982) 66 *ILR* 519 and *Journal du Droit International* 869, 889 [90] (2)). The argument was dismissed in both the *Aminoil* (*ibid*) and *Texaco* awards, 53 *ILR* 420 and (1977) *Journal du Droit International* 350, [80–91]). See also Paasivirta, *Participation of States* (n 3) 182–96.

[49] See Weil, 'Le droit international en quête de son identité' (n 4): 'the protected individual [by human rights] . . . far from being the subject, *that is, the creator of international norms relative to human rights . . .*' (at 121) (emphasis added). And yet if one thinks like Weil that 'international contract law is as much international law as international law of treaties, or of the sea, or of war' (*ibid*, 98), a company that concludes a state contract, governed by international contract law, is as much involved in creating international norms as a state or organisation that makes a treaty. But Weil, who is reticent even about intergovernmental organisations being international legal persons, refuses absolutely to draw such conclusions (*ibid*, 104).

constitute subjects of law in any legal order. A subject of law is a person on whom the legal order bestows rights and obligations. They are not in principle organs by which law is produced, except to the extent that, as Kelsen explains, they have 'the legal power to assert (by taking a legal action) the fulfilment of a legal obligation, that is, the legal power to participate in the creation of a judicial decision'.[50] Subjects of law may, therefore, take part in creating individual norms; they are not producers of general norms.

In international law, states are in a position where they are both producers of norms and subjects of the legal order, that is, bearers of obligations and of rights they themselves have created. This does not mean this situation is exclusive of any other and that, in the international legal order, there cannot be envisaged subjects of law in the domestic law sense. For that, it suffices to show that, under certain circumstances, international law imposes obligations directly on certain individuals and also invests individuals with rights they can enforce directly in international courts. For the first hypothesis, this has long been borne out in international criminal law, with the case of piracy but above all with international conventions or decisions entrusting the punishment of certain offences they define to international courts (Nuremberg and Tokyo Tribunals, International Tribunals for Former Yugoslavia or Rwanda).[51]

---

[50] H Kelsen, *Pure Theory of Law* trans M Knight (Berkeley, University of California Press, 1967) 168. See also Kelsen's analyses of the notion of 'Right' (*ibid*, 134–38 and in particular at 135) where Kelsen emphasies that 'right', in the technical sense, is defined as 'the legal power conferred for the purpose of bringing about by a law suit the execution of a sanction as a reaction against the non fulfillment of an obligation'. Similarly one can refer to his development of the 'concept of organ' (*ibid*, 150–58 and in particular at 153): 'the individual who exercises a legal power by bringing a law suit against somebody or by conducting a legal transaction may be designated as "legal organ" and the legal power bestowed upon him as his "competence" '. Ultimately in the domestic legal order, on which Kelsen reasons here, individuals are organs of the order, because the order confers on them a 'capacity to act', a power; and conversely, if in the international legal order it is observed that individuals henceforth have, even in a restricted domain, such capacity to act, it must be inferred that they are from now on organs of the order that has conferred legal power and therefore competence on them.

[51] On the international repression of war crimes see C Rousseau, *Le droit des conflits armés* (Paris, Pedone, 1983) 179ff, with the cited references. The Yugoslavia and Rwanda Tribunals were created by decisions of the UN Security Council: see P Weckel, 'L'institution d'un tribunal international pour la répression des crimes de droit humanitaire en Yougoslavie' (1993) *Annuaire Français de Droit International* 232; M Mubiala, 'Le tribunal international pour le Rwanda: vraie ou fausse copie du tribunal pénal international pour l'ex-Yougoslavie?' (1995) *Revue Générale de Droit International Public* 929.

As for the second, it too is old, since the Treaty of Versailles and other peace treaties that followed the First World War provided that the subjects of the Allied Powers could apply for reparations for damages caused by extraordinary wartime measures taken by Germany. To this end, mixed arbitration tribunals were set up, where individuals could sue Germany directly.[52] Moreover, there is hardly need to dwell on the development of the international protection of human rights that has gone on since 1945 according individuals, at least in a regional context, rights by virtue of international conventions and the means to uphold them against states in international courts.[53] The exceptional situation of the post-1918 peace treaties has now become almost commonplace and Kelsen rightly emphasises that 'To the extent that [contemporary] international law penetrates areas that heretofore have been the exclusive domain of national legal orders, its tendency toward obligating or authorizing individuals directly increases'.[54]

It should be remembered from this, and within the most restrictive understanding of it, that a subject of international law may be *any person on whom the international legal order bestows rights and obligations and that is able to take action directly with another subject of international law in such capacity and, possibly, to bring that subject before an international court of law* (conditional on consent given by the latter in some form or other).[55] From these premises it can be understood how the evolution that has occurred with state contracts authorises one to consider individuals as (limited) subjects of international law.

[52] H Kelsen, *General Theory of Law and State* trans A Wedberg (Russell & Russell, New York, 1961) 347–48. Kelsen cites the German–Polish Convention of 15 May 1922 regarding Upper Silesia authorising individuals to bring suits before an international court for failure by either of those states to meet their treaty commitments (at 348). See also C Rousseau, *Droit international public* (Paris, Sirey, 1983) t 5, 381–83.

[53] F Sudre, *Droit international et européen des droits de l'homme* 9th edn (Paris, PUF, 2008). It is only in the context of the European Convention on Human Rights that judicial control by individual action has really been imposed. However, the inter-American system is beginning to be implemented. See G Cohen-Jonathan, 'Cour inter-américaine des droits de l'homme: l'arrêt Velasquez' (1990) *Revue Générale de Droit International Public* 455.

[54] Kelsen, *Pure Theory* (n 50) 527.

[55] See Kelsen, *General Theory* (n 52) 347, which presents the cases where individuals must be considered 'direct subjects of international rights'. He writes: '[i]ndividuals can have international rights only if there is an international court before which they can appear as plaintiffs'. *Mutatis mutandis*, this could explain why, say, disputes between civil servants of international organisations and their organisations can be governed by a branch of international law from the moment the administrative tribunals of international organisations are considered to be international courts. See below, ch 4, fn 55 (at 120).

But closer scrutiny shows it is across the whole domain of international investment law that individuals increasingly enjoy privileges of direct action against states through bilateral or multilateral treaties and so accede to the same standing of subjects of international law.

The Mixed Arbitration Revolution

It is first in state contracts that a phenomenon is observed that has taken on considerable scope in recent years: the overturning of the impossibility, asserted by classical international law, save the exceptions cited above (p 25), for an individual to have a dispute with a state adjudicated other than by the domestic courts of that state. In the event of failure and of exhaustion of domestic remedies, the only solution was for the investor's home state to take up its cause, through diplomatic protection, and to transform the dispute between a state and a private person into a dispute between states.

Transnational or 'mixed' arbitration has made this process virtually obsolete.[56] Any company that invests by contracting with a state knows it has a legal instrument allowing it to bring the state before a judicial instance outside that state for adjudication of a claim opposing it to the state. This mechanism first arose on a purely contractual basis and with ad hoc arbitration. It is understandable that there was reluctance, or even outright hostility, to considering that arbitration

---

[56] See SJ Toope, *Mixed International Arbitration. Studies in Arbitration between States and Private Persons* (Cambridge, Grotius Publications, 1990). Care must be taken not to confuse what are traditionally called mixed arbitration tribunals for liquidating disputes arising after military conflicts (see n 51) and mixed arbitration in the contemporary sense of arbitration about a state contract, that is also called transnational arbitration. In this respect, it can be noted that the Iran–United States Claims Tribunal is in many ways akin to mixed arbitration tribunals. See JA Westberg, *International Transactions and Claims Involving Government Parties. Case Law of the Iran–United States Claims Tribunal* (Washington DC, International Law Institute, 1991) 11–13. However, the exact nature of that Tribunal has come into question; see in *Le tribunal des différends irano-américains* (CEDIN, University of Paris 10, 1985), the opinions of P Fouchard, 'La nature juridique de l'arbitrage du Tribunal des différends irano-américains' 27–48, who inclines towards the *sui generis* character of the institution whereas M Virally, in the discussion of P Fouchard's contribution, sees in it 'a quite classical institution and well known to international lawyers . . . arbitration of public international law' of the same type as the mixed arbitration tribunals set up after conflicts (at 50). However, even if the vast case law engendered by the Iran–United States claims concerns but marginally the issue of state contracts (and mostly for matters of expropriation) its influence will certainly be felt in future in all transnational claims. See B Audit, 'Le Tribunal des différends irano-américain (1981–1984)' (1985) *Journal du Droit International* 791; JR Crook, 'Applicable Law in International Arbitration: The Iran–US Claims Tribunal Experience' (1989) *American Journal of International Law* 278.

tribunals set up on this basis might be international tribunals on the same footing as tribunals created by treaty, as in the examples cited above (p 25). And yet, if one considers that these are contracts made by states as subjects of international law, it is not illogical to consider that the law applicable to the arbitration clause is not national but international law. That, at any rate, is the reasoning the arbitrators followed in the *Aramco, Texaco* and *Liamco* awards.[57] In *Aminoil*, the parties had themselves given the Court the power to 'decide on the procedure applicable to arbitration on the basis of natural justice and the principles of transnational procedure it held applicable'. The arbitrators concluded that 'Given the way the Tribunal was set up, its international or rather transnational character is obvious . . .'.[58]

We shall return to the Tribunal's hesitation between 'international' and 'transnational'. What should be noted is that the Tribunal did not rule out the possibility for a state, in its capacity as a sovereign power, to see its dispute with a company submitted to the decision of an arbitration instance not governed by any domestic law.[59] If, like Mayer, one thinks that the international character of an arbitration tribunal depends on the law governing the arbitration clause,[60] it can be argued that, even with ad hoc arbitration, we are dealing with the configuration of the individual who can bring the state before an international court.

---

[57] For the *Aramco* award see (1963) *Revue Critique de Droit International Privé* ('The arbitration tribunal, considering the arbitration is subject to the rules of international law on the grounds that one of the parties is a state' at 277) and ('It ensues that the arbitration institution cannot but come directly within the remit of international law' at 305). For *Liamco*, the formula was a little more complex: 'the arbitrator in the procedure he follows, must be guided, as far as possible, by the general principles contained in the draft convention on arbitration procedure drawn up by the United Nations International Law Commission in 1958' (1980) *Revue de l'Arbitrage* 147 and also Stern, 'Trois arbitrages' (n 6) 10). This is the famous draft by G Scelle for interstate arbitration that was never adopted (see (1958) *Annuaire Français de Droit International* 441ff).

[58] See the *Aminoil* award of 24 March 1982, 66 *ILR* 519 at 560 reprinted in (1982) *Journal du Droit International* 869, paras 4 and 5, 872.

[59] It was the state in its capacity as a sovereign power since what was in cause was the possibility for the state to make a commitment, in a contract, not to nationalise. This possibility was acknowledged in para 90 of the award on certain conditions stated in para 95, see (1982) *Journal du Droit International* 894–95.

[60] Mayer, 'La neutralisation' (n 4) 32. Mayer, 'Contract claims' (n 13) 35, however, returns to a more conventional conception by considering that the 'most plausible and most widespread [definition] is that a court is an international court when its power to adjudicate is founded by treaty'.

If, on the other hand, one considers like Rigaux that the only inter-national arbitration instances are those set up by an interstate agree-ment, like the ICSID or the Iran–United States Claims Tribunal,[61] one will notice that the success of the Washington Convention (123 ratifications by states representing just about all legal cultures by the end of 1995; 143 ratifications by the end of 2008) leads to a conse-cration of the possibility of direct action by investors against host states and particularly as the ICSID arbitration clause has become commonplace in major investment contracts. While not going so far as to say that the 'international community' has ratified this mech-anism, at least it is now among the common and widely accepted techniques of international economic relations. In any event, it is indeed the state as a subject of international law that is brought by the private person (investor) before an international arbitration tribunal set up under the aegis of the Washington Convention.[62]

The Ongoing Revolution: Bilateral and Multilateral Treaties for the Protection of Investments

The capacity of private persons to act directly against states is under-going considerable development because of the inclusion in a new generation of bilateral treaties for promoting and protecting invest-ments made between investment source states and host states of clauses allowing investors to take cases to the ICSID for any alleged breach by the state of its obligations under the treaty. This is no longer a matter of a contract binding the investor with the host state but of the possibility for individuals to have an arbitration tribunal rule on the state's observance of its international commitments.

---

[61] F Rigaux, 'Contrats d'Etat et arbitrage transnational' (1984) *Rivista di diritto internazionale* 489, 502 and 'Souveraineté des Etats et arbitrage transnational'in *Etudes offertes à B Goldman* (n 4) 269. See also Rousseau, *Droit international public* (n 52): 'the true criterion of the nature of the tribunal [is] a formal one and reside[s] not in the law applied by it or in the capacity of the litigants but in the act that is the source of its creation and its power: it is the existence of an international treaty that constitutes in this respect the decisive criterion' (at 382).

[62] A Giardina, 'L'exécution des sentences du centre international pour le règle-ment des différends relatifs aux investissements' (1982) 71 *Revue Critique de Droit International Privé* 273, 276 dealing with the enforcement of ICSID awards notes that 'the ICSID system has (. . .) its specific connotations that make it not so close to inter-national commercial arbitration as to certain recent achievements in the domain of international courts before which individuals may be parties. The examples are essen-tially that of the Court of Justice of the European Communities, as concerns the enforceability of awards including orders to pay monies and that of the tribunal of the sea that is to be set up by the draft convention drawn up by the third United Nations Conference on the law of the sea'.

This possibility was confirmed in *AAPL v Sri Lanka* (ARB/87/3).[63] In this case arbitration proceedings had been brought for the first time before the ICSID not through an arbitration clause or agreement, but on the basis of the undertaking given in the treaty for protection of investments between the investment source and host states. On the law governing the claim presented by the investor (a Hong Kong company) against the Sri Lankan Government, the arbitrators decided that in view of the arguments exchanged between the parties, they agreed to consider that the provisions of the bilateral convention were the main source of law governing the issue, given that the convention referred also to other sources such as general international law and other conventions.[64] So not only did the investor act directly against the state over an international commitment by the state, but their dispute was subject essentially to international law.

Now it happens that every year a growing number of bilateral protection treaties, some 300 at least, contain the same possibility for an investor to bring a case before the ICSID on the basis of the covering treaty should the private person complain of the breach by the host state of a right conferred by the bilateral investment protection treaty.[65] Furthermore, multilateral treaties are appearing, offering the same options to individuals. Thus, the North American Free Trade

[63] Award 27 June 1990. See E Gaillard, 'Chronique' (1992) *Journal du Droit International* 216 and (1991) 5 *ICSID Review* 526.

[64] Gaillard, *ibid*, 217.

[65] The figure of 300 treaties is given by Shihata and Parra, 'Applicable Substantive Law' (n 22), who estimate that of the 700 bilateral investment protection treaties some 300 contain clauses allowing investors to bring cases before the ICSID (185–86). They further note (at 209) that the United States conclude a growing number of bilateral treaties that all provide the possibility for investors to resort to ICSID arbitration or to other forms of arbitration should they think rights conferred by the treaty are not observed by the state. This is true also of France. See the examples given by P Juillard, 'Chronique' (1994) *Annuaire Français de Droit International* 735 and (1995) *Annuaire Français de Droit International* 607–609. Similarly for Spain, see JA Vives Chillida, *El Centro internacional de arreglo de diferencias a inversions (CIADI) y los tratados de promocion y proteccion de inversions concluido por Espana* (Universitat Pompeu Fabra, Barcelona, 1996) 92ff; see also A Escobar, 'Introductory note on bilateral investment treaties recently concluded by Latin American States' (1996) *ICSID Review* 86 with the texts of 14 recent treaties 95–220 and the standard treaty used by Germany 221–32. E Gaillard in his chronicle of ICSID case law estimates 350 bilateral treaties refer to the Centre: 'Chronique' (1996) *Journal du Droit International* 274. There were more than 2676 investment protection treaties at the end of 2008 (See UNCTAD, *Recent Developments in International Investment Agreements* (2008–June 2009), UNCTAD, IIA Monitor No 3 (2009), UN 2009. The increase since 2008 when this chapter was first written needs no comment. For a recent study of these treaties see UNCTAD, *Bilateral Investment Treaties 1995–2006: Trends in Investment Rulemaking* (New York and Geneva, UN, 2007).

Agreement (NAFTA) Treaty Chapter 11 Section B (settlement of disputes between a party and an investor of another party) sets up a procedure giving investors the possibility to ask for the establishment of an arbitration tribunal either under the Washington Convention or under the supplementary mechanism (provided by the ICSID when states that are not parties to the Convention are involved) or by reference to the UNCITRAL arbitration regulation.[66]

As regards governing law, article 1131(1) refers to the provisions in the NAFTA Treaty and the relevant rules of international law without any reference to the municipal law of states.[67] And likewise in the Energy Charter Treaty, an international convention opened for signature in December 1994 which aimed to set the rules for investment in energy for 41 West and East European states as well as Australia, the United States and Japan, article 26 on dispute settlement provides investors with a choice of action against the state it claims has failed to comply with its commitments about promoting and protecting investments (Energy Charter Treaty title III). The company may bring the dispute either before the domestic courts of the state or resort to dispute settlement mechanisms previously stipulated by the parties, or use those provided for in the Energy Charter Treaty itself. In this event the dispute may be brought before the ICSID (arbitration or supplementary mechanisms) or before an ad hoc arbitration body abiding by the UNCITRAL rules, or before the Arbitration Institute of the Stockholm Chamber of Commerce (article 26(4)).[68]

Notice that, since the Energy Charter Treaty applies in the same way to all states, should it come into force,[69] it would not be impossible for Australian or US investors to bring disputes with, say, the French government before an ICSID arbitration tribunal. The law

---

[66] NAFTA art 1120, text in (1993) *ILM* 643. On this matter see G Burdeau, 'Nouvelles perspectives pour l'arbitrage dans le contentieux économique intéressant les Etats' (1995) *Revue de l'Arbitrage* 3, 20ff. On the ICSID supplementary mechanism see P Rambaud, 'Note sur l'extension du système CIRDI' (1983) *Annuaire Français de Droit International* 290 and A Broches, 'L'évolution du CIRDI' (1979) *Revue de l'Arbitrage* 323.

[67] 'A Tribunal established under this Section shall decide the issues in dispute in accordance with this Agreement and applicable rules of international law' (1993) *ILM* 645.

[68] See P Juillard, 'Chronique' (1994) *Annuaire Français de Droit International* 736, 741 fn 42; T Wälde, 'International Investment under the 1994 Energy Charter' (1995) 29 *Journal of World Trade* 5, 47–50 and 'Investment Arbitration under the Energy Charter Treaty: From dispute settlement to treaty implementation' (1996) *Arbitration International* 429, 457 on governing law.

[69] It did come into force in 1998.

governing the dispute as provided for by article 26(6) is worded exactly like NAFTA article 1131: *the treaty and the relevant rules of international law.* Provisions of the same kind are found in a treaty on reciprocal protection of investments within Mercosur.[70] Likewise, in the multilateral agreement on investments being negotiated within the OECD (Organisation for Economic Co-operation and Development) and whose final conclusion was postponed until spring 1998, it is a question also of inserting provisions of the same type on dispute settlement. But, as is well known, the 1998 OECD draft for a Multilateral Investment Agreement failed.[71]

Lastly, to return to a very specific bilateral treaty, namely the Franco–British treaty on the Channel Tunnel and its operation by concessionary companies, article 19(1)(b) gives jurisdiction to an arbitration tribunal whose establishment is provided for in the treaty to settle 'disputes between the Government and Concessionaires relating to the concession'. The governing law is provided for in article 19(6):

> To settle the disputes relating to the Concession, application is made of the relevant provisions of the Concession Treaty [that is international law]. The rules of French law or of English law may be used, if need be, when recourse to such rules is required by the enforcement of specific obligations of French or English law. The relevant principles of international law may also be applied and, should the parties to the dispute agree thereon, the principle of equity.[72]

---

[70] Colonia Protocol on the Reciprocal Promotion and Protection of Investments within Mercosur, cited by E Gaillard, 'Chronique' (1996) *Journal du Droit International* 274. In quite another domain see art 187 of the Montego Bay Convention and Annex VI of the Convention on the statute of the International Tribunal for the Law of the Sea, art 20(2), which gives access to the Tribunal to entities other than state parties. In this case the applicable law provided for by art 293(1) of the Convention is made up of 'this Convention and the other rules of international law not incompatible with this Convention'.

[71] See TL Brewer, 'International Investment Dispute Settlement Procedures' in *Towards Multilateral Investment Rules* (OECD, Paris 1996) 89 and see the report of working group D, 163. On the 1998 OECD draft see P-M Dupuy and C Leben (SFDI), *Un accord multilateral sur l'investissement: d'un forum de négociation à l'autre?* (Paris, Pedone, 1999).

[72] Treaty between the United Kingdom of Great Britain and Northern Ireland and the French Republic concerning the construction and operation by private concessionaires of a channel fixed line with exchanges of notes, signed at Canterbury on 12 February 1986, HMSO Treaty Series No 15 (1992) and (1987) *Revue Générale de Droit International Public* 1395. See R Goy, 'Le tunnel sous la Manche' (1986) *Annuaire Français de Droit International* 741; G Marcou, R Vickerman and Y Luchaire, *Le Tunnel sous la Manche entre Etats et Marchés* (Villeneuve d'Ascq, Presses Universitaires de Lille, 1992).

The upshot of all this is that private persons (investors) increasingly have the capacity to act directly against states as subjects of international law, not only on the basis of state contracts, but on the basis of treaties that bestow this capacity directly on them. In addition, in both cases, application of international law to this type of dispute is becoming commonplace. Lastly, if one thinks of the number of treaties that allow cases to be taken to the ICSID, it can be predicted that the *AAPL v Sri Lanka* case law will be greatly expanded in the future.[73]

Under these circumstances I see no reason to continue to refuse to see what is the true position of current international law, namely that through entirely different means from those used in the sphere of human rights, private persons have acquired (limited) legal personality in the legal institution of state contracts and more generally in the sphere of investment law by virtue of their *capacity to act directly against states* in international courts in defence of their rights.[74]

On the Preference Given to Public International Law Rather than Transnational Law for Governing State Contracts

Many scholars who accept the specific character of state contracts at the same time dismiss the argument that such contracts can be governed by public international law, either because they do not envisage international law can truly apply in mixed relations, or because they consider it does not contain sufficiently precise rules in the domain of contracts, or, more often than not, for both reasons at once. They propose this new category of contract should be governed by a third legal order, often named transnational law. But this expression covers various concepts and here transnational law as a synonym for *lex mercatoria* must not be confused with transnational law as a law peculiar to mixed relations between states and private persons, nor with Mayer's specific theory of the principles of transnational law.

Dismissal of The *Lex Mercatoria*

Lex mercatoria here means the set of rules and principles arising from the practices of international trade such as they are formulated by

---

[73] See E Gaillard, 'Chronique' (1996) *Journal du Droit International* and Burdeau, 'Nouvelles perspectives' (n 66) 14. Events since this was written in 1998 have borne this out.

[74] The comparison is also made by Burdeau, 'Nouvelles perspectives', *ibid*, 16 and Lillich, 'The Law Governing Disputes' (n 2) 67–68.

private professional and scholarly institutions (see recently the
UNIDROIT principles on international commercial contracts,
Rome 1994) and by arbitrators who accept to adjudicate in the name
of this *lex mercatoria*, which some commentators also call transnational law.[75]

There are both theoretical and practical reasons for considering
that state contracts, as defined here, cannot be contracts made in the
legal order of the *lex mercatoria*. As they are contracts entered into by
states as subjects of international law it is inconceivable they can be
governed by a legal order born from the *societas mercatorum*, that is,
from international trade among private persons.[76] Notice that article
42(1) of the Washington Convention makes no allusion to this type of
transnational law. The Athens (1979) and Santiago de Compostella
(1989) resolutions of the Institute of International Law probably refer
to it but without using the expressions *lex mercatoria* or transnational
law.[77]

However, observing governing law clauses in state contracts of
which I am aware, there are barely any express references to the *lex
mercatoria*, but occasionally expressions that might have that meaning.

This is the case in the contract between the State of Gabon,
Petrogab and Swiss Oil Corp as revealed by a 1987 International
Criminal Court (ICC) award, where the governing law was 'the law
of the Gabonese Republic and the universally recognised laws and
practices of international trade'.[78]

Similarly in a contract of 23 July 1989 between the Sultanate of
Oman and an oil company, article 24(3) contained the ambiguous
clause:

[75] On the *lex mercatoria* see B Goldman, 'La *lex mercatoria* dans les contrats et l'arbitrage international' (1979) *Journal du Droit International* 475; E Gaillard, 'Trente
ans de *lex mercatoria*. Pour une application sélective de la méthode des principes
généraux de droit' (1995) *Journal du Droit International* 5; I Strenger, 'La notion de
lex mercatoria en droit du commerce international' (1991) 228 *Recueil des Cours de
l'Académie de Droit International* 211–355; A Giardina, 'Les principes UNIDROIT
sur les contrats internationaux' (1995) *Journal du Droit International* 547.

[76] See also Weil, 'Droit international et contrats d'Etat' (n 4) 387, 407: '[I]t is difficult to support the idea that the law applicable to state contracts can be likened to
that governing relations among private traders to the point it forms one and the same
"set of rules of law"'.

[77] See art 2 of the Athens resolution of the Institute of International Law in 1979
about the law governing agreements between states and private persons, (1979)
(58/II) *Institute of International Law Yearbook* 194 and art 6 of the resolution adopted
at Santiago de Compostella in 1989 on arbitration among states and foreign companies, (1989) (63/II) *Institute of International Law Yearbook* 330.

[78] See Paris (1ère Ch. suppl.) 16 juin 1988, Société Swiss Oil c/ Société Petrogab
et République du Gabon; C Jarrosson 'Note' (1989) *Revue de l'Arbitrage* 309.

> In construing and interpreting this Agreement, the arbitrators shall apply the generally accepted customs and usages of the international petroleum industry and principles of law generally recognized by the nations of the world.

The first part of the sentence suggests the *lex mercatoria* while the second part suggest rather the principles of public international law.

Equally ambiguous wording is found in the 1993 standard Chinese contract for petroleum exploration. Its article 28 provides that the governing law is the law of the People's Republic of China but adds:

> Failing the relevant provisions of the laws of the People's Republic of China for the interpretation or implementation of the contract, the principles of the applicable laws widely used in petroleum resources countries acceptable to the parties shall be applicable.

The notion of state contract being both a notion that has been under construction for 50 years and a subject on which there is nothing nearing consensus in doctrine, it is hardly surprising to find that state contracts contain clauses that are neither fish, flesh nor fowl. However, in most cases, what the authors have taken to be references to transnational law was a reference to the general principles of law in which, for theoretical reasons, they have refused to see principles of international law (text to nn 82–83).[79]

One might anyway think that the role assigned initially to the *lex mercatoria* in state contracts stems from a historical combination of circumstances. At about the same time as scholars like Goldman or Schmitthoff were observing the development of an a-national law in international trade, there appeared the first petroleum arbitration awards wherein arbitrators sought principles outside the law of a contracting state to settle disputes submitted to them. As the arbitrators justified their dismissal of the host state's law by its inadequacy (an argument used generally by proponents of the *lex mercatoria*: the inadequacy of domestic laws for international trade relations) and they invoked the usages of the profession (some spoke of a *lex petrolea*) and the general principles of law that are also the

---

[79] On the ambiguities of references to general principles of law see Weil, 'Droit international et contrats d'Etat' (n 4). He notes that while reference to general principles of law alone is not necessarily a reference to international law, in some instances it may be if we are dealing with a contract that is 'rooted in the international legal order' (at 408–409). For me, the wording might be modified slightly to read 'if it is a contract made with a state as a subject of international law'.

sources invoked for the *lex mercatoria*, commentators conflated the two phenomena. As no distinction was drawn between contracts made by states for ordinary commercial transactions (purchase of plant or equipment, licensing agreements, etc) where it might be meaningful to invoke the *lex mercatoria* and investment contracts, which by their specific characteristics appeared to be undertakings of states as subjects of international law, scholars included 'state contracts' in their reasoning on the *lex mercatoria*.

And conversely, some scholars, observing that the reasons that had impelled the early arbitrators to take refuge in what they thought was a third legal order no longer existed because all the countries concerned had adopted a modern and complete law, therefore concluded state contracts were no more.[80] But this is to lump together two phenomena that are actually unrelated: the early petroleum arbitration awards demonstrated the emergence of a new type of contract in which states as subjects of international law contracted outside their own legal orders. And the legal order that accommodated this new type of contract was gradually to prove to be none other than public international law. The existence nowadays of developed municipal laws has no repercussion on this analysis.

Dismissal of Transnational Law as Specific Law in Mixed Relations

First, it should be noticed again that this transnational law (distinct from the *lex mercatoria*) is not invoked to govern just any old contract between a state and an individual but solely the specific type of contract that is isolated in some way or other and designated as a state contract. Practically, it is for petroleum concession contracts (and for international loan agreements too) that legal scholars, in doctrine, have proposed to apply general principles of law supposedly situated in a third legal order between the municipal order and the international order.[81]

---

[80] See AS El-Kosheri and TF Riad, 'The Law Governing a New Generation of Petroleum Agreements: Changes in the Arbitration Process' (1986) *ICSID Review* 257; G Delaume, 'The Proper Law of State Contracts and the Lex Mercatoria: A Reappraisal' (1988) *ICSID Review* 79.

[81] See JF Lalive, 'Contrats entre Etats ou entreprises étatiques et personnes privées. Développements récents' (1983) 181 *Recueil des Cours de l'Académie de Droit International* 9 (at 31 for the definition of transnational law). Other workers speak of quasi-international law. See H Pazarci, 'La responsabilité internationale des Etats à l'occasion des contrats conclus entre Etats et personnes privées étrangères' (1975) *Revue Générale de Droit International Public* 354.

This proposal in fact covered a desire to internationalise such contracts, a desire that dared not come out into the open because, in principle, it excluded individuals from the sphere of international law. This is particularly clear in McNair's 1957 paper (one of the pioneering papers on the issue) about the general principles of law recognised by civilised nations. On contracts between states and foreign companies and that had certain specific features such as that they relate to the long-term exploitation of a country's natural resources, the acquisition of property rights over large tracts of territory, the enjoyment of certain semi-political privileges such as tax exemptions, etc, McNair says:

> [I]t is submitted that the legal system appropriate to the type of contract under consideration is not public international law but shares with public international law a common source of recruitment and inspiration, namely, 'the general principles of law recognised by civilized nations'.[82]

And he further specifies it can only be a third system and not '*public international law stricto sensu* as at present understood, *because the contracts do not deal with interstate relations*' (emphasis added).[83]

In reality the reference to this type of general principle recognised by civilised nations (in some contracts the adjective is omitted) was subsequently more generally considered to be a reference to public international law itself.[84] Likewise, scholars favourable to this approach to transnational law proposed to apply international law by 'analogy'. What might this mean other than that arbitrators are invited to reason as if they were in the international legal order but that a veil of modesty is thrown over this fact by speaking of transnational law so as not to have to accept private persons as recipients of an international contract law, which was certainly in limbo in the 1950–60s but no more so than transnational contract law?[85]

---

[82] AD McNair, 'The General Principles of Law Recognised by Civilized Nations' (1957) *British Yearbook of International Law* 1, 6.

[83] McNair, *ibid* 19.

[84] See rapport van Hecke, (1977) (57/I) *Insititute of International Law Yearbook* 195. The rapporteur notes that 'On the whole the answers [of the Institute of International Law Commission members] were more favourable to the notion of general principles of law considered as a part of international law than to the notion of general principles considered to form a third legal order that would be neither national nor international'.

[85] Pazarci, 'La responsabilité internationale' (n 81), while rejecting transnational law (at 387–88) pleads for a 'quasi-international' law. The idea is not remote: one reasons as if it were international law while saying it is not. One can return on this point to the hestitation noted (n 58) of the arbitration tribunal in the *Aminoil* case on the 'international or rather transnational' character of the tribunal. Notice that in

Again it must be observed that when the Washington Convention setting up the ICSID was negotiated, the positions of the states were quite clear: some were for municipal law and others for international law. There was no question of a specific transnational law, just as there is no question of it in article 42(1) of the Washington Convention nor in bilateral treaties for investment protection nor in multilateral treaties like the NAFTA or the Energy Charter Treaty.

However, it should be added that the adjective 'transnational' must be reserved not to designate any legal order specific to state contracts but to designate *one of the contemporary branches of public international law*. This covers interstate relations, relations between states and international organisations or between international organisations themselves, and relations between states and individuals. It is convenient for designating this last specific branch of public international law to say that it applies to transnational relations.

Dismissal of Mayer's Theory

In his paper on the neutralisation of normative power, Mayer takes a highly original stance. While considering that 'transnational relations' [and this means state contracts *stricto sensu*] call for their own rules, he proposes 'to call those rules transnational principles' while reminding readers that he does not see in them 'the content of a third legal order, but legal proposals only by their object, intended for arbitrators and established by doctrine and by themselves'.[86] These rules do not derive from any autonomous legal order and the state contract proves to be a *contrat sans loi* that has 'as a disconcerting particularity', notes Mayer, 'that it only finds its principle of validity on the day the arbitrator makes an adjudication'. Again this assertion needs to be supplemented because the arbitrator's decision 'being private, can found nothing in itself, but [it is] state rules that recognise the award has binding force [that] indirectly confer its binding force on the contract'.[87] The contractual relations between the state and the foreign company are not subject to any law but it is for the arbitrators to invent the proper rules for transnational relations drawing inspiration from the general principles of law and adapting them to the specificities of state contracts.

reasoning on the merits, the tribunal refers constantly to public international law (see paras 70(1), 78, 90, 101, 142 and 157). The only time the tribunal refers to a third legal order, 'a *lex petrolea* that [is supposedly] a sort of specific branch of a general and universal *lex mercatoria*' is to dismiss it (paras 155–56).

[86] Mayer, 'La neutralisation' (n 4) 29.
[87] *Ibid*, 25.

Although Mayer invites us to shake off our 'theoretical scruples about *contrats sans loi*' one cannot help feeling most reticent about a construction in which the mandatory character of state contracts becomes apparent only when the arbitrator intervenes or perhaps even only when the award, a pure private dictum, receives the authority for enforcement in a municipal legal order. Mayer further asserts:

> The important thing is to have a judge and a system of constraint outside of the parties. The rules are very useful, but when they have to be invented anyway, it does not matter whether this is in the name of some legal order or autonomously.[88]

This assertion is debateable. For the invention of rules in the name of a legal order provides its basis both to the action of the judge/arbitrator and to the mandatory character of the contractual relations on which the judge/arbitrator adjudicates. If it is true that the rules to apply to state contracts are largely uncovered by arbitration case law, it is more consistent to enshrine such contracts and this case law within a legal order that alone is liable to impart the character of a mandatory contract to the expression of the agreement between the parties. It can even be added that the parties present, states and companies, will find it more legitimate and will more readily accept to see their relations placed within a clearly identified legal system. The many references to international law that are found in contracts, in various forms, and the wording of the second sentence of article 42(1) clearly express this desire of contracting parties (states and companies) to come within a specific legal order.

Against this is very often opposed the indigence of international contract law that allegedly comes down to a few vague general principles of law.[89] Two remarks can be made on this. First, it will be recalled with Lauterpacht that 'the history of law teaches us that courts preceded codes and the establishment of detailed rules of law'. And the fact is 'an elementary legal system, with only a few very general rules to guide the court is complete when the members of the community are bound by the duty to submit their disputes to the

---

[88] *Ibid.*

[89] See J Combacau and S Sur, *Droit international public* 2nd edn (Paris, Montchrestien, 1995) 322: 'an essential condition is missing for such contracts to be characterised as formal international acts: the existence of a body of international rules in which one can reasonably see a "law of contracts" analogous to that the various municipal laws propose'. See also J Verhoeven, 'Droit international des contrats et droit des gens' (1978/9) *Revue Belge de Droit International* 209.

court's decision'.[90] Now if one considers, for example, the system deriving from the Washington Convention, we are in exactly this position and it is for the ICSID tribunals to elaborate, in a judicial fashion, the rules of international contract law, since it is indeed international law that ultimately governs article 42(1) (text to note 35).

And already commentators have been able to establish various rules from the case law of this tribunal (*pacta sunt servanda*, observance of acquired rights, allowance for changed circumstances, validity of stabilisation clauses and even, under certain circumstances, of non-nationalisation, the amount of compensation and means of calculating it in the event of nationalisation, observance of financial balance of the contract, obligation to negotiate and cooperate in good faith, prohibition of self-contradiction to the detriment of others, etc).[91]

This would not be the first time either in international law or in municipal law that the content of a law has been developed by the activity of courts. But in reality things have already gone beyond this point. The law of state contracts lies within investment law and arbitration tribunals are increasingly led to take account of the provisions of international conventions that number in their thousands. The World Bank has engaged in an exercise of unofficially codifying the principles that flow from the vast network of bilateral treaties for protecting investments and from the existing arbitration case law. This resulted in the publication in 1992 of *Guidelines on the Treatment of Foreign Direct Investment*, whose title IV (*Expropriation and Unilateral*

---

[90] H Lauterpacht, 'La théorie des différends non justiciables en droit international' (1930) 34 *Recueil des Cours de l'Académie de Droit International de La Haye* 539.

[91] M El Younsi, 'Les règles matérielles du droit des contrats d'Etat à la lumière de la jurisprudence arbitrale contemporaine' (Thesis, University of Paris 2, 1994). See also E Gaillard, 'Chronique' (1987) *Journal du Droit International* 155–56 on *Amco Asia v Indonesian Republic* in which he lists no fewer than nine principles of international law that can be derived from the award. But it is true that for him these are principles belonging to the *lex mercatoria*. (See also Gaillard, 'Trente ans' (n 75)). I have stated my reasons for rejecting this (text to nn 74–75). But independently of this question of principle, there is nothing to prevent several such rules deduced from the general principles of law from being both in international contract law and in the *lex mercatoria*. This is even inevitable as in any event the general principles are abstracted from features shared by the main national legal systems. This does not mean, though, that the principles apply in exactly the same way in either order. For example, the presence of the state in a state contract may lead to a different interpretation of a principle applicable also in relations between private persons. On all these issues see Weil, 'Droit international et contrats d'Etat' (n 4) and the somewhat different approach of M Virally 'Un tiers droit? Réflexions théoriques' also in *Etudes offertes à B Goldman* (Paris, Litec, 1982) 373, 380ff.

Alterations or Termination of Contracts) may be considered an important fragment of customary international contract law.[92] To this
should be added the principles deriving from the multilateral treaties
(NAFTA, Energy Charter Treaty, the failed OECD multilateral
agreement on investments and also the GATT agreement on trade-
related measures concerning investment) to realise that the situation
is now very different from that of the 1950–60s when arbitrators had
virtually complete creative freedom. It is clear that an international
contract law is now being consolidated independently of judge-made
rules based on general principles of law, even if we are still obviously
a long way from having a full set of international norms.

Ultimately, the major hurdle for commentators like Mayer to the
inclusion of state contracts as he himself defines them in international law is a conception of international law as a purely interstate
law; or, from another perspective, the refusal to consider it is possible for individuals to be limited subjects of public international law
is the alpha and omega of this attitude.[93] This may never have been
better put than in a 1959 course at The Hague by the Italian scholar
Sereni in which he explained:

> Each legal system serves the purpose of regulating the status and relations
> of social entities for which and among which it exists. An attempt at
> applying international law to private relations would be tantamount to
> seeking to apply the matrimonial laws of France or England to relations
> between cats and dogs.[94]

[92] See the text of the *Guidelines* in (1992) *Annuaire Français de Droit International*
801 together with P Juillard, 'Chronique' 779. The studies that served as a basis for
the ICSID in formulating these Guidelines are reproduced in a special issue of that
institution's journal (1992) 2 *ICSID Review*.

[93] Notice that to formulate his principles of transnational law, Mayer (n 4) finds
nothing better than to take inspiration from public international law. Thus, for the
acceptance of an abritration clause by a state that is contrary to the legislation in force,
the best solution seems to be that set out by treaty law in art 46 of the Vienna
Convention. And he adds: 'there is in fact no reason to apply a different rule when the
state's partner is not another state but a foreign company' (at 47). And likewise for
illegal acts likely to implicate the state's extra-contractual liability relative to a contract
made with one of its emanations, the rules of public international law seem equally
appropriate to him (at 60–62). The rules therefore seem transposable but the coexis-
tence of these beings (states and private persons) in the international legal order seems
impossible to him (at 77).

[94] AP Sereni, 'International Economic Institutions and the Municipal Law of
States' (1959-I) 96 *Recueil des Cours de l'Académie de Droit International de La Haye*
133, 210. That an Italian should express this opposition so strongly will not be
surprising if it is realised that this ultimately expresses a dualist doctrinal position.
See H Triepel, 'Les rapports entre le droit interne et le droit international' (1923) 1
Recueil des Cours de l'Académie de Droit International de La Haye 77, 80: '. . . public

One could of course retort that state contracts are not 'private relations' but Sereni's jibe was directed at discussion about the governing law of petroleum concessions. We have here two implacable
conceptions of what international law should and could be: a law
essentially confined to interstate relations or a law whose expansion
is boundless, that can cover any domain, a law of which individuals
may be direct subjects, with the sole proviso, as Kelsen noted, that
this possibility must remain exceptional on pain of seeing the borderline between international law and national law disappear.[95] And
it is that very phenomenon that is observed with the very peculiar
form of international law that we know as Community law.

international law governs the relations between states and only between perfectly
equal states. . . . Individuals, from the point of view of a community of law binding
states as such, are unable to be invested with their own rights and duties deriving from
a legal system of *this* community'. This assertion can be compared with Kelsen's position in his first lesson at The Hague: 'Les rapports de système entre le droit interne et
le droit international public' (1926) 14 *Recueil des Cours de l'Académie de Droit
International de La Haye* 231, 283–86 where he argues that the fact that international
law applies immediately to states and only mediately to individuals 'is not inherent to
international law [and] does not constitute a necessary feature of its norms' (at 284).
A fuller demonstration is given in the 1932 course: 'Théorie générale du droit international public. Problèmes choisis' (1932) 42 *Recueil des Cours de l'Académie de Droit
International de La Haye* 121, 141–72 with the same conclusion: 'International law
has, as a general rule, for subject states, that is individuals in a *mediate* manner (ie,
individuals whose action or inaction shall be counted as actions or inactions of the
state since the state can act only through individuals)—exceptionally also individuals
in an *immediate* way. *It is not contrary to the nature of international law that what is today
an exception should one day become the rule*' (at 270) (emphasis added). Beware that the
notion of mediate application of international law has not quite the same meaning in
the 1926 course as in the 1932 course.

[95] Kelsen, General Theory (n 52) 348.

2

The International Responsibility of States based on Investment Promotion and Protection Treaties*

ANYONE INTERESTED IN international investment law knows there has been a tremendous change in their discipline, a change that entails major implications for the nature and workings of international law, even if not all internationalists yet realise or acknowledge this.

International investment law had already undergone remarkable change during the twentieth century, change that led to the invention of mixed (or transnational) arbitration between states and private persons (investors), to the advent of a certain type of internationalised contract known as 'state contracts' and to the creation of an arbitration centre established by international treaty, the International Centre for Settlement of Investment Disputes (ICSID), set up by the Washington Convention of 18 March 1965 and now ratified by 142 states.[1] But it is a pity this change has been too widely disregarded.

This initial movement has been compounded since the final decade of the twentieth century by the rush to conclude bilateral

---

* First published as 'La responsabilité internationale de l'Etat sur le fondement des traités de promotion et de protection des investissements' (2004) *Annuaire Français de Droit International* 683.
[1] There were 144 members in July 2009 but with the departure of Bolivia in 2007 and Ecuador in 2009, the two big multilateral conventions of international economic law have a comparably large number of subscribers: the WTO had 153 members in July 2008. On the ICSID see E Gaillard, *La jurisprudence du CIRDI* (Paris, Pedone, 2004); S Manciaux, *Investissements étrangers et arbitrage entre Etats et ressortissants d'autres Etats. Trente années d'activités du CIRDL* (Dijon, CREDIMI, Paris, Litec, 2004); W Ben Hamida, 'L'arbitrage transnational unilatéral' (Thesis, University of Paris 2, 2003). On the development of investment law in the twentieth century see C Leben, 'La théorie du contrat d'Etat et l'évolution du droit international des investissements' (2003) 302 *Recueil des Cours de l'Académie de Droit International de La Haye* 197.

treaties for the promotion and protection of investments.[2] These surged from 385 in 1989 to 2181 in 2002 (and numbered 2676 by the end of 2008), while 176 states are contracting parties to at least one bilateral treaty.[3] Allowance must be made too for the appearance of several multilateral conventions that include provisions of the same type: NAFTA (1994, Chapter 11); Energy Charter Treaty (1994); Colonia Protocol for the Promotion and Protection of Investment in Mercosur (1994); investment treaty concluded among ASEAN (The Association of Southeast Asian Nations) member countries (1987), not to mention the OECD's still-born attempt to draw up a multilateral agreement on investments (1998).[4]

This movement, whose positive effect on international investments from north to south is much discussed,[5] accompanied the failure of the New International Economic Order of the mid-1970s–mid-1980s and confirmed the acceptance, *nolens volens*, by virtually all states—whether from north or south, whether former (eastern European) or still officially communist states (China, Vietnam, Cuba)—of a liberal (in the economic sense) set of rules for international investment flows. To promote such flows, firms are offered both economic incentives (such as tax breaks) and legal incentives. The latter usually include the possibility for firms, in the event of a dispute with investment host states, to implement arbitration proceedings ensuring any dispute is settled by a neutral arbitration panel applying law that is not controlled by the host state.

The movement was given further impetus when the ICSID arbitration panels accepted jurisdiction no longer exclusively on the basis

---

[2] Hereinafter referred to as protection treaties or BITs.

[3] See UNCTAD, *World Investment Report* 89 (Geneva, 2003).

[4] The Lisbon Energy Charter Treaty of 17 December 1994 includes 51 EU states, text in OJ L380/24, 31 December 1994; the Colonia Protocol of 17 January 1994 brings together Argentina, Brazil, Paraguay and Uruguay; the 1987 ASEAN Treaty among Brunei, Indonesia, Malaysia, the Philippines, Singapore and Thailand (1998) *ILM* 612. For the aborted multilateral investment agreement see Société Française pour le Droit International, *Un accord multilatéral sur l'investissement: d'un forum de négociation à l'autre?* (Paris, Pedone, 1999).

[5] There is an abundant legal and economic literature on the effectiveness of bilateral treaties in attracting investment. The tone is generally more sceptical. See J Salacuse and N Sullivan, 'Do BITs Really Work: An Evaluation of Bilateral Investment Treaties and their Grand Bargain' (2005) *Harvard Journal of International Law* 67. For a very negative answer see AT Guzman, 'Why LDCs Sign Treaties that Hurt Them' (1998) *Virginia Journal of International Law* 637. See also UNCTAD, *Bilateral Investment Treaties in the Mid-1990s* (New York, UN, 1998); UNCTAD, *Bilateral Investment Treaties 1995–2006: Trends in Investment Rulemaking* (New York and Geneva, UN, 2007).

of an arbitration clause inserted in an agreement between investor and state, but on the basis of a national statute (*SPP v Egypt*, 1988) or a bilateral treaty (*AAPL v Sri Lanka*, 1990) by which states expressed their intention to settle disputes of this type by arbitration.[6] Rightly or wrongly some scholars thought such intent in itself was not enough to bestow jurisdiction on the arbitration tribunal, before which cases could only be brought on the basis of an arbitration clause contained in an investment agreement.[7] The emergence of what has been called *arbitration without privity* or *unilateral transnational arbitration*, while it may have shocked some, is nowadays (some 15 years' later) the leading form of settlement of international investment disputes.[8] More particularly, the ICSID has become the world's leading centre for the settlement of this type of dispute and handles an increasing case load: 19 in 2002, 31 in 2003 including 17 for the Argentine Republic alone and 27 in 2004.[9] These are disputes involving sometimes very substantial sums not only between developing states and multilateral firms, but also between multinational firms and the USA and Canada under the NAFTA Treaty.[10] It should be noticed that other arbitration centres, like that of the Stockholm Chamber of Commerce or the ICC Court of Arbitration, also benefit from this movement, as do ad hoc arbitration tribunals set up under the UNCITRAL arbitration rules.

That, briefly then, is the background to any legal study of international investment law. The issue to be addressed here is what is the

---

[6] See 'Southern Pacific Properties (Middle East) Ltd (SPP) v Arab Republic of Egypt, 14 April 1988' 3 *ICSID Reports* 131; (1994) *Journal du Droit International* 220; E Gaillard, *La jurisprudence du CIRDI* (n 1) 347; 'Asian Agricultural Products Limited (AAPL) v Socialist Democratic Republic of Sri Lanka, award of 27 June 1990' (1992) *Journal du Droit International*; Gaillard, *La jurisprudence du CIRDI* (n 1) 216 and (1991) *ILM* 577.

[7] See G Burdeau, 'Nouvelles perspectives pour l'arbitrage dans le contentieux économique intéressant les Etats' (1995) *Revue de l'Arbitrage* 3; B Stern, 'Le consentement à l'arbitrage CIRDI en matière d'investissement international: que disent les travaux préparatoires?' in *Souveraineté étatique et marchés internationaux à la fin du XXe. Mélanges en l'honneur de Philippe Kahn* (Dijon, CNRS & Litec, 2000) 119.

[8] See J Paulsson, 'Arbitration without Privity' (1995) 2 *ICSID Review* 232. Two good general studies are available in French: Manciaux, *Investissements étrangers* (n 1) and Ben Hamida, 'L'arbitrage transnational unilatéral' (n 1) and see also P Kahn and T Wälde (eds), *Les aspects nouveaux du droit des investissements internationaux* (Leiden, Martinus Nijhoff, 2007).

[9] E Gaillard, 'Chronique' (2005) *Journal du Droit International* 135.

[10] It is ironic that at present North America is the part of the world with most claims involving expropriation: some ten cases against the USA alone, whose liability for expropriation was challenged for the first time in its history on the basis of an international treaty in *Loewen v US*, award of 26 June 2003; Gaillard, *La jurisprudence du CIRDI* (n 1) 775; (2004) *Journal du Droit International* 219; (2003) *ILM* 881.

nature of state responsibility when implicated by investors on the basis of protection treaties? Of course, such treaties between investment source states and host states belong to the realms of international law. But what of the relations that are established between the host state and the investor, either because of a contract or (although the two may be compounded) because of referral of a dispute by the private party to an arbitration tribunal provided for in the protection treaty? Is the investor's action also in the international legal order? Some commentators doubt this because in their view private persons cannot accede to the international legal order. I shall try to show, to the contrary, that it is indeed in this international legal order that the private person's action is situated, and that a new chapter must be added to the study of the international responsibility of states, which the International Law Commission (ILC) alluded to when it declared in its *Articles on State Responsibility for Internationally Wrongful Acts* (2001) article 33 (2): 'This part (part 2) is without prejudice to any right, arising from the international responsibility of a State, which may accrue directly to any person or entity other than a State'. It shall then be seen how a state's international responsibility squares with its responsibility in the internal legal order.

State Responsibility in the International Legal Order

Anyone failing to comply with the law and wronging another is under an obligation to right the wrong so caused. This is the basic mechanism of civil responsibility (to keep to the name used in law in the French tradition) in any legal order. The obligation to right the wrong may have a contractual basis where there is an agreement between the two persons, or it may be founded in tort where, in the absence of any such agreement, a wrongful act has been committed that has caused some loss or damage. The involvement of a person's responsibility invariably lies within a given legal order, whether a national (the law of some state or other) or the international order. In the latter case, it is public international law that governs state responsibility for internationally illegal acts. This responsibility concerns the acts of one state with regard to another state, and customary international law—on which much of this responsibility still relies—has been the subject matter of a very substantial attempt at codification by the ILC for more than 40 years.[11]

[11] J Crawford, *The International Law Commission's Articles on State Responsibility* (Cambridge, Cambridge University Press, 2002).

These rules of general international law do not concern just relations among states, which are the hard core of international relations. The question arises as to whether these rules are appropriate for governing the other subjects recognised by the law of nations, namely intergovernmental organisations in their mutual relations or in their relations with states. More complex still is the matter, which arose several decades ago, of state responsibility in states' relations with private persons, when such relations do not lie within a municipal legal order. But can such a hypothesis even be conceived of? There is an already long-standing controversy on this topic as to the possibility of encompassing a contractual relation within the international legal order, whether it is termed a state contract, an internationalised contract or an economic development agreement. I have dealt with this question elsewhere and shall not dwell on it here.[12]

More recently, the development of bilateral or multilateral treaties for promoting and protecting investments has given rise to a new question: does state responsibility on the basis of such treaties lie within the general regime of the states' international responsibility as it has been constructed over the last 100 or 150 years and such as it arises from the ILC's codification work? It is true that responsibility on the basis of investment protection treaties has specific characteristics that set it apart from the law of responsibility as it has developed, in the same domain of international investments, but via the mechanism for diplomatic protection. In practice, nothing in these specific characteristics precludes us from seeing in treaty-based responsibility a sub-system within the general international law system of state responsibility.

Characteristics of States' International Responsibility on the Basis of Protection Treaties

So far we have spoken of state responsibility on the basis of treaties as if this responsibility covered just one type of relation between states and investors. But scrutiny of contractual clauses shows there are actually three separate types of relation that may give rise to three

[12] See Leben, 'La théorie du contrat d'Etat' (n 1) and its references. For the first major summary on the question see P Weil, 'Problèmes relatifs aux contrats passés entre un Etat et un particulier' (1969-III) 128 *Recueil des Cours de l'Académie de Droit International de La Haye* 96. See also AFM Maniruzzaman, 'The Relevance of Public International Law in Arbitrations covering International Economic Development Agreements' (2005) 2 *Journal of World Investment and Trade* 263.

different types of dispute between the host state, the investor and the state of origin. These three types of dispute are liable to involve the state's international responsibility under circumstances other than those surrounding the classical implementation of diplomatic protection.

Three Types of Dispute

There are, in respect of state responsibility on the basis of a protection treaty, two levels of relations that must be clearly distinguished, the distinction having consequences on the way certain complex matters are treated, such as the way the different procedures for implementing responsibility hinge together, or the determination of the nature of disputes as contract-based or treaty-based disputes. There are, therefore, at a first level, the relations between the investor and the host state and, at a second and third level, the relations between the investor's home state and the host state.

Disputes between Host State and Investor

It should first be recalled that, regardless of the existence of an investment protection treaty, an investor may invoke its state partner's responsibility on the basis of the agreement it has entered into with the state. If the agreement provides for redress through international arbitration, and more specifically through ICSID arbitration, and if the governing law is international law or the principles common to municipal law and international law, or any other expression of the kind,[13] we are dealing with a situation resembling a dispute on the basis of a protection treaty. What is at issue in both instances is the international 'conventional' responsibility (in the widest sense) of the state, that is, both on the basis of a contract and on the basis of a treaty. In both cases the private person is itself entitled to invoke that responsibility before an international arbitral tribunal. The difference between the two cases is that in the first, that of a state contract, the investor may invoke the breach of the actual contract before the arbitrators whereas, in the absence of any such contract, the investor will have to base its claim on the violation of a protection treaty.

Protection treaties invariably contain two types of dispute settlement clause: one between the investor and the host state; the other between the two states signatories of the treaty.

[13] See Leben, 'La théorie du contrat d'Etat' (n 1) 264.

The dispute between the investor and the host state may be brought unilaterally by the investor before an international arbitration tribunal; and that is the most revolutionary feature of the entire system. Sometimes too an alternative avenue is open to the private person. Thus, to cite just two examples concerning a bilateral and then a multilateral treaty, article 8 of the treaty between France and Chile of 14 July 1992 (*Journal Officiel*, 8 November 1995):

> 1. Any dispute relating to investments between one of the contracting parties and a national or a company of the other contracting party is, as far as possible, to be settled amicably between the two parties concerned. 2. If it has not been possible to settle such a dispute within six months from the time it was raised by either of the parties to the dispute, it is submitted at the request of the national or of the company either to the competent court of the contracting party in the territory of which the investment was made or to the arbitration of the International Centre for Settlement of Investment Disputes (ICSID) [. . .]. 3. The arbitration decision is final and mandatory.

Article 26 (3a) of the Energy Charter Treaty states:

> Subject only to subparagraphs (b) and (c), each Contracting Party hereby gives its unconditional consent to the submission of a dispute to international arbitration or conciliation in accordance with the provisions of this Article.

The Two Tiers of Dispute between Host State and Investor Home State
To the first level, protection treaties add a second level which is that between the two states, the investor's home state and the investment host state, which relates to the settlement of a dispute between states themselves, disputes that may arise in particular from their differing interpretations of the terms of the treaty to which they are parties and of their respective obligations. Should disputes continue beyond a certain time (say, six months) all treaties contain a clause providing for the dispute to be submitted, at the request of one of the contracting parties, to an arbitration tribunal.[14]

---

[14] Art 11(2) of the France/Chile Treaty: 'If the dispute is not settled within six months of the time it was raised by either of the Contracting Parties, it shall be submitted at the request of either Contracting Party, to an arbitration tribunal'. Similarly, art 27(2) of the Energy Charter Treaty: 'If a dispute has not been settled in accordance with para (1) within a reasonable period of time, either party thereto may . . . submit the matter to an ad hoc tribunal under this Article'.

To this must be added a third level, should the host state not accept the arbitration procedure provided for in the protection treaty or refuse to execute the award. In this event, we return to the traditional mechanism for implementing international responsibility by the classical scheme of things as presented in the ILC articles on state responsibility, including the possibility of engaging in countermeasures proportionate to the violation of international law.[15]

In particular, the mechanism of diplomatic protection, which is the prime means of invoking the responsibility of a state that fails to comply with its international obligations with respect to a foreign national, is suspended by article 27(1) of the Washington convention under which no contracting state shall give diplomatic protection in respect of one of its nationals or bring any international claim in respect of a dispute between its nationals and another contracting state. However, should a contracting state fail to comply with an award made in a dispute with the investor, the conventional dispute settlement procedures between states may be activated.

The second and third levels concern relations between states and so are incontestably governed by the rules of public international law, especially the rules concerning international liability for illegal international acts. The first level, on the contrary, concerns relations between the investor (private person) and the investment host state. This is where the question arises as to the nature of the ties between state and investor. Are they ties governed by public international law, or by municipal law, or even by a third legal order? But what is the point of asking such a question, one might think? To my mind it is fundamental. Situating a legal relationship within a certain legal order indicates in what general legal context the judicial instances are to interpret the law. The law is not construed in the same way within a state order or an international legal order or even in some third order (transnational law or *lex mercatoria*, provided it is clearly defined what this means).

For example, in the event the judge or arbitrator feels there is a lacuna, they may want to look to custom or to the general principles of law. But in doing so, a municipal court will not reason like an

---

[15] This hypothesis was allowed for in the OECD draft Multilateral Agreement on Investments, which envisaged suspending rights derived from the MIA in reaction to any failure by one of the parties to comply with its obligations in the area of dispute settlement. See J Kokott, 'Interim Report on the Role of Diplomatic Protection in the Field of the Protection of Foreign Investment' (2000) *ILA Report of the 70th Conference, New Delhi* 259, 275.

international court, if only because the municipal court may be very reticent to call on custom, which plays a very limited role in a state order such as that of France, whereas custom is a major source of international law. And this remark holds for resort to the general principles of law too. Everything hangs on what type of international court one finds oneself before: the judge of a permanent court, an arbitrator set up by international treaty (ICSID or 1981 Algiers Accords on the settlement of disputes between Iran and the USA), an ICC arbitrator adjudicating under ICC arbitration rules or an ad hoc tribunal governed by UNCITRAL rules or by rules established by the parties themselves.

To answer this question one must set this responsibility of the state with regard to the investor on the basis of protection treaties against what for more than a century has been the most important mechanism for implicating the international responsibility of a host state, namely the exercise of diplomatic protection in favour of the investor by its home state.[16]

Responsibility on the Basis of an Investment Protection Treaty and Responsibility arising from the Exercise of Diplomatic Protection

The comparison must necessarily be made because, as regards state responsibility in the area of investments, international law has been developed by a long succession of interstate arbitral awards resulting from the exercise of diplomatic protection of investors' home states. Are the rules of this international law, which in large measure form part of customary international law, relevant in respect of arbitration on the basis of protection treaties? One recent commentator denies this, considering there is a difference in kind between the rules of state responsibility for internationally unlawful acts laid down in the context of diplomatic protection and the rules that apply where a state is in cause on the basis of protection treaties.[17]

It is sure and certain that the basis for the two actions is not the same. On one side, for the implementation of diplomatic protection, the very generally accepted scheme is that the state that defends its national does not defend the national's right but the right, which is the state's, to ensure compliance with the international rules on the

---

[16] See Kokott, 'Interim Report', *ibid.*
[17] See Z Douglas, 'The Hybrid Foundations of Investment Treaty Arbitration' (2003) *British Yearbook of International Law* 151.

treatment of foreigners which have allegedly been breached by the host state with respect to one of the home state's nationals. From this ensues the implication of the host state's responsibility by the investor's home state. As the Permanent Court of International Justice (PCIJ) puts it in a famous dictum in the *Mavromatis* case (PCIJ Reports, Series A No 2, at 12):

> By taking up the case of one of its subjects and by resorting to diplomatic action or international judicial proceedings on his behalf, a State is in reality asserting its own rights—its right to ensure, in the person of its subjects, respect for the rules of international law.

The drawbacks of such a mechanism are too well known to need underlining here: the discretionary character of the home state's action, the change in character of the dispute, the non-participation of the private person in proceedings, the acceptance by the state of lump-sum compensation in an amount lower than that claimed by the investor, and so on.

The advancement of international law has consisted entirely in establishing treaty-based regimes allowing direct action by individuals against states. This advance was first made in the area of human rights, then in the area of investment protection.[18] In the latter area, the importance of the change was not understood at first. Accordingly, the 1981 Algiers Accords giving rise to the Iran–United States Claims Tribunal were perceived as setting up an ad hoc mechanism that was not representative of the state of international law.[19] As for investment protection treaties, it was only in the late 1990s, when they began to thrive and when the *AAPL/Sri Lanka* case opened up the ICSID forum to all investors relying on a protection treaty between their home state and the host state that the true scope of the change was to become apparent.[20]

---

[18] For a recent study see G Cohen-Jonathan, 'L'individu comme sujet de droit international. Droit international des contrats et droit international des droits de l'homme' in *Mélanges Paul Amselek* (Brussels, Bruylant, 2005) 223.

[19] See P Fouchard, 'La nature juridique de l'arbitrage du Tribunal des différends irano-américains' (1984) *Cahiers du CEDIN*, 'Le tribunal des différends irano-américains' 27, who saw it as a *sui generis* institution while for M Virally (*Cahiers du CEDIN*, ibid, 50) it was public international law arbitration. See also CN Browner and JD Brueschke, *The Iran-United States Claims Tribunal* (The Hague, Martinus Nijhoff, 1998).

[20] See the disillusioned conclusion in Kokott, 'Interim Report' (n 15): 'in the context of foreign investment, the traditional law of DP [diplomatic protection] has been to a large extent replaced by a number of treaty-based dispute settlement procedures'.

The most important point of all is, of course, that protection treaties create a right that directly benefits investors who, depending on their interests alone and independently of their home state, may go before an arbitration tribunal and force the host state to defend itself in that forum.[21] Such recourse may be exercised without having to exhaust all domestic remedies, unless such an obligation is expressly provided for in the treaty itself.[22] And the issue to be tried before the court is nothing other than the lawfulness of the state's action in respect of the rules established in the protection treaty, that is, the rules of international law. In other words, it is indeed the international responsibility of the host state that is at issue before the arbitration tribunal; its responsibility on the basis of investment protection treaties, and its responsibility on the basis of customary rules of responsibility in public international law.

It is at this juncture that there arises a strand of thought hostile to the present evolution and hostile to the multiplication of protection treaties—which are perceived at best as ineffective in their stated aim of increasing investment flows—and more generally hostile to a change in international law as it is traced out at the present time; this evolution makes room for redress by private persons, which are in

---

[21] This is, of course, merely a legal obligation and nothing can compel a defaulting state to come and explain itself before the tribunal. See, eg, the *Texaco, BP* and *Liamco* awards where Libya had defaulted; see B Stern, 'Trois arbitrages, un même problème, trois solutions: les nationalisations pétrolières libyennes devant l'arbitrage international' (1980) *Revue de l'Arbitrage* 3. It seems to me, but it needs to be checked, that this situation has not occurred in ICSID arbitration.

[22] See P Peters, 'Dispute Settlement Agreements in Investment Treaties' (1991) *Netherlands Yearbook of International Law* 91 and Douglas, 'The Hybrid Foundations' (n 17) 178–79. The question of the exhaustion of domestic remedies was discussed in *Maffezini v Spain*, decision on objections to jurisdiction of 25 January 2000, (2001) *ICSID Review* 212. Article X, paras 2 and 3a, of the treaty between Spain and Argentina required that any dispute be brought first before the domestic courts with the possibility of then going to an arbitration tribunal if, after 18 months, a decision had not been rendered or if, despite the decision, the dispute persisted. But see above all *Loewen v United States*, award of 26 June 2003 (ARB(AF)/98/3), 7 *ICSID Reports* 442; Gaillard, *La jurisprudence du CIRDI* (n 1) 775. The arbitration tribunal had dismissed the idea, in an opinion from Sir Robert Jennings that 'the local remedies rule is essentially confined to cases of diplomatic protection' (para 150). But the situation was quite special in this case as it was a question of whether an action based on the NAFTA Treaty could be brought against the United States and on the basis of the denial of justice while remedies existed in US law against the judgment that for *Loewen* constituted such a denial. On this matter see the observations in Gaillard, *La jurisprudence du CIRDI* (n 1) 786–92; AA Bjorklund, 'Waiver and the Exhaustion of Local Remedies Rule in NAFTA Jurisprudence' in T Weiler (ed), *NAFTA Investment Law and Arbitration: Past Issues, Current Practice, Future Prospects* (New York, Transnational Publishers, 2004).

actual fact just multinational corporations looking to defend their interests at the expense of developing countries.[23]

Justification of Recourse to International Law

There have always been scholars favourable to the expansion of international law beyond the sphere of interstate relations and others, on the contrary, anxious to confine this law to such relations.[24] More specifically with regard to state responsibility on the basis of protection treaties, it is worth giving an account of a very lengthy study published recently in the *British Yearbook of International Law* and which very clearly illustrates the restrictive position of some scholars, but which has failed to convince the present author.[25]

Douglas' Criticism

An Essentialist Conception of International Law

If one posits as a starting point the idea that individuals can never have direct access to the international legal order, which is accessible to states (or interstate organisations) alone, the regime applicable to disputes taken to arbitration on the basis of (bilateral or multilateral) investment protection treaties could not be a regime of public international law; and particularly so if the arbitrators have to examine questions bearing on private rights for which international law has no rules.

This is how Douglas argues that 'the investment treaty regime for the arbitration of investment disputes . . . cannot be adequately rationalised either as a form of public international or private transnational dispute resolution'.[26] And indeed because the dispute between a host state and an investor allegedly always bears on the investor's

---

[23] See n 5. One representative of this hostile strand is M Sornarajah, *The International Law on Foreign Investment* (Cambridge, Cambridge University Press, 2004).

[24] This contention is found, eg, over the question of the international personality of private persons. Favourable to it is H Kelsen, *General Theory of Law and State* trans A Wedburg (Russell & Russell, New York, 1961) 343–47; the Italian dualist school is opposed: D Anzilotti, *Cours de droit international* (Paris, Université Panthéon-Assas (Paris 2), 1999) 132–36.

[25] Douglas, 'The Hybrid Foundations' (n 17).

[26] Douglas, *ibid*, 152. Douglas bases his opinion on a citation from Paulsson, the 'inventor' of the idea of arbitration without privity: 'This is not a sub genre of an existing discipline. It is dramatically different from anything previously known in the international sphere'.

private interests, the law applicable to this type of dispute could only be a 'hybrid' of international law and domestic law and not solely international law as in interstate arbitration.[27]

It follows from this overall conception that the customary rules of state responsibility in the area of investments, rules which have developed in the context of interstate arbitration set up further to the exercise of diplomatic protection, supposedly have no relevance for actions based on investment protection treaties. The customary rules, on which the work of the ILC focused, concerned interstate relations and not mixed relations between a private person and a state, which relations by their nature lie outside the sphere of public international law.[28]

Such exclusion from the law of nations concerns not just the law applicable to the merits of the dispute, but the law applicable to the arbitration proceedings (*lex arbitri*). This seems an astonishing assertion at first sight as regards the procedure before ICSID arbitrators governed by the Washington Convention. Admittedly, it is argued, ICSID arbitration is indeed international arbitration in the sense that it stands apart from any domestic law; but that does not mean that its *lex arbitri* is international law.[29] International law on arbitration developed from interstate disputes and its rules—those

---

[27] Douglas, *ibid*, 195, 197: 'Customary international law contains no substantive rules of property law. . . . Nor do investment treaties purport to lay down rules for acquiring rights in rem'.

[28] A rather curious argument has been made for removing responsibility under protection treaties from the sphere of public international law. For Douglas the rules of state responsibility for an internationally wrongful act cannot be relied on because they were developed, as concerns state responsibility towards investors, in the context of diplomatic protection. One of the arguments used is that the rules codified by the ILC do away with the damage condition, whereas this condition is central to dispute settlement on the basis of protection treaties. However, there is a consensus of the most eminent french speaking legal scholars to challenge whether this condition can be removed from the law of international responsibility. See D Alland, *Droit international public* (Paris, PUF, 2000) 411 fn 376; J Combacau and S Sur, *Droit international public* 6th edn (Paris, Monchrestien, 2006) 525ff; P Daillier and A Pellet, *Droit international public* 7th edn (Paris, LGDJ, 2002) 484; PM Dupuy, *Droit international public* 7th edn (Paris, Dalloz, 2004) 481ff; J Verhoeven, *Droit international public* (Brussels, Larcier, 2000) 616ff. In any event, there is nothing there to exclude the rules governing state responsibility on the basis of investment protection treaties from the main body of rules on international responsibility.

[29] Douglas, 'The Hybrid Foundations' (n 17) 225: 'International procedural rules for admissibility of claims, such as the rules on the nationality of claims and the exhaustion of local remedies, have developed in the context of diplomatic protection . . . there is no reason to import such concepts into investment treaty arbitration. An analysis of the lex arbitria of ICSID arbitrations thus requires a far more nuanced approach to reflect the complexities of this *sui generis* regime'.

rules, for example, concerning continuous national identity, the exhaustion of domestic rights of redress, etc—cannot be applicable to state/investor arbitration based on protection treaties. In this way Douglas criticises, for example, the *Loewen* award for referring, outside of any textual basis in the NAFTA Treaty, to customary rules on the admissibility of claims 'because it [the tribunal] fails to acknowledge the distinct and independent nature of the investment treaty regime for the resolution of investor/state disputes'.[30] The tribunal probably did not share Douglas' conception of the specific character of arbitration on the basis of treaties.

In the face of what he sees as an illegitimate incursion of international law, Douglas invokes the application of a *sui generis* regime that supposedly corresponds to the hybrid nature of the relationship between state and investor.

Love of Hybrids

Notice first that we have here a type of argument encountered in certain analyses of state contracts. State contracts are objects which, as contracts, supposedly fall within the sphere of domestic law but which, because of their governing law clauses when they refer to international law, would seem to come under international law. Some commentators have thought to have come up with a solution by relating state contracts to a transnational law with very hazy contours and of a markedly hybrid character.[31] Naturally enough, hybrids do occur in nature and in thought, but before reaching such a characterisation, one should make sure it is really required. Do we not resort too readily to *sui generis* claims because we fail to grasp the full extent of the concepts we do have and their ability to cover new fields as and when they arise?

In the case at hand, everything rests on and everything relates to an 'essentialist' conception of international law as an exclusively interstate law to which individuals have no access. There is little point expending energy in saying this is a conception that does not square with the reality of contemporary international law.[32] So instead of constructing a 'hybrid' regime of state responsibility on the basis of investment protection treaties, it is better, as it is closer to the actual state of things, to anchor state responsibility firmly in

---

[30] Douglas, *ibid*, 193.
[31] Leben, 'La théorie du contrat d'Etat' (n 1) 314–21.
[32] *Ibid*, 264ff.

the sphere of international law, of which it is one of the major developments of the last two decades.

The proponents of the specific and hybrid character of the law of state responsibility on the basis of treaties bolster their argument by emphasising that the disputes arising between host states and investors relate to private rights, usually property rights, for which international law has no rules.[33] Here again is the transposition of an argument already encountered in the theory of state contracts: just as international law supposedly has no rules about contracts, making it impossible for there to be any specific international law of contracts, likewise, in investment law, there are allegedly no provisions bearing on the substantive law governing relations between individuals and states, thus necessitating the involvement of domestic law. But when it comes down to it, what are the issues subjected to arbitration on the basis of protection treaties? Is it a matter of deciding between private rights? Not at all. Even when disputes relate to expropriation, it is not the actual law of property that comes under scrutiny, but the lawfulness of the state's act of expropriation in respect of its international obligations in treaty or custom, or again, the possibility that legislative acts of general interest may result in an indirect expropriation of an investment. Moreover, questions of nationalisation are no longer the most common ones. Cases relate to the application of the most-favoured nation clause, or to national treatment, or to fair and equitable treatment, or to the obligation to ensure full protection and security for the investment, or to denial of justice, or to the consequences of an umbrella clause, and so on; all things to which the state has made commitments by treaty and which fall squarely within the ambit of international law.

State Responsibility on the Basis of Protection Treaties: A Sub-System within the General Regime of States' International Responsibility

The case law of the arbitration tribunals confirms that the regime of state responsibility on the basis of protection treaties is indeed a subsystem of the international legal order.

A Sub-System within and not apart from International Law

It is quite clear that an international treaty can create a specific system of international responsibility both in respect of the primary

---

[33] Douglas, 'The Hybrid Foundations' (n 17) 155.

rules (the substantive obligations subscribed to by the parties), the breach of which entails state responsibility and in respect of secondary rules about the implication of state responsibility. Thus, any international organisation—the World Trade Organisation, say, or the European Union—puts in place both a system of primary obligations its members must abide by and a system of secondary rules for determining whether or not there has been a violation of the primary rules and the consequences such violation entails. This is equally true for treaties that do not create an international organisation with a set of organs but which provide, though, forms of conflict resolution and specific consequences for recognised violation of their obligations by the parties.

This is precisely the case of investment protection treaties, treaties entered into by states but which have the peculiarity of allowing individuals to seize an arbitration court to adjudicate on any possible violation by a state of its obligations. This hypothesis is covered by article 33(2) of the ILC articles on state responsibility which provides that: 'This part (part 2) is without prejudice to any right, arising from the international responsibility of a State, which may accrue directly to any person or entity other than a State'. This is developed by the commentary emphasising that 'where the primary obligation is owed to a non-State entity, it may be that some procedure is available whereby that entity can invoke the responsibility on its own account and without the intermediation of any State'.[34] And the commentator cites as an example, alongside treaties on human rights 'bilateral or regional investment protection agreements'. And he adds '[i]t will be a matter for the particular primary rule to determine whether and to what extent persons or entities other than States are entitled to invoke responsibility on their own account'.[35]

In other words, putting in place a 'sub-system of responsibility' as Douglas calls it, does not release us from the responsibility of public international law, even when individuals are entitled to invoke this responsibility. Individuals do invoke the international responsibility of states in the relation linking the individual and the state, even if this relation is not by definition an interstate relation. It should be deduced from this too that the specific rules about responsibility put in place by a treaty apply, first, in place and stead of the customary rules of international responsibility such as described by the ILC

---

[34] Crawford, *The International Law Commission's Articles on State Responsibility* (n 11) 250–51.
[35] *Ibid*, 252.

articles. However, in the absence of specific treaty-based rules, it is the general rules that are to apply. And for example, if the state refuses to apply an award made by an arbitral tribunal in a dispute opposing it to an investor (level one), the investor's home state may implement the dispute settlement clause and bring the matter before the arbitration tribunal provided for by the protection treaty (level two). If this second award is itself refused, the refusal may give rise to invocation of responsibility at the interstate level (level three), whether this is expressly provided for in the treaty or not.

ICSID Case Law

This analysis is largely confirmed by examining the case law of ICSID arbitration tribunals. These apply both treaty-based and customary public international law massively and without any qualms, without drawing any distinction between whether they are adjudicating in matters opposing an individual and a state or two states. In one case at least they were led to rule on an argument invoking the specific character of this type of arbitration. This was *Loewen v United States* (award rendered on 26 June 2003) [36] where the investor had been treated in a particularly scandalous fashion, as the arbitrators themselves said, by a Mississippi court. One approach that would have allowed the court to declare it had jurisdiction, although Loewen had not exhausted all domestic remedies, would have been to consider that the customary rule of exhaustion was 'essentially confined to cases of diplomatic protection'. This was the line taken in an opinion of Sir Robert Jennings (award, paragraph 150). But this argument had been explicitly dismissed by the tribunal when invoking a different doctrine (Garcia-Amador, Sohn and Baxter, Crawford) and then studying long-established arbitral case law, constituted in disputes opposing two states on the basis of diplomatic protection (paragraphs 151–53 and 155 for the Iran–United States Claims Tribunal).

Notice that from the first time a case was brought before an arbitration tribunal on the basis of a protection treaty (*AAPL v Sri Lanka*, 1990), the majority of arbitrators clearly situated themselves within the legal order of international law. And so after noting that the damage caused to the investor could not be made good on the basis of the protection treaty, which excluded damage caused by

---

[36] *The Loewen Group, Inc. and Raymond L. Loewen v United States of America*, final award of 26 June 2003, (2003) *ILM* 811; (2004) *Journal du Droit International* 219 (with E Gaillard's observations); Gaillard, *La jurisprudence du CIRDI* (n 1) 775.

combat, the tribunal sought whether there were any customary rules in the matter. To do this, it examined the precedents in arbitration awards since the early twentieth century, all of which, needless to say, were rendered in matters opposing two states (award, paragraph 73ff).[37] It deduced there was a rule of customary international law allowing it to invoke the state's international responsibility on the basis of failure to comply with the duty to exercise due diligence.

Thus, in the absence of any treaty-based provisions, the tribunal quite naturally examined general international law, without being in the least perturbed by the fact that it was not dealing with a relation between two states.

Nowhere can it be observed that arbitration tribunals consider the rules of classical international law, governing interstate relations, are separate from the (hybrid) rules applicable to relations between states and investors. Nowhere is it to be seen that there is any difference depending on whether we are in the presence of interstate arbitration or mixed arbitration, as regards, say, the interpretation of most-favoured nation clauses, or national treatment, or full protection and security, or rules about expropriation, etc. And where the old-established customary rule has evolved, it is not because of any specific character of arbitration based on protection treaties, but because the multiplication of such treaties has come to modify the rule within the international legal order itself. As the tribunal noted in *Pope & Talbot Inc. v Canada* (award rendered 31 May 2002, on compensation) 'the content of custom in international law is now represented by more than 1800 bilateral investment treaties' (paragraph 62, cited in *Loewen* paragraph 131).

This does not mean there is no difference between the general rules of international law of responsibility governing the relations between states and those governing relations between states and investors on the basis of protection treaties. It is manifest that the consequence of a breach of an obligation is not the same in both instances. In one instance, a state may be authorised to resort to countermeasures against the state responsible for the wrongful act (see ILC articles 49–54). That cannot be the case in state–investor relations where a dispute must be brought before a mixed arbitral tribunal or an interstate arbitral tribunal depending on whether it is the

---

[37] See *AAPL v Sri Lanka*, award of 27 June 1990 (ARB/87/3) in 4 *ICSID Reports* 246 at 278, Gaillard, *La jurisprudence du CIRDI* (n 1) 322ff, paras 73–74, where the tribunal cites the *British Goods in Spanish Morocco, Melilla-Ziat, Ben Kiran and Sabiaggio* cases, all with the most classical doctrine of public international law.

first or second level of the dispute. It is only if such actions fail to find a solution that there is a return to the general regime of state responsibility and that rules on the consequences of internationally wrongful acts might apply.

Similarly, some rules initially laid down in the context of diplomatic protection do not find application, as is the case with the rule on the exhaustion of domestic remedies, unless the parties elect otherwise.[38] In other cases, and in the absence of any contractual indication, the arbitration tribunal will apply the received customary rule. This is what happened in the *Loewen* case where the tribunal applied the customary rule on continuous national identity, a rule laid down in classical case law on diplomatic protection. It may be, as has been argued, that the tribunal misinterpreted the customary rule, or that it should have set it aside because of the specific character of responsibility on the basis of protection treaties;[39] but what matters here, and it could be borne out by other examples, is that in the absence of any specific contractual provisions, the tribunal quite naturally examined general international law, without any misgivings about it not dealing with a relation between two states.

State Responsibility on the Basis of Protection Treaties and State Responsibility in Municipal Law

The implication of states' international responsibility on the basis of investment protection treaties raises almost all the questions that are studied in respect of responsibility in customary international law, whether they are questions of substantial or procedural law (see the sizeable case law on indirect expropriation, calculation of compensation, national treatment, the minimum standard for treatment of aliens, denial of justice, the rules on continuous national identity, state of necessity, etc).[40] It is presently impossible to address any of

---

[38] Likewise art 26 of the Washington Convention provides that: 'A contracting state may require the exhaustion of local administrative or judicial remedies as a condition of its consent to arbitration under this Convention'.

[39] See Gaillard, *La jurisprudence du CIRDI* (n 1) 787–90; M Mendelson, 'The Runaway Train: The Continuous Nationality Rule from the Panevezys-Saldutiskis Railway Case to Loewen' in T Weiler (ed), *International Investment Law and Arbitration: Leading Cases from the ICSID, NAFTA, Bilateral Treaties and Customary International Law* (London, Cameron, 2005) 97; Bjorklund, 'Waiver and the Exhaustion of Local Remedies Rule' (n 22); Douglas, 'The Hybrid Foundations' (n 17) 193.

[40] For a study of some of these problems see C Leben and J Verhoeven (eds), *Nouveaux développements dans le contentieux arbitral transnational relatif à l'investissement international* (Paris, Larcier/LGDJ, 2005).

these matters in international law without taking account of the awards made under international law by the arbitral tribunals set up on the basis of protection treaties, whether ICSID tribunals or tribunals of other arbitration instances or even ad hoc tribunals (mostly using UNCITRAL arbitration rules). It might be pointed out by way of example that there are over thirty arbitration proceedings against Argentina as the upshot of its decision to devalue the peso in January 2002. Foreign businesses, often concessionaries of public services, found themselves trapped by prices set in contracts entered into at a time when the peso was on level footing with the US dollar. The arbitration awards are beginning to be rendered and the latest ICSID decision of 20 April 2005 includes a very lengthy passage on the state of necessity invoked by Argentina because of the serious political, economic and social crisis in which the country was mired.[41] That passage of the award contains a long discussion on the conditions on which a state may invoke such circumstances to set aside its responsibility (paragraphs 304–31 with a negative conclusion by the tribunal). It is likely that in the other matters currently under examination, the defences derived from the state of necessity, but also from *force majeure* or distress, shall be discussed and will provide public international law with developments of great importance on all these points.

A full examination of state responsibility on the basis of protection treaties would therefore take into account all these questions; but that is not the purpose here. Here the purpose is more simply to ask how international law procedures mesh together with domestic law procedures in implicating state responsibility on the basis of investment protection treaties. So long as the investors were backed by their home state's channels of diplomatic protection, the procedures of international law and of domestic law were quite separate: on one side was an international action governed by international law and opposing two states before a permanent international court or inter-

---

[41] See AA Escobar, 'Argentina's Multiplication of Investor–State Arbitration Proceedings' in Leben and Verhoeven (eds), *Nouveaux développements* (n 40) 219. For an initial review of arbitration awards in the Argentinian cases see L Achtouk-Spivak, 'Arbitrage en matière d'investissement et crise argentine: un bilan d'étape' (2007) *Les Cahiers de l'Arbitrage* 55. In the case *LG&E v Argentina* (ARB/021), decision on liability 3 October 2006, 11 *ICSID Reports* 414, the tribunal decided that the Argentine economic crisis constituted a state of necessity exonerating Argentina from liability. The exact opposite of the *CMS v Argentina* decision. See D Foster, 'Necessity Knows No Law: LG&E v. Argentina' (2006) *International Arbitration Law Review* 149; JE Alvarez and K Khansi, 'The Argentine Crisis and Foreign Investors' (2008–2009) *Yearbook on International Investment Law and Policy* 379.

state arbitration tribunal; on the other, an action by the investor before the host state's courts or before arbitrators governed by domestic law and adjudicating by application of domestic law.

Arbitration on the basis of treaties calls this distinction into question. Investors themselves may now bring international actions against host states, which actions are governed by the rules of international law and which are ultimately determined by the application of public international law.[42] This means that the two spheres of international law and domestic law are brought into contact; in principle this did not happen, or only marginally so, in the context of diplomatic protection. This coming together of the two spheres did not fail to raise the problem of how rules of international law square with rules of domestic law. More specifically, the problem arose over dispute settlement. Here two arrangements can be distinguished: either there is a contract between the investor and the host state (or public entities) with an attribution of jurisdiction clause providing for the host state's domestic courts to have jurisdiction; or there is no such contractual tie and it is the protection treaty which, usually but not always, settles the matter of possible jurisdictional recourses and how they fit together.

In the Absence of any Contractual Connection between Investor and State

Most protection treaties include a clause expressly providing that the investor may seek redress in the event of a dispute with the host state before various courts or tribunals at its option: ICSID, UNCITRAL or some other arbitration mechanism and the state's domestic courts. The bilateral treaty between France and Argentina (n 42) provides in its paragraph 2 that any dispute shall be 'submitted at the investor's request: (i) either to the national courts of the Parties

---

[42] On the place of public international law in arbitration pertaining to state contracts see Leben, 'La théorie du contrat d'Etat' (n 1) 264–321. The conclusions are also valid for treaty-based arbitration. For a detailed study of arbitral solutions see C Crépet, 'Investissements internationaux et arbitrage. La détermination du droit applicable' (2003) 2 *Les Cahiers de l'arbitrage (Gazette du Palais)* pt 2, 17–20. For an example of clauses determining the law applicable to a dispute between an investor and a state on the basis of a protection treaty, see art 8(4) of the France/Argentina Agreement of 3 July 1991 (*Journal official*, 5 June 1993): 'The arbitration organ shall adjudicate on the basis of the provisions of this Agreement, of the law of the Contracting Party that is a party to the dispute—including the rules on conflict of laws—of the terms of any particular agreements that might have been concluded on the subject of the investment, and of the principles of international law on the subject matter'.

involved in the dispute, (ii) or to international arbitration under the circumstances described in para. 3'. That paragraph 3 provides for the possibility of bringing the matter before an ICSID tribunal or an ad hoc arbitration panel formed on the basis of UNCITRAL rules.

But two positions must then be distinguished depending on whether the investor's choice of procedure is irrevocable or, on the contrary, leaves the way open to another procedure.

Irrevocable Choice of Procedure

Under some protection treaties, the investor is left the option of bringing its case before one of several dispute settlement bodies. It therefore implements the procedure that seems in its best interests and, it shall be recalled, with no need to exhaust the avenues of redress available in domestic law if it opts to go to arbitration, unless otherwise stated in the treaty. However, many treaties, like the treaty between France and Argentina, provide that 'once an investor has submitted the dispute either to the courts of the relevant contracting Party or to international arbitration, the choice of either procedure is firm and final' (article 8, paragraph 2). This irrevocable choice clause is known as 'a fork in the road': for the investor two courses of action lie open and when he has taken the one, there is no turning back.[43]

There are cases, though, where the seizure of the state's courts is not considered as a waiver of arbitration proceedings. Such cases may be provided for by the treaties themselves or laid down by arbitral case law. Thus, the ICSID tribunals have considered that the investor's resort to the state's courts to apply for interlocutory or preventive measures does not constitute an irrevocable choice of domestic courts.[44]

Likewise, although the investor may have accepted the state's courts for a specific dispute, it will be quite at liberty to choose another form of dispute settlement in a separate matter. This is self-evident but in fact raises the question of when two cases are the same or different. For example, the action brought by a subsidiary in the host state is not the same as that brought by foreign shareholders of

---

[43] On all these questions I am indebted to the analyses in Ben Hamida, 'L'arbitrage transnational unilatéral' (n 1) 374ff.

[44] Ben Hamida, *ibid*, 375, fn 620. This is provided for expressly in article 26(3) of the bilateral treaty between Uruguay and the United States concluded on 25 October 2004, (2005) *ILM* 286.

that subsidiary (*Alex Genin v Estonia*, 2001); or again, the action against the state as a subject of international law is not the same as the action against a territorial subdivision of the state in domestic law (*Compania de Aguas del Aconquija S.A. and Compagnie générale des eaux v Argentina*, 2000). It was in this case too that a distinction was clearly established among the investor's grounds for action. The enterprise may have waived international arbitration for disputes pertaining to the contract (improper performance, termination, etc) but not for disputes pertaining to the state's failure to comply with its international obligations under the protection treaty (breach of the minimum standard of treatment, of the protection clause, prohibition of any discrimination, clause providing for full safety and protection of the investment, etc).

Concurrent Procedures

Some bilateral treaties and two big multilateral treaties provide for the possibility of concurrent avenues of redress before the domestic courts and before an international arbitration instance. Thus, article 26 of the Energy Charter Treaty in its many subparagraphs offers to investors a choice of procedures ranging from judicial or administrative courts to ICSID, UNCITRAL, or Stockholm Chamber of Commerce arbitration proceedings. However, subsection 3b of this article gives states the possibility of refusing international arbitration if the investor has previously brought an action before its courts.

This generosity in dispute settlement provisions raises the daunting problem of the possible rank ordering of international arbitral awards and domestic judicial decisions. The contact between the domestic and international spheres in arbitration on the basis of protection treaties implies, and shall increasingly imply in the future, with the development of this type of arbitration, that the problem shall recur in many cases. At present, arbitrators exercise exceeding care and have stated on several occasions that arbitration is not some sort of final court of appeal from decisions entered by state courts.[45]

NAFTA includes a more complex clause on the relations between domestic proceedings and international arbitration. For it to be possible to seize an arbitration tribunal as provided for in article 1116 of the agreement, the investor—and this is provided for in article 1121

---

[45] Crépet, 'Investissements internationaux et arbitrage' (n 42) 15–17, referring to the *Mondev International Ltd v United States* (2002) and *Robert Azinian v Mexico* (1999) cases.

(2b)—must expressly waive its right to 'initiate or continue before any administrative tribunal or court' proceedings brought against the state over the measure challenged before the arbitral tribunal. 'Continuing' implies that the investor has already introduced the matter before the state courts and then decided to seize an arbitration body provided for by the NAFTA Treaty. The reason given, in *Waste Management Inc. v United Mexican States* (award of 2 June 2000) for the requirement to waive, in this instance, the domestic proceedings is that it must be precluded that an enterprise can be compensated twice over, once by the domestic courts and again by an arbitral tribunal.[46] In any event, an investor may, after beginning proceedings in the state courts, turn to the arbitration proceedings by waiving the domestic action. But there is (in addition) an exception for disputes with Mexico. Mexico does not accept this mechanism and once a case has been begun before the Mexican courts, it cannot be continued before an arbitral tribunal (NAFTA annex 1120.1).

The problem evoked earlier arises here as to whether the investor's waiver is valid for the actions based on the protection treaty alone (NAFTA here), which would leave open the possibility of seizing the state's domestic courts in actions based on the state's domestic law, or even in actions based on international sources other than NAFTA. This is what the enterprise argued in *Waste Management Inc. v United Mexican States* (2000). The arbitration tribunal rejected the argument and stated that 'the waiver must extend to national proceedings brought on the basis of domestic law alone'.[47]

Recourse of the Public Person against the Investor

There is an imbalance in unilateral transnational arbitration between the possibilities of action by the state and by the private party. The private party, in bringing its case before the arbitral instance provided for by the treaty, accepts the offer of arbitration made by the state and so 'forces' the state to follow it to arbitration. The state, on the contrary, cannot 'force' the investor so long as the investor has not consented to arbitration. However, the state is always free to bring the dispute opposing the state and the investor before the host state's own courts. The investor, to defend itself, will be led to accept the arbitral instance provided for by the protection treaty. There will,

---

[46] Quoted by Ben Hamida, 'L'arbitrage transnational unilatéral' (n 1) 382–83.
[47] *Ibid*, 383.

therefore, be two parallel actions, one before the state courts and one before the arbitral tribunal provided for by treaty. Again we have two proceedings, domestic and international, dealing with one and the same matter. It is logical enough, on this assumption, that each court should adjudicate depending on the requirements of its own order. Thus, the international courts are inclined to consider the action brought in the international order should take precedence over that brought in the municipal order. There is an example of this in the very first case submitted to the ICSID, *Holiday Inns SA and others v Morocco* (1973). The ICSID arbitration tribunal invited the Moroccan courts to,

> stay proceedings until the arbitration tribunal had decided these questions [those on which the arbitration court would itself be led to adjudicate], and if the tribunal had already determined them, the Moroccan courts should concur in its opinion. Any other solution would bring or would risk bringing into question the responsibility of the Moroccan state and threaten the principle of the primacy of international proceedings over municipal proceedings.[48]

This principle—which was confirmed in *Victor Pey Casado and President Allende Foundation v Republic of Chile* (2001) and is also found in the context of the Iran–United States Claims Tribunal— operates here as it operates *mutatis mutandis* and relatively speaking in the Community legal order to justify the primacy of the decisions of the European Court of Justice (ECJ) over national decisions. Naturally the arbitration tribunals have none of the means available to the Luxembourg court to ensure its superiority over reticent state courts; but ultimately, and where municipal courts fail to acknowledge this primacy, it is indeed the international responsibility of the state that is at issue, because of the decisions of its courts.

In the Presence of a Contractual Connection between State and Investor and with a Separate Dispute Settlement Clause from that provided by the Protection Treaty

This hypothesis is probably the most common one. On one side, the protection treaty contains a dispute settlement clause referring more often than not to arbitration and especially ICSID arbitration; on the

---

[48] P Lalive, 'The First World Bank Arbitration (*Holiday Inns v Morocco*. Some Legal Problems' (1980) *British Yearbook of International Law* 123; Ben Hamida, 'L'arbitrage transnational unilatéral' (n 1) 390.

other side, the contract with the state, or a state organism,[49] which provides recourse to the host state's national courts or arbitration in municipal law (as in *SGS v Pakistan*, 2003).[50]

The inconsistency between clauses as to jurisdiction can be resolved by special provisions in either instrument. Thus, US bilateral investment protection treaties contain clauses giving priority to the dispute settlement procedure provided for in the contract rather than in the treaty.[51] It seems, though, that recent US treaties opt rather for maintaining the jurisdiction of the arbitration tribunals provided for in the treaty, even if the investor has accepted a contract with a clause reserving jurisdiction for other courts, and particularly the host state's courts.

Another way of articulating the various courts and tribunals is that already seen in NAFTA article 1121(2) asking investors to waive their right to initiate or continue proceedings before an administrative tribunal or court under the domestic legislation of one party or other dispute settlement procedures. Conversely, is it possible that in the investment agreement, the enterprise might waive the benefit of an arbitration clause provided for in a protection treaty? The question, already raised in the OECD's talks on a draft multilateral agreement on investments, is an intricate one as host states might be tempted to put pressure on enterprises, or at any rate on the weakest enterprises, to void a protection treaty of its substance. Such an attitude could give rise to a dispute with the home state, with recourse to the arbitration instance provided for under this hypothesis.

The problem encountered earlier recurs of the possibility of bringing a case before the arbitration tribunal provided for by the

[49] One of the most important questions in all these cases is the imputation to the state of actions of its emanations or territorial divisions. See Y Nouvel, 'L'arbitre à la recherche du fait étatique' in Leben and Verhoeven (eds), *Nouveaux développements* (n 40); A Cohen-Smutny, 'State Responsibility and Attribution: When is a State Responsible for the Acts of State Enterprises?' in Weiler, *International Investment Law and Arbitration* (n 39) 17.

[50] The hypothesis is ruled out here that the contract between investor and state includes a dispute-settlement clause referring to an international tribunal, such as the ICSID tribunals, for in this case, and if the applicable law were international law in part or in full, this would be a state contract, that is an internationalised contract, a position that is equivalent, in my view, to that existing on the basis of a protection treaty. See Leben, 'La théorie du contrat d'Etat' (n 1) 264ff.

[51] Ben Hamida, 'L'arbitrage transnational unilatéral' (n 1) 393 and 'L'arbitrage Etat-investisseur étranger: regards sur les traités et projets récents' (2004) *Journal du Droit International* 419, 432. This includes an important innovation: the institution of a 'super' arbitration tribunal before which all proceedings on the same dispute would be consolidated.

protection treaty after having brought it before the host state's courts. The host state may consider the referral to its courts implies waiving the referral to the arbitration tribunal provided for by the treaty, particularly if the treaty contains a 'fork in the road' clause. However, in at least two instances (*Lanco v Argentina*, decision rendered 8 December 1998[52] and *Salini v Morocco*, decision on jurisdiction of 23 July 2001)[53] the ICSID arbitration tribunals considered that the acceptance in a contract of the exclusive jurisdiction of the administrative tribunal, mandatorily competent under the host state's law, did not express a true choice, that is by mutual agreement, of a previously agreed dispute-settlement procedure, and made it impossible to seize the ICSID tribunal.

All of these hypotheses may be complex, but we shall not dwell on them but rather draw attention to a matter that very directly raises the problem of how the domestic and international legal orders hinge together. This is the famous umbrella clause or compliance-with-commitment clause whose presence or absence in a protection treaty may have far-reaching consequences.[54] It is an old clause that is found already in the first bilateral treaty between the Federal Republic of Germany and Pakistan (25 November 1959) and which is adopted in a number of protection treaties even if it seems it is barely found in bilateral treaties entered into by France. Switzerland, on the contrary, resorts to it quite often, for instance in article 11 of its bilateral treaty with Ukraine (1995): 'Each of the Contracting Parties shall permanently ensure that it observes its commitments with regard to the investments of investors of the other Contracting Party'.

Or again article 11 of the treaty between Switzerland and Pakistan: 'Each of the Contracting Parties shall at all times ensure that it observes the commitments it has given with regard to the investments of the other Contracting Party'.

The clause is also found in some multilateral protection treaties such as the Energy Charter Treaty whose article 10(1) provides:

[52] *Lanco v Argentina* (2001) *ILM* 457.

[53] Gaillard, *La jurisprudence du CIRDI* (n 1) 627.

[54] See A Sinclair, 'The Origins of the Umbrella Clause in the International Law of Investment Protection' (2004) 4 *Arbitration International* 411; T Wälde, 'The "Umbrella" Clause in Investment Arbitration' (2005) 2 *Journal of World Investment and Trade* 183; W Ben Hamida, 'La clause relative au respect des engagements dans les traités d'investissements' in Leben and Verhoeven (eds), *Nouveaux développements* (n 40); E Teynier, 'Les umbrella clauses' (2004) 2 *Les Cahiers de l'arbitrage (Gazette du Palais)* pt 2, 29.

'Each Contracting Party shall observe any obligations it has entered into with an Investor or [in respect of] an Investment of an Investor of any other Contracting Party'.

And again article III of the investment protection treaty of ASEAN member countries states: 'Each Contracting Party shall observe any obligation arising from a particular commitment it may have entered into with regard to a specific investment of nationals or companies of the other Contracting Parties'.

The major question raised by this umbrella clause is that of the internationalisation of all the state's commitments and especially its contractual commitments with regard to an investor: should it be considered that because of this umbrella clause all the obligations assumed by the state, internally, become international obligations. And consequently shall state responsibility in its relations with investors invariably be, through the effect of this clause in a protection treaty, a responsibility grounded in the international legal order whereas in classical international law, breach of contract is not governed by international law unless it entails also a breach of a rule of international law, such as the prohibition of the denial of justice or failure to comply with the minimum standard of treatment of aliens.[55]

A distinction must be drawn, then, in respect of the articulation of proceedings in municipal law and in international law, depending on whether or not the protection treaty contains such an umbrella clause.

In the Absence of an Umbrella Clause in the Treaty

The situation contemplated here is one where there is both a protection treaty including a dispute settlement clause between the host state and the investor attributing jurisdiction to one or more international arbitration tribunals and a contract between the investor and the same state assigning jurisdiction to the state's domestic courts or more rarely to arbitration tribunals in municipal law (see *SGS v Pakistan*, decision of 29 January 2004, ARB/02/6, 8 *ICSID Reports* 518).

---

[55] There is a wealth of scholarship on this point including Gaillard, *La jurisprudence du CIRDI* (n 1) 833; Ben Hamida, 'L'arbitrage transnational unilateral' (n 1) 579 and Ben Hamida, 'La clause relative au respect des engagements', *ibid*, 53; for a study of case law see Gaillard, *ibid*, 832, 900; Teynier, 'Les umbrella clauses', *ibid*, 29 and (2006) 3 *Les Cahiers de l'arbitrage* 38; Sinclair, 'The Origins of the Umbrella Clause', *ibid*; Wälde, 'The "Umbrella" Clause in Investment Arbitration', *ibid*.

In the event of a contractual dispute, can the investor bring the case before the arbitration tribunal provided for by the treaty, invoking either breach of the contract or of the treaty, or both, while the contract provides exclusively for recourse to the domestic courts and the host state rejects the jurisdiction of the arbitration tribunal? The ICSID tribunals' answer involves the distinction between treaty claims and contract claims. This answer to the problem, although upheld by several arbitration awards, raises doctrinal criticisms that must be addressed.

The Treaty Claims/Contract Claims Distinction

The conflict between a jurisdictional clause in a protection treaty and in an investment agreement is encountered in several cases submitted to the ICSID, including *Salini v Morocco* of 23 July 2001; *Compania de Aguas v Argentina* of 21 November 2000, annulled in part by the decision of 3 July 2002; *CMS v Argentina* of 17 July 2003; *SGS v Pakistan* of 6 August 2003 and *SGS v Philippines* of 29 January 2004. And also more rapidly in *Generation Ukraine v Ukraine* of 16 September 2003; *Azurix Corp. v Argentina* of 8 December 2003; *Enron Corp. v Argentina* of 14 January 2004 and 2 August 2004; *Siemens AG v Argentina* of 3 August 2004, and more recently still *CMS v Argentina* of 20 April 2005 and *Impregilano v Pakistan* of 22 April 2005.[56]

What is viewed as the authoritative decision on the subject is that of the ad hoc Committee in *Compañia de Aguas del Aconquija SA & Vivendi Universal v Argentine Republic* of 3 July 2002 on the application for annulment of an ICSID award of 21 November 2000.[57] It was a dispute between the Argentine province of Tucumán and a subsidiary of the French company Vivendi over the cancellation of a water concession agreement. The agreement included a clause attributing exclusive jurisdiction to the Argentinean administrative

---

[56] For a commentary on several of these awards see F Yala, 'Fondement des demandes des investisseurs (Treaty claims/Contract claims)' (2003) 2 *Les Cahiers de l'arbitrage* pt 2, 12–15 and C Crépet, 'Treaty claims/contract claims' (2004) 2 *Les Cahiers de l'arbitrage* pt 2, 23.

[57] See Gaillard, *La jurisprudence du CIRDI* (n 1) 719ff and C Schreuer, 'Investment Treaty Arbitration over Contract Claims—The Vivendi I Case Considered' in Weiler (ed), *International Investment Law and Arbitration* (n 39) 281. See also the major contributions to doctrine by I Fadlallah, 'La distinction "Treaty claims–Contract claims et la compétence de l'arbitre (Cirdi: faisons nous fausse route?)' (2004) 2 *Les Cahiers de l'arbitrage* pt 2, 3 and P Mayer, '*Contract claims* et clauses juridictionnelles des traités relatifs à la protection des investissements' (2009) *Journal du Droit International* 71.

tribunals whereas the bilateral investment protection treaty between France and Argentina (3 July 1991) allowed the matter to be brought before the ICSID. After cancellation of the agreement, the investor invoked the arbitration clause of the protection treaty and an arbitral tribunal was formed.

In its award of 21 November 2000 the arbitration tribunal considered that in this matter it was impossible to separate breaches of the protection treaty from alleged breaches of the concession agreement, which the administrative tribunals of Tucumán province alone could determine. It also refused to consider that Argentina could be internationally responsible on the basis of the protection treaty alone.

Vivendi appealed to have the award annulled and the ad hoc committee rendered its decision on 3 July 2002. It partly annulled the award of November 2000 for excess of powers constituted by the arbitration tribunal's refusal to examine the claims on their merits about the acts of Tucumán province by virtue of the bilateral investment treaty (paragraph 119c). The committee was to state the distinction between contractual disputes and disputes based on the breach of the treaty very clearly and systematically. It thus declared, in paragraph 96:

> [W]hether there has been a breach of the BIT and whether there has been a breach of contract are different questions. Each of these claims will be determined by reference to its own proper or applicable law—in the case of the BIT, by international law; in the case of the Concession Contract, by the proper law of the contract, in other words, the law of Tucumán.[58]

On the merits, the Committee states, the fact that acts are consistent with internal law in no way precludes them from being contrary to international law, such that Argentina cannot 'rely on an exclusive jurisdiction clause in a contract to avoid the characterisation of its conduct as internationally unlawful under a treaty' (paragraph 103). Where a claim is based exclusively on the contract it is for the court deciding on the contract to give a ruling. Conversely,

> where 'the fundamental basis of the claim' is a treaty laying down an independent standard by which the conduct of the parties is to be judged, the existence of an exclusive jurisdiction clause in a contract between the claimant and the respondent state or one of its subdivisions cannot operate as a bar to the application of the treaty standard' (paragraph 101).

---

[58] Vivendi (2002) 6 *ICSID Reports* 340 at 365; Gaillard, *La jurisprudence du CIRDI* (n 1) 744.

The trickiest problem remains: what happens if the claim is based on both contract and treaty, or even if the breach of the treaty arises from the breach of contract. The first ICSID arbitration tribunal seemed to have given priority in this event to the court adjudicating on the contract. The ad hoc committee was to oppose this and reassert that the possible jurisdiction of a national court did not preclude the ICSID tribunal from determining the matter and so interpreting and applying the concession agreement 'at least so far as necessary in order to determine whether there had been a breach of the substantive standards of the BIT' (paragraph 110). It is, therefore, on the entire dispute, both contract and treaty, that the arbitration tribunal can adjudicate.[59]

Doctrinal Criticism

This case law of ICSID arbitration tribunals has come in for sharp criticism in French doctrine. Several commentators have called into question the idea that the dispute between an investor and a host state may be broken down into a contractual dispute submitted to the contract judge—usually the host state courts applying municipal law—and a treaty dispute over the jurisdiction of the tribunals provided for by treaty—and usually an arbitration treaty, whether ICSID or other—applying international law.[60] Fadalallah, for instance, writes that 'the distinction between contract claims and treaty claims, while it may be of interest when examining the merits of a case, appears to be radically artificial in respect of jurisdiction'.[61]

He observes that, in this respect, the problem raised here cannot be resolved by observance of an obligations clause (umbrella agreement), for such a clause, if it is properly understood, by raising breaches of contract to the rank of treaty violations, presupposes that

[59] In support of this Fadlallah, 'La distinction "Treaty claims–Contract claims" et compétence de l'arbitre' (n 57): 'The ICISID arbitrator may hear all treaty violations, including those resulting from a breach of contract'.

[60] Wälde, 'The "Umbrella" Clause in Investment Arbitration' (n 54) seems favourable to maintaining the distinction. He criticises the tribunal in *SGS v Pakistan* for abandoning 'the very useful distinction between contract disputes—to be decided under applicable jurisdiction by the competent adjacatory body—and treaty disputes—distinct and separate, to be heard by a treaty-based arbitration tribunal' (at 230). Gaillard also seems favourable to this distinction in his chronicles. See Gaillard, *La jurisprudence du CIRDI* (n 1) 759ff, 859ff and 892ff, and E Gaillard 'L'arbitrage sur le fondement des traités de protection des investissements' (2003) *Revue de l'Arbitrage* 853, 864–72.

[61] Fadlallah, 'La distinction "Treaty claims–Contract claims" et compétence de l'arbitre' (n 57) 5.

it has been accepted to split the dispute in two, between a purely contractual dispute and a separate purely treaty-based dispute.

In doing so 'an artificial carve-up' is made, whereas we are dealing, as Mayer too observes, with 'what is in fact a single dispute as it arises out of the same facts and the investor makes the same claim: the awarding of damages'.[62] The governing law alone differs between international law for the dispute arising out of the treaty and domestic law (usually) for the dispute arising out of the contract (unless it is a state contract and so internationalised). Now, both commentators observe, it is paradoxical to restrict the jurisdiction of ICSID arbitration tribunals to conflicts based on treaty, reserving contractual disputes to state courts, when the Washington Convention of 18 March 1965 was devised precisely to provide an arbitral instance for contractual disputes between states and investors.

The difficulty here arises, in fact, because we are in a situation that had not really been envisaged in 1965. The ICSID was indeed to act as an arbitration court for settling contractual disputes between states and investors. There had, then, to be a contract and it had to contain an ICSID arbitration clause. The arbitrators were to apply the legal rules adopted by the parties (article 42(1) first sentence) and, failing agreement between the parties, the law of the contracting state 'and such rules of international law as may be applicable' (article 42(2) second sentence). Arbitral case-law was to put this latter source in a pre-eminent position.[63]

In other words, the ICSID mechanism was not devised to take account of contracts that did not refer to its competence and even less to contracts that provided that, in the event of a dispute, jurisdiction was to be that of the domestic law courts (state courts or domestic arbitration tribunals) adjudicating by application of state law. The problem arose with *AAPL v Sri Lanka* (1990) which authorised investors to take their case to the ICSID even in the absence of any contractual connection with the host state and on the basis of the protection treaty alone. It was just a few years before enterprises (or their counsel) understood how they could benefit from this case law

---

[62] Contribution to the conference on *Nouveaux développements dans le contentieux arbitral transnational relatif à l'investissement international* (n 40) 197 and Mayer 'Contract claims et clauses juridictionnelles des traités relatifs à la protection des investissements' (n 57) 71.

[63] See C Schreuer, *The ICSID Convention: A Commentary* (Cambridge, Cambridge University Press, 2001) 608, paras 103ff and Leben, 'La théorie du contrat d'Etat' (n 1) 276ff, and above 17.

and from more than two thousand bilateral treaties that could hence-forth be activated. And so the late 1990s and early 2000s saw a surge in the number of cases brought before the ICSID arbitration tribunal on the basis of one of these treaties although initially arising from contractual disputes for which domestic law courts had jurisdiction. Indeed, this is now the way most cases come before the ICSID.

The attitude of the ICSID arbitrators may be explained, I believe, by their trying to be respectful of the jurisdiction of municipal courts; this led them to this distinction between disputes based on contract and disputes based on treaty, meaning their own involvement could be confined to the domain of treaties alone, so giving their action greater legitimacy. But this distinction gave rise to substantial diffi-culties and in particular difficulties concerning its implementation where there is a 'fork in the road' clause or an umbrella clause in the contract. All of this does indeed lead to a 'carve-up' of disputes on investments in a quite artificial way.

Now, as Fadalallah and Mayer assert, there is nothing to stop an ICSID tribunal, when a case relating to an investment dispute comes before it, from dealing with both the treaty and contract-based aspects of the dispute since the ICSID was set up to settle contrac-tual disputes. Simply, instead of coming to it by way of an arbitra-tion clause, the dispute comes to it via a protection treaty. It should be added, though—if we accept this way of seeing things—that it would be best if the state accepting an arbitration clause in the treaty were aware that, by the same token, it accepts to appear in front of an international arbitration tribunal for all disputes opposing it to investors of the state with which it has concluded a protection treaty, regardless of whether or not there is a contract between a particular investor and the state. It might be difficult to obtain an explicit clause to this effect. Clearly, everything depends here on the balance of power between states. It is not surprising that in two recent protec-tion treaties to which the United States is party (with Chile and Singapore) a clause has been included giving jurisdiction to a 'super' tribunal to deal with all proceedings pending for a given dispute.[64]

What happens, lastly, where there is a contract between the invest-ment host state and the investor, but where the contract provides that, in the event of a dispute, the host state's domestic courts have jurisdiction and that municipal law applies? If such a contract is entered into after conclusion of the bilateral treaty, it might bring to

[64] See Ben Hamida, 'L'arbitrage Etat-investisseur étranger' (n 51) 432.

nought the benefit provided by the protection treaty, for the investor could be deemed to have waived the protection offered by the treaty at its own discretion. But seeing that the possibility of recourse to an international arbitration tribunal is in fact, as observed, the main benefit investors derive from the treaty,[65] one may wonder whether enterprises should not be released from the pressure exerted by those host states that may require their private partners to waive treaty protection.[66] Once again, Mayer suggests, one might insert a clause in the treaty providing that the jurisdiction provided for by the treaty (say the ICSID tribunal) could only be set aside by an explicit clause in the investment contract. Naturally enough, such a clause would not be easy to secure either.

Another way forward might be, as Ben Hamida shows,[67] to define the dispute open to arbitration more broadly in the protection treaty so as to extend jurisdiction *ratione materiae* to all or part of contractual disputes. This is the direction supposedly taken by the new generation of investment protection treaties entered into by the United States. Thus, in the US/Uruguay bilateral treaty,[68] the investor may seize the arbitration tribunal for (i) disputes relating to violations of the BIT; (ii) disputes concerning investment authorisations and (iii) disputes relating to contracts entered into between one of the contracting states and the investors of the other. In addition, the court may apply international law (and not just treaty law) but also, if need be, the domestic law chosen by the parties in the contract. In this event, it should be added that the internationalist logic of arbitration tribunals should prompt them to give precedence to

---

[65] See the declaration by Professor Crivellaro, appended to the decision on jurisdiction in *SGS v Pakistan* 8 *ICSID Reports* 568, para 2; Gaillard, *La jurisprudence du CIRDI* (n 1) 894. More explicitly, the author refers to 'the right to choose among the various alternative courts and tribunals made available by the BIT'.

[66] Wälde, 'The "Umbrella" Clause in Investment Arbitration' (n 54) indicates that some central Asian countries, after having lost at arbitration, put pressure on investors to give a written waiver of the right they derive from the BIT to seize an arbitration tribunal. Can this clause be considered a modern form of the Calvo clause leading us to conclude that investors cannot waive the treaty's protection? But the reasoning used for diplomatic protection, that the investor cannot waive a right he does not have, cannot be served up again here as it is indeed a right the private person derives directly from the protection treaty. The question is an intricate one. However, should a tribunal say that the investor had managed to waive its right, its home state could begin proceedings criticising the host state for an attitude contrary to the investment protection and promotion treaty. The issue would be settled by the interstate arbitration tribunal provided for by the treaty.

[67] See Ben Hamida, 'La clause relative au respect des engagements' (n 54) 260.

[68] (2005) *ILM* 268.

international law over municipal law, as can be seen in the ICISD tribunals' case law applying article 42 of the Treaty of Washington,
supposing there is a contradiction between these laws (n 63).

In the Presence of a Specific Contractual Commitment on Observance of Obligations

This question recently came under lively scholarly discussion after
several cases that caused quite a stir.[69] Mention has already been
made of the meaning of such articles which, in various wordings,
crop up in many protection treaties whether bilateral or multilateral
and by which states declare they wish to abide by all their obligations
listed in the treaty. The clause in the first bilateral investment
protection treaty, the one concluded between West Germany and
Pakistan (1959), provides an example: 'Either party shall observe
any other obligation it may have entered into with regard to investments by nationals or companies of the other party'. Such clauses
sound odd, like a superfluous statement that the state undertakes to
comply with its contractual commitments, that is, it reasserts that
pacta sunt servanda. And indeed, as Wälde observes, this clause subscribed to by the states parties to protection treaties and by which
they made mutual commitments, was a form of exhortation by
which states expressly said what went without saying. It is likely too
that in north–south relations, the provision was intended to set aside
the spectre of nationalisation or at least of expropriation without adequate compensation. But it had few real legal consequences. Again it
was *AAPL/Sri Lanka* that was to rouse the clause from its slumber
and to impart effects to it that had until then been only potential.

Effects of an Umbrella Clause

From the moment an investor could unilaterally bring a dispute
before the arbitral tribunal provided for by the protection treaty, it
could also invoke before the tribunal the specific undertaking that
the state had subscribed to in the treaty to abide by its commitments.
But which commitments? Did this cover its legislative provisions at
the time the agreement was entered into or the provisions of treaties
entered into by the state? The question is under discussion.[70]
However—and it is this that is of interest to us here—it most certainly covers the commitments made in the contract concluded with

---

[69] There is an abundant literature on this topic; see n 54.
[70] See Ben Hamida, 'La clause relative au respect des engagements' (n 54).

the investor, with the result that, what were initially just contractual obligations were raised to treaty status and so protected by international law. Consequently, in the event of a breach of the word given by the state, there is a shift from the uncertain involvement of state responsibility on the basis of its law before its municipal courts to international responsibility before an international arbitration tribunal (ICSID) and by application of international law.

There is a shift too from disputes relating almost exclusively to questions of expropriation to contractual disputes, as may arise between ordinary contracting parties; disputes that will be adjudicated by the arbitrators provided for in the protection treaty and applying international law, which will not preclude referral to municipal law where necessary.

Another consequence of the insertion of umbrella clauses in a protection treaty is the outdistancing (although not the demise) of the technique of the state contract in the strict sense of the term, that is, of a certain type of internationalised agreement. State contracts are characterised essentially as contracts concluded with the investment host state, as a person of international law and containing clauses referring disputes to an international arbitrator (ICSID, say) who decides matters by applying not municipal law alone but a stabilised municipal law or by reference in one way or another to international law.[71] For an investor to secure a contract of this type presupposes that the enterprise has substantial bargaining power, for few states readily accept to relinquish their legal control over the contracts they conclude. That means in practice that small or medium-sized investors can never secure state contracts in this sense.

The umbrella clause then brings about a situation similar to that under a state contract. And this time, all investors, big and small, can benefit from it because the clause has been negotiated between states and leads to a stabilisation of obligations that goes further than the clauses of this type included in a contract.[72] But this can only be if it is considered that the umbrella clause effectively transforms contractual obligations into treaty obligations. This, though, is where opinions differ: whereas some scholars continue to be favourable to the internationalisation of contractual obligations via the umbrella clause, recent ICSID case law shows that arbitrators are very reluctant to accept this mechanism.

---

[71] See Leben, 'La théorie du contrat d'Etat' (n 1) 264ff, and see above 17ff.
[72] See Ben Hamida, 'La clause relative au respect des engagements' (n 54) 205.

The Question of the Effect of the Umbrella Clause in Doctrine
The idea that an obligation–observance clause entails the internationalisation of contractual commitments was asserted very early in doctrine. In his 1969 course at The Hague, Weil wrote:

> Involvement of the covering treaty transforms the contractual obligations into international obligations and so ensures . . . the contract is intangible under pain of breach of the treaty; any non-performance of the contract, be it lawful in the eyes of the municipal law of the contracting state, involves the state's international responsibility with regard to the home state of the contracting party.[73]

Similarly, Mann wrote:

> This is a provision of particular importance in that it protects the investor against any interference with his contractual rights, whether it results from a mere breach of contract or a legislative or administrative act, and independently of the question whether or not such interference amounts to expropriation. The variation of the terms of a contract or licence by legislative measures, the termination of the contract or the failure to perform any of its terms, for instance, by non-payment, the dissolution of the local company with which the investor may have contracted and the transfer of its assets . . . these and similar acts the treaties render wrongful.[74]

Wälde presents a middle-of-the-road opinion considering that the clause does not internationalise every 'merely commercial' contractual dispute but only disputes arising from the host state's use of its 'governmental powers'. If we look at the history of the umbrella clause, he argues, it can be seen that it was introduced in the minds of its proponents not to cover any ordinary commercial commitment but only 'a contract dealing with matters *iure imperii*, a public concession or contrat administratif, ie, not a commercial contract outside the normal scope of international law but a contract that involves the powers of government'.[75]

I am not convinced that this is a really useful distinction, if only because it introduces a distinction which in other areas, like that of sovereign immunities, has given rise to extremely complicated case law. This is not desirable if investors and states are to be provided with straightforward rules whose operation is understandable and

---

[73] Weil, 'Problèmes relatifs aux contrats passés entre un Etat et un particulier' (n 12) 130.
[74] FA Mann, *Further Studies in International Law* (Oxford, Clarendon Press, 1990) 234–51, 240.
[75] See Wälde, 'The "Umbrella" Clause in Investment Arbitration' (n 54) 215.

predictable. Moreover, looking at ICSID case law, it has several times covered what could be characterised as 'commercial' cases: in *Klöckner v Cameroon* (1983) over a common dispute in the business world with each side accusing the other of failing to meet its obligations that led to the failure of a project to build a large production plant, or *Fedax v Venezuela* over non payment of endorsed bills of exchange, or for a more recent example *Salini v Jordan* (2004)[76] (not to be confused with *Salini v Morocco*, 2001) over the company's claims for monies for additional work that had been asked for. That these were commercial disputes in no way prevented the arbitration tribunal, admittedly provided for by the arbitration clause in the contract between the host state and investor, from deciding these matters. It can be seen from this, I feel, that such disputes could equally well benefit from the internationalisation effected by an umbrella clause. The only valid limitation would be that relating to the definition of investment: treaty or case law would need to provide a narrower interpretation of the notion of investment so that not just any type of interest claimed by the private party could be characterised as an 'investment' and so be secured in the international arena, which would be reserved for investment disputes and not open to any 'merely commercial dispute'.

In any event, if it is accepted that the umbrella clause internationalises the state's contractual obligations, we are left with a legal regime that runs counter to the traditional customary rule of international law that considers that a breach of contract by a state does not involve its responsibility if it is not compounded by an international wrong such as a denial of justice or more generally the breach of a minimum standard of treatment of aliens. The umbrella clause would certainly bring any breach of contract by the state within the ambit of international law.

Case Law

Only very recently have the ICSID tribunals had to rule on the effects of umbrella clauses. This was in *SGS v Pakistan* (6 August 2003),[77] *SGS v Philippines* (29 January 2004)[78] and *Joy Mining v*

---

[76] Decision on jurisdiction of 29 November 2004, 20 *ICSID Review* (2005); *Fedax v Venezuela* 11 July 1997, 5 *ICSID Reports* 186; (1999) *Journal du Droit International* 278; (1998) *ILM* 1378.

[77] *SGS v Pakistan* (ARB/01/13), 8 *ICSID Reports* 406; Gaillard, *La jurisprudence du CIRDI* (n 1) 815ff.

[78] *SGS v Philippines* (ARB/02/06), 8 *ICSID Reports* 518; Gaillard, *ibid*, 865ff.

Egypt (6 August 2004)[79]. In all three cases, the arbitrators were reluctant to recognise the internationalisation mechanism that doctrine attributes to umbrella clauses.

The two most important cases involved SGS, first against Pakistan and then the Philippines. In both cases the Société Générale de Surveillance SA seized the ICSID on the basis of the bilateral protection treaty between Switzerland and in one instance Pakistan, in the other the Philippines. In the first treaty, article 11 provided that 'Either Contracting Party shall constantly guarantee the observance of the commitments it has entered into with respect to the investments of the investors of the other Contracting Party'. In the second, article X(2) stated: 'Each Contracting Party shall observe any obligation it has assumed with regard to specific investments in its territory by investors of the other Contracting Party.'

This is not the place to comment on these two important awards. It will suffice for present purposes to remark that, somewhat surprisingly, both tribunals, following different and even opposing lines of reasoning, managed to paralyse the effect of the umbrella clause. Thus, in *SGS v Pakistan* paragraph 167 of the award very clearly reveals the spirit in which the tribunal examined the clause:

> Considering the widely accepted principle . . . that . . . a violation of a contract entered into by a State with an investor of another State, is not, by itself, a violation of international law, and considering further that the legal consequences that the Claimant would have us attribute to Article 11 of the BIT are so far-reaching in scope, and so automatic and unqualified and sweeping in their operation, so burdensome in their potential impact upon a Contracting Party, we believe that clear and convincing evidence must be adduced by the Claimant . . . that such was indeed the shared intent of the Contracting Parties to the . . . Investment Protection Treaty . . .[80]

The tribunal considered such evidence had not been adduced. Elsewhere, it emphasises the 'extraordinarily expansive manner' in which the claimant read article 11 (award, paragraph 171) and considers that 'Article 11 of the BIT should be read in such a way as to enhance mutuality and balance of benefits in the interrelation of different agreements located in legal orders' (award, paragraph 168). The arbitration tribunal's aim to maintain what it conceives of

---

[79] *Joy Mining v Egypt* (ARB/03/11), 13 *ICSID Reports* 123.
[80] 8 *ICSID Reports* 443, Gaillard, *La jurisprudence du CIRDI* (n 1) 820.

as a balance of power between the host state and the investor is obvious and the whole legal argument is built upon this aim.

In *SGS v Philippines*, the arbitration court was first to wrong foot the *SGS v Pakistan* award and then, by an odd reversal of its position, to arrive at a conclusion that was not very far removed.

In its interpretation of article X(2) of the Switzerland–Philippines treaty, the tribunal first came to the provisional conclusion that 'Article X(2) means what it says', in other words that it ensures the internationalisation of contractual obligations (paragraph 119). But as the defendant, the Philippines, invoked the *SGS v Pakistan* case law, the tribunal was to go through the grounds for the earlier decision and dismiss them one by one (paragraphs 110–24). It eventually came to the conclusion that 'Not only are the reasons given by the Tribunal in *SGS v. Pakistan* unconvincing: the Tribunal failed to give any clear meaning to the "umbrella clause" ' (paragraph 125). Indeed the tribunal acknowledged the clause had only an implied affirmative effect whereas jurisdiction granted to an international tribunal, if it is to be recognised as having any effect at all, must confer jurisdiction with adequate certainty (paragraph 125).

One then thinks the tribunal in *SGS v Philippines* is preparing to confer its full effect on the umbrella clause. But in examining the final ground of the previous tribunal, it makes an unexpected U-turn. The tribunal in *SGS v Pakistan* feared that a broad interpretation of the umbrella clause might lead to 'instant transubstantiation' of all domestic contracts into international contracts; but not so explains the tribunal in *SGS v Philippines*. The clause does not convert questions of contract law into questions of treaty law (paragraph 126). It simply provides an international guarantee as to *performance* of contractual obligations. However, the *scope* of these obligations is to be determined by the court ruling on the contract. And to cite the tribunal again:

> Article X(2) makes it a breach of the BIT for the host State to fail to observe binding commitments, including contractual commitments, which it has assumed with regard to specific investments. But it does not convert the issue of the *exten*t or *content* of such obligations into an issue of international law.[81]

The arbitration tribunal in *SGS v Philippines* was also to stay proceedings and refer the case to the domestic courts for them to determine whether there had been a breach of contract and, in that

---

[81] 8 *ICSID Reports* 553, para 128.

case, to determine any compensation that should be awarded. And it was only the state's failure to comply with that judgment that could provide grounds to take the matter before an arbitration tribunal provided for under the protection treaty.

The relevance of the SGS case law and the effect it will have on future cases is debatable. All that can be ascertained for the time being is that arbitrators hesitate to give full international effect to umbrella clauses. It will be noticed in this respect that state contracts (in the strict sense of internationalised contracts) here retain an advantage over BITs insofar as they set the contractual relation within the orbit of international law, a move that is not guaranteed with the implementation of protection treaties.

This chapter set out, as said, only to make students of general international law more familiar with the major developments in international investment law that are occurring at the present time both through the intermediary of bilateral and multilateral agreements for the promotion and protection of investment and through the intermediary of rapidly expanding arbitration case law. There is some reluctance in our discipline to accept into the international law 'club' tribunals that are not interstate tribunals in the narrow sense and that do not decide disputes between states but disputes between states and individuals. Obviously, one can discuss endlessly the underlying nature of international law, the possibility for private persons to accede to it or the appropriate character of this law for ruling on question raised by disputes between states and foreign investors. But practice does not wait. Regardless of these doubts, arbitration tribunals almost naturally apply international law to solve the disputes before them. Let us take two examples, the most recent ones available: *CMS v Argentina*, final award rendered 12 May 2005 and *Impregilo v Pakistan* of 22 April 2005.

The first case pertained to the consequences to be drawn from the economic crisis in Argentina and the measures the Argentinean Government took from 1999 to 2002 and especially the devaluation of the peso. CMS, like some thirty other companies currently in dispute with Argentina, argued that these measures amounted to expropriation of its investment without compensation (and see supra note 41). What was discussed before the arbitrators? Questions of nationalisation and compensation that are classical questions of international law, but also questions of *force majeure*, of the state of necessity in customary international law with reference to old-established arbitration case law (*The Caroline* 1905; *Company General of the Orinoco* 1905;

War Compensation (*Russia/Turkey*) 1912; *French Company of Venezuelan Railroads* 1905; *Properties of the Bulgarian minorities in Greece*). The arbitrators also called on decisions by the Permanent Court of International Justice (*Société commerciale de Belgique* 1939), the International Court of Justice (*Gabcikovo-Nagymaros* 1997) and works of the International Law Commission. Ultimately the award develops at length the conditions for resort to the notion of the state of necessity in international law and for reparations owed in the event of nationalisation.

In the second case, where it was what one might call a purely commercial matter of a joint venture for the construction of a hydroelectric facility that went wrong in a very ordinary way, what was at issue? Mainly decisions of the International Court of Justice: the *Ambatielos* 1953; *Petroleum platforms* (Iran v US) 1996 and *Legality of the use of force in Yugoslavia* 1999 cases; decisions cited equally as often as those of the ICSID tribunals (*SGS v Pakistan, SGS v Philippines, Wena v Egypt, Vivendi v Argentina*, etc). Noticeable too in both cases, as in other recent ones (eg, *CMS v Argentina*, May 2005) is the participation in ICSID arbitration tribunals of judges of the International Court of Justice who do not seem like fish out of water and who, perhaps, even leave their own mark on the decisions (eg, *Impregilo v Pakistan* of 22 April 2005).

These are most clearly questions that pertain to public international law. And so it can be observed that the two most important economic flows in the world economy—the flow of trade in goods and services on the one side and the flow of investments on the other—are now the subject matter of international regulation. World trade is under the sway of the World Trade Organisation's (WTO) rules, and investment flows under the sway of the rules in bilateral and multilateral treaties for the promotion and protection of investments. In addition, in both cases—and this is not the least important point—case law takes on considerable importance which was hitherto unknown in international law: case law of the Dispute Settlement Body in one instance; case law of the arbitration tribunals, and primarily of the ICSID tribunals in the other. It can be further noticed that each of the two systems looks somewhat covetously at the success of the other. Thus, in the WTO some envy the possibility investors have of bringing a state before an international court; conversely, others envy the existence of an avenue for appeal within the Dispute Settlement Body, which is currently lacking in the ICSID, which has only an annulment procedure.

When it comes down to it, the current changes are only logical: an international phenomenon calls for international law and not municipal law, or even 'transnational law'; for where are the rules and the case law that compose such law? No-one knows. But international law, for its part, has its customary rules as revealed through more than a century of arbitration case law; it benefits from the codification work of the International Law Commission, and it relies on a network of investment protection treaties that is almost unparalleled in history. Yes, it is time to wake up to the fact that international law, Grotius' good old law of nations, has been given new impetus in the area of international economic relations.

3

The State's Normative Freedom and the Question of Indirect Expropriation*

IN APRIL 1997 Ethyl, a US firm that had invested in Canada, announced it was to claim compensation at arbitration from the Canadian Government under NAFTA Chapter 11 for the loss it had allegedly incurred because of a Canadian statute prohibiting Canadian provinces from importing and trading in the petroleum additive MMT. The Canadian authorities justified the ban on environmental grounds and out of concern to replace the additive by ethanol. The Canadian subsidiary that imported the product from the US to mix with petroleum and distribute the fuel in Canada saw its prospects of profits seriously jeopardised. It argued it was the victim of a measure that was tantamount to expropriation and claimed $250 million in compensation.[1]

This claim caused something of a rumpus coinciding as it did with the big campaign then being conducted by non-governmental organisations against the adoption of the draft Multilateral Agreement on Investments (MAI) by the OECD. This draft agreement included provisions similar to the one allowing Ethyl to act against Canada on the basis of the NAFTA Treaty. The spectre of multinational firms claiming compensation from states as victims of

* First published as 'La liberté normative de l'Etat et la question de l'expropriation indirecte' in C Leben (ed), *Nouveaux développements dans le contentieux arbitral transnational relatif à l'investissement international* (Paris, IHEI, 2006).

[1] The arbitration tribunal ruled it did have jurisdiction in a decision of 24 June 1998. See (1999) *ILM* 70ff and (1999) 3 *Journal of International Arbitration* 149ff. A $13 million settlement was reached; a far cry from the $250 million claimed. But Canada withdrew its legislation, which oddly banned imports of MMT and trade in it between Canadian provinces, but not its production in Canada. The Canadian authorities acknowledged in a letter to Ethyl that there was no scientific proof that MMT was a human health risk.

the economic repercussions of legislative reforms adopted in the realms of environmental or health protection, and more generally in areas where the state acts in defence of a nation's general interest, was apparently one of the factors that put paid to the project.[2] The problem raised by Ethyl's claim was not a new one, though. For almost a century, the question has been around of the treatment of indirect expropriation (or nationalisation—no distinction shall be drawn here),[3] that is, of measures which, while not having as their stated purpose to deprive persons of their property, do have that effect in practice. This is the case especially when, further to the passing of new legislation or regulations in a state, a person loses the effective control and enjoyment of his property.

The question has been a familiar one in the United States since 1922 and the Supreme Court has developed very substantial case law about what it calls 'regulatory takings', that is, dispossessions further to general normative activity by the power of the states or of the federation that have the result of depriving citizens of their property in breach of the Constitution's Fifth and Fourteenth Amendments.[4] Similarly, Article 1 of the first additional protocol to the European Convention on Human Rights, after stating that:

> Every natural or legal person is entitled to the peaceful enjoyment of his possessions. No one shall be deprived of his possessions except in the

---

[2] See R Geiger, 'Regulatory Expropriations in International Law: Lessons from the Multilateral Agreement on Investments' (2002) *New York University Environmental Law Journal* 94. On the MAI and its failure, see Société Française pour le Droit International (SFDI), *Un accord multilatéral sur l'investissement: d'un forum de négociation à l'autre?* (Paris, Pedone, 1999).

[3] D Carreau and P Juillard, *Droit international économique* (Paris, Dalloz, 2003) 499, no 1375 distinguish between expropriations that are administrative measures and nationalisations decided by the legislator. See also S Manciaux, *Investissements étrangers et arbitrage entre Etats et ressortissants d'autres Etats. Trente années d'activités du CIRDI* (Dijon, CREDIMI, Paris, Litec, 2004) 457, noting that the distinction is more in the civil law tradition and is seldom made in common law literature. From the standpoint of international law it matters little whether the deprivation was by the executive or the legislative body. For Higgins, the term 'nationalisation' indicates a direct take-over of a sector of activity by legislative or regulatory means, while 'expropriation' designates 'a taking by the State which does not result in the direct management and control of the property by public bodies': R Higgins, 'The Taking of Property by the State: Recent Developments in International Law (1982) 176 *Recueil des Cours de l'Académie de Droit International de La Haye* 259, 376 fn 2.

[4] For an initial approach see *New York University School of Law Environmental Law Journal*, proceedings of April 2002 conference, and especially E Shenkman, 'Could principles of fifth amendment takings jurisprudence be helpful in analysing regulatory expropriation claims under international law? 174ff. See also papers in (2003) 3 *Forum du Droit International: International Law Forum* 150–214.

public interest and subject to the conditions provided for by law and by the general principles of international law.

specifies in a second subparagraph:

> The preceding provisions shall not, however, in any way impair the right of a State to enforce such laws as it deems necessary to control the use of property in accordance with the general interest or to secure the payment of taxes or other contributions or penalties.

Admittedly, it is a question there only of statutes governing the use of property. This is a more restricted category than in the problem raised here which potentially concerns all statutes that may have an effect on property; but it can be seen that the law of property is subjected to statutes and is so subjected in the general interest.[5] International law too was to see this problem raised before its courts from the 1920s and 1930s.[6] They gave an outline response that was to be taken up again and confirmed, as shall be seen, by the arbitration awards that from the late 1990s were to deal with this problem either on the basis of bilateral investment treaties (BITs) or in the context of the arbitration mechanism set up by NAFTA Chapter 11 to settle disputes between state parties and investors. The outline response is that indirect expropriation is included in the notion of expropriation, the only factor to be taken into account being whether or not the owner of the property really has been deprived of it. But this does not mean that courts or arbitration tribunals readily recognise that dispossession can be effected by means of legislation or regulations adopted for an altogether different purpose than that of transferring property.[7]

---

[5] On this point see F Sudre, *Droit international et européen des droits de l'homme* 6th edn (Paris, PUF, 2003) 446–80.

[6] See G Fouilloux, *La nationalisation et le droit international public* (Paris, LGDJ, 1962) 140ff; S Petrén, 'La confiscation des biens étrangers et les réclamations internationales auxquelles elle peut donner lieu' (1963) 109 *Recueil des Cours de l'Académie de Droit International de La Haye* 492–571; G White, *Nationalization of Foreign Property* (London, Stevens, 1961) 41ff.

[7] See Y Nouvel, 'Les mesures équivalant à une expropriation dans la pratique récente des tribunaux arbitraux' (2002) *Revue Générale de Droit International Public* 80; A Lemaire, Chronique, 'Investissements internationaux et arbitrage' (2003) 2 *Les Cahiers de l'Arbitrage (Gazette du Palais)* part 2, 20; T Wälde and A Kolo, 'Environmental Regulation and Modern Investment Treaties: "Regulatory Taking" as a New International Law Discipline' (2001) *International & Comparative Law Quarterly* 811; T Wälde, 'Nouveaux horizons pour le droit international des investissements dans le contexte de la mondialisation de l'économie' in *Cours et travaux de l'Institut des Hautes Etudes Internationales de Paris* (Paris, Pedone, 2004) 62; and see also for the entire question Manciaux, *Investissements étrangers et arbitrage entre Etats et ressortissants d'autres Etats* (n 3).

We find ourselves here, rather unwittingly, in the domain of states responsibility for their legislative activity. Now, as scrutiny of comparative law shows, such responsibility can be incurred in exceptional cases only.

Indirect Expropriation in International Law

Until the multiplication of bilateral investment promotion and protection treaties (BITs) and the emergence of a few big multinational treaties (especially NAFTA and the Energy Charter Treaty), the question of indirect expropriation only arose from time to time in international law by dent of the diplomatic protection mechanism. And yet, case law and doctrine rapidly reached an outline answer that has been confirmed both in the case law of a regional court like that of the European Convention on Human Rights and in the transnational arbitration awards of the last decade.

In International Law in General

PCIJ/ICJ Case Law

Questions pertaining to the indirect expropriation of goods are found in a handful of decisions of the two permanent courts of international justice. In all instances, the courts endeavoured to check there really had been dispossession, even if it was effected mediately only. In *Certain German Interests in Polish Upper Silesia* (25 May 1926), the Court recognised that the nationalisation of *Oberschlesische Stickstoffwerke* entailed the nationalisation of *Bayerische Stickstoffwerke* that ran it. While Poland maintained it had never sought to expropriate the latter company, the Court recognised there had been an indirect expropriation because:

> [i]t is clear that the rights of the Bayerische to the exploitation of the factory and to the remuneration fixed by the contract for the management of the exploitation . . . have been directly prejudiced by the taking over of the factory by Poland.[8]

In *Oscar Chinn* (12 December 1934), on the contrary, the Permanent court declined to find the Belgian Government had indirectly expropriated the British subject in question, who had been

---

[8] *Certain German Interests in Polish Upper Silesia* (Merits) PCIJ Rep Series A No 7, 44.

bankrupted because of the reduction in prices Belgium had required of Chinn's sole competitor, that price cut being accompanied by subsidies that were not available to Chinn.[9] The question of indirect expropriation might have been raised before the International Court of Justice (ICJ) in *Barcelona Traction*[10] (5 February 1970, *Recueil* 1970, at 3) had the matter come to trial on the merits. The situation in which the Barcelona Traction Company was placed in Spain—refusal of an authorisation to transfer the sums needed to pay interest on a loan by the company and bankruptcy of the company—could have been construed as a disguised expropriation. The same could have been true in *Elettronica Sicula* (20 July 1989) if the Court had not considered the company had voluntarily gone out of business but rather that it had been bankrupted by decisions of the Italian Government.[11]

European Court of Human Rights Case Law

The European Court of Human Rights extends its control not only when there is deprivation of property (article 1, paragraph 1 of the First Protocol) or control of the use of property (article 2, paragraph 2) but also where there is an infringement of the law of property. This is what happened in *Sporrong and Lönnroth v Sweden* (23 September 1982), which covers hypotheses of indirect expropriation. In the case in point, for example:

> Although the expropriation permits left intact in law the owners' right to use and dispose of their possessions, they nevertheless in practice significantly reduced the possibility of its exercise. They also affected the very substance of ownership in that they recognised before the event that any expropriation would be lawful and authorised the City of Stockholm to expropriate whenever it found it expedient to do so. The applicant's right of property thus became precarious and defeasible (paragraph 60).[12]

Iran–US Claims Tribunal Case Law

Naturally enough, matters raising the problem of indirect expropriation are found in the mass of litigation opposing US firms and Iran

---

[9] *Oscar Chinn* PCIJ Rep Series A/B No 63, 65.
[10] Barcelona Traction 5 February 1970, Recueil 1970, at 3
[11] See *Elettronica Sicula* (1989) *Recueil* 13, paras 99–100.
[12] Case of *Sporrong and Lönnroth v Sweden* (App nos 7151/75, 7152/75) (1982) Judgment (1982) para 60. See Sudre, *Droit international et européen des droits de l'homme* (n 5) 454, no 262ff and F Sudre *et al*, *Les grands arrêts de la Cour européenne des droits de l'homme* 2nd edn (Paris, PUF Thémis, 2004) no 57, para 63, 527.

before the Claims Tribunal. Here again the Tribunal has decided this question on the basis of international law. Thus, in *Tippetts*, the Tribunal stated:

> A deprivation or taking of property may occur under international law through interference by a state in the use of the property or with the enjoyment of its benefits, even where legal title to the property is not affected; . . . such conclusion is warranted whenever events demonstrate that the owner was deprived of fundamental rights of ownership and it appears that this deprivation is not merely ephemeral. The intent of the government is less important than the reality of their impact.[13]

Doctrine

This case law which, admittedly, is not very abundant, is confirmed even so by almost unanimous scholarly opinion. Article 10 (3)(a) of the Harvard Law School draft convention on the international responsibility of states for injuries to aliens, drawn up by Sohn and Baxter, reads:

> 'A taking of property includes' not only an outright taking of property but also any such reasonable interference with the use, enjoyment, or disposal of property as to justify an inference that the owner thereof will not be able to use, enjoy, or dispose of the property within a reasonable period of time after the inception of such interference.[14]

In the same sense the Third Restatement of Foreign Relations Law of the United States (1987) (paragraph 712, commentary g) declares:

> A state is responsible for an expropriation of property . . . when it subjects alien property to taxation, regulation, or other action that is confiscatory, or that prevents, unreasonably interferes with, or unduly delays, effective enjoyment of an alien's property or its removal from the state's territory.[15]

---

[13] Tippetts, 6 Iran–US Claims Tribunal Rep 225–26 and see also *Biloune v Ghana* (1989) 95 *ILR* 209. See also V Heiskanen, 'The Contributions of the Iran–United States Claims Tribunal to the Development of the Doctrine of Indirect Expropriation' (2003) 3 *Forum du Droit International/International Law Forum* 176. Generally see Nouvel, 'Les mesures équivalant à une expropriation' (n 7) 88ff and H Sedigh, 'What Level of Host State Interference Amounts to a Taking under Contemporary International Law' (2001) 2(4) *The Journal of World Investment* 631.

[14] See Harvard Law School draft convention on 'the international responsibility of states for injuries to aliens' (1961) *American Journal of International Law* 545, 553.

[15] The Third Restatement of Foreign Relations Law of the United States (1987), as adopted and promulgated by the American Law Institute at Washington DC (14 May 1986) 200.

It is not over-adventurous to consider then that general international law does indeed include a rule that indirect expropriation should be treated as direct expropriation whenever it leads to the effective deprivation of property. This point was to be picked up on and confirmed by the many bilateral and then multilateral treaties that are the basis of international investment law today.

In International Investment Law

International investment law has been profoundly marked in recent decades by the tremendous development of bilateral treaties for promoting and protecting investments. These treaties, plus certain multilateral treaties (NAFTA, Energy Charter Treaty), have largely contributed, through the arbitration case law they have engendered, to enhancing investment law to an extent unknown heretofore.[16]

Bilateral Protection Treaties

There are currently more than 2000 treaties[17] for the promotion and protection of investments and they are no longer made just between developed and developing states but between developing states themselves, China alone having entered into a hundred or so of them.

These treaties provide that no investment can be expropriated or nationalised except under certain conditions, including the payment of adequate compensation (there are various formulae for specifying what adequate means). In many instances, the treaties stipulate that they also cover 'all other measures whose effect is to directly or indirectly dispossess the investors' (China–Pakistan BIT), or 'any other measures tantamount to expropriation or nationalisation' (UK–Panama BIT), or again 'any other form of direct or indirect dispossession' (France–South Korea BIT), or 'any other measure, direct or indirect . . . if the effect of such measure, or a series of such

[16] On the development of bilateral and multilateral agreements, see UNCTAD (2003) *World Investment Report* 88; see also C Leben, 'L'évolution du droit international des investissements' in *Un accord multilatéral sur l'investissement* (n 2) 7; P Juillard, 'L'évolution des sources du droit des investissements' (1994) 250 *Recueil des Cours de l'Académie de Droit International de La Haye* 13; G Sacerdoti, 'Bilateral Treaties and Multilateral Instruments on Investment Protection' (1997) 269 *Recueil des Cours de l'Académie de Droit International de La Haye* 255.

[17] There were 2676 such treaties by the end of 2008 and probably more than 3000 in 2010., V. UNCTAD, *Recent Developments in International Investment Agreements* (2008–June 2009), UNCTAD, IIA Monitor No 3 (2009), U.N. 2009.

measures, would be tantamount to expropriation or nationalisation' (Egypt–US BIT), or finally 'Neither Party shall expropriate or nationalize a covered investment either directly or indirectly through measures tantamount to expropriation or nationalization' (US–El Salvador).[18]

Multilateral Investment Treaties: NAFTA and Energy Chapter Treaty

The North American Free Trade Agreement (NAFTA) treaty (in force since 1994) includes a Chapter 11 establishing a common regime for investments in the zone by investors from each of the three parties (Canada, United States and Mexico).[19] The chapter forces each state to grant favourable treatment to investments and especially national treatment (article 1102); most-favoured-nation treatment (article 1103); treatment consistent with international law, and especially fair and equitable treatment as well as full protection and security (article 1105). Article 1110 (1) on nationalisation provides that:

No Party may directly or indirectly nationalize or expropriate an investment of an investor of another Party in its territory or take a measure tantamount to nationalization or expropriation of such an investment except:

(a) for a public purpose; (b) on a non-discriminatory basis; (c) in accordance with due process of law and the general principles of treatment provided in Article 1105; an (d) upon payment of compensation in accordance with paragraphs 2 to 6.[20]

[18] These examples are borrowed from W Ben Hamida, 'L'arbitrage transnational unilatéral' (Thesis, University of Paris 2, 2003) 557.

[19] See T Weiler (ed), *NAFTA Investment Law: Past Issues, Current Practice, Future Prospects* (New York, Transnational Publishers, 2004); A Lemaire, 'Le nouveau visage de l'arbitrage entre Etat et investisseur étranger : le chaptire 11 de l'ALENA' (2001) *Revue de l'Arbitrage* 43; C Levesque, 'Investor-state Arbitration under NAFTA Chapter 11: What Lies Beneath Jurisdictional Challenges' (2002) *ICSID Review* 320; B Legum, 'The Innovation of Investor-state Arbitration under NAFTA' (2002) 2 *Harvard International Law Journal* 531; PG Foy and R Deane, 'Foreign Investment Protection under Investment Treaties: Recent Developments under Chapter 11 of the North American Free Trade Agreement' (2001) *ICSID Review* 299.

[20] It might be wondered, on the basis of the NAFTA Treaty and on the basis of certain other treaties, whether there had not been a shift from two to three types of measure: (i) direct expropriation measures, (ii) indirect expropriation measures and (iii) measures tantamount to expropriation. An ICSID tribunal, in *Tradex v Albania*, seems to have gone down this road (See Ben Hamida, 'L'arbitrage transnational unilatéral' (n 17) 557 fn 8. By contrast, two tribunals set up under the NAFTA Treaty (in *Pope & Talbot*, and *S.D. Myers*) considered, rightly I feel, that the 'tantamount' measures were another way of saying indirect expropriation.

Similarly, article 13 of the Energy Charter Treaty (which is known to have been influenced by the NAFTA Treaty) covers investments allegedly 'nationalized, expropriated or subjected to a measure or measures having effect equivalent to nationalization or expropriation . . .'.

To return to the NAFTA Treaty (although the following observations largely hold for the Energy Charter Treaty too), compliance with obligations by states is ensured by the implementation of a unilateral arbitration mechanism allowing any investor from one of the parties to seek a ruling from an arbitration tribunal that the state has failed to comply with any of its obligations under Chapter 11 (articles 1116 ff) and to obtain compensation for any injury incurred.

From 1997 arbitration tribunals were to be formed (either under the UNCITRAL arbitration regulation or on the basis of the supplementary ICSID mechanism) to adjudicate on claims from investors. Complaints from investors were to increase over time and implicate the three NAFTA partners almost equally. The website for investment disputes handled by this international organisation lists (by early 2004), excepting tallying errors, 32 cases (ranging from those for which there is as yet but a declaration of intent to go to arbitration to cases on which final decisions have been rendered). Of these, 11 involve Canada, 10 Mexico and 12 the US (with a margin of error of one or two cases).

Moreover, of these 32 cases, only five do not include claims based on article 1110. In most applications to go to arbitration, investors invoke one or more of articles 1102 to 1105 (national treatment, most-favoured-nation treatment, etc) but also article 1110 on expropriation or measures tantamount to expropriation. Thus, the 10 cases begun against Mexico all refer to article 1110 as do eight out of the 11 cases against Canada, and 10 of the 12 against the US.

Barring a few exceptions, the measures invoked are not direct outright expropriations. Usually investors accuse states of adopting measures of various sorts, the effects of which are tantamount to expropriation. To cite but a few cases, states are variously accused of: banning the sale of a product manufactured by the investor (*Ethyl, S.D. Myers, Sun Belt, Crampton, Methanex, Knex*); imposing export quotas (*Pope & Talbot* and several other cases brought by forestry companies); subjecting investors' products to anti-dumping duties (*Doman, Canfor*); refusing the opening of a waste processing site for which a prior authorisation had been granted (*Metalclad*); refusing to grant certain tax breaks to which the investor was allegedly entitled (*Roy Feldman Karpa*); refusing to apply certain legislation on sugar prices to the investor (*Gami*); or investors complain of being victims of groundless legal decisions (*Loewen, Mondev, Calmark*), or of incurring losses amounting to expropriation further to legislative measures adopted in the United States for the benefit of four big cigarette manufacturers (*Grand River*).[21]

What is important is to observe that these claims brought by investors against states often call into question legislation or regulations made by various state organs, whether the legislator, a government agency or even a judicial decision. The crucial problem is clearly framed: under what circumstances can an enterprise challenge a state's normative action when that action is conducted in the general interest and does not aim to expropriate any particular enterprise?

It is a question that is the subject today of very lively debates in the United States and Canada. Some circles, especially environmentalist circles, challenge the constitutionality of arbitration tribunals formed on the basis of the NAFTA Treaty, call into question arbitrators who allegedly provide none of the guarantees of independence required for judicial instances, and denounce the power they are given to question acts of the local, national and federal authorities.[22] Are these fears justified on examination of the data by the arbitration tribunals that have had to deal with these issues? Have arbitrators set strict limits to the normative freedom of states? It seems not.

Maintaining the State's Normative Freedom

An examination of recent case law of transnational arbitration tribunals reveals that, while the expropriation argument is used by claimants in most claims, it has been approved by the arbitrators in a very small number of cases only. This is particularly true of arbitration on the basis of the NAFTA Treaty, as in one case only (out of some 20 already heard where expropriation was invoked) was such expropriation recognised by the arbitrators. Admittedly, that

---

[21] It is something of an irony that North America is the part of the world where there are currently most claims for expropriation at the present time (10 cases against the US alone, whose responsibility for expropriation is under question for the first time in its history on the basis of an international treaty).

[22] A glance at various NGO sites indicates the hostility towards NAFTA, both outside and inside the United States. For a more academic study see A Milanova, 'Le règlement des différends dans le cadre de l'ALENA: les atours discrets d'une hégémonie' (2003) *Journal du Droit International* 87.

can be explained by various considerations of legal technique. But more fundamentally, I feel, a restrictive attitude of the sort relates to the limits of implication of states' liability for their legislative activities, such limits being found in most legal orders.

Results of Case Law

Let us look very briefly at the reasons why arbitration tribunals have dismissed claims based on measures tantamount to expropriation.

The Essential Elements of the Right of Ownership must have Disappeared

This point has long been established in general international law. If it is argued that some normative act of the state has caused de facto expropriation, it must be proved that the essential attributes of the right of ownership have disappeared or been seriously jeopardised. This is a rule that probably exists in most domestic legal orders. It occurs for instance in the US Supreme Court decision in *Lucas v S.C. Coastal*:

> [F]or there to be compensation in the case of regulatory taking, there must be deprivation of all economic benefit of the property; . . . if there was some other use available for the property, there was no compensable taking.[23]

And similarly in the case law of the European Court of Human Rights in *Katte Klitsche de la Grange v Italy* (1995):

> Where, following an administrative decision concerning specific property, the owner retains the ownership subject to restrictions which reduce to virtually nothing the economic value of the use or exchange of the property, this is known as a 'value expropriation' (espropriazione di valore) and it gives rise to an entitlement to compensation.[24]

In an investment dispute, the *Tecmed v Mexico* (interim award of 13 November 2000) case opposed a Spanish company and the Mexican Government on the basis of the bilateral investment treaty between Spain and Mexico.[25] The Tribunal held that for a state measure to be characterised as expropriation, the investor had to be

---

[23] *Lucas v S.C. Coastal*, 505 US 1003 (1992) and see the commentary on art 10 of the Harvard Law School draft convention (n 13) 554ff.

[24] *Katte Klitsche de la Grange v Italy*, 27 October 1994, A 293B para 26d. See also *Fredin v Sweden*, 18 February 1001, A 192.

[25] Award of 29 May 2003 (ARB(AF)/00/2), 10 *ICSID Reports* 134; (2004) *ILM* 133. For the original Spanish text see the ICSID web site: www.worldbank.org.icsid.

'radically deprived of the economical use and enjoyment of its investments, as if the rights related thereto—such as the income or benefits related to the [investment] or its exploitation—had ceased to exist' (paragraph 115).

In most cases these stringent conditions are not met and on this ground various compensation claims for expropriation have been dismissed by arbitrators. In *S.D. Myers v Canada* (award of 13 November 2000), a US company complained it was banned temporarily from exporting a certain toxic waste, PCB, by a decision of the Canadian Environmental Protection Agency.[26] The Tribunal, while acknowledging there was a breach of the principle of national treatment in this case, dismissed the expropriation argument. The ban in question had certainly affected the company temporarily but never had as its consequence the transfer of ownership of the company to Canada (paragraph 287). The Tribunal went on to distinguish between expropriation and regulation. In the first case there was deprivation of the property, that is 'a lasting removal of the ability of an owner to make use of its economic rights' (paragraph 283). In the second case, on the contrary, there was merely interference by the state to a lesser extent in the company's economic activity. This distinction had to be made, the arbitrators emphasised, to avoid the risk that 'governments will be subject to claims as they go about their business of managing public affairs' (paragraph 282).

Similarly again in *Pope & Talbot v Canada* (award of 26 June 2000), the Tribunal held that export quotas on timber to the United States introduced on the basis of an agreement between the United States and Canada, could not be deemed to have led to partial expropriation of the company that continued to be able to export substantial amounts of timber to the United States.[27]

In *Feldman v Mexico* (award on objections to jurisdiction of 6 December 2000),[28] the US claimant complained it had been refused a certain reduction, granted to others, on taxes applicable for cigarette exports. This allegedly resulted in a large economic loss, tantamount, it argued, to an expropriation. But the Tribunal held that the enterprise created by the US investor continued to do business:

---

[26] First Partial Award on Liability, 13 November 2000, 8 *ICSID Reports* 18; (2001) *ILM* 1408ff.

[27] Interim award of 26 June 2000, 7 *ICSID Reports* 69, available at www.naftacmaims.com.

[28] Interim award of 6 December 2002 (ARB(AF)/99/1); Interim Decision on Preliminary Jurisdictional Issues, 6 December 2002, 7 *ICSID Reports* 327; Award, 16 December 2002, 7 *ICSID Reports* 341, (2001) *ILM* 615.

The claimant's 'investment', the exporting business known as CESM . . ., remains under the complete control of the claimant, in business with the apparent right to engage in exportation of alcoholic beverages, photographic supplies, contact lenses, powdered milk, and other Mexican products.[29]

A Simple Loss of Value of the Investment is not Tantamount to Expropriation

This is an argument found in the decisions of various international courts. In *Oscar Chinn*, the Permanent Court of International Justice ruled:

No enterprise . . . can escape from the chances and hazards resulting from general economic conditions. Some industries may be able to make large profits during a period of general prosperity, or else by taking advantage of a treaty of commerce or of an alteration in customs duties; by they are also exposed to the danger of ruin or extinction if circumstances change. Where this is the case, no vested rights are violated by the State.[30]

Under the European Convention on Human Rights, for example, the Court in *Pine Valley Developments Ltd v Ireland* (1991) declared that 'the applicant was engaged in a business, which, as in any business, involved and element of risk'.

The same argument was used in the cases just spoken of: a simple reduction in profits for investors cannot be deemed an expropriation under pain of turning investment host states into insurers for investors' economic risks.

In *Feldman v Mexico* (2000), the Tribunal devoted a whole paragraph of its award to making a clear statement of this idea:

[N]ot every business problem experienced by a foreign investor is an indirect or creeping expropriation under art. 1110 . . . not all government regulatory activity that makes it difficult or impossible for any investor to carry out a particular business, change in the law or change in the application of existing laws that makes it uneconomical to continue a particular business, is an expropriation under art. 1110. Governments in their exercise of regulatory power, frequently change their laws and regulations in response to changing economic circumstances or changing political, economical or social considerations. Those changes may well make certain activities less profitable or even uneconomic to continue (paragraph 112).

---

[29] Award of 16 December 2002 (ARB(AF)/99/1), 7 *ICSID Reports* 341 at 370, para 111.
[30] PCIJ Series A/B No 63, 88 (1934); see also Nouvel, 'Les mesures équivalant à une expropriation' (n 7) 83ff.

Such considerations are found in many other awards. In *Maffezini v Spain* (award of 13 November 2000),[31] the Tribunal stated: 'Bilateral investment treaties are not insurance policies against bad business judgements' (paragraph 64).

The State Must be Left Room for Manoeuvre

The two criteria just stated are in practice quite difficult to apply outside cases of flagrant deprivation. Even in terms of an investor's loss of the essential profit it derives from its property in contrast to the reduction in its value, diverging appreciations may be given in all good faith. As can be seen in the first arbitration award rendered on the basis of the Energy Charter Treaty (award of 16 December 2003). This case opposed a western company and one of the former Soviet Union republics. The firm had invested in an electricity power station and had been assured it would be able to sell its electricity to the distributing company (a state company having a monopoly of distribution) at twice the base tariff.[32]

However, new legislation was passed subsequently whereby the firm was compelled to sell its electricity at just 75 per cent of the base tariff. In its arbitration claim, the investor argued that 'The Republic cannot, and must not, however, use its power in order to change the expectations of an investor in a way so as to undermine, or destroy the economic viability of the investment'. And as Wälde and Hobér observe, the new tariff had the same effect as an extra 65 per cent tax on the investor's income. Now, a substantial rise in taxation applied to a firm is generally considered to constitute expropriation.[33]

The arbitration tribunal, noting that the investor had knowingly run the risk of investing in the country, dismissed the claim on this point, stating:

[31] Final award of 13 November 2000, available in Spanish on ICSID website and in English in (2001) *ICSID Review* 248. See also *CMS v Argentina*, award of 6 May 2003 (2004) *ILM* 771, para 29; T Wälde and K Hobér, 'The First Energy Charter Treaty Arbitral Award' in C Leben (ed), *Le contentieux arbitral transnational relatif à l'investissement* (n 1) 307.

[32] Wälde and Hobér, 'The First Energy Charter Treaty Arbitral Award', *ibid.*

[33] Wälde and Hobér, 'The First Energy Charter Treaty Arbitral Award' (n 30) 323; see also the Harvard Law School draft convention (n 13) arts 10(5) 554, 561. This was the case, eg, in *Revere* between this company and the US investment insurer OPIC, where the arbitration tribunal recognised a tax could be tantamount to expropriation even if it was not the case in the matter before it. See award of 24 August 1978, (1978) *ILM* 1321ff, and see WW Park, 'Expropriation and Taxation under NAFTA' in Weiler, *NAFTA Investment Law* (n 18) 93. See also Nouvel, 'Les mesures équivalant à une expropriation' (n 7) 87. NAFTA contains a special provision (art 2103(6)) for investors to invoke expropriation by fiscal measures.

There was no possession taking of Windau B [the enterprise] or its assets, no interference with the shareholder's right or with the management's control over and running of the enterprise, apart from ordinary regulatory provisions laid down in the production licence, the off-take agreement, etc.[34]

This decision may be explained, as Wälde and Hobér point out, on tactical grounds: the arbitration tribunal was, in this case, to find against the state on the basis of article 10(1) (prohibition of discriminatory treatment) and probably did not want to hammer the state on every point.[35] It may also be that the tribunal considered, in keeping with well-established case law, that the state enjoyed a certain margin of appreciation in the conduct of its affairs, that international courts must observe, or again that, in the fine balancing act between protecting the legitimate interests of investors and the deference owed to the state as sole judge of its general interest, it was the latter factor that carried most weight.

Such an attitude was to be more readily adopted by arbitrators when they had other grounds for finding against reprehensible action by the state. This was the case here, as it was in *S.D. Myers*, where Canada was found guilty of discriminatory treatment, contrary to the national treatment provided for under NAFTA article 1102 (see paragraphs 238ff of the award). Canada was also held to have violated article 1105 of the norm on minimal treatment,[36] as in *Pope & Talbot*.

Presumption in Favour of Measures of General Interest adopted by States

What I shall call 'general interest measures' are what Americans call 'policy measures'. The long-established idea in domestic law and international law alike is that the state is not responsible for its general normative action whether by legislative or regulatory channels if that action is conducted in good faith, even if it causes injury to private interests. US doctrine also speaks of police power exception.[37] Thus, article 712, commentary of the Third Restatement reads:

A state is not responsible for loss of property or for other economic disadvantage resulting from bona fide general taxation, regulation, forfeiture

[34] *Nykomb Synergetics Technology Holding AB, Stockholm v The Republic of Latvia*, award of 16 December 2003, 11 *ICSID Reports* 158 at 194, para 4.3.

[35] Wälde, and Hobér, 'The First Energy Charter Treaty Arbitral Award' (n 30) 323.

[36] See (2001) *ILM* 1435–39, paras 258ff.

[37] On this question, see Nouvel, 'Les mesures équivalant à une expropriation' (n 7) 92–101. He speaks of 'measures taken in the preeminent interest of the host state'.

for crime, or other action of the kind that is commonly accepted as within the police power of states . . .

Here we are at the heart of the problem raised by consideration of indirect expropriation, especially fears that protection granted to investors should paralyse states' action on environmental matters or on public health. It is to allay these fears that NAFTA article 1114(1) provides:

> Nothing in this Chapter [Chapter 11] shall be construed to prevent a Party from adopting, maintaining or enforcing any measure otherwise consistent with this Chapter that it considers appropriate to ensure that investment activity in its territory is undertaken in a manner sensitive to environmental concerns.

And similarly the OECD draft Multilateral Agreement on Investment provided:

> A Contracting Party may adopt, maintain or enforce any measure that it considers appropriate to ensure that investment activity is undertaken in a manner sensitive to health, safety or environmental concerns, provided that such measures are consistent with this agreement (article 3 of Annex 3).

And again, in the Multilateral Investment Guarantee Agreement (MIGA) offering international cover for political risk, article 11(a)(ii) excludes:

> Any legislative action or administrative action or omission attributable to the host government which has the effect of depriving the holder of a guarantee of his ownership or control of, or a substantial benefit from, his investment [but] with the exception of non-discriminatory measures of general application which governments normally take for the purpose of regulating economic activity in their territories.[38]

The legitimacy of the general normative action of states is constantly reaffirmed in arbitration awards but it is at the same time confronted, on a case by case basis, with the necessity of defining the interests legitimately acquired by investors. There is no question then of accepting a general exception in favour of the normative action of states. As the Tribunal in *Pope & Talbot* observed:

---

[38] Although not altogether the same subject, see the statement by the British Minister of Agriculture dismissing any compensation for businesses hit by BSE: 'no government [is] under any obligation to pay compensation to a business for any loss of opportunity of carrying on that business which may arise from Parliament's properly considered legislative decisions' (cited by H Mountfield, 'Regulatory Expropriations in Europe: The Approach of the European Court of Human Rights' (2002) *New York University Environmental Law Journal* 136, 144.

Regulations can indeed be characterized in a way that would constitute creeping expropriation. Indeed much creeping expropriation could be conducted by regulation, and a blanket exception for regulation measures would create a gaping loophole under protection against expropriation (paragraph 99).

Similarly in the arbitration award *Compañia del Desarrollo de Santa Elena v Republic of Costa Rica* (17 February 2000), the Tribunal ruled:

> While an expropriation or taking for environmental reasons may be classified as a taking for a public purpose, and thus may be legitimate, the fact that the property was taken for this reason does not affect either the nature or the measure of the compensation to be paid for the taking. That is, the purpose of protecting the environment for which the property was taken does not alter the legal character of the taking for which adequate compensation must be paid.[39]

Notice too that in NAFTA article 1114(1) (and in article 3 of the Annex to the MIA) reasserting the power of states to legislate, it is nonetheless provided that the measures adopted must be consistent with the agreement itself, including its provisions on expropriation.

Ultimately arbitrators are to be led to assess factors such as the burden that state legislation or regulation places on the investor alone, the proportionate character of restrictions compared with the commanding purpose pursued by state legislation, the legitimate expectations the investor might entertain given the former conduct of the state authorities, and so on. All these are highly subjective factors and allowance for them is accepted when it is made by domestic judicial institutions or international courts such as the European Court of Human Rights, but may surprise when made by arbitration tribunals composed of private persons and with no appellate or review mechanism.

The Prudence of Arbitrators

It is, therefore, an immense power that arbitrators have inherited because of the provisions on expropriation contained in bilateral or multilateral investment treaties. It should be observed that, thus far, they have wielded it with a great deal of moderation.

---

[39] *Compañia del Desarrollo de Santa Elena (SA) v Republic of Costa Rica*, award of 17 February 2000, (2000) *ICSID Review* 169.

Cases where Claims based on Expropriation were Admitted

This has happened just once under the NAFTA Treaty in *Metalclad v Mexico* (award of 30 August 2000).[40] A US enterprise had purchased a site in the state of San Luis Potosi to set up a big toxic waste processing plant. It made its investment after receiving the necessary federal authorisations. But strong local opposition meant the project was halted by various legal actions including a decree by the governor classifying the site as an area for the protection of rare cacti. The Tribunal reasserted in its award that:

> [E]xpropriation under NAFTA includes not only open, deliberate and acknowledged takings of property . . . but also covert or incidental interference with the use of property which has the effect of depriving the owner, in whole or in significant part, of the use or reasonably-to-be-expected economic benefit of property even if not necessarily to the obvious benefit of the host State.[41]

> By permitting or tolerating the conduct of Guadalcazar in relation to Metalclad which the Tribunal has already held amounts to unfair and inequitable treatment breaching Article 1105 . . . Mexico must be held to have taken a measure tantamount to expropriation in violation of NAFTA Article 1110(1).[42]

More recently an arbitration tribunal set up under the ICSID supplementary mechanism was again led to rule on a question about a toxic waste processing site. The case opposed a Spanish investor (Tecnicas medioambientales Tecmed S.A.) and Mexico (award of 29 May 2003).[43] In this case, the National Ecological Institute (a state organ), after authorising the implantation of the site and so the investment in 1996, refused to renew that authorisation in 1998, as a result of objections to the project. The Spanish company argued this decision (a resolution in Mexican terminology) was tantamount to expropriation (paragraph 39).

Mexico argued before the Tribunal to the contrary that the Institute's 'resolution':

> [W]as a regulatory measure issued in compliance with the State's police power within the highly regulated and extremely sensitive framework of

---

[40] See E Gaillard, *La jurisprudence du CIRDI* (Paris, Pedone, 2004) 669ff; (2001) *ILM* 37ff. See also P Dumberry, 'Expropriation under NAFTA Chapter 11 Investment Dispute Settlement Mechanism: Some Comments on the Latest Case Law' (2001) *International Arbitration Law Review* 96.

[41] 40 *ILM* 50 (2001), para 103.

[42] *Ibid*, para 104.

[43] Award of 29 May 2003, (2004) *ILM* 133ff. The Spanish original can be consulted on the ICSID website.

environmental protection of public health. In those circumstances, the Respondent [Mexico] alleges that the Resolution is a legitimate action of the State that does not amount to expropriation under international law (paragraph 97).

The Tribunal found otherwise and ruled the Institute's resolution and the effects it wrought were a violation of the BIT and of international law (paragraph 151).

The ICSID arbitration in *Middle East Cement Shipping and Handling Co. S.A. v Egypt* (award of 12 April 2002) might also be cited here.[44]

But in truth, none of these three cases seems relevant, to me, to the problem of the general normative activity of the state. Our starting point was the *Ethyl* case and the question of the limitation of the state's legislative or regulatory activity and not the question of individual decisions (for example, a refusal to grant or renew an operating licence) regardless of a general legal text. In practice, while the general issue has already been raised before umpires (for instance in *S.D. Myers*, *Feldman* or *Pope & Talbot*), it has never been tried on its merits since the expropriation was not recognised.

The question might crop up again in the *Grand River* case in which the legislative measures taken by the United States for the benefit of four major cigarette manufacturers are contested,[45] or in *Terminal Forest Products*, in which the Canadian company argues that anti-dumping measures and compensatory measures adopted by the United States on the basis of its legislation, itself derived from the Marrakech Accords, constitute expropriation.[46] However, I feel it is doubtful this type of argument will prosper.

Appreciation of States' General Normative Activity

Some commentators have deplored the timidity of arbitrators when it comes to recognising that the general normative activity of states

---

[44] Award of 12 April 2002, 7 *ICSID Reports* 178.

[45] *Grand River Enterprises Six Nations Ltd.* filed a claim for UNCITRAL arbitration on the basis of NAFTA art 1120(1)(c) on 10 March 2004. It complained that the agreement made in November 1998 between 48 federated states and six territories of the United States and that country's four largest cigarette manufacturers (the MSA agreement) implemented in those states by uniform legislation, entailed a situation such that, for small manufacturers, it breached NAFTA arts 1103, 1104, 1105 and 1110. For the latter article, the plaintiffs argued 'By essentially banning the purchase and sale of the Investors' products in the MSA states and the operation of their investment enterprises unless they make prohibitive MSA or escrow payments, the MSA states have effectively expropriated their business . . .' (para 77). Text of claim, available on the US State Department site.

[46] UNCITRAL arbitration application of 30 March 2004, available on the US State Department site.

might have effects tantamount to expropriation. I believe, though, that arbitrators are justifiably cautious, first for reasons of common sense: it is hard to see how an arbitration tribunal, with none of the legitimacy that surrounds national courts and even less national courts of last instance, could challenge any statutory or regulatory provision of a state if the matter submitted to it is not a flagrant case of infringement of a private person's property.

To understand the position of arbitration tribunals in this area, they need to be compared with the position of domestic courts with regard to statutes. In all legal systems, the legislator's acts either escape from any mechanism entailing its responsibility or can only entail it under extraordinarily stringent circumstances. Thus, one of the finest scholars of French administrative law, Professor Chapus, observes that if one tries to list, in French law, cases where the Conseil d'Etat has effectively recognised the state's responsibility for the doings of its statutes 'it is enough to know how to count on the fingers of one hand', while the principle itself had been accepted in the famous *La Fleurette* decision of 1938.[47]

Under another system, Community law, the European Court of Justice recognised in 1971 that individuals could invoke the injury caused to them by an invalid act of the Community. In *Zuckerfabrik* of 2 December 1971 it stated that:

> Where legislative action involving measures of economic policy is concerned, the Community does not incur noncontractual liability for damage suffered by individuals as a consequence of that action, by virtue of the provisions contained in article 215, second paragraph, of the Treaty, unless a sufficiently flagrant violation of a superior rule of law for the protection of the individual has occurred.[48]

This case law, albeit in the context of liability for fault (unlike the *La Fleurette* decision in French law) imposes highly restrictive conditions for attributing responsibility to the Community for its normative activity.[49] Thus, the European Court of Justice expressly indicated:

---

[47] See R Chapus, *Droit administratif général* 15th edn (Paris, Montchrestien, 2001) vol 1 no 1516, 1375 and Conseil d'Etat, 14 janvier 1938, *Société anonyme des produits laitiers 'La Fleurette'*; M Long, P Weil, G Braibant, P Delvolvé and B Genevois, *Les grands arrêts de la jurisprudence administrative*, 17th edn (Paris, Dalloz, 2009) 311ff.

[48] Judgment of 2 December 1971, *Aktien-Zuckerfabrik Schöppenstedt v Council of the EC*, Case 5/71, [1971] ECR 975.

[49] See D Simon, *Le système juridique communautaire* 3rd edn (Paris, PUF, Droit fondamental, 2001) 601 fn 3.

Individuals may be required . . . to accept within reasonable limits certain harmful effects on their economic interests as a result of a legislative measure without being able to obtain compensation from public funds even if that measure has been declared null and void.[50]

The reason being, in Community law as in national law:

[T]o allow the legislative power to adopt normative measures in the general interest even if liable to adversely affect individual interests, without being hampered by the prospect of action for damages . . .[51]

As for the no-fault liability of the Community, on the basis, say, of a breach of equality in the face of public charges, even if not ruled out in principle, it has not to date been accepted in any decision.[52]

And so, it seems to me, it is in very limited and quite flagrant cases that transnational arbitrators could go down the road leading to censorship of the general legislative activity of states. Any other attitude would be unreasonable and would lead transnational arbitration into conflict with most states, whether developed or developing states. And, in such conflict, the very existence of transnational arbitration might be called into question. Moreover, states fearing that arbitration may drift in that direction can pre-empt it, of course, and make bilateral investment protection treaties containing provisions very clearly recognising their freedom to subject the investment in their territory to the observance of their general legislation, whether in environmental matters or matters of public health, to take just two examples. This was the road taken by the United States in its two 2003 treaties with Chile and Singapore.[53]

---

[50] Judgment of 25 May 1978, *(Fourth Dried Milk Cases) Bayerische HNL Vermehrungsbetriebe GmbH & Co. KG and others v Council and Commission of the European Communities*, Joined Cases 83 and 94/76, 4, 15 and 40/77, [1978] ECR 1209 at 1225, para 6.

[51] A Barav in V Constantinesco, J-P Jaqué, R Kovar and D Simon (eds), *Traité instituant la CEE—commentaire par article* (Paris, Economica, 1992) 1334 (commentary of ex article 215 (2)) and *Bayerische NHL, ibid.*

[52] Simon, *Le système juridique communautaire* (n 48) 603.

[53] Gaillard, *La jurisprudence du CIRDI* (n 39) 771–72; W Ben Hamida, 'L'arbitrage Etat-investisseur étranger: regards sur les traités et projets récents (2004) *Journal du Droit International* 419, 430; T Weiler, 'Interpreting Substantive Obligations in Relation to Health Safety Issues' in Weiler, *NAFTA Investment Law* (n 18) 107. In a recent case (*Methanex v United States*, award of 3 August 2005) the Tribunal dismissed the Canadian company's claim, among others, for indirect expropriation because of California's ban on a certain petroleum additive. The company was even ordered to pay costs of several million dollars.

Part II

Advances in the Theoretical Analysis of International Law

4

Some Theoretical Reflections on State Contracts*

In chapter one[1] I argued that:

(a) As Mayer was the first to show, state contracts in the strict sense of the term are agreements entered into with a private person by the state as a subject of international law (the state as sovereign within the international legal order) in contradistinction to the state as 'administration'. Contracts entered into by the state as administration are contracts concluded within the state's domestic legal order and are subject to national law (for example, the country's law of administrative contracts, where such a category exists). By contrast, contracts concluded by a state as sovereign are concluded outside its legal order. In my opinion, and contrary to Mayer's presentation, such contracts are made within the legal order of public international law.

(b) State contracts form a new category of international legal acts. They are governed, as such, by international law in various ways, the most common of these currently being set out in the second sentence of article 42(1) of the Washington Convention establishing the International Centre for Settlement of Investment Disputes (ICSID): the law of the contracting state combined with the principles of international law on the subject.[2]

---

* First published as 'Quelques réflexions théoriques à propos des contrats d'Etat' in *Mélanges offerts à P Kahn* (Paris, Litec, 2001). *Souveraineté étatique et marchés internationaux à la fin du 20ème siècle* (Paris, CREDIMI, Litec, 2000) 119.

[1] First published as 'Retour sur la notion de contrat d'Etat et sur le droit applicable à celui-ci' in *Mélanges offerts au Professeur H Thierry: l'évolution du droit international* (Paris, Pedone, 1998) 247.

[2] For an exhaustive analysis of art 42(1) see the commentary on the Washington Convention by CH Schreuer, *The ICSID Convention: A Commentary* 2nd edn (Cambridge, Cambridge University Press, 2009).

(c) It ensues from this conception—which I tried to show accounted for contractual practice and arbitral case law—that private persons (in practice business corporations) have acquired a limited but real international personality in the field of state contracts.[3] This personality can be inferred from the fact that private persons can rely on rights (or be subject to obligations) set out in an international act (a state contract or a bilateral or multilateral investment promotion and protection treaty) and have the capacity to sue their state partner before an international arbitration tribunal. The combination of these two factors (having rights or being subject to obligations defined in an international act and being able to bring a case in an international forum) is conclusive evidence of international personality.[4]

Readers may like to refer to chapter one, then, for the details of the proof (or attempted proof) of these arguments. Here I wish to go further and clarify my thinking on the subject of state contracts by allowing for the remarks and criticisms made after that study was first published.[5] I would also like to include objections found in two

---

[3] State contracts are usually investment contracts. But not all investment contracts are necessarily state contracts, and state contracts can be imagined in other domains, such as international loan contracts. See above, ch 1, fn 6.

[4] Combacau defends a broader conception of what constitutes a subject of law: 'To say of individuals or of collective entities that they receive the quality of person or subject of a legal order is to assert, and is only to assert that this order sets itself up as apt to endow them with rights and obligations'. And he adds: 'Personality must not be confused with capacity to act which is just one aspect of it that is variable in its existence and in its scope': J Combacau and S Sur, *Droit international public* 4th edn (Paris, Montchrestien, 1999) 308. This position had been defended by H Lauterpacht, 'The Subjects of the Law of Nations' (1947) 63 *Law Quarterly Review* 438, 455: 'Important as is the recognition of the procedural capacity of aliens—and of individuals generally—before international tribunals, there is no reason to exaggerate its bearing on the questions of the subjects of international law. The two questions are not identical. . . . There is a clear distinction between procedural capacity and the quality of subject of law'. The paper is continued in the same journal in 1948, 97. I understand the arguments of both commentators. However, it must be observed that the international personality of domestic subjects has only really been taken seriously and defended in doctrine from the time those subjects enjoyed procedural capacity giving them access to organs specific to the international order, to use Combacau's terms (*ibid*, 318–19). It should be noticed in this respect that on the issue of court actions, Combacau cites the domain of the protection of human rights 'but also [that] of the treatment of foreign investments and of the law of the international civil service', *ibid*, 319.

[5] My special thanks to P Mayer whose insightful remarks have led me to reword some of my assertions.

theses: one dating from before my paper but that I had been unaware of at the time of writing; and one defended quite recently.[6]

The Concept of State in State Contracts

The entire thesis of state contracts *stricto sensu*, as presented by Mayer and as I have taken it up, rests on the distinction between contracts entered into by the state as administration and contracts entered into by the state as a subject of international law. This distinction refers back to two passages in the *Pure Theory of Law* where Kelsen introduces alongside a broad notion of the state, which is the sovereign state of international law, a narrow notion of the 'state as a bureaucratic apparatus of officials with the government at its head'.[7]

Before returning to the exact meaning of this distinction in Kelsen's work, we now need to introduce the very astute thesis defended recently by Sophie Lemaire on *Les contrats internationaux de l'administration*.[8] Her line of argument might minimise or even reduce to nothing the idea of state contracts as contracts concluded with the state as a subject of international law. Let me summarise the essential points of this thesis, or at least those that are relevant here.

---

[6] See L Lankarani El-Zein, *Les contrats d'Etat à l'épreuve du droit international* (Brussels, Bruylant, éd de l'Université de Bruxelles, 2001); S Lemaire, *Les contrats internationaux de l'administration* (Paris, LGDJ, 2005). I was also unaware of papers by JM Jacquet, 'Contrats d'Etat' (1998) *Jurisclasseur de Droit International* fascicule 565–60 and D Berlin, 'Contrats d'Etat' (1998) *Répertoire Dalloz de Droit International*. Each of these papers considers the problem of state contracts acceding to international law. Berlin considers it is impossible (at 6–26) while observing a 'slow creation of an international regime' (at 27–53). Jacquet considers the objections to the internationalisation of state contracts can be overcome (at 25–28). See also the interesting work by M Audit, *Les conventions transnationales entre personnes publiques* (Paris, LGDJ, 2002).

[7] See H Kelsen, *Pure Theory of Law* trans M Knight (Berkeley, University of California Press, 1967) 266, 291. The distinction between the state as the personification of the total legal order and the state *stricto sensu*, as an apparatus of state organs and public agents is already to be found in 'Aperçu d'une théorie générale de l'Etat' (1926) *Revue du Droit Public* 561 para 14, 575–76. See also M Troper, 'Réflexions autour de la théorie kelsénienne de l'Etat' in *Pour une théorie juridique de l'Etat* (Paris, PUF, 1994) 143. 'Alongside the formal concept of state, which plays a decisive role in the solution of problems of his general theory, there is a second narrower material concept of state which, however, presupposes the first' *ibid*, 153 (fn 11). And for a critical study of the difficulties raised by the narrow concept of state (as a set of organs) in Kelsen, see *ibid*, 153.

[8] Lemaire, *Les contrats internationaux de l'administration* (n 6).

The Double Personality of the State in Anzilotti

Lemaire begins from Anzilotti's theoretical position as expressed in his international law courses that 'the term "state" in the sense that it designates . . . the subject of a state legal order, determines a subject that is wholly different from the state as a subject of international law'. In particular, where national laws apply to foreign states (for example, if the foreign state acquires goods or enters into contracts), 'the word state designates a different legal subject from that to which the same word refers in international law'. Legal science, adds Anzilotti, 'cannot fail to see two separate subjects where ordinary language seems to denote just one'.[9]

Lemaire devotes a preliminary chapter (at 12–74) to defending Anzilotti's opinion about the state's double domestic and international personality against all possible objections. To what end? Her aim is to show that doctrine, which fails to make this distinction, might, without realising it, have conflated contracts entered into with the state as a person of domestic law and contracts with the state as a person of international law. And in any event, that same doctrine might have exaggerated 'the role played by the state as the subject of the law of nations to the detriment of the role of the state-administration, as a person of domestic public law' (at 6). She adds:

> Assuming the hypothesis is true that at least some international state contracts have been imputed to the state as an international person in place and stead of its homonym as a subject of domestic law, serious consequences would ensue (at 6). [Notably] [s]uch a demonstration would overturn, first of all, the sense of debate about state contracts. Imputing such agreements to the state as a subject of domestic law would give rise to analyses remote from those that until now have been based on the involvement of the international sovereign state. The question would no longer be to think about the relationship between the state and its co-contractor as a subject of private law by reference to treaties entered into between states as persons of the law of nations (at 7). [And further] Imputing international state contracts, or at least some of them, to the administration would lead more naturally to likening these agreements to

---

⁹ D Anzilotti, *Cours de droit international* trans Gidel (Paris, Sirey, 1929) reprinted in the collection 'Les introuvables' (Paris, Université Panthéon-Assas (Paris 2), 1999) 53–54. See also at 405 [contrary to treaties] 'the statute contemplates the behaviour of entities subjected to the legislator's authority, including the state itself, the word 'state' then indicating a subject other than the state as a subject of international law'.

understandings between simple subjects of domestic law. As international agreements, state contracts could, in today's absence of any true international administrative law, be set against international contracts between private persons. Given, in addition, that they are binding on the state-administration, they could justifiably be compared with domestic contracts on the same subject matter (at 7).[10]

I have cited Lemaire's starting hypotheses at length to make clear the challenge these hypotheses, if they were borne out, would present to a conception of the state contract as I have developed it. Admittedly, Lemaire remains cautious: she does not deny there may be contracts made with sovereign states in international law; but she sets about showing that, in most cases probably, it is the state-administration that is involved. So what needs to be developed is a theory of international contracts of the administration—that is where the major doctrinal interest lies—and not a theory of state contracts over which she implicitly leaves a doubt as to their real importance, and even, in the extreme, as to their very existence.

In Lemaire's presentation—and I repeat its great qualities—I am in no way troubled by the focus on international contracts entered into by domestic public persons. However, I cannot accept the basic idea underpinning the entire thesis, namely the double domestic and international personality of the state,[11] and I must dismiss the

---

[10] See also Lemaire, *Les contrats internationaux de l'administration* (n 6) 123 where she reasserts that 'the vast majority of state contracts' are in fact made with the domestic administration and that alone should entail 'a fundamental upheaval of most studies of such contracts, which are generally based on the principle that they are made with the state as a sovereign international entity'.

[11] Some hesitation is apparent in Lemaire's terminology. Several times she speaks of the two faces of the state. For example: the state is 'a Janus, a being with two faces' (at 73). See also Lemaire, *Les contrats internationaux de l'administration* (n 6) 31 where she cites R Carré de Malberg, *Contribution à la théorie générale de l'Etat* (Paris, Sirey, 1920, reprint, Paris, CNRS, 1969) 71, fn 26 speaking of the 'two faces', internal and external, of the state. But Carré de Malberg writes very pointedly: 'Thus sovereignty has two faces. And yet, two separate sovereignties should not be seen in internal and external sovereignty'. And in his lengthy discussion of the state's personality (at 35–51) he never alludes to a double personality of the state in the way Anzilotti means. So two faces does not mean two separate persons. This can be seen in another citation she gives from J Combacau, 'Pas une puissance, une liberté: la souveraineté internationale de l'Etat' (1993) 67 *Pouvoirs*: 'sovereignty . . . contains two aspects, in which classical public law doctrine has clearly seen two faces of the *same state object* etc.' (at 49–50, emphasis added). See also S Rials, 'La puissance étatique et le droit dans l'ordre international. Eléments d'une critique de la notion usuelle de "souveraineté externe"' (1987) *Archives de Philosophie du Droit* 189. On this entire question see below, ch 8.

argument that the distinction presented by Kelsen, in the passage cited above, is equivalent to Anzilotti's doctrine.[12]

Kelsen's Dismissal of the Double Personality of the State Presented by Anzilotti

Kelsen denounced Anzilotti's thesis on several occasions. Already in his 1936 paper on the transformation of international law into domestic law, Kelsen dismissed the 'overly renowned theory of the double aspect of the nature of the state, the *Zwei-Seiten-Theorie*'.[13] If it is maintained both that the state has a double (internal and international) legal personality and that it is indeed one and the same state, then it must be admitted that there is a substance of the state that is independent of its legal personality, which, for Kelsen, is theoretically out of the question:

> The state . . . exists for the theory of law only as a subject of law (or as a legal order . . .). And if in a legal theory two different subjects of law are both characterised as 'state', they can only be two separate states. The elimination of the identity of the state as a subject both of the international legal order and of the domestic legal order is, in truth, just an inevitable consequence of the dualist conception by which international law and the domestic law of the state are two quite different systems of norms and are isolated from one another. But it is precisely this consequence to which the dualist conception inevitably leads that brings out its absurdity.[14]

[12] Lemaire does not say so in as many words but in her preliminary chapter on the double internal and international personality of the state she examines in section 1 all the authors in favour of 'the principle of a double personality of the state' and cites Anzilotti (at 19) and Kelsen (at 24, also cited indirectly at 19 by the reminder of Mayer's thesis distinguishing between the sovereign state in the law of nations and the state-administration).

[13] H Kelsen, 'La transformation du droit international en droit interne' (1936) *Revue Générale de Droit International Public* 5, 22. The theory was also defended by Jellinek; see CM Herrera, *Théorie juridique et politique chez Hans Kelsen* (Paris, Kimé, 1997) 106. In his 1926 course at The Hague, Kelsen reacted as follows to the theory of states having two forms of sovereignty: 'A wholly untenable doctrine, because it is self-contradictory. It does not reflect a simple attenuation of the state's sovereignty; it contains a contradiction between the principle of such sovereignty and an opposing principle'. The state is supposedly the supreme power internally but only an independent power, equal to other powers, outside. But this is only possible if one accepts 'the existence above all the states of a legal order coordinating them and in respect of which each of them is but a delegated partial legal order'. This implies that the state ceases to be a supreme order even internally. It is dependent in its totality on international law which is superior to it in its totality: H Kelsen, 'Les rapports de système entre le droit interne et le droit international public' (1926) 14 *Recueil des Cours de l'Académie de Droit International de La Haye* 260.

[14] Kelsen, 'Les rapports de système', *ibid*, 23.

Similarly, in his *General Theory of Law and State*, Kelsen returns to this matter:

> If, then, there were no unifying relation between international and national law, [the dualist theory] the State, in its former capacity, would have to be an entity totally separate from the State in its latter capacity. From the juristic point of view, there would then exist two different States under the same name, two Frances, two United States, and so on, a France of national law, and a France of international law, etc.[15]

One might even imagine—why not—these two Frances entering into contracts with one another . . . Consequences that it is difficult to take seriously. Admittedly a state has both an international and a domestic personality, but simply in the sense that a human being is both a moral subject, that is, the addressee of moral norms, and a legal subject, because also the addressee of legal norms.

The Double Theory of the State in Kelsen

Kelsen quite clearly, then, wholly eschews any idea of the double—national and international—personality of the state. What then is the meaning of the distinction Kelsen draws between the state in the narrow sense of the term 'the state as a bureaucratic machinery, headed by the government' and the state in the broad sense of the term?[16] One must begin from Kelsen's identification of the state with its legal order. There is no pre-existing substratum of the state that supposedly gives rise to a legal order. The legal order is the state itself, or in other words, the state is the personification of the legal order. It is not composed of three elements (population, territory and power) as the traditional theory asserts, but the state's legal order is defined by its spheres of personal and territorial validity and by its centralisation and efficacy.[17]

---

[15] H Kelsen, *General Theory of Law and State* trans A Wedberg (Russell & Russell, New York, 1961) 376–77.

[16] Kelsen, *Pure Theory of Law* (n 7) 266, 293. Lemaire has misunderstood these passages of Kelsen. See, eg, at p 28 where she writes that Kelsen subscribes to the idea that the state is composed of three elements, 'the people, the territory and the power of the state exercised by an independent government'. But in this passage from *The Pure Theory of Law* Kelsen writes this is 'the traditional theory' whereas he says these elements can be conceived of 'only as the validity and the spheres of validity of a legal order', which is something else entirely. In particular, for Kelsen, the state is not the 'personification of the nation'. See Kelsen's rejection of this thesis (an implicit rejection as Kelsen does not name it although it is that that is in question) in *Pure Theory of Law, ibid*, 287–88 when dealing with 'the state's population'.

[17] Kelsen, *Pure Theory of Law, ibid*, 287–90.

This legal order is the total state legal order. Within it, Kelsen distinguishes a partial legal order, which is the state in the narrow sense of the term, namely 'the state as a bureaucratic machinery, headed by the government'. This state 'is the personification of the partial legal order that settles only the functions of individuals with the quality of public officials'. But as Troper notes, this narrower material concept of the state necessarily presupposes the formal concept of the state as a total legal order.[18] Kelsen does indeed specify:

> The attribution of these [bureaucratic] functions to the state means the relation to the unity of this partial legal order. But by relating these functions to the unity of the partial legal order, they are at the same time related to the unity of the total legal order that includes this partial order. The attribution to the state in the narrower sense implies the attribution to the state in the wider sense.[19]

In other words, any action by the state in the narrow sense of the term is *ipso facto* also an action of the state in the broad sense.

Consequently, when Kelsen distinguishes between the state as a subject of international law, which is nothing else than the total state legal order acting in its spheres of validity and the state-administration, he speaks only of a nesting of legal orders, just as the total legal order is itself nested in the international legal order to form a single universal legal order:[20]

> The identity of the State as subject of international law and as subject of national law means that, finally, the international legal order obligating and authorizing the State and the national legal order determining the individuals who, as organs of the State, execute its international duties and exercise its international rights, form one and the same universal order.[21]

Lemaire senses the problem when she notes 'there is no denying that organically the highest state instances, ministers, represent the state, as a subject of international law, at the same time as they represent the administration'. And how can anyone imagine that the France that concludes a treaty with a foreign country through these organs is not the same person that performs the treaty through the same organs in its national legal order? But since the state as a subject of international law and the state-administration are decidedly not two separate persons, how can we

---

[18] Troper, Pour une théorie juridique de l'Etat (n 7).
[19] Kelsen, *Pure Theory of Law* (n 7) 266.
[20] Kelsen, *General Theory of Law and State* (n 15) 373.
[21] Ibid.

imagine relations between them? In the form of a 'corporation' in national law, replies Kelsen. Corporation must be understood as a juristic person like an association or a company. The corporation is first off formed pursuant to the laws of the state that govern its operation, appoint its organs, etc and constitute in respect of it a total legal order. But at the same time, it is governed by its articles of association, which are the foundation of its internal partial legal order:

And thus external and internal obligations and rights may be distinguished with respect to the state as a corporation subject to international law just as with respect to a corporation subject to the national legal order: external obligations and rights of the state are stipulated by the international [legal order], internal [rights and obligations] by the national legal order.[22]

This presentation of Kelsenian theory of the state seems to answer the difficulties Lemaire raises in her preliminary chapter. In any event, I do not feel the theory of the double personality of the state is defendable. As regards contracts, what are the consequences of these analyses? It is clear first of all that a contract can be concluded *within* the total legal order of the state, by an individual (a national or a foreigner) with the state as the personification of the partial legal order (state-administration).[23] Such contracts, whether or not they are called administrative contracts (and possibly international administrative contracts) are governed by the rules of the state.

But it is equally clear, to my mind, that the contract can be concluded by an individual with the state within the meaning of international law, that is, with the total state legal order. And in this case, the proposal that the contract is governed by public international law is reinforced, for it is only in the eyes of that law that the state can be apprehended as a subject of international law. The international legal order alone fully knows the special being that is the sovereign state, and it alone is liable to produce a legal regime that can govern the contracts entered into by this entity with private persons. If it is admitted, then, that a contract is concluded with that being (the

---

[22] Kelsen, *Pure Theory of Law* (n 7) 290.

[23] It should be observed that the state-administration as Kelsen means it does not correspond to the 'administration' in the meaning of French administrative law. The legislator and the courts themselves are also organs of this partial legal order called state-administration. It could be suggested that this partial legal order is that made up of all the secondary norms in Hart's sense of the word, insofar as these secondary norms command the workings of the 'state apparatus': production and modification of primary norms and their application via the administration and the courts. See below, ch 8.

sovereign state), the operation can only be situated within the legal order of public international law and not within a vacuum as Mayer claims.[24]

The presentation just made of the question of the double personality of the state has proved inadequate. I have since come to realise that the two concepts of the state in Kelsen do actually correspond—and in contradistinction to what he himself said (or did not say)—to a double personification of the state. This is explained below in chapter eight.

Individuals as Subjects of Public International Law

One of the important characteristics, to my mind, of the theory of state contracts is that it confirms, in the area of international economic law, that individuals (natural or juristic persons) may be subjects of international law with limited capacity, as is observed in other areas of law such as international human rights law or international criminal law.

In both cases, it can be seen either that individuals have rights granted to them by an international convention and that they can rely on those rights in an international court of law and against a state that has failed to observe them (this reasoning is based on the example of the European Convention of Human Rights); or conversely, that individuals are the addressees of obligations of international criminal law and that any violation of those obligations can lead to them being tried by international courts, such as the courts for former Yugoslavia and for Rwanda today and perhaps in the near future by an International Criminal Court set up by the 1998 Convention of Rome.[25]

---

[24] Lemaire, *Les contrats internationaux de l'administration* (n 6) presents another argument (at 157) relating to the comparison between states and international organisations. Like states, international organisations supposedly have a double personality: they are international persons subject to the law of nations and internal personalities within their own legal order. Now, according to the two commentators she cites (S Bastid and Glavanis) contracts with private persons are supposedly always entered into by the organisation as an internal person. I have shown (see above ch 1) this is not always the case and that, surprisingly, some organisations (such as the European Bank for Reconstruction and Development: EBRD) do indeed seem to foresee the possibility of contracts between the organisation as a subject of international law and private co-contractors (ch. 1 'External Confirmation', fn 24 (at 20).

[25] On the International Criminal Court see JF Dobelle, 'La Convention de Rome portant statut de la Cour pénale internationale, présentation générale' (1998) *Revue Générale de Droit International Public* 983; the discussion on the International Criminal Court in (1999) *Revue Générale de Droit International Public* 7–45, with the papers by

Definition of the Subject of International Law

In a true state contract, that is, a contract entered into by a private person and a state as subject of international law, it can be seen that, thanks to the arbitration clause and especially such a clause referring to the ICSID, a company in dispute with its state co-contractor can escape from the national courts and bring the state before an international arbitration tribunal.[26]

On this basis, and bearing in mind the examples from international human rights law and international criminal law, I defined the subject of international law as *'any person able to take action directly with another subject of international law in such capacity and, possibly, to bring that subject before an international court of law (conditional upon consent given by the latter in some form or other)'*.[27]

It has rightly been observed that the definition presupposes there are 'true' subjects of international law, or 'natural' subjects, for whom the problem of international personality is not raised, that is, in plain language, states. And it is only through this presupposition that we can deduce that those who can bring these 'true' subjects before an international court (or be brought there by them) are themselves subjects of international law. The definition, not being of equal value for all subjects in the same way, purportedly loses its relevance.

The criticism is fair, but the conclusion is not. All international law scholars know that the international legal order has just one category of 'primary', 'original', 'plenary' or 'specific' subjects, namely, states. States have *ab initio* and without any need for prior accreditation, full rights and competences recognised by the law of nations and are

L Condorelli, J-A Carillo-Salcedo and S Sur. For a general study see R Maison, *La responsabilité individuelle pour crime d'Etat en droit international public. De la sanction pénale des individus par les juridictions internationales*, (Brussels, Bruylant, 2004). Maison defends a restrictive interpretation of the individual's criminal liability that supposedly exists only when the person acts in his or her capacity as a de jure or de facto state organ. For a contrary opinion see, eg, Lauterpacht, 'The Subjects of the Law of Nations' (n 4) 106: 'A soldier who, for the satisfaction of private gain or lust, is guilty of murder or plunder in occupied territory or, generally, in the theatre of operations, is guilty of a war crime *jure gentium*'. And it is only afterwards that Lauterpacht examines the case of individuals acting in their capacity as state organs. See also A Cassese, *International Criminal Law* (Oxford, Oxford University Press, 2008).

[26] See above ch 1, 26.

[27] See above ch 1, 24. In fact, to allow for international criminal law, one should add: 'any person able to bring a subject of international law before an international court of law *or liable to be brought by that subject before an international court*'.

subject to all the obligations of general international law. Interstate organisations are but 'derived' subjects whose range of competences, rights and obligations varies with their constituent instrument. There would seem to be nothing inconsistent in thinking that individuals too could, under certain circumstances, be derived subjects of international law. Speaking more particularly of the agreements between states and private persons, Jacqué noticed back in 1972 that 'accepting that individuals might, in the context of contractual relations, be recognised as subjects of law, with limited capacities, does not require new concepts to be introduced into international law'.[28]

One might even go further and consider that any legal order has both primary subjects, namely those necessary to the order's existence, and 'secondary' or 'derived' subjects that only appear subsequently. Thus, national law has individuals as its primary subjects just as international law has states. But that in no way precludes 'secondary' or 'derived' subjects from being accommodated in an order constructed foremost around its primary subjects. This is the case, in national law, for legal entities as opposed to natural persons. National law like international law accommodates a variety of legal subjects.

So I have no qualms about specifying the definition given above: private persons may be considered subjects of international law with limited capacity whenever (a) it is shown that, in a given domain, they may be in direct dispute with a primary subject of international law (that is a state) or with a derived subject whose personality is already recognised by general international law (interstate organisations); and (b) they may bring either of these subjects before an international court of law (still upon condition of consent) or themselves be brought there by those subjects.[29]

---

[28] JP Jacqué, *Eléments pour une théorie de l'acte juridique en droit international public* (Paris, LGDJ, 1972) 282–83; JA Barberis, 'Nouvelles questions concernant la personnalité juridique internationale' (1982) 174 *Recueil des Cours de l'Académie de Droit International de La Haye* 145, 206 shares that opinion: 'Given that quasi-international accords [that I call state contracts] are part of the law of nations, it follows, and this is a logical consequence, that the contracting parties are holders of rights and obligations in international terms. That means therefore that private persons who enter into quasi-international accords with states or with other international entities acquire, by so doing, the capacity of subjects of the law of nations'.

[29] This clarification leads me to take up an expression used by F Rigaux, 'Des dieux et des héros—Réflexions sur une sentence arbitrale' (1978) *Revue Critique de Droit International Privé* 435, 446: indeed it is states that give the international 'club member card' to individuals (and to a lesser extent to interstate organisations). But whereas Rigaux found this situation intolerable, I see it as the consequence of a development of international law that one may regret (which is not my case) but cannot deny.

Subjects of International Law and 'Legal Communities' of International Law

Kelsen goes even further in differentiating the subjects of international law. In his 'Contribution à la théorie du traité international', he presents an original distinction between the subjects of international law and legal communities able to participate in the conclusion of treaties.[30] Kelsen reasserts that individuals are subjects of international law insofar as they are the addressees of international rights or obligations and as they have also received the option of appearing before international courts.[31] But individuals do not have for all that the capacity to conclude a treaty with a state. Just as customary international law pertains only to the practices of state, 'international convention law (of treaties) is itself created only by states or by legal communities which, during the development of the law of nations, have obtained, beside states, the capacity to create international law . . .'. Among these legal communities Kelsen lists the Roman Catholic Church, certain unions of states such as the Society of Nations and certain entities such as the British dominions.[32]

[30] H Kelsen, 'Contribution à la théorie du traité international' in C Leben (ed), *Hans Kelsen. Ecrits français de droit international* (Paris, PUF, 2001) 121, 130, para 13. See also the lengthy developments on the subjects of international law in the (1932) 42 *Recueil des Cours de l'Académie de Droit International de La Haye* 141 and in a more succinct form in (1953) 84 *Recueil des Cours de l'Académie de Droit International de La Haye* 93. See also H Lauterpacht 'Règles générales du droit de la paix' (1937) 62 *Recueil des Cours de l'Académie de Droit International de La Haye* 215 and especially 240–43.

[31] Kelsen, 'Contribution à la théorie du traité international', *ibid*, 261, para 13. See also H Kelsen, 'Théorie du droit international coutumier' (1939) *Internationale Zeitschrift für die Theorie des Rechts/Revue Internationale de la Théorie du Droit* 253, para 22. However, on individuals' international capacity from the procedural viewpoint not being for some commentators a necessary condition for acquiring international personality, see above (n 4).

[32] Kelsen, 'Contribution à la théorie du traité international', *ibid*, 130, para 13. One might also think of the current (2001) status of the special administrative region of Hong Kong which can be part of international organisations like the World Trade Organisation, sign international trade agreements or renew and amend agreements for air services to Hong-Kong or even conclude new ones. See L Focsaneanu, 'La déclaration conjointe du gouvernement de la République populaire de Chine et du gouvernement du Royaume-Uni sur la question de Hong Kong, signée à Pékin, le 19 décembre 1984' (1987) *Revue Générale de Droit International Public* 479, 494–97. On the problem of the *jus contractus* of infra-state entities see P Gautier, *Essai sur la définition des traités entre Etats. La pratique de la Belgique aux confins du droit des traités* (Brussels, Bruylant, 1993) 102ff for the communities and regions in Belgium. See also M Audit, *Les conventions transnationales entre personnes publiques* (n 6) and Lemaire, *Les contrats internationaux de l'administration* (n 6).

So there appear to be, on one side, *legal communities* that are seemingly both subjects of international law and that could participate in the creation of law in the form of treaties (notice that international organisations are still not mentioned generally but just in the instance of the Society of Nations); and, on the other, subjects of international law, private persons (natural persons or legal entities) who supposedly do *not yet* have this status of being a fully-fledged legal community of international law. But clarifications need to be added: in his paper on the theory of custom, Kelsen notes that when individuals are granted by treaty the possibility of suing states in international courts, they necessarily participate in the creation of the individual norm of international law that the court will lay down. Through this, they participate in creating international jurisprudential law even if they 'are not, or *not yet*, organs for the creation of customary [or . . .] contractual international law' (emphasis added).[33]

It is plain what the 'not yet' means. And indeed in the study of the theory of the international treaty Kelsen elaborates:

> The fact that international treaties are concluded only by states or legal communities that are assimilated to them in this respect, is not a limitation resulting from the essence of the law of nations, but simply the current state of positive law of nations, as it is currently constituted. There is no reason why this state of things should not change by the path of custom, that is, why the circle of subjects able to create international treaty law should not shrink or—what is more likely—expand, by the fact that for example national or religious minorities acquire the right to feature as parties to treaties.[34]

The hypotheses Kelsen contemplated did not come about, although the case of the status of national liberation movements at one time suggested they might enter the circle of 'legal communities' in the Kelsenian sense. However, it is now clear that all interstate

[33] Kelsen, 'Théorie du droit international coutumier' (n 31) 268, para 22.
[34] Kelsen, 'Contribution à la théorie du traité international' (n 30) 130, para 13. Similarly see P Weil, 'Un nouveau champ d'influence pour le droit administratif français: le droit international des contrats' (1970) *Etudes et Documents du Conseil d'Etat* 13ff: 'It is not of its essence . . . but because of fluctuating historical givens that classical international law governs only interstate relations and nothing precludes accepting that its field of application can extend to other subjects of law: it has already integrated international organisations and one fails to see by virtue of what *a priori* "transnational" contractual relations could not in turn fall within its orbit' (at 18). Weil seems to have adopted a more restrictive position on the personality of individuals in international law in his course at The Hague: 'Le droit international en quête de son identité' (1992 V-I) 237 *Recueil des Cours de l'Académie de Droit International de La Haye* 110. See also above ch 1 (n49).

organisations do make up such communities. Questions are beginning to be raised about some at least of the non-governmental organisations and henceforth an eminent doctrine recognises the International Red Cross Committee has international personality.[35] As for individuals, while the International Court of Justice ruled out their entering into treaties with states in *Anglo-Iranian Oil Co*,[36] it does seem, as I tried to show in an earlier study, that they can enter into agreements governed, in various ways, by international law with state partners. Such *state contracts*, to call them by their name, purportedly then form a new category of international legal acts in respect of which individuals are reportedly both subjects of international law and 'legal communities' able to create law through contract channels and so not only through their involvement in the legal function.[37]

It has also been objected that if individuals are in certain cases subjects of international law, they would be in that peculiar situation sometimes subjects of national law and sometimes subjects of international law. I see nothing impossible nor any *non sequitur* in that. Suppose there are firms forming cartels on the French market. They can fall foul of French anti-trust regulations without also falling foul of Community law (for example, if their effect on the relevant market is weak and does not affect trade among Member States). But should those same firms increase their activity and make access to the national market more difficult in a way that is no longer insignificant, they shall be apprehended also by community law.[38]

[35] See P Reuter, 'La personnalité juridique internationale du Comité international de la Croix rouge' in *Le développement de l'ordre juridique international. Ecrits de droit international* (Paris, Economica, 1995) 205. Reuter notes that the 'possibility of concluding agreements subjected to rules of public international law is the touchstone of international legal personality' (at 214) and observes that some agreements entered into by the International Committee of the Red Cross (ICRC) with states have been assimilated by the states in question to international treaties. The same is true of agreements with intergovernmental organisations (at 213). The particular international status of the ICRC was recently recognised by a decision of 1 October 1999 of the third chamber of first instance of the Criminal Court for Former Yugoslavia. See 'Chronique des faits internationaux' (1999) *Revue Générale de Droit International Public* 984. See also R Sogno-Bezza, 'La personnalité juridique du Comité international de la Croix rouge' (Thesis, University of Paris 2, 1974) 202–23.

[36] See the *Anglo-Iranian Oil Co* case, decision of 22 July 1952, *ICJ Reports* 112: 'The Court cannot accept the view that the contract signed between the Iranian Government and the Anglo-Persian Oil Company has a double character. It is nothing more than a concessionary contract between a government and a foreign corporation'.

[37] For a defence of this argument see above, ch 1.

[38] See L Dubouis and C Blumann, *Droit matériel de l'Union européenne* (Paris, Montchrestien, 2004) 401ff.

What is there surprising about that?[39] What is there surprising about people being at one and the same time subjects of some domestic law, of a regional law like that of the European Communities and of public international law, or even of a transnational legal order, like athletes belonging to a national and international sports federation?[40] Such multi-membership may create difficulties but it does reflect the true state of things.[41]

Objections Raised by the Dualist Doctrine

In fact, and as already said, the major obstacle to those who refuse to accept that individuals may, under certain circumstances, be subjects of international law lies in the dualist conception whereby international law and municipal law are watertight worlds each reigning over different subjects. I feel that the advancement of international

[39] Some commentators have even wanted to see in the whole discussion about the subject of international law something peculiar (or even bizarre) about international law since the expression 'subject of law', they argue, is not used in municipal law. But what is a subject? It is a person, in the eyes of a legal order which recognises he has rights, imposes obligations on him and allows him to act before the organs that apply the law. In domestic law, the subjects are *almost* self-evident: they are (since slavery was abolished) all natural persons (barring the case of people with no capacity to act such as the mentally handicapped, say); they are also legal entities. But when the question arose of apprehending legal entities, a protracted debate opposed the proponents of the fiction of juristic personality and the school that claimed this personality was real. See M Cozian and A Viandier, *Droit des sociétés* (Paris, Litec, 1995) 84ff; B Oppetit, 'Les rapports des personnes morales et de leurs membres' (Thesis, University of Paris, 1963). And in the end, what was the crux of the problem? Are legal entities really independent of their members? In other words, are legal entities true subjects of municipal law? Once this had been answered in the affirmative, the quality of subject of law disappeared beneath the characterisation of 'natural or juristic persons'. On this issue see L Michoud, *La théorie de la personnalité morale* (Paris, LGDJ, 1924) (eg vol 1, at 7 where the author notes that in the legal sense of the term the juristic person 'is nothing other than a subject of law').

[40] For a defence of individuals belonging to multiple legal orders see F Rigaux, 'Les situations juridiques individuelles dans un système de relativité générale' 'Les situations juridiques individuelles dans un système de relativité générale' (1989) 213 *Recueil des Cours de l'Académie de Droit International de La Haye* 283–91. See also G Simon, *Puissance sportive et ordre juridique étatique. Contribution à l'étude des relations entre puissance publique et les institutions privés* (Paris, LGDJ, 1990); F Latty, *La lex sportiva: recherche sur le droit transnational* (Leiden, Martinus Nijhoff, 2007).

[41] Eg, in the *Bosman* case, the contrast between national measures designed to dissuade footballers from leaving their home country and Community law condemning any impediment to the free movement of workers, even if they are not discriminatory impediments: ECJ C-415/93, ECR [1995] I-4921 (15 December 1995). On the 'transnational legal order of professional football', see Rigaux, 'Les situations juridiques individuelles', *ibid*, 283–91; F Latty, *La lex sportiva, ibid*.

law militates against such a conception of the systemic relations, even if dualism still has its talented defenders. This is the case, to my mind, of Mayer whose arguments have been discussed in chapter one.[42] I would just like to recall here a remark by Lemaire. She recalls the question of her thesis supervisor asking: 'How could international society devise norms for people it has no power over, not just in practice but through the very structure of the legal ordering?'[43] She goes a step further that, adding:

[I]t seems to me the same question could be asked in the diametrically opposed hypothesis of the submission of subjects of international law (with the implication the 'true' subjects, states) to the rules of the municipal order. How could the internal legal order devise norms for international persons over whom it has no power, not just in practice but again through the very structure of its ordering.[44]

Both questions seem to me typical of the dualist conception of system relations, and both also seem wrong. If we take, for example, the rule of municipal law about state immunities, whether formulated by the legislator or by case law, and if we make allowance for the developments in recent decades that have led several states to move from an absolute to a restricted conception of sovereign immunities, one can see domestic law rules that are intended to apply whenever a state claiming its sovereign prerogatives, as traditionally recognised in international law, appears before a domestic court.[45]

Conversely, for the norms of international law aimed at individuals, one can naturally evoke the true power of constraint that appears with the working of the international criminal courts, but also all the instances where municipal courts of the state accept to apply the international treaty-based or (less easily) custom-based norm as it

[42] Ch 1, fn 42 (at 7).

[43] P Mayer, 'La neutralisation du pouvoir normatif de l'Etat' (1986) *Journal du droit international* 5, 21.

[44] Lemaire, *Les contrats internationaux de l'administration* (n 6) 97.

[45] On such matters see M Cosnard, *La soumission des Etats aux tribunaux internes face à la théorie des immunités de l'Etat* (Paris, Pedone, 1996); I Pingel-Lenuzza, Les immunités des Etats en droit international (Brussels, Bruylant, 1998); H Fox, *The Law of State Immunity* (Oxford, Oxford University Press, 2004). Moreover, to follow Lemaire's reasoning, it would be quite inconceivable that national judges rule on the international lawfulness of an act of a foreign state. Yet it is a hypothesis that arises quite regularly, see P Weil, 'Le contrôle par les tribunaux nationaux de la licéité internationale des actes des Etats étrangers' (1977) *Annuaire Français de Droit International* 9 where Weil notes in particular: 'Far from being impervious to one another or to the international order, national legal orders constantly collaborate with the international order . . .' (at 44).

stands (without transforming international law into national law). This system is taken to its extremes by Community law, where the European Court of Justice sees that national courts give maximum effect to the Community norm to the detriment of the national norm. Now, and I have often argued this, Community law is not an essentially different species from international law. It is a (regional) international law to which states have given the means to be more effective without any of those means being unimaginable for 'classical' international law; but, of course, within a monistic view of the law of nations.

Relations between Private Persons and their Home State from the Standpoint of International Law

Lankarani El-Zein argues, in criticising it, that the granting of a limited international personality to the co-contractor in an internationalised contract would consequently give rise to 'two separate subjects of international law on the international level, the private co-contractor and its national state [and] would create an international obligation in favour of both these subjects at once'.[46]

As Weil notes:

Whenever a contract is internationalised . . . this circumstance also produces effects as to the appreciation of the unlawful act in terms of classical international responsibility among states, because it will be through a single legal approach that the conformity of the litigious action to obligations arising from the contract and to those emanating from general international law shall be appreciated, and that the same act may entail both the international responsibility of the state in respect of the other state and its [international] contractual responsibility in respect of its co-contractor.[47]

It should be specified, however, that this situation cannot arise all at once. If the dispute relates only to the non-performance of the contract invoked by the private partner, that partner's home state cannot intervene for it is generally accepted that such non-performance is not a delict in the eyes of general international law (which is one of the reasons for the invention of the internationalised contract and for transnational arbitration to allow individuals to invoke the state's contractual liability before a judicial instance

---

[46] Lankarani El-Zein, *Les contrats d'Etat* (n 6) 152.

[47] P Weil, 'Problèmes relatifs aux contrats passés entre un Etat et un particulier' (1969-III) 128 *Recueil des Cours de l'Académie de Droit International de La Haye* 94, 157–58.

independent of that state).[48] If, however, the dispute bears on an expropriation without compensation pursuant to international law, there will be scope for the private person's home state to intervene, through the exercise of diplomatic protection. But, once again, the existence of arbitration clauses will not allow the firm's home state to intervene unless the host state refuses to go to arbitration. This is what is provided for, in particular, in article 27(1) of the Washington Convention:

> No Contracting State shall give diplomatic protection, or bring an international claim, in respect of a dispute which one of its nationals and another Contracting State shall have consented to submit or shall have submitted to arbitration under this Convention, unless such other Contracting State shall have failed to abide by and comply with the award rendered in such dispute.[49]

All the bilateral or multilateral conventions that provide for dispute settlement between the host state and the investor by ICSID arbitration imply compliance with this article 27(1) of the Washington Convention, whether implicitly or explicitly.[50]

---

[48] See SM Schwebel, 'On Whether the Breach by a State of a Contract with an Alien is a Breach of International Law' in *Le droit international à l'heure de sa codification. Etudes en l'honneur de Roberto Ago* vol III (Milan, Giuffrè, 1987) 401; Weil, 'Problèmes relatifs aux contrats passés entre un Etat et un particulier', *ibid*, 133–47.

[49] For a commentary on this article see Schreuer, *The ICSID Convention* (n 2) 640 and also JV Chillida, *El centro internacional de arreglo de diferencias relativas a inversiones (CIADI)* (Madrid, Ciencias juridicas/McGraw Hill, 1998) 151–56; M Hirsch, *The Arbitration Mechanism of the International Centre for the Settlement of Disputes* (Dordrecht, Martinus Nijhoff, 1993) 116. For a study of the ICSID in French, see Manciaux, *Investissements étrangers et arbitrage entre Etats et ressortissants d'autres Etats. Trente années d'activité du CIRDI* (Dijon, CREDIMI, Paris, Litec, 2004).

[50] See, eg, art 8(6) of an investment protection treaty concluded with Chile in 1994: 'Once a dispute has been submitted to the competent tribunal or international arbitration in accordance with this Article, neither Contracting Party shall pursue the dispute through diplomatic channels unless the other Contracting Party has failed to abide or comply with any judgement, award, order or other determination made by the competent international or local tribunal in question' in *International Investment Instruments: A Compendium* vol III (New York, UNCTAD, 1996) 147. Similarly, in a bilateral treaty entered into by Switzerland, art 9: 'Neither Contracting Party shall pursue through diplomatic channels a dispute submitted to the Centre [ICSID], unless . . . (b) the other Contracting Party does not abide and comply with the award rendered by an arbitral tribunal', *ibid*, 181. NAFTA art 1136 provides for settlement of disputes between a state party and a national investor of another state party by arbitration (ICSID or ad hoc arbitration under UNCITRAL rules). Art 1136(5) provides that if a state party fails to abide by an arbitration award, the investor's national state may require the formation of a panel under art 2008 to settle the dispute between the two states. For the NAFTA text see (1993) 3 *ILM*, 605ff.

On the Inequality between States and Private Persons

Another of Lankarani El-Zein's arguments that has often been presented is that, through the international legal status granted to the private party in the theory of state contracts as international legal acts, that party supposedly has only rights and no obligations in the international sphere. Thus, 'public international law supposedly comes to recognise that a contractual act, celebrated under its aegis, consecrates the legal inequality of the parties in respect of the act'. The state alone purportedly has to bear the consequences in international law of the principle that *pacta sunt servanda*.[51] In reaching this conclusion, the author relies on paragraph 47 of the *Texaco* award that consecrates, in her view, the fact that only the private person has 'specific international capacities'. The private person supposedly enjoys international rights without being subject to international obligations. But she reads into the award something it does not say. The arbitrator (René-Jean Dupuy), in this paragraph, seeks above all to show that the private co-contractors do indeed have specific international capacities. But he quite simply does not discuss international obligations, which does not mean they are non-existent. The arbitrator simply observes that 'unlike the state, the private person has only a limited capacity and its quality as a subject of international law entitles it merely to rely on the rights it has under the contract in the field of international law'.[52]

More practically, it has been denounced that arbitration clauses in state contracts allowed the private co-contractor to bring a state before an arbitration tribunal whereas the opposite seldom happened. Yet it must be admitted that the state and the private person are placed on an equal footing as regards bringing a dispute before an arbitration tribunal. Article 36(1) of the Washington Convention expressly provides the procedure for '[a]ny *Contracting State or national of a Contracting State* wishing to institute arbitration proceedings' (emphasis added). And the same is true of ad hoc arbitration.

If, in practice, it is often the state that is brought before the arbitration tribunal and not the opposite, that is either because the state has acted in a manner contested by its co-contractor (unilateral change of contract, for example) or because it has not acted as

---

[51] Lankarani El-Zein, *Les contrats d'Etat* (n 6) 159.
[52] *Texaco-Calasiatic (TOPCO) v Libyan Government*, award of 19 January 1977, (1977) 104 *Journal du Droit International* 351, 361; (1978) 17 *ILM* 1.

expected, for example by refusing to pay the contract price.[53] Its partner must therefore take the initiative but there is nothing to prevent it being first the state that goes to the arbitration tribunal, suing the private party for breach of contract.

The problem, it is said, is more serious in arbitration without a prior contractual tie between the firm and the investment host country (arbitration without privity).[54] This possibility was recognised in ICSID arbitration of *AAPL v Sri Lanka* (ARB/87/3, award of 27 June 1990)[55] and *SPP v Egypt* (ARB/84/3, award on merits of 20 May 1992).[56] It has been noted that this case law meant investment host states having concluded bilateral investment protection treaties (and there were more than 1500 of them in December 1997)[57] providing for the acceptance of ICSID arbitration were in the hands of a unilateral seizure of the ICSID by firms they themselves could not bring before the arbitration tribunal for want of any contractual tie.[58]

---

[53] See, eg, *Klöckner v United Republic of Cameroon and SOCAME* (ARB/81/2, award of 21 October 1983) (1984) 111 *Journal du Droit International* 409; 2 *ICSID Reports* 9. Cameroon's refusal to pay for work done by Klöckner, accused of misleading it, brought Klöckner to bring the dispute before the ICSID.

[54] See J Paulsson, 'Arbitration without Privity' (1995) 2 *ICSID Review* 526.

[55] See E Gaillard, 'Chronique' (1992) *Journal du Droit International* 216 and (1991) *ICSID Review* 526.

[56] See E Gaillard, 'Chronique' (1994) *Journal du Droit International* 229; G Delaume, 'L'affaire du plateau des pyramides et le CIRDI. Considérations sur le droit applicable' (1994) *Revue de l'Arbitrage* 39. Some commentators are surprised by this ICSID case law. It derives, though, from a quite straightforward reading of art 25. Reuter in presenting the ICSID tribunals at a 1968 conference, envisaged this case explicitly: 'The great freedom given by the Convention allows all manner of consent to be contemplated. The simplest would be an arbitration clause in an "investment agreement"; but there may be many others; for example a state lays down by statute the rule that some investment agreements . . . shall include as of right the Centre's jurisdiction to hear certain disputes arising from it: the day an individual national of a contracting state enters into such an agreement . . . he gives his consent which will join that which the state gave before. By slightly altering the foregoing example, we can imagine a bilateral treaty wherein two states give their prior consent to the centre's jurisdiction in respect of their nationals; the nationals' consent shall be given as in the previous example'.(P Reuter, in *Investissements étrangers et arbitrage entre Etats et personnes privées*, Travaux du CREDIMI (Paris, Pedone, 1969)) 14. However, there is an ambiguity in Reuter's paper, for it is unclear whether he is talking solely about an investment agreement made with the host state or whether he means also an investment agreement where the state is not a party. I do not think Reuter's reasoning would have been different in this case.

[57] More than 2676 in 2009 (UNCTAD, *Recent Developments in International Investment Agreements* (2008–June 2009) and see C Leben, 'L'évolution du droit international des investissements' in *Un accord multilatéral sur l'investissement: d'un forum de négociation à l'autre ? Journées d'étude de la SFDI* (Paris, Pedone, 1999) 7, 9.

[58] See G Burdeau, 'Nouvelles perspectives pour l'arbitrage dans le contentieux économique intéressant les Etats' (1995) *Revue de l'Arbitrage* 3, 15.

But is the state not, in this hypothesis, in a position of weakness? Not at all. In the event the state has anything against a given investor, it can simply act unilaterally by bringing the matter before its own courts. As Jacquet astutely remarks:

> While it is true that the procedure can only be triggered by one of the parties (the investors) . . . still the state shall hardly be to pity if it is led to bring disputes before its own courts, which the investor meanwhile cannot complain of if it itself has waived bringing the matter before the ICSID.[59]

Consequently the state can always either bring a dispute before the ICSID directly (on the basis of an arbitration clause) or indirectly by unilaterally taking measures that will prompt the investor to turn to the ICSID. This is what happened in the Klöckner case.[60]

---

[59] Jacquet, 'Contrats d'Etat' (n 6) 23, para 110. It should be recalled too that under art 26 (second sentence) of the Washington Convention: 'A Contracting State may require the exhaustion of local administrative or judicial remedies as a condition of its consent to arbitration under this Convention'. In this instance we are in the presence of a mechanism comparable to that of the European Convention on Human Rights. But if this condition has not been expressly stipulated: 'Consent of the parties to arbitration under this Convention shall unless otherwise stated, be deemed consent to such arbitration to the exclusion of any other remedy' (art 26, first sentence). If, therefore, a state that has not inserted in its arbitration clause or in the bilateral investment protection treaty the obligation to exhaust domestic remedies brings a dispute before its own courts, the investor shall seize the ICSID which shall reassert it has exclusive jurisdiction. The arbitration may be put in place and go ahead even if the state objects (see arts 37 to 40 on the constitution of the tribunal, art 45(2) on the procedure in the absence of a party, etc). The question is more complex when the texts provide a choice for the parties between a national procedure and ICSID proceedings. Depending on the wording of the clauses, the ICSID tribunal may hear cases as an appeal court for national decisions or, on the contrary, it may be considered that the investor having opted for a national procedure has waived any action before the ICSID. See C Schreuer, 'Commentaire de l'article 26 de la Convention de Washington' (1997) *ICSID Review* 154, 170–75; H Hellio, 'L'Etat un justiciable de second ordre? A propos des demandes étatiques dans le contentieux arbitral transnational relatif aux investissements étrangers' (2009) 4 *Revue Générale de Droit International Public* 589.

[60] This point was raised very early on by Reuter in *Investissements étrangers* (n 56) 7. In presenting the ICSID mechanism at a conference in Dijon in 1968 he observed: 'the Convention protects not only the investor but it also protects the state; the state may be the plaintiff and one can be just about sure from the standpoint of procedural technique that the day an individual starts in motion the protection provided for under the [Washington] Convention and triggers, say, arbitration, the state attacked would immediately file a counterclaim'.

Private Persons Bringing Proceedings before International Courts

The central feature in my conception of state contracts as international acts and of the individual as a subject of international law with limited capacity is that the individual may unilaterally bring a case before an international court to adjudicate on a dispute with the state.[61] This raises the intricate problem of determining what exactly is an international court.

Dismissal of the Petitio Principii *that Individuals can never Bring Proceedings before International Courts*

The possibility of individuals having access to international courts was granted principally with the formation of mixed arbitral tribunals for dispute settlements between individuals and states, even if examples dating from the nineteenth century can also be found.[62] By contrast, the possibility for international courts to judge individuals on the basis of international law was recognised in its full scope only with the creation of the Nuremberg and Tokyo international military tribunals. In both cases (mixed arbitral tribunals and international military tribunals), the international characters of these courts was brought into doubt by the dualist-inspired internationalist doctrine for which individuals can never accede to the sphere of public international law.

This is what Anzilotti wrote in his *Cours de droit international*:

As for the mixed arbitration tribunals set up by the recent peace treaties, these are legal organs common to two states and not international legal organs . . . The provisions of the treaties in question, that grant individuals the right to resort to mixed arbitration tribunals and lay down the rules applicable by such tribunals have become internal norms of each of the contracting states thanks to the regular approval and publication of the treaty in the forms required by the constitution and compose a uniform

---

[61] There is no need for this reasoning to contemplate the reverse situation, ie, the possibility in international criminal law of prosecuting an individual before an international court. See supra 165.

[62] See S Seferiades, 'Le problème de l'accès des particuliers à des juridictions internationales' (1935) 51 *Recueil des Cours de l'Académie de Droit International de La Haye* 5; FA von der Heydte, 'L'individu et les tribunaux internationaux' (1962) 107 *Recueil des Cours de l'Académie de Droit International de La Haye* 297, 313–19.

internal law, the uniform realisation of which is guaranteed by the existence of the common legal organ.[63]

Some post-war Italian scholars continued to refuse to characterise the international military tribunals as international courts and considered them to be municipal courts set up by the supreme authority exercised by the Allies in Germany and Japan.[64]

Such a position is untenable in view of the development of international law either as regards the international criminal courts or as regards the pecuniary disputes between states and private persons, not to mention the international procedures for the protection of human rights. Short of resorting to somewhat extravagant legal constructions, it must be acknowledged that the position Kelsen took in the 1920s, recognising the possibility for international law to impose obligations directly on private persons and to invest them with rights that they could rely on before international courts does indeed reflect the state of positive international law today.[65]

Can Mixed 'Tribunals' be considered International Courts? The Case of ICSID Tribunals

This is the question that must now be answered once it has been accepted that individuals can have access to such courts. It will be

---

[63] Anzilotti, *Cours de droit international* (n 9) 135–36. Lauterpacht, 'The Subjects of the Law of Nations' (n 4) 452 argues: 'These explanations cannot be accepted as expressing the correct legal position. Although the claimants could avail themselves of the assistance of the agents appointed by their governments, there was nothing to prevent them from pursuing their claims unaided'. See also H Lauterpacht, *International Law and Human Rights* (London, Stevens, 1950) 65, fn 10 where he criticises the dogmatic statements of Anzilotti that are 'out of date . . . with the recent developments and trends of international law'.

[64] See the commentators cited by Maison, *La responsabilité individuelle pour crime d'Etat* (n 25) 346, fn 5. For a contrary opinion see G Balladore-Pallieri: 'It can under no circumstances be said that the Nuremberg Tribunal (and the Tokyo Tribunal) were extraordinary tribunals of France, the United States, Great Britain and the Soviet Union, fitted into the domestic orders of those states and that they passed sentence in the name of those municipal orders. That would be entirely fanciful. On the contrary, the four states mentioned declared they were fulfilling an international function in the interest of the whole of the United Nations and they drew the constitution of the tribunals directly from the international act they had concluded' *Diritto internazionale pubblico* (Milan, Giuffrè, 1962) 221 cited in Maison, *ibid*, 347, fn 7.

[65] See Kelsen, *General Theory of Law and State* (n 15) 343–47. So it is not 'the positivist conception of international law' as exclusively interstate law that is responsible for the refusal to recognise the character of international courts to those courts that are accessible to individuals, as claimed by L Cavaré, 'La notion de juridiction internationale' (1956) *Annuaire Français de Droit International*, 496, 506, but solely the dualist branch of positivism.

remembered that courts set up to settle disputes between states and individuals, mostly in the domain of international investments, are currently referred to as 'mixed' or 'transnational' tribunals.[66] To answer the question (are they international courts?) we shall reason first on the case of ICSID tribunals so as to follow the method that consists in beginning with the easiest cases and then moving on to the less easy ones.[67] In the case of ICSID tribunals we are dealing with: (a) tribunals set up on the basis of an international treaty; (b) whose procedure is itself provided for by the treaty; (c) tribunals that apply international law; (d) tribunals that deal with international issues, and (e) that have specific appeal procedures laid down by treaty.

Tribunals created on the Basis of a Treaty

It seems there could be courts or tribunals set up by treaty and that even so are municipal courts. This is the case, essentially, where a treaty sets up a federation. As Von der Heydte writes: 'Almost all federal . . . constitutions appear first of all to be public international law treaties. But as soon as . . . the federation [has been formed], the treaty that was until then a feature of public international law changes nature'.[68]

A recent example of such an operation is provided by the reunification of Germany by the treaty of 31 August 1990 between the Federal Republic of Germany (FRG) and the German Democratic Republic (GDR), which came into force on 3 October 1990, and has

---

[66] See SJ Toope, *Mixed International Arbitration: Studies in Arbitration between States and Private Persons* (Cambridge, Grotius Publications, 1990).

[67] The Iran–US Claims Tribunal shall not be dealt with here for want of space. But I fully share the view of M Virally in CEDIN, *Le tribunal des différends irano-américains* (University of Paris 10, 1985) 50, who sees in it 'a quite classical and well known institution for international law scholars . . ., public international law arbitration' of the same type as mixed arbitration tribunals set up after the First and Second World Wars. A differing opinion is given by P Fouchard, 'La nature juridique de l'arbitrage du Tribunal des différends irano-américains' (1984) *Cahiers du CEDIN* Le tribunal des différends irano-américains 27, who inclines towards a *sui generis* institution.

[68] Von der Heydte, 'L'individu et les tribunaux internationaux' (n 62) 309. He reasons on both 'federal and confedaral institutions', but that is a mistake. There is no constitution (in the municipal sense) in a confederation as it does not form a state. The founding treaty of a confederation remains a treaty. See Kelsen, *General Theory of Law and State* (n 15) 316–24. Conversely, the founding treaty of a federation changes into the internal constitution of a new state. See L Le Fur, *Etat fédéral et conféderaton d'Etats* (Thesis, Paris, Marchal et Billard, 1896) reprinted by University Panthéon-Assas (Paris 2, 2000) 564–89; and more recently C Eisenmann, *Cours de droit administratif* (Paris, LGDJ, 1982) t1, 429.

international effects as a treaty (disappearance of the GDR as a sovereign state) and is at the same time a text of constitutional value for the FRG.[69] Another slightly more complex example is that of the Constitution of Bosnia-Herzegovina, set out in Annex 4 of the Framework Agreement negotiated at Dayton and signed in Paris on 14 December 1995, which, in its article VI.1, provides for the setting up of a constitutional court.[70]

However, apart from these very specific instances (and others may be found), there is a strong presumption that a court set up by treaty actually is an international court. This is what Rousseau thought when he wrote:

> The true criterion of the nature of a tribunal [is] of a formal order and reside[s] . . . in the act that is the source of its creation and of its powers: it is the existence of an international treaty that constitutes the decisive criterion in this respect.[71]

That, too, is the opinion of Rigaux who concludes that the only 'mixed' but international arbitration tribunals are those of the ICSID and the Iran–United States Claims Tribunal.[72]

We could end our enquiry there. However, it is interesting to review other criteria that further confirm the characterisation of an international court and that could be useful should one find oneself before a tribunal created by treaty.

An Arbitration Procedure governed by International Law

Here again, in the case of the ICSID, the situation is plain enough. Most of the procedure is set out in the Washington Convention: the way to bring arbitration proceedings (article 36); the constitution of the tribunal (articles 37–40); the tribunal's powers and functions (articles 41–47); the making of the award (articles 50–52); the replacement and disqualification of arbitrators (articles 56–58). Article 44 provides in addition that the arbitration procedure is to be conducted in accordance with the provisions laid down by the treaty 'and, except as the parties otherwise agree, in accordance with the

---

[69] See M Fromont, 'Les techniques juridiques utilisées pour l'unfication de l'Allemagne' (1991) 8 *Revue française de droit constitutionnel* 579. The entire issue is useful reading.

[70] See Maison, *La responsabilité individuelle pour crime d'Etat* (n 25) 347, fn 6.

[71] C Rousseau, *Droit international public* (Paris, Sirey, 1983) tV, 382.

[72] F Rigaux, 'Contrats d'Etat et arbitrage transnational' (1984) *Rivista di diritto internazionale* 489, 502.

Arbitration Rules in effect on the date on which the parties consented to arbitration'.[73] If any question arises that is not settled by any text, 'the Tribunal shall decide the question'.

There is hardly need to say anything more, other than that the governing law of the ICISID arbitration clause is indeed international law, in the case in point the law laid down by the Washington Convention.[74]

For the Iran–US Claims Tribunal, it is the UNCITRAL arbitration rules that were adopted with a number of modifications.[75] Even if this text may just as well be adopted in international trade arbitration between private parties, it is still a text devised in an international arena and does not have the nature of a domestic legal text. Adopted by an arbitration tribunal constituted by treaty, the rules have the full character of an international legal text.

A Court applying International Law

For some commentators:

> An international court applies international law. There is here a criterion that remains essential. If it adjudicates on the basis of municipal law (except for the hypothesis where reference to the rules of municipal law is explained to demonstrate the existence of a general principle of law), it is not an international court.[76]

---

[73] On 26 September 1984 the ICSID adopted rules for the introduction of cases and arbitration rules: see the texts in *Juri classeur de Droit International* 588. See the new procedural rules adopted in 2006.

[74] Mayer initially argued that the international character of an arbitration tribunal depends on the law governing the arbitration clause: see Mayer, 'La neutralisation du pouvoir normatif de l'Etat' (n 43) 32. He has recently dismissed this view; see 'Contract claims et clauses juridictionnelles des traités relatifs à la protection des investissements' (2009) *Journal du Droit International* 71, 86 and seems to have moved closer to (what he considers) 'the most plausible analysis' that a court or tribunal is international when 'its power to adjudicate arises from a treaty' (at 85). But subsequently, and with a reference to Anzilotti and to dualist conceptions, he argues that a court or tribunal 'even if set up by treaty, ruling on relations between a state and an individual . . . cannot derive its power to adjudicate from the international order' (at 86). This viewpoint is debatable but any discussion of it will have to wait for some other opportunity.

[75] See B Audit, 'Le tribunal des différends irano-américains (1981–1984)' (1985) *Journal du Droit International* 791, 800: of the 41 articles adopted 'almost two-thirds were taken up unchanged' from the UNCITRAL rules.

[76] See C Philip and JY de Cara, 'Nature et évolution de la juridiction internationale' in *La juridiction international permanente*, colloque SFDI de Lyon (Paris, Pedone, 1987) 3.

This assertion is far from unanimously accepted and other commentators argue that it is 'impossible to deny the international character of a tribunal for the simple reason that it implements certain rules of municipal law'.[77] It is noticeable, conversely, that for municipal courts to apply international law, which is a quite common practice, in no way makes them international courts.[78]

Whatever the problem for domestic courts, how is the problem posed for ICSID arbitration tribunals? Article 42(1) of the Washington Convention comprises two sentences referring to two possibilities as to the law applicable to the dispute. Either (the first sentence):

> The Tribunal shall decide a dispute in accordance with such rules of law as may be agreed by the parties.

or (the second sentence):

> In the absence of such agreement, the Tribunal shall apply the law of the Contracting State party to the dispute (including its rules on the conflict of laws) and such rules of international law as may be applicable.

It was shown in our earlier study, on the basis of ICSID case law and of scholarly opinion alike, that the second sentence of article 42(1) implied that in any event a state's national law could only be applied provided it was consistent with public international law. In other words, the state's commitment to the investor is governed, in the last resort, by international law. Here we can reproduce the *dictum* of the second arbitration tribunal (presided by Rosalyn Higgins) in the *Amco Asia v Indonesia* (ARB/81/1, award of 31 May 1990) which states that:

> Article 42 (1) refers to the application of the law of a host state and of international law. If there is no relevant provision of the host state's law on an issue, the relevant dispositions of international law must be sought. If there are applicable provisions of the host state's law, they must be appreciated in respect of international law which prevails in the event of conflict. So international law is fully applicable and to characterise its role as 'merely supplementary and corrective' is a vain distinction. In any event,

---

[77] See Cavaré, 'La notion de juridiction internationale' (n 65) 507 citing the case of the ECSC Court of Justice which 'when adjudicating on redress for excess of power . . . operates as an administrative tribunal, but still as an International Court of Justice. The role of administrative jurisdiction it fulfils does not change anything in its nature'.

[78] The problem is different in community law: see A Barav, 'La plénitude de compétence du juge national en sa qualité de juge communautaire' in *L'Europe et le droit. Mélanges en l'honneur de J Boulouis* (Paris, Dalloz, 1991) 1.

the Tribunal considers that its task is to assess any legal claim in this matter first in respect of Indonesian law and then in respect of international law.[79]

However, the first sentence of article 42(1) implies that the parties, being free to choose the governing law, may opt for some national law. This has indeed happened in a few cases.[80] That an ICSID tribunal is sometimes led to apply some municipal law, as said, is of no consequence to its possible character as an international court. But it must be added that even if the parties make such a choice, the municipal law necessarily remains under the control of international law. For how can it be imagined that an arbitration tribunal, created by treaty to offer investors the guarantee of international protection for their rights, can uphold provisions of municipal law that are clearly contrary to international law?

Think, for example, of an investment contract governed by the law of a state X. That state, through legislative channels, expropriates the investment without paying any compensation in compliance with the express provisions of the statute. Should an ICSID tribunal called on to adjudicate in the ensuing dispute uphold this confiscation, because it rules on the basis of article 42(1), first sentence of the Washington Convention? Such an outcome would deny much of the interest of the Convention. Doctrine and case law have come out clearly against such an interpretation. Thus, in the decision of 16 May 1986 of the ad hoc committee in *Amco Asia v Indonesia* (ARB 81/1), the arbitration tribunal pointed out that,

---

[79] *Amco Asia v Indonesia* (ARB/81/1, award of 31 May 1990), (1991) *Journal du Droit International* 173, 176; E Gaillard, *La jurisprudence du CIRDI* (Paris, Pedone, 2004) 302. This award was also annulled (decision on annulment, 3 December 1992, 9 *ICSID Reports* 3). For the doctrine, see A Broches, 'The Convention on the Settlement of Investment Disputes between States and Nationals of Other States' (1972) 136 *Recueil des Cours de l'Académie de Droit International de La Haye* 333, 392, who considers that the relation between the law of the state and international law is: 'The Tribunal will first look at the law of the host State and that law in the first instance be applied to the merits of the dispute. Then the result will be tested against international law. That process will not involve the confirmation or denial of the validity of the host State's law, but may result in not applying it where that law, or action taken under that law, violates international law. In that sense . . . international law is hierarchically superior to national law under article 42(1)'. See also I Shihata and A Parra, 'Applicable Substantive Law in Disputes between States and Private Foreign Parties: The Case of Arbitration under the ICSID Convention' (1995) *ICSID Review* 183, 192; Schreuer, *The ICSID Convention* (n 2) 486, para 146, for a long commentary on art 42(1) with the conclusions drawn from this general review.

[80] See above ch 1, 15.

[. . .] the national State of the investor is precluded from exercising its normal right of diplomatic protection during the pendency of the ICSID proceeding and even after such proceeding in respect of the contracting state which complies with the ICSID award (a.27 of the convention). The thrust of article 54(1) and of article 27 of the convention makes sense only under the supposition that the award involved is not violative of applicable principles of international law.[81]

In the end, even in the case of the first sentence of article 42(1), municipal law must be controlled for compliance with international law. Such was my conclusion above in chapter one. To the doctrine cited in that study, should be added the following passage from a study by Reuter dating from 1974 (I was unaware of it at the time). Dealing with article 42(1) of the Washington Convention, he wrote:

It can be seen then—which is logical for an *international* tribunal—that the state's law is never applied originally and unreservedly; what takes precedence is the intentions of the parties, but when there is a referral under the 1965 Convention itself to the law of a state, the state party to the dispute, it is invariably conditional upon the principles of international law.[82]

Reuter adds that accession to the Washington Convention implies that 'states do not object to the rules of international law supplementing, tempering and if need be correcting the rules of national law'.

A Tribunal ruling on an International Legal Dispute

There are international courts that do not decide disputes of an international order in the narrowest sense of the word. This is the case of disputes submitted to the administrative tribunals operating as part of international organisations like the United Nations or the International Labour Organization (ILO).[83] But ordinarily one of

---

[81] *Amco Asia v Indonesia* (ARB/81/1, decision of 16 May 1986), 1 *ICSID Reports* 515, para 21; Gaillard, *La jurisprudence du CIRDI* (n 79) 178, para 21.

[82] P Reuter, 'L'extension du droit international aux dépens du droit national devant le juge international' in *Mélanges offerts à Marcel Waline* (Paris, LGDJ, 1974) t1, 251, reprinted in P Reuter, *Le développement de l'ordre juridique international, Ecrits de droit international* (n 35) 598, 609.

[83] See Cavaré, 'La notion de juridiction internationale' (n 65) 506. But how can it be explained that such administrative tribunals are indeed international tribunals? (See the acceptance of this characterisation by the ICJ in its advisory proceedings on *Judgements of the administrative tribunal of the ILO*, Reports 1956, 97. On international administrative courts see CF Amerasinghe, *The Law of International Civil Service as Applied by International Administrative Tribunals* (Oxford, Clarendon Press, 1988) t1, 49ff). The answer is, in my view, that the statutes of these tribunals allow private persons to bring before them, unilaterally, a subject of international law (the organisation) and that the law applied is a branch of international law.

the criteria used for defining an international tribunal is that it adjudicates in disputes within the sphere of the international legal order. From this standpoint, Virally, at the Société française de droit international conference on the permanent international courts, underscored that ICSID tribunals intervene in an area that was traditionally subject to public international law cases. Referring to the 'mixed arbitration that is ever more important in contemporary international society' he said:

> If one deplores the narrow range of action of the International Court of Justice or even of inter-governmental arbitration tribunals, which barely occupy themselves with what, during the entire nineteenth and a large part of the twentieth centuries were most of the cases submitted to those courts—I refer to those concerning the treatment of aliens—it is because diplomatic protection is ever less used. Since diplomatic protection is not exercised, one no longer goes to the inter-state courts. The same matters are nonetheless increasingly submitted to international courts, but this time directly by the interested firm, without any need for it to secure the state's approval and pursuit of its claim. In practice, what made up the most part of international claims have been taken up by courts that obviously fail to correspond to the definition adopted [by the rapporteurs of permanent international courts].

And after evoking the activity of the ICSID but also of other arbitration centres, Virally concluded his intervention:

> The boundaries between institutional courts and others are weakening just as the classical distinction between inter-state or inter-governmental courts and other forms of court is weakening too. These, it cannot be denied nowadays, are also international courts because they deal with international matters, because they do so in conditions such that states' actions are very seriously limited and that we never remain within the framework of some national law.[84]

A Tribunal with Autonomous Avenues of Appeal

It should further be recalled, to complete the picture, that the ICSID arbitration system has an autonomous system, provided for by articles 50 to 52 of the Washington Convention, for all the remedies that a party may implement against an award (request for interpretation, revision and annulment).[85] This system is also exclusive and article 53(1) states that:

---

[84] Virally, in La juridiction internationale permanente (n 76) at 83.
[85] See Broches, 'The Convention on the Settlement of Investment Disputes between States and Nationals of Other States' (n 79) 387: 'As to these matters [remedies against

The award shall be binding on the parties and shall not be subject to any appeal or to any other remedy except those provided for in this Convention. Each party shall abide by and comply with the terms of the award except to the extent that enforcement shall have been stayed pursuant to the relevant provisions of this Convention.

Each state party to the Convention must recognise and enforce ICSID awards 'as if it were a final judgment of a court in that State' (article 54). Only the issue of state immunity from execution is left hanging by the Convention (article 55).[86]

In view of all these points, it seems most reasonable to me to conclude, as it seems Reuter and Virally did before, that ICSID tribunals are a new form of international court, that is, a court of public international law ruling on disputes not between states but between states and private persons (here investors).[87]

Can 'Mixed' Courts be considered International Courts? The Case of Ad Hoc Tribunals

It has just been shown that ICSID tribunals are courts set up under an international treaty, whose procedure is itself, for the most part, provided for by the treaty, and that they are courts that apply international law, that deal with international questions and that have specific appeal procedures laid down by treaty.

Which of these points are altered when it comes to ad hoc tribunals? Two of them: (i) ad hoc tribunals are not set up by treaty but under arbitration clauses in some contract and (ii) they do not provide any specific appeal procedures. Similarly two points are common to both situations. Since we are dealing here with ad hoc tribunals that have had to adjudicate on disputes concerning investment contracts, (i) these tribunals deal with international disputes (they play the same role as substitutes for diplomatic protection referred to in supra 176 for ICSID tribunals) and (ii) they have been

---

an award and its recognition and enforcement], too, the Convention provides a special regime insulating the proceedings from review by national courts, although calling on these courts in connection with recognition and enforcement'.

[86] See the commentary on arts 54 and 55 by Schreuer, *The ICSID Convention* (n 2) 1115.

[87] Remember here the citation from Reuter (n 82) who in speaking of an ICSID tribunal for which 'state law is never applied originally' adds 'which is logical as it is an *international* arbitration tribunal', emphasising the adjective 'international' himself. For Virally see the quotations in supra, 192.

led to apply the principles of international law, more or less sharply, it is true.[88]

If we take the standpoint defended by Rigaux and Rousseau, the point that these tribunals were not set up by international treaty is enough to exclude any international characterisation for these courts.[89] One could readily accept this way of seeing things were it not the fairly frequent provisions of bilateral treaties for the promotion and protection of investments that leave parties to investment contracts with the choice between an ICSID clause and one or more other possibilities, in particular an *ad hoc* procedure governed by the UNCITRAL arbitration regulation.[90] Should it be considered that the choice of an arbitration tribunal other than the ICSID, which is often explained by the fact that the state is not yet party to the Washington Convention, is enough to establish a difference in kind between procedures and awards which, otherwise, display many similarities?

It is probably examination of the second characteristic point (see above 136) of the ICSID arbitration that provides an answer to this question: the procedure applicable to such arbitration is an international procedure (in this specific case, a procedure laid down by the Washington Convention and the two arbitration regulations adopted subsequently).[91] Now, we can consider, as Mayer does, that

---

[88] See in particular *Texaco-Calasiatic (TOPCO) v Libyan Government*, award of 19 January 1977, (1977) 104 *Journal du Droit International* 350; (1978) 17 ILM 1; 53 ILR 420; *Libyan American Oil Co (LIAMCO) v Government of the Libyan Arab Republic*, award of 12 April 1977, 62 ILR 140; (1980) *Revue de l'Arbitrage* 132; *BP Exploration Company v Government of the Libyan Arab Republic*, award of 10 October 1973, 53 ILR 300; (1980) *Revue de l'Arbitrage* 117; *Government of the State of Kuwait v American Independent Oil Co (Aminoil)*, award of 24 March 1982, 66 ILR 519; (1982) *Journal du Droit International* 869.

[89] Rigaux, 'Contrats d'Etat et arbitrage transnational' (n 72) 502 and F Rigaux, 'Souveraineté des Etats et arbitrage transnational' in *Le droit des relations économiques internationales. Etudes offertes à Berthold Goldman* (Paris, Litec, 1982) 269. See also Rousseau, *Droit international public* (n 71) 382: 'The true criterion of the nature of a court [is] formal and reside[s] not in the law applied by it or in the capacity of those who appear before it but in the act that lies behind its creation and its powers: it is the existence of an international treaty that is the decisive criterion in this respect'.

[90] See art 1120 of the NAFTA Treaty (choice between ICSID arbitration, arbitration under the ICSID additional facility rules and ad hoc arbitration under the UNCITRAL arbitration rules). An almost identical choice was provided for in the aborted draft of the OECD multilateral agreement on investment, which added an extra choice with the ICC arbitration rules. Art 26 of the Energy Charter Treaty also refers to the arbitration rules of Stockholm Chamber of Commerce. See F Poirat, 'L'article 26 relatif à la Charte de l'énergie: procédures de règlement des différends et statut des personnes privées' (1998) *Revue Générale de Droit International Public* 45, 52.

[91] See above, n 73.

the international character of an arbitration tribunal depends on the law applicable to the arbitration clause.[92] If this procedure is provided for by treaty (as with the ICSID) the condition is obviously fulfilled. But one can easily imagine that—and one can find in arbitral practice cases where—the arbitration procedure is subject to non-treaty public international law. That, at any rate, is what the arbitrators held in several petroleum awards that lie behind the theory of state contracts.

Thus, in the *Aramco* award, the arbitration tribunal considered that:

> Although the present arbitration was instituted, not between States, but between a State and a private American corporation, the Arbitration Tribunal is not of the opinion that the law of the country of its seat should be applied to the arbitration. The jurisdictional immunity of States (. . .) excludes the possibility, for the judicial authorities of the country of the seat, of exercising their right of supervision and interference in the arbitral proceedings which they have in certain cases.[93]

This explains why the arbitration tribunal concluded that the arbitration [*Aramco v. Saoudi Arabia*], as such, can only be governed by international law . . .' 27 *ILR* 156.

In the *Texaco* case, the sole arbitrator took up the reasoning followed in the *Aramco* award, then, after adding a few additional arguments, concluded:

> Therefore if it is appropriate for the Tribunal to declare that this arbitration . . . is governed by international law, it is because—the parties wanting to remove the arbitration from any national sovereignty—one cannot accept that the institution of arbitration should escape the reach of all legal systems and be somehow suspended *in vacuo*.[94]

In the *Liamco* arbitration award, the formula adopted also removes the procedure from any national law since the arbitration tribunal decided that:

[92] See Mayer, 'La neutralisation du pouvoir normatif de l'Etat' (n 43) 32. But see his change of view on this (n 74).

[93] Arbitration award made in the dispute between the Government of Saudi Arabia and the Arabian American Oil Company, 23 August 1958, 27 *ILR* 117 at 155, and in French: (1963) *Revue Critique de Droit International* Privé 272, 305. The Tribunal further noted: 'Considering the jurisdictional immunity of foreign States, recognized by international law in a spirit of respect for the essential dignity of sovereign power, the Tribunal is unable to hold that arbitral proceedings to which a sovereign State is a Party could be subject to the law of another State', 27 *ILR* 155–56.

[94] *Texaco-Calasiatic (TOPCO) v Libyan Government*, award of 19 January 1977; (1978) *ILM* para 16.

[. . .] the principal proper law of the contract in said Concessions is Libyan domestic law. But it is specified in the Agreements that this covers only the principles of law of Libya common to the principles of international law. Thus, it excludes any part of Libyan law which is in conflict with the principles of international law.[95]

In the three Libyan awards—*Aramco*, *Liamco* and *BP*—only the latter saw the arbitrator take up the solution adopted previously in the *Sapphire* arbitration and apply the national law of the seat of arbitration to govern the procedure.[96] To this must be added the *Aminoil* award of 24 March 1982 that clearly underscores that even if the arbitration is submitted to all the mandatory provisions of the place of arbitration (that is, Paris):

This does not in the least entail of itself a general submission to the law of the tribunal's seat which was designated as Paris. In fact the parties themselves gave the tribunal the power 'to prescribe the procedure applicable to the arbitration on the basis of natural justice and of such principles of transnational arbitration procedure as it may find applicable'. The arbitrators went on to add: 'Having regard to the way in which the Tribunal has been constituted, its international or rather, transnational character is apparent'.[97]

Independently of the hesitation between 'international' and 'transnational', what must be remembered from this is that the Tribunal did not rule out the possibility for a state, in its capacity as a sovereign power, seeing its dispute with a corporation being submitted to the adjudication of an arbitration panel not governed by a national law.[98]

So it seems quite feasible and even logical to characterise as international ad hoc tribunals operating in accordance with a procedure

[95] *Libyan American Oil Co (LIAMCO) v Government of the Libyan Arab Republic*, award of 12 April 1977, 62 ILR 141, 173; (1980) *Revue de l'Arbitrage* 132, 139.

[96] For a study of these three cases see B Stern, 'Trois arbitrages, un même problème, trois solutions: les nationalisations pétrolières libyennes devant l'arbitrage international' (1980) *Revue de l'Arbitrage* 3, 10. See also *Sapphire v NIOC*, award of 15 March 1963, (1962) *Annuaire Suisse de Droit International* 273 and observations by JF Lalive, 'Un récent arbitrage suisse entre un organisme d'Etat et une société privée' (1962) *Annuaire Suisse de Droit International* 293.

[97] *Government of the State of Kuwait v American Independent Oil Co (Aminoil)*, award of 24 March 1982, 66 ILR 519 at 560, paras 4–5; (1982) *Journal du Droit International* 869, paras 3–5, 871–72.

[98] See ch 1, fn 98 (at 27). The reason it must be considered it is the state as sovereign that was in cause in this case is that it was about the possibility for the state to undertake not to nationalise, a possibility recognised by the Tribunal under certain circumstances set out in para 95; see (1982) *Journal du Droit International* 894–95.

governed by international law, when they apply principles of international law to disputes that belong to the sphere of the international legal order. For if we remember that we are discussing only state contracts in the narrow sense of the term, that is, contracts where it is considered it is the state as sovereign in international law that has entered into the contract with respect to a private partner, it seems normal that arbitration should escape from any municipal law, whether that of the state of the place of arbitration or some other state.

Let us finish this point with a prophecy (an eminently dangerous genre). The increasing participation of states in the Washington Convention (131 ratifications and 147 signatures by 1 March 2000 [134 ratifications in 2009], with the accession in recent years of countries like China, Saudi Arabia and several countries of Latin America and central and eastern Europe, etc)[99] and the inclusion in the more than 1500 bilateral investment protection treaties (more than 2676 in 2009) of arbitration clauses referring almost invariably, so it seems, to ICSID arbitration at least as one of the possible forms of arbitration, shall mean that the very great majority of disputes over investments shall be brought before the courts of the Washington Convention for which the characterisation as international is least contested.[100]

Of the Incapacity of General Principles of Law to Internationalise State Contracts

Lankarani El-Zein's Argument

In her highly critical thesis on the internationalisation of state contracts,[101] Lankarani El-Zein develops the following reasoning, among others. State contracts in the sense of investment contracts and the disputes relating to state contracts belong to the state's reserved domain, that is, the domain which, from the standpoint of international law, is left to the normative jurisdiction of each state. Whenever the question has arisen of internationalising state con-

---

[99] (2000) 1 *Revue de l'Arbitrage* 167.

[100] Berlin, 'Contrats d'Etat' (n 6), while arguing 'it is impossible for state contracts to accede to the status of international law emphasises the importance of the change made in international law by the 'institution of an arbitration forum called the ICSID' fn 46ff.

[101] Lankarani El-Zein, *Les contrats d'Etat* (n 6).

tracts (and so the disputes arising from them), this has been done through resort to the general principles of international law, in the meaning given to that idea in article 38(1)(c) of the Statute of the International Court of Justice as the third source of public international law applicable by the ICJ.[102] Lankarani El-Zein says:

> Before one can claim a subject is internationalised through the extraction of general principles of law recognised by civilised nations, one must first

[102] This third source of law applicable by the ICJ has been accepted with great reluctance by various positivist scholars. Kelsen does not even mention it in the first edition of his *Principles of International Law* (New York, Rinehart, 1952). In the 2nd edn (ed RW Tucker) (New York, Holt, Rinehart and Winston, 1966), he comments: 'As to the "general principles of law recognized by civilized nations" (clause [c]), it is doubtful whether such principles of the civilized nations exist at all, especially in view of the ideological antagonism which separates the communist from the capitalist, and the autocratic from the democratic legal systems' (at 539–40). It is interesting to notice that Kelsen's doubt about the possibility of formulating general principles of law was shared at the same time, and for the same reasons, by some soviet scholars, and in particular Tunkin. See B Vitanyl, 'Les positions doctrinales concernant le sens de la notion de principes généraux de droit reconnus par les nations civilisées' (1982) *Revue Générale de Droit International Public* 48, 56–57. Kelsen adds that resort to the general principles of law supposes that the judge has spotted gaps in existing international law and has decided to fill them by formulating such a principle by his own initiative. But Kelsen says: 'it is, however, doubtful whether the framers of the statute really intended to confer upon the Court such an extraordinary power' (at 540). Then he reminds us that art 38(1) indicates that 'The Court, whose function is to decide in accordance with international law such disputes as are submitted to it' and deduces from this that the general principles are only applicable if they are part of treaty law and custom law. And he concludes that clause (c) of art 38(1) referring to general principles of law is quite simply superfluous. There is a fine illustration of reasoning contrary to the interpretative maxim *ut res magis valeat quam pereat*: instead of deriving some sense from the article being interpreted, he destroys it. Another reason for Kelsenian thinkers objecting to general principles as an autonomous source of law is given by P Guggenheim *Traité de droit international public* (Geneva, Georg & Cie, 1953) tI, 150. He remarks that, supposing clause (c) of art 38(1) was introduced to make good the shortcomings of international law and to avoid any *non liquet*: 'As there are no gaps in the law of nations based on customary law and treaty law, all disputes submitted to the international court can be resolved. There is therefore no room for the *non liquet*'. The same idea is found in Anzilotti, *Cours de droit international* (n 9) 119. However, Guggenheim recognises a juridico-political interest in the third source. 'The exclusive application of treaty law and customary law would mean that many disputes would have to be settled in the sense of there being no legal duty of an obligation. Now, resort to the general principles of law often allows us to presume there is a legal duty in place and stead of a discretionary power' (*ibid*). Having admitted the worth of these principles, Guggenheim tries to show that in fact the basis for the validity of general principles can be found in treaty law or customary law (at 152). He invokes in support Lauterpacht's opinion that 'the general principles of law are legal analogies in the private law of civilised nations, analogies adapted to the needs of the law of nations and that have been incorporated into international customary law', *Private Law Sources and Analogies in International Law* 71, cited by Guggenheim, 153 fn 1; see also on this topic, A Pellet, *Recherche sur les principes généraux de droit en droit international* (Thesis, University of Paris 2, 1974) 373–80.

question the system of the law of nations on the matter of whether or how this third source of international law can extend the domain of normative competence of international law at the expense of municipal law.[103]

And she adds that 'The deliberate choice of international law no more than the deliberate choice of any other law is not enough to affect the nature of the contractual legal act'.[104] We can follow her on this last point. From the beginning of the doctrine of internationalisation of state contracts Mann had argued that the state and its co-contractor could choose international law as the applicable law, just as two private persons could do on the basis of freedom of contract if they found any point in doing so.[105] It is clear that, under this hypothesis, the choice made by such private persons would not indeed change the character of their contractual tie.

Is the same true when one of the parties to the contract, governed by international law or, to follow the author's reasoning, by the general principles of international law, is a state? Lankarani El-Zein says yes, because for her the contract entered into by the state comes within the reserved jurisdiction that international law recognises the state has. But additionally—and this is an important second argument—if international law can reduce the domain reserved for the state's exclusive jurisdiction, it can only do so, she says, via the first two sources of international law (treaty and custom) and not via the third (general principles of law): 'The third source of international law is only operational [that is can shift the boundary between the national and international domains] if the question for which the absence of treaty law and customary law is observed is not part of the reserved domain'.[106]

What reason is there for such discrimination between the first two sources of international law and the third, when international law establishes no, or little, hierarchy among its sources? Why can a gen-

---

[103] Lankarani El-Zein, *Les contrats d'Etat* (n 6) 180.

[104] *Ibid*, 181.

[105] See FA Mann, 'The Law Governing State Contracts' in *Studies in International Law* (Oxford, Clarendon Press, 1973) 179.

[106] Lankarani El-Zein, *Les contrats d'Etat* (n 6) 206. This supposes there is a fundamental heterogeneity between the general principles of law and the other two sources. We have seen, though, that some scholars, and not the least of them, considered that the general principles in fact found their valid basis in the norms of customs or treaties of the law of nations. See Pellet, *Recherche sur les principes généraux* (n 103) 373–80 and Vitanyl, 'Les positions doctrinales concernant le sens de la notion de principes généraux de droit reconnus par les nations civilisées' (n 103) 56–64.

eral principle of law, in the meaning of the ICJ statute, exist 'only to settle disputes whose subject matter is part of the domain of international law, to settle issues of international law or matters arising from international law'.[107]

The author evokes two reasons. One is technical: the general principles of law require a work of abstraction by the international law judge from national laws, then the transposition of those principles to the specific structure of international law. All that supposes that the judge adjudicates on a dispute that is itself, clearly, one of international law. Besides, the general principles of law were supposedly only mentioned in the ICJ statute to avoid the judge 'pronouncing a non liquet when faced with the non existence—and/or obscurity—of rules of treaty and custom'.[108]

In other words, the general principles of law would only allow the international judge to play a legislative role (since he makes good the absence or obscurity of rules of custom and treaty) for questions that already belong to international law; but he is supposedly not authorised to modify the dividing line between the municipal and international domains through such general principles. If that were allowed—and this is the second (and probably the more important) reason—this judge-made law 'would become the main and most expansionist source of international law'.[109] Thus, through this source, and depending on the arbitrary wont of judges 'any legal relation—in the case in point state contracts—could come within the orbit of international law'.[110]

Dismissal of this Argument

Lankarani El-Zein's very tightly worked argument fails to convince me, though. The argument presupposes, first of all, a priori knowledge of which issues belong to the state's reserved domain and can only be submitted to municipal law and which issues belong to the international legal order and are governed by international law. But such an outlook is unacceptable, at least if one takes a monistic view

---

[107] Lankarani El-Zein, ibid, 189.

[108] *Ibid*, 186.

[109] *Ibid*, 190 and the strange note 2, that goes so far as to imagine that states could deliberately widen 'the gap between their internal legislations' to preclude the emergence of general principles of law leading to the restriction of their domain of reserved jurisdiction.

[110] *Ibid*, 182.

(with the primacy of international law) of relations between international and municipal law.[111] As Kelsen emphasises:

> It is incorrect to say that a matter can be settled by international law because it is an external matter and another may be settled by national law because it is an internal matter. One should say on the contrary that a matter is external when it is settled by international law and another is internal so long as it actually is settled by national law alone.[112]

It follows, as Reuter noted, that 'while some matters cannot be settled by national law, the opposite is not true: there is no issue that cannot be submitted to a rule of international law by reason of its subject matter'.[113] And likewise the International Law Institute, in a 1954 resolution on determining the reserved domain and its effect, said that 'the scope of this domain depends on international law and varies with its development' (article 1(2)).[114]

If I support this position myself, it is not (or not just) out of ideological bias but because it seems to me that the whole development of municipal/international law relations for the last century confirms the accuracy of this argument.[115]

In fact, Lankarani El-Zein would be ready to accept this point of view (at 184) provided that for international law, one considers only norms derived from treaty and custom. We are dealing here with an objection on principle to the production of law by the courts and with a voluntarist conception of international law. While willing to understand this objection, it must be observed it is not based on any

---

[111] Even if this doctrinal position should be re-examined generally in view of recent developments of international law in its relations with municipal law, it still remains, to my mind, the best founded doctrine for thinking out the role and the position of international law.

[112] H Kelsen, 'Théorie du droit international public' (1953) 84 *Recueil des Cours de l'Académie de Droit International de La Haye* 116–17. See also 'Théorie générale du droit international public. Problèmes choisis' (1932) 42 *Recueil des Cours de l'Académie de Droit International de La Haye* 298–311 on the determination of the domain of material validity of the state order by international law.

[113] Reuter, 'L'extension du droit international aux dépens du droit national devant le juge international' (n 82) 248. It is an opinion shared by many internationalists See Weil, 'Un nouveau champ d'influence pour le droit administratif français' (n 34) 18: 'It is not by essence . . . but because of fluctuating historical givens that international law governs only interstate relations, and there is nothing to prohibit admitting its field of application to extend to other subjects of law'.

[114] See (1954) 45 *Annuaire de l'Institut de Droit International* t II 299–300.

[115] See, though, for the exact opposite argument (dualism with primacy of the state's reserved domain) G Arangio-Ruiz, 'Le domaine réservé. L'organisation internationale et le rapport entre droit international et droit interne' (1990) 225 *Recueil des Cours de l'Académie de Droit International de La Haye* 9.

text. At any rate, article 38(1)(c) of the ICJ statute, as it is currently worded, does not introduce any discrimination among the three sources to which the Court is authorised to resort.[116] Pellet, after a study of doctrine and case law, concludes that even if this third source generally gives way to a treaty-based or custom-based norm, that 'does not, for all that, strip the simultaneous existence of a principle of all significance'. Principles 'are used in a complementary way, to complete a line of argument, to support the other reasons invoked by the international legal organ that applies them—they help to satisfy the court'.[117]

This is true in the context of the international legal system as a whole where the judge may encounter treaty rules, customary rules and general principles. But when it comes to the development of a new branch of law, and unless the development of all judge-made law is to be excluded on principle, legal history, in both municipal and international law, shows that whenever a court is in a position of adjudicating, where the domain is still lacking in primary norms, it will be forced to turn almost to the general principles of law. In addition, as Lauterpacht observed:

> [H]istory teaches us that the courts preceded codes and the development of detailed rules of law; [indeed] an elementary legal system, with just a few very general rules to guide the judge, is complete when the members of the community are bound by the duty to submit their disputes to a judge's decision.[118]

[116] It is true that the initial draft planned that 'the Court applies in successive order, etc'. See Pellet, *Recherche sur les principes généraux* (n 103) 411.

[117] Pellet, *ibid*, 411 and 420. We should notice, in passing, that unlike the ICJ, many domestic and international courts are not authorised in the texts to resort to the general principles of law but do so nonetheless. See D Simon, 'Y a-t-il des principes généraux de droit communautaire?' (1991) 14 *Droits* 73. For an overview relating to international law and community law, see P Morvan, *Le principe de droit privé* (Paris, Editions Panthéon-Assas, LGDJ, 1999) 649. For public law, see P Avril and M Verpeaux, *Les règles et principes non écrits en droit public* (Paris, Editions Panthéon-Assas, LGDJ, 2000).

[118] H Lauterpacht, 'La théorie des différends non justiciables en droit international' (1930) 34 *Recueil des Cours de l'Académie de Droit International de La Haye* 539. This is how the general principles of law were used by international administrative courts to develop international civil service law, see Pellet, *Recherche sur les principes généraux* (n 103) 150–60; see Amerasinghe, *The Law of International Civil Service* (n 83) 151–58. On recourse to the general principles of law in the area of contracts, see P Weil, 'Principes généraux du droit et contrats d'Etat' in *Le droit des relations économiques internationales. Etudes offertes à Berthold Goldman* (Litec, Paris, 1982) 387 and M Virally, 'Un tiers droit ? Réflexions théoriques' in *Le droit des relations économiques internationals, ibid*, 373, 380–85.

Would we then be delivered up to the 'government of judges' or rather of arbitrators who—without proving anything, without setting about this double task of comparing national systems of law and then adapting principles for their proper transposition into international law—would freely 'invent' principles for the sole purpose of reducing the states' 'reserved domain'?

It is true there has never been seen (or let's say almost never in case of exceptions we are unaware of) a judge, whether in municipal or international courts, going into great demonstrations to prove the existence of a general principle whose existence he purely and simply asserts. But is it much more common for judges (or arbitrators) to go into demonstrations to prove the existence of sufficient practice accompanied by an adequate *opinio juris*, and so to prove the existence of an international customary rule? And is there much difference between a judge who, after a process where intuition plays a large part, comes up with a custom-based on precedent and an *opinio juris* and a judge who extracts a general principle of international law because of its presence, which is more a matter of feeling than of proof, in most major systems of municipal law?[119]

If, then, Lankarani El-Zein wants to protect the state's reserved domain from the arbitrariness or arbitrators, she should go further and rule out the possibility that unwritten customary norms ('discovered' by an arbitrator fortuitously when dealing with some case) may reduce this reserved domain. But why stop short? Do realist theorists of interpretation not explain that judges (or arbitrators) enjoy the greatest freedom even with regard to written sources of law that for them are but 'proposals' that only truly become norms after their intervention. Thus, *all law is judge-made law*.[120] The best protection

---

[119] See on this the argument on the general principles of law in Pellet, *Recherche sur les principes généraux* (n 103) 434: 'In theory it is possible to discover and apply a principle on the basis of thorough scientific reasoning drawing on the resources of comparative law and the process of analogy. In fact, the occurrence of such a rule in the international legal order results from an empirical transposition: the jurist guesses more than proves the general character of the norm and has no measuring instrument to know whether international society is ready to accommodate the principle. It is a matter of sensitivity and intuition'.

[120] On the realist theory of interpretation see C Leben, 'Le principe d'égalité devant la loi et la théorie de l'interprétation judiciaire' in G Haarscher (ed), *Chaïm Perelman et la pensée contemporaine* (Brussels, Brulant, 1993) 215; M Troper, 'Kelsen, la théorie de l'interprétation et la structure de l'ordre juridique' (1981) 138 *Revue Internationale de Philosophie* 518; HLA Hart, 'American Jurisprudence through English Eyes: The Nightmare and the Noble Dream' in *Essays in Jurisprudence and Philosophy* (Oxford, Clarendon Press, 1983) 123.

of the state's reserved domain would therefore be ultimately to exclude all possibility for any judge whatsoever ruling on this issue.

But suppose, without going so far, that what is objected to are the general principles of law alone. It must be noticed, then, that for the (international or municipal) domain in which the question of state contracts lies, and beyond the question of international investment law, the delimitation is settled—even by Lankarani El-Zein's criteria—largely in favour of the international legal order. What should be concluded from the more than 1500 [2676 in 2008] bilateral investment protection and promotion treaties (without counting any multilateral conventions) that provide that host states undertake to settle any disputes opposing them and the investors, whether there is a contractual tie between them or not, through arbitration and generally by the ICSID?[121]

For me, the answer suffers no doubt: the question of state contracts no longer belongs, and has not belonged for some time now, to the state's 'reserved domain'; and it never did belong to it if one considers state contracts in the strict sense of the term. If such contracts are defined as agreements in which the state as an international person contracts with a private person, such contracts cannot be part of the reserved domain, for that would be to deny their very reason for being. If one thinks there can be a special category of contracts in which the sovereign state of international law subscribes to obligations towards a private person, that can only be done if the state comes out of its reserved domain.

On Stabilisation Clauses in State Contracts

One of the necessary consequences of the existence of state contracts, in the narrow meaning, is that the governing law is not simply the law of the contracting state. I have tried to show that it could be international law, in one form or another.[122] In very many cases, though, the applicable law clause specifies not international law (or the general principles of law or the principles of international law on the subject, or principles common to municipal law and international law, etc) but

---

[121] See *Un accord multilatéral sur l'investissement : d'un forum de négociation à l'autre*, SFDI (Paris, Pedone, 1999) with the paper by D Small, 'Réglement des différends entre investisseurs et Etats d'accueil dans un accord multilatéral sur l'investissement' 79 and Leben, 'L'évolution du droit international des investissements' (n 57) 7.

[122] See above, ch 1, 99.

stabilised law of the state, in part or in full. Therein lies a clear indication that a contract can be characterised as a state contract.[123]

Stabilisation Clauses are Purportedly not Characteristic of a New Category of Contracts

In her thesis, Lemaire (above, note 6) seeks to show that such clauses are not all characteristic of a specific category of contract. Then she argues that, even if in some cases these clauses refer to a specific category, they are of such limited effect in practice that it is impossible to construct a new legal category of contracts on such insubstantial clauses.[124]

As regards stabilisation clauses, Lemaire begins with the distinction presented by Weil, among others, between clauses that resort to the incorporation technique and those that resort to the non-enforcement technique (*technique de l'inopposabilité*).[125] In the incorporation technique, the two parties (the state and the private person) agree that the law governing the contract is the state's law frozen, in part or in full, at a given date, usually the date the contract was concluded. To take up Mayer's analysis, he argues that incorporation is not a technique specific to the contracts under study and that it is commonly used in contracts between private persons. It is not the state as an international person but the state as a public person in municipal law (the administration) that is contracting, and we are therefore not dealing with a state contract. Mayer justifies this position by explaining that, in such cases, it is not the state's legislative competence that is in question, but only its 'competence in the sense of private international law, that is, applicability by a judge or an arbitrator'.[126]

I cannot accept such an analysis. When two private persons adopt a national law frozen at a certain date as the governing law of their contract, it is true that there is a choice of a system of reference that is incorporated into the contract as if the system had been copied by

---

[123]   See Mayer, 'La neutralisation du pouvoir normatif de l'Etat' (n 43) 34–36, fns 41–44.

[124]   See Lemaire, *Les contrats internationaux de l'administration* (n 6) 87–104.

[125]   See P Weil, 'Les clauses de stabilisation ou d'intangibilité insérées dans les accords de développement économique', in *Mélanges offerts à Charles Rousseau* (Paris, Pedone, 1974) 301, 310ff; Lemaire, *ibid*, 87–88; Mayer, 'La neutralisation du pouvoir normatif de l'Etat' (n 43) 34–35, fn 41; and against N David, 'Les clauses de stabilité dans les contrats pétroliers. Questions d'un praticien' (1986) *Journal du Droit International* 79.

[126]   Mayer, 'La neutralisation du pouvoir normatif de l'Etat' (n 43) 34, fn 41.

the parties in the governing law clause; it may be any system of law past or present (Hammurabi's Code of Laws, the Twelve Tables, Swiss law, etc). Such a mechanism implies nothing for the parties if not the necessity to observe the legal provisions incorporated and the obligation for an arbitrator to apply them (under reservation of any difficulties arising from immediately applicable statutes). But things are quite different when it is a state that accepts a freezing clause. Is such a clause truly any different from a non-enforcement clause by which the state undertakes not to apply certain provisions of its law to the contract concluded with the foreign partner? What is the important point? What is the point at issue here? Can the state use its legislative power to alter its position with respect to its co-contractor? It is clear that legally it cannot when it has accepted a non-enforcement clause in the contract. But neither can it when it has accepted a freezing clause. Because of such a clause, the state accepts that its new fiscal, customs, welfare, provisions, etc are not applicable (by the arbitrator) to the contract.

That means that the state accepts to see the contract leave its legal order and refrains from giving binding force over its co-contractor to any new legislation it might adopt. Where, then, is the difference with the non-enforcement clause? Lemaire writes that stabilisation clauses are clauses 'whereby the state undertakes not to modify the contract's legislative environment'. And in this part of her thesis she refers both to freezing clauses and to non-enforcement clauses.[127] And rightly so, the two categories of clause have the same effect.[128]

[127] Lemaire, *Les contrats internationaux de l'administration* (n 6) 139.

[128] What seems to me to be a misunderstanding must be cleared up. Whatever the wording of the stabilisation clause, it cannot neutralise in any general way the state's normative power. It can only neutralise it in respect of the company that benefits from the stabilisation clause. For it is of little matter to the company that the conditions change for others (at least if the change does not bring any extra advantages) as long as it does not change for it. An illustration of this can be found in a 1979 mining contract: 'During the period of application of this Agreement, unless a derogation is provided for by mutual consent, it is guaranteed to the Company, for the activities that are the subject matter of this Agreement, that fiscal, parafiscal and customs charges of any kind resulting directly from taxes and duties such as they exist at the date the Agreement comes into effect, both in terms of their base and their rates and the arrangements for payment and inspection . . . shall be stabilised. During the period of application of this stabilised fiscal regime, the Company cannot be subject to fiscal charges resulting for the activity that is the subject matter of this Agreement from taxes and duties *whose creation may result from a provision subsequent to the start date of the regime thus decided*'. It is clear that the state retains its normative power (and how could it be otherwise?). It is just that that power is suspended (unless it violates the agreement, for which the state would be answerable) with respect to the company benefiting from the stabilised regime.

And it is precisely this effect that is not achieved in a freezing clause between two private individuals, for in this case neither of them is in the position of legislator with respect to the governing law. That law is completely extrinsic to them.

When, on the contrary, one of the parties is a state, the problem arises immediately as to the effect of the state's action as legislator on the contract. Is the state bound or not by the stabilisation clause accepted in some form or another? If so, then the state that entered into the contract can only be the state as subject of international law, for it alone can validly give such an undertaking. The state as legislator, which is the state-administration (see above note 23) cannot do so, for *lex posterior derogat priori*.[129]

Stabilisation Clauses Purportedly do not Imply the Internationalisation of State Contracts

Another attack on the effect of stabilisation clauses on the international character of state contracts is led by Lankarani El-Zein. She argues:

> Either the agreement is an international agreement in which case the [stabilisation] clause is superfluous, *pacta sunt servanda* including it by definition and beforehand; or *pacta sunt servanda* is inapplicable and the clause will be of use, that is, it will constitute a contractual obligation whose non-performance will entail consequences that would not have occurred on the same terms had it not been included in the contract. In either case, the clause has no effect on the location of the order in which the contract is rooted, on the basis of its mandatory force.[130]

---

[129] See below, ch 8 for a fuller discussion. Clear evidence of this state of affairs is provided by the dispute over mining concessions in Australia. In this country, it is the federated states that own the mining resources. They grant concessions which are adopted by the local legislator and therefore have legislative value. These concessions often contain intangibility clauses by which the local legislator undertakes not to adopt measures that may have consequences for the concession holder without its consent. As might be expected, the legislator is led (for example for tax reasons) to renege on its promise. In several instances, the supreme courts of the various mining states in Australia have had to rule on the force to be granted to such legislative commitments. Thus, for example, the supreme court of South Australia responded: 'As far as alterations to the provisions of the indenture are concerned, no doubt the parties to the indenture are bound by it, but that does not stop the Parliament of South Australia from amending that indenture or any other indenture, whether given statutory status or not, by amending Act of the Parliament'. In other words, the legislator, being all-powerful, is unable to give a firm undertaking to a private partner. See for this question in Australia, Y Nouvel, *La souveraineté minière de l'Australie* (Thesis, University of Paris 1, 1996) 182–93, quotation 185–86.

[130] Lankarani El-Zein, *Les contrats d'Etat* (n 6) 157.

I confess I fail to understand. Under what hypothesis would *pacta sunt servanda* not be applicable? If the agreement is not an international agreement, it is subject to some municipal law and, in practice (for investment contracts more often that not, to the law of lost state etc), to the law of the host state. This obviously comprises the *pacta sunt servanda* principle; but the state is in a position to act, in particular through legislative channels, on a stabilisation clause so as to eliminate any effect it might have both before its own courts and before arbitration tribunals. Under these circumstances, if it is considered that the stabilisation clause is not an indication that the contract is internationalised, the private partner is left at the mercy of the good will (or good faith) of the state co-contractor. If one thinks, things being what they are, that this is not an ideal solution, one must interpret the inclusion of such a clause as an indication that the contract is internationalised, for it is the only way to maintain, in any event, the useful effect of the clause. That is the first part of the reasoning. Once this is accepted, the clause will also reinforce the legitimate expectations of the private co-contractor and so make allowance, for example, for *lucrum cessans* in calculating compensation.[131]

On the Validity and Efficacy of Stabilisation Clauses

After attempting to neutralise one part at least of stabilisation clauses (freezing clauses), Lemaire sets out to cast doubt on the legal validity of such clauses. To do so, she needs only to recall the doctrinal controversy that is still smouldering on this subject. Should one, as Weil and Mayer think, for example, accept the principle of these clauses without which one 'would make the State incapable'[132] or should one consider, like the dedicatee of these lines, that because of the 'state's unshared and unlimited primacy, [the state] cannot alienate its sovereignty for the benefit of private interests generally', a position shared by many scholars.[133]

---

[131] See the *Aminoil* award where the arbitration tribunal, while asserting that the stabilisation clause did not prohibit nationalisation, acknowledged that '. . . the stabilization clauses . . . were nevertheless not devoid of all consequence, for they prohibited any measures that would have had a confiscatory character. These clauses created for the concessionaire a legitimate expectation that must be taken into account. In this context they dissipate all doubts as to the srentgh of the respect due to the contractual equilibrium', 66 *ILR* 519 at 607, para 159; (1982) *Journal du Droit International* paras 159, 905 and see also para 148.

[132] Mayer, 'La neutralisation du pouvoir normatif de l'Etat' (n 43) 141.

[133] P Kahn, 'Contrats d'Etat et nationalisation. Les apports de la sentence arbitrale du 24 mars 1982' 109 (1982) *Journal du Droit International* 844, 850.

All the arguments have already been exchanged on this question and commentators' replies depend on their ideological and theoretical commitments and on the analysis they make of actual practice. I would simply like to recall here that it is necessary to take account of the historical dimension if one wishes to understand the way the question of state contracts arose and developed. This contractual feature appeared in the post-war years over a small number of petroleum contracts. The first major papers and the earliest leading synthetic studies (those of Mann, Weil and JF Lalive) were published before the petroleum awards of the 1970s and 1980s and the very substantial development of ICSID case law.[134]

Yet very often, we go no further than the arguments developed at the time, without considering either the recent changes or the circumstances under which the discussion took place. Thus, for example, Lemaire regrets that the International Law Institute, at its 1979 Athens session, and in its resolution on 'The Proper Law of the Contract in Agreements Between a State and a Foreign Private Person' failed to clearly settle the validity of freezing clauses and did not give its opinion more broadly on clauses for neutralising the state's normative power.[135] But it must not be forgotten that the discussions at the Institute took place at the time of the major onslaught from the ideology of the New international economic order. And, it should be added, at a time when arbitration case law had been enhanced by the three Libyan oil awards alone. It would be interesting to see the question reviewed afresh within this eminent body.[136]

It should be pointed out, though, that over the last five decades, a very large number (certainly several hundred) of contracts entered into between host states and foreign investors have included such stabilisation clauses. They are also found in petroleum contracts of

---

[134] See above, ch 1, fn 134 (at 5). For JF Lalive, I am thinking of his paper 'Contracts between a State or a State Agency and a Foreign Company' (1964) *International and Comparative Law Quarterly* 987 and not his course at The Hague: 'Contrats entre Etats ou entreprises étatiques et personnes privées. Développements récents' (1983) 181 *Recueil des Cours de l'Académie de Droit International* 9.

[135] Lemaire, *Les contrats internationaux de l'administration* (n 6) 93, para 302.

[136] I tried to do this in ch 1. On the Libyan awards see Stern, 'Trois arbitrages, un même problème, trois solutions' (n 97) 3. For a recent review of the scope and validity of stabilisation clauses see Jacquet, 'Contrats d'Etat' (n 6) fn 49 and 131–9 and Berlin, 'Contrats d'Etat' (n 6) 73–74. With all the nuances necessary for each case, none of these scholars challenges the validity and even the effectiveness (maintaining the contract's financial equilbrium) of stabilisation clauses. Berlin also emphasises the historical dimension of the problem by showing the 'slow genesis of an international regime' of state contracts (fn 27ff).

the 1990s.[137] Under the circumstances, it would be strange for doctrine to invalidate (on paper) so significant a contractual practice and to fail to take account of the needs of each of the co-contractors (developing states want and/or need to attract investment and investors want to guard against risk). One can protest at the asymmetry of power between northern and southern nations, but to no real avail. It seems to me that the way to proceed is by promoting trade and investment by coming up with legal arrangements whereby each party can find what it needs (but not necessarily the ideal, which is out of reach).

However, continuing with some very methodical demolition work and after casting doubt on the validity of stabilisation clauses, Lemaire goes on to attack their effectiveness, assuming, that is, that any such clauses have remained standing (by which I mean legally valid) after her previous offensive. She begins, it should be noted, by simplifying her task by taking, in defence of her argument, only the arbitration awards relating to contracts including non-binding clauses and that alone allegedly commit the legislator,[138] and by excluding those that contains freezing clauses. This allows her to eliminate important arbitration awards in favour of the validity and effectiveness of stabilisation clauses. *Sapphire v NIOC*, *Texaco v Libya* and the ICSID arbitration awards *Alcoa Minerals*, *Kaiser Bauxite*, *Reynolds Jamaica*, *Klöckner*, *Letco* and also the American Arbitration Association award *Revere Copper and Brass* (4 August 1978) are all excluded in this way.[139]

Let us accept this bias and examine the author's arguments on the two arbitration awards containing 'legislator commitment' (sic) clauses: *Agip v Congo* (award of 30 November 1979) and *Aminoil v Kuwaitt* (award of 24 March 1982). In these instances, Lemaire concedes the arbitration tribunals did recognise the validity of the clauses but stripped them of any real effectiveness.

In the *Agip v Congo* award, the recognition of validity of the stabilisation clause led the arbitrator to award a nominal franc in compensation for *lucrum cessans*. Now, since the allowance for

---

[137] See above, ch 1, fn 137 (at 10). There is also a trend to replace stabilisation clauses by renegotiation clauses, inserted—oddly enough—in clauses that retain the name of 'stabilisation clauses'.

[138] But it has been seen (n 130) that the state, as the internal legislator, simply cannot give a firm and final undertaking to the private partner. Only the state as subject of international law can give such a commitment in the international legal order.

[139] Lemaire, *Les contrats internationaux de l'administration* (n 6) 94ff.

lucrum cessans is the main positive outcome that a firm can expect from a stabilisation clause, Lemaire draws the conclusion that this hope is vain. The issue before the arbitrators was different in *Aminoil*. The contract includes a clause (article 17) of a very general character, it seems, by which 'The Shaikh shall not by general or special legislation or by administrative measures or by any other act whatever annul this Agreement . . .'[140] The arbitration panel recognised the clause was entirely valid but considered that the nationalisation by Kuwait did not come within its scope as it referred only to acts to cancel the agreement, not to nationalisations. Admittedly, the panel acknowledged, a state may also undertake not to nationalise, but given that it is a 'particularly serious undertaking, it should be expressly stated'.[141]

Lemaire comments on this award:

> We think a decision asserting the theoretical validity of a promise not to alter the terms of a contract—so as to better remove the promise not to nationalise from its domain of application despite the general character of the terms of the undertaking—leaves an essential doubt as to the effectiveness of this type of promise.[142]

It is to be remembered, therefore, that in both these awards the stabilisation clauses (in the narrow sense of the term as interpreted by the author) are recognised as valid. Should it be considered that what was granted to validity was denied to effectiveness? I do not think so. Returning to *Aminoil*, the arbitration tribunal's interpretation of article 17 of the contract may be regretted.[143] Rightly or wrongly, two of the three arbitrators considered the clause did not cover nationalisation. That is the interpretation given by the jurisdictional body provided for by the contract and it is at least equal to the value of any interpretation given by any commentator.

---

[140] Award, 66 *ILR* 519 at 586, para 88; (1982) *Journal du Droit International* 892.

[141] Award, para 95; (1982) *Journal du Droit International* 894.

[142] Lemaire, *Les contrats internationaux de l'administration* (n 6) 96, para 308.

[143] On this, see the dissenting opinion of G Fitzmaurice, (1982) *ILM* 1049–53 and the severe commentary by FA Mann, 'The Aminoil Arbitration' (1982) *British Yearbook of International Law* 213 reprinted in *Further Studies in International Law* (Oxford, Clarendon Press, 1990) 252, 257. For an opinion close that of the solution adopted by the majority of the arbitration tribunal, see the consultation by M Virally in this case reported by AS El-Kosheri, 'Quelques réflexions à propos d'un texte inédit de Michel Virally' in *Le droit international au service de la paix, de la justice et du développement* (Paris, Pedone, 1991) 297, 306.

But above all, should one, in theoretical and practical terms, conclude such clauses are wholly ineffective? No. From this award, a jurist will determine (a) that stabilisation clauses are valid, (b) that it seems, from the *Aminoil* case law, that they do not cover the instance of nationalisation; that it is necessary, if one wishes to guard against this possibility when negotiating an agreement, to add a non-nationalisation clause to the stabilisation clause. Such clauses do exist, even if they are rare, and we know from the *Aminoil* award that, under certain conditions, they are valid too. The remainder is a question of drafting of the contract. It can be added that there is no telling whether, in some more or less distant future, another arbitration panel will necessarily confirm the distinction between stabilisation clause and non-nationalisation clause.

Again in the *Aminoil* award, Lemaire denigrates the Tribunal's dictum that stabilisation clauses 'are far from having lost all their value and efficacity on that account since . . . they re-inforce the necessity for a proper indemnification as a condition of it (nationalisation)' and they have as an effect to 'dissipate all doubts as to the strength of the respect due to the contractual equilibrium'.[144] But, she claims, that is just a repetition of an accepted legal rule about compensation in the event of nationalisation as provided for by resolution 1803 of 14 December 1962 of the General Assembly of the United Nations.

This appraisal betrays a flagrant lack of historical perspective. Resolution 1803 was followed in the 1970s by several resolutions (in particular that on the New international economic order, that adopting the Charter of states' economic rights and duties) that called into question the contents of resolution 1803 and proposed new rules, leaving the conditions for compensation in particular to the appreciation of the nationalising state.[145] And it was precisely the arbitration awards of the 1970s and 1980s (the three Libyan and especially *Texaco* awards, the *Aminoil* and *Agip* awards and several awards of the Iran–United States Claims Tribunal) that reasserted the legal rule in resolution 1803. The passage cited from the *Aminoil* award is therefore not a simple repetition of a well-established rule but on the

---

[144] *Aminoil* award, 66 *ILR* 519 at 589–90, para 96 and 607, para 159; Lemaire, *Les contrats internationaux de l'administration* (n 6) 146.

[145] For some historical perspective, see D Carreau and P Juillard, *Droit international économique* 3d edn (Paris, Dalloz, 2007) 432ff. See also M Virally's opinion in the consultation cited (n 144) 298–300. A summary of the development of law on this topic is to be found in Jacquet, 'Contrats d'Etat' (n 6).

contrary a reaffirmation of the positive character of a rule that was largely contested at the time.[146] But if a stabilisation clause reinforces the need for adequate compensation, what is to be made of the award of a nominal franc in the *Agip v Congo* award? Again it is a choice by the arbitrator dependent on the facts of the case and that has no repercussion on the validity of the stabilisation clause. By way of comparison, in some defamation cases, plaintiffs claim or are awarded just one franc in nominal damages. That naturally has no implication as to the existence of the offence itself or as to the realilty of the defamation in the particular case. In other words, if for reasons of legal policy, the sole arbitrator in this case did not want to go further in allowing for *lucrum cessans*, that in no way means the same will apply in future for other cases.

Whatever, one point is very clear: for arbitrators to recognise that stabilisation clauses have some effect on compensation, such clauses must be valid. They must, consequently, be granted by an instance able to make such a promise and unable to renege on that promise *without certain legal consequences arising*. Lemaire considers that if stabilisation clauses ultimately have the effect only of ensuring compliance with the financial balance of the contract (and not of preventing the state from acting, but who can prevent a state from acting?) they cannot be used as an argument to prove the presence of the state as a subject of international law. Indeed 'such an obligation (maintaining the financial balance of a contract) may be that of any contractor' and suggests rather the involvement of the state-administration, as a person of municipal public law.

---

[146] *Texaco-Calasiatic (TOPCO) v Libyan Government*, award of 19 January 1977, For an English translation of the French original: (1978) 17 *ILM* 1; 53 *ILR* 420; (1977) 104 *Journal du Droit International* 350; *Libyan American Oil Co (LIAMCO) v Government of the Libyan Arab Republic*, award of 12 April 1977, 62 *ILR* 141; (1980) *Revue de l'Arbitrage* 132; *BP Exploration Company v Government of the Libyan Arab Republic*, award of 10 October 1973, 53 *ILR* 300; (1980) *Revue de l'Arbitrage* 117; *Government of the State of Kuwait v American Independent Oil Co (Aminoil)*, award of 24 March 1982, 66 *ILR* 519; (1982) *Journal du Droit International* 869; *AGIP s.p.a. v Governnment of the People's Republic of Congo*, award of 30 November 1979, 67 *ILR* 318; (1989) *Revue Critique de Droit International Privé* 92; see also the awards of the Iran–United States Claims Tribunal on the question of nationalisation, especially *Amoco International Finance Corporation v Islamic Republic of Iran* (1978) *ILM* 15. On these awards see JA Westberg, *International Transactions and Claims Involving Government Parties. Case Law of the Iran-United States Claims Tribunal* (Washington DC, International Law Institute, 1991) 101.

It is obvious, though, that if it is the state-administration—the legislator for example[147]—that grants such a guarantee, it is able to renege on the guarantee as it wants and when it wants and without any financial consequence if it so desires. It votes a new statute, altering the conditions of performance of the contract and provides that no compensation shall be paid.[148] If it is wished to safeguard these stabilisation clauses from any intervention *without financial consequences* by the state person, the state contract must be concluded outside the state's legal order and, for me, in the international legal order. The presence of such clauses is prima facie evidence of this.

To all these arguments, Lemaire adds an observation drawn from the practice of bilateral investment promotion and protection treaties. They commonly contain,

> clauses whereby the state which is the place of the investment, undertakes, in respect of the state from which the private co-contracting person comes, not to alter its legislation or not to enforce certain changes to existing contracts.[149]

She deduces from this that the undertakings given by the states in the contract are given by the public person of municipal law and that it is only in the context of treaties that the state as a person of international law intervenes.

But the phenomenon she reports can be construed in a quite different way. The fact that the hundreds of bilateral treaties (in 1997 there were said to be 1507 such treaties, 2676 in 2009) confirm the stabilisation mechanism in the contracts can equally constitute the recognition, consecration and accommodation in treaty law of a widespread contractual practice the validity of which was already the subject of a customary rule of international contract law.

This custom was not born with the making of bilateral treaties (and their proliferation in the 1990s) but with the practice of state contracts where the state intervenes as a subject of international law. The only reason to object to such an analysis is once again because of a refusal to consider that a private person can enter the sphere of the international legal order. This is clear from the unreserved

---

[147] We shall see in detail below in ch 8 that the notion of state-administration does not mean the administration in the ordinary sense of the term (the offices of the executive) but means all of the functions of the state whether legislative, executive or judicial forming the state's state's internal legal order.

[148] See Nouvel, La souveraineté minière de l'Australie (n 130).

[149] Lemaire, *Internationaux de l'administration* (n 6) 101, para 324.

approval by Rigaux and other members of the Institute of International Law of the practice of stabilisation by treaty[150] and their denial of the validity of such clauses in contracts. And yet the result is the same in the end; or rather it is more radical when a treaty has been concluded since it covers all contracts, even those which do not contain a stabilisation clause, or better still, it covers situations even where there is no contract between the state and the investor.[151]

What is at issue, therefore, is not so much the protection of host states—developing states—against legal practices that might be unfavourable to them; it is the defence of an ideological position that is fundamentally averse to the presence of private persons generally in the sphere of public international law.

---

[150] See Rigaux, 'Les situations juridiques individuelles' (n 40) 229–30, fn 165.
[151] See the turning point of the ICSID arbitration award *AAPL v Sri Lanka* (ARB/87/3) (1992) *Journal du Droit International* 216 and (1991) *ICSID Review* 526.

5

Hans Kelsen and the Advancement of International Law*

FOR ANYONE WISHING to go beyond an empirical approach to law, to examine its concepts in depth and develop an overview which may provide a guide through the mass of facts, reading Kelsen will always prove a worthwhile occupation. This is so even for those who subscribe only in part, or indeed not at all to his views. And what it is true of his theory of law as a whole is possibly even more true of his theory of international law. This subject is genuinely central to Kelsen's theory of law, which sets him apart from other legal theorists who usually disregard international law or at best (as with Hart) accord it very limited treatment.[1] Kelsen, however, devoted a great deal of space to reflections on international law and to ways of incorporating this specific topic into the general theory of law. Of the 387 titles listed by the Hans Kelsen Institute of Vienna 106 deal with international law, ahead of legal theory (96 titles) and constitution law (92 titles).[2]

The purpose of this chapter is not to make a tally of everything international law owes to Kelsen's writings. I shall endeavour instead to show why Kelsen's tenets are valuable for viewing international

---

* First published in (1998) 9 *European Journal of International Law*, 287

[1] Thus, see, eg, R.Carré de Malberg, *Contribution à la théorie générale de l'État* (Paris, Sirey, 1920, reprint, Paris, CNRS, 1962). This author, probably the leading French theorist of public law, presents no development of international law, despite a passing mention in discussion about sovereignty. See also HLA Hart, *The Concept of Law* (Oxford, Clarendon Press, 1961) 208–31. In contrast, Dworkin seems unaware of the existence of international law, or at least has no interest in it. Similarly, J Raz, *The Concept of a Legal System. An Introduction to the Theory of Legal System* 2nd edn (Oxford, Clarendon Press, 1980) fails to develop the question. Other examples could be cited.

[2] See H Kelsen, *General Theory of Norms*, trans M Hartney (Oxford, Oxford University Press, 1991) 440. These bibliographic indications are not given in the French translation of the work: *Théorie générale des norms*, trans O Beaud (Paris, LGDJ, 1996).

law both as *positive law* and *evolving law*. Kelsen's theoretical analyses allow us not only to consider international law as law proper, but they also provide insight into how such law can evolve and be improved. I shall show in particular how these analyses account for certain recent legal developments which have created considerable surprise as they have not been consistent with the traditional conception of international law as law between states.[3]

The Nature of International Law

Law in its Own Right

Already in his earliest writings Kelsen claimed that international law was law in its own right. What was original and paradoxical about this stance was that he viewed international law as law in the strict sense of the term for the *very reasons* that prompted many positive theorists to question legal status of international law.[4]

It is well known that Kelsen defines a legal obligation by the sanction it entails. Law is therefore a 'coercive legal order'. He further defines a sanction in a very narrow sense as the exercise or threat of physical coercion. In the nineteenth century, Austin had also defined law as a 'wish conceived by one and expressed or intimated to another with an evil to be inflicted and incurred in case the wish be disregarded'.[5]

Austin deduced that because international law had no sovereign capable of sanctioning the violation of its rules, it could not be true law but only 'positive morality'.[6]

It is the conclusion that Kelsen forcefully dismisses, whether it be reached by strict positivists (like Austin) or by realists who hold that there can be no international law until such time as the power to coerce states is concentrated in the hands of a single authority (Raymond Aron).[7]

---

[3] See also P Visscher, 'Observations sur la contribution de Hans Kelsen au droit international positif' (1981) 4 *Revue Internationale de Philosophie* 530.

[4] H Bull, 'Hans Kelsen and International Law' in R Tur and W Twining (eds), *Essays on Kelsen* (Oxford, Clarendon Press, 1986) 321, 323.

[5] J Austin, *The Province of Jurisprudence Determined* (Cambridge, Cambridge University Press, 1995) 24.

[6] *Ibid*, 112.

[7] R Aron, *Guerre et paix entre les nations* 3rd edn (Paris, Calmann-Levy, 1962) 704–12.

Against these arguments Kelsen asserts that law is defined by sanction, that sanction consists of physical coercion and that international law does indeed have this type of sanction available to it. This is probably Kelsen's most famous tenet, but also the one that has given rise to the most serious misunderstanding of his theory.

Reprisals and War: Sanctions of Decentralised International Law

For Kelsen the sanctions available under international law are reprisals and war:

> These sanctions like the sanctions of national law consist in the forcible deprivation of life, liberty, and other goods, notably economic values. In a war human being are killed, maimed, imprisoned and national or private property is confiscated and other legal rights are infringed.[8]

These are sanctions of a 'primitive', that is, 'decentralised' legal order: a legal order in which the functions of the creation of law and administration of justice have not yet been concentrated in the hands of central organs. This means that law is both created and applied by the subjects of law themselves who resort to reprisals and war to exact their own justice.

This conception of international law and sanctions came in for harsh criticism from almost all sides from the time it was first presented. I myself have been very critical of Kelsen's argument about sanctions in international law.[9] Nevertheless, it now seems more worthwhile to concentrate on the rationale of the argument and the service it renders all those who want to 'take international law seriously'.

Commentators focus primarily on the gloomy view that Kelsen seems to take of primitive, that is, decentralised or anarchical, international law. But it can be argued that it is precisely this same view that allows Kelsen to imagine relations between states as being subjected to law proper and above all to law amenable to progress. That there is no sovereign above the states to enforce sanctions on them does not in Kelsen's view preclude the conception of interstate relations being governed by law since, and here lies the difference with Austin, law involves submission to rules and not to the person of the

---

[8] H Kelsen, 'The Essence of International Law' in KW Deutsch and S Hoffmann (eds), *The Relevance of International Law: Essays in Honor of Leo Gross* (Cambridge MA, Schenkman, 1968) 87.

[9] C Leben, *Les sanctions privatives de droits ou de qualité dans les organisations internationales spécialisées* (Brussels, Bruylant, 1979) 41–45.

sovereign (*non sub homine sed sub lege*).[10] This means that even a decentralised legal order can be conceived of as a true legal order. The difference between this sort of primitive order and an advanced order such as that of the state is one of degree and not of kind. While this reasoning may leave us sceptical at this point, it goes further. Kelsen argues that any use of force in the international community must be characterised either as a sanction or a delict, that is, a violation of international law. It is important to understand the theoretical consequences of this perception. It leads, as Bull has shown, to ranking Kelsen's thinking in the 'Grotian' tradition of international law, that is, a tradition that asserts international law is true law and that denies states the right to wage war indiscriminately.[11] And this is the essential point that is often overlooked by critics of Kelsen's presentation of sanctions of international law: the assertion that those sanctions are reprisals and that war *is made only as a lead-up* to the assertion that international law in the twentieth century has emerged from the state of anarchy and no longer authorises indiscriminate resort to such sanctions.

Centralisation of International Law: Collective Security and Compulsory Jurisdiction

At this juncture it is necessary to sketch out a side of Kelsen that is little known to legal scholars, that of political militant for democracy within states and for peace in the international community.[12] It should be recalled in this respect that particularly in the 1930s and 1940s Kelsen actively supported this setting up of the collective security system in the international community. He wrote exten-

---

[10]   H Kelsen, *Principles of International Law* (New York, Rinehart, 1952) 104.
[11]   Bull, 'Hans Kelsen and International Law' (n 4) 329.
[12]   Carlos Miguel Herrera's valuable study of the 'political' side of Kelsen. *Théorie juridique et politique chez Hans Kelsen* (Paris, Kimé, 1997). It is regrettable though that the author does not address the question of Hans Kelsen and the advancement of international law in Kelsen's work. See also the special issue of the journal (1990) 17 *Cahiers de Philosophie Politique et Juridique*: 'La pensée politique de Kelsen'. On the pacifist presuppositions of Kelsen's theory of sovereignty see Herrera, *ibid*, 115–18 and A Carrino, 'Le positivism critique de Hans Kelsen: une foundation logico-formelle des normes' (1991) 20 *Cahiers de Philosophie Politique et Juridique* 77–78, 88. The pacifist and anti-imperialist creed is particularly obvious in his conclusion to the 1926 Hague Lectures 'Les rapports de système entre le droit interne et le droit inter-national public' (1926-IV) 14 *Recueil des Cours de l'Académie de Droit International de La Haye* 231, 320–31.

sively on the issue.[13] In his early work he takes a position 'politically' for the *bellum justum* theory, which restricts the discretionary power of state to resort to war and only justifies this course of action when it is in response to an earlier breach of international law, and therefore a sanction. It is a political statement since Kelsen acknowledges that in the 1920s examination of positive law does not lead to the 'scientific' conclusion that war can only be either a legal sanction or a violation of law.

In his final works, however, he takes the view that this 'political' position henceforth reflects positive law. Considering the effects in general international law of the Covenant of the League of Nations, the Briand-Kellog Pact and the United Nations Charter, [i]t is hardly possible to say any longer today that according to valid international law any state [. . .] may wage war against any other state for any reason without violating international law; it is hardly possible, in others words, to deny the general validity of the *bellum justum principle*'.[14]

Some observers criticise Kelsen's doctrine of *bellum justum* as 'the product of wishful thinking'.[15] It could be countered that it accurately anticipated the process of change in the international community during its darkest hours. The important point to emphasise in any case is, that the conception of the interstate order as a primitive legal order with war and reprisals as its sanctions, exists for Kelsen alongside a dynamic conception of international law as evolving law, *advancing law*, and of a society that may have been completely anarchical in the past but is no longer.

With regard to international law, therefore, Kelsen actually ascribes central importance to the institution of a compulsory jurisdiction responsible for settling disputes that threaten international peace. This is another little understood aspect of his history, although it is set out in Kelsen's many works on the idea of 'peace through law'. In the most important of these, published in 1944, he proposes a draft Pact to supersede the League of Nations, in which he devotes 33 articles to the future Court of Justice, as opposed to one article for the Council and one for the Plenary Assembly![16]

[13] See Kelsen's 1940s writings, such as *Peace through Law* (North Carolina, University of North Carolina Press, 1944); 'The Strategy of Peace' (1944) 5 *American Journal of Sociology* 381.
[14] Kelsen, 'The Essence of International Law' (n 8) 87. For a full discussion of the role of war in international law see *Principles of International Law* (n 10) 25–44.
[15] Bull, 'Hans Kelsen and International Law' (n 4) 329.
[16] *Peace through Law* (n 13). For a study of this work see C Tournaye, *Kelsen et la sécurité collective* (Paris, LGDJ, 1995).

There is no need to underscore the utopian and unrealistic character of such a construction. However, it should be recalled that for Kelsen '[t]he foundation of all legal organisation as any legal community is the judicial process'.[17] In this he falls in with legal theorists who like Bobbio and (probably) Hart consider that the turning point in the transition from a simple (or primitive) form of law to a more complex form occurs with the centralisation of the function of application of law in the courts.[18] This led Kelsen to write in 1932 that it is '. . . much more important to get states to renounce deciding by themselves whether there has been a violation of law than abolish the right to exact justice themselves'.[19] This assertion was confirmed later during the International Law Commission proceedings where, on the question of countermeasures without the use of armed force, the Special Rapporteur for the draft articles on the international responsibility of states, Professor Arangio-Ruiz, was unable to obtain support for the point that the process of countermeasures as a response to an unlawful act should be strictly governed by resort to judicial proceeding.[20]

But whatever the still utopian character of the introduction of a compulsory jurisdiction within the universal interstate community, two remarks need to be made which confirm the idea that the introduction of such a jurisdiction is the turning point in the transition from a decentralised legal order to a more centralised, and therefore more effective, legal order. Everyone is aware that the very special characteristics of the European Community legal order are primarily the result of the role of the European Court of Justice. However,

---

[17] *Peace through Law* (n 13) 73. See also the valuable paper by O Pfersmann, 'De la justice constitutionnelle à la justice internationale: Hans Kelsen et la seconde guerre mondiale' (1993) 16 *Revue Française de Droit Constitutionnel* 760, 776–79.

[18] See N Bobbio, 'Kelsen et les source du droit' (1981) 4 *Revue Internationale de Philosophie* 474, 482: '. . . Courts are not only a source of law . . . they are the necessary condition for the existence of a legal order'. See also by the same author, this time on a study of Hart: 'Nouvelles réflexions sur les normes primaires et secondaires' in C Perelman (ed), *La règle de droit* Brussels, Bruylant, 1971) 104, 121. It will be recalled that for commentators like Kantorowicz, the main characteristic of a rule of law is to be *subject to justice*, ie, to the subject of a judgment by a third party, at least potentially. See H Kantorowicz, *The Definition of Law* (Cambridge, Cambridge University Press, 1958) 79.

[19] H Kelsen, 'La technique du droit et l'organisation de la paix: la théorie du droit devant le problème du désarmement' (1932) (3 February) *Journal des Nations* 61.

[20] For an overview of the controversies raised by the report of Professor Arangio-Ruiz, see (1994) 5 *European Journal of International Law* 20–119; 'Remarques sur une revolution inachevée. Le projet d'articles de la CDI sur la responsabilité des États' (1996) *Annuaire Français de Droit International* (1996) 7, 18–32; C Leben, 'Contremesures' in *Nouveau Répertoire Dalloz de droit international public*

it has been convincingly argued that the setting up of the Court and the different procedures for bringing cases before it (especially that of Article 177 EC Treaty) presupposed a unified vision of the founder states of the Communities. In other words, it was not the setting up of the European Court of Justice that produced this remarkable legal order but the prior political will among the states that allowed this order to be constructed.

This is hardly disputable. However, it will be observed that within the universal interstate community phenomena occur which give rise to compulsory quasi-tribunals that completely transform the topography of international law. Such is the effect produced by the creation within the World Trade Organization of an effective mechanism for the settlement of disputes which, within the space of two years, has led to no fewer than 100 cases (more than 300 in 2003) being brought before the Dispute Settlement Body. In striking contrast, the previous ineffective GATT (General Agreement on Tariffs and Trade) procedure dealt with a mere 195 procedures in 46 years of existence.[21]

These points confirm that 'the foundation of all legal organisations . . . is judicial process' and that international law is at one and the same time the law of a decentralised society and of a society in the process of centralisation.

Changes in International Law: Towards what sort of *Civitas Maxima*?

Given the importance of the theory of the state in Kelsen's work and the fact that he characterises general international law as primitive law, it is often thought that Kelsen only envisaged the development of international law along the lines of the state model. This is an error of appreciation. Kelsen considers that there is only a difference of degree and not a difference of kind between the state legal order and the international legal order: both are merely specific cases of a general phenomenon which is centralisation and decentralisation of legal orders. It is by analysing this phenomenon that the specificity of the state can be understood and the ways forward for international

---

[21] See H Ruiz Fabri, 'Le règlement des différends dans le cadre de l'organisation mondiale du commerce' (1997) 3 *Journal du Droit International* 709. See also WTO, *Focus* no 21 (August 1997) which announced that the 100th dispute was reported on 19 August 1997. All proceedings brought under Article XXIII of the GATT (1947) are listed in *Guide to GATT Law and Practice* (6th edn, 1994) 719–34.

law can be conceived. These lead to a *civitas maxima* which is definitely not conceived of along the lines of the nation state.

Centralisation/Decentralisation of Legal Orders

As Kelsen pointed out, any legal order which is based on a territory invariably consists of combination of norms, some of which are valid for the entire territory (known as 'central norms) while others are valid for part of the territory only (and known as 'local' or 'partial' norms). A wholly centralised legal order with local norms is virtually impossible to set up. Conversely, a fully decentralised legal order with no central norm is simply inconceivable since a legal order must have at least one central norm to ensure the unity of the territory which is the basis of that order.[22]

Thus, the two 'bounds' (in the mathematical sense) of the range of variation of the function are excluded from the range of possibilities. However, within these bounds, the function can take any value, that is, the degree of decentralisation or decentralisation of a legal order can be a continuum. This contrast within any legal order between a central order and a number of local (or partial) orders based on the criterion of the spatial validity of the norms is the 'static' conception of the notion of centralisation/decentralisation. As ever, Kelsen adds a 'dynamic' conception based on a way norms are created and executed.[23]

This presentation of the structure of the legal orders allows Kelsen to bridge the gap which in classical theory, and in a particular dualist theory, separates the nature of the state and the nature of the international legal order: *both orders* are partly centralised and partly decentralised. While the international legal order is more decentralised (and that is all is meant when it is said to be 'primitive') the internal legal order is never fully centralised: the difference between the two is one of degree and not of kind. The state is the model for the future development of the international legal order in that it is a more centralised legal order and in that the development of international law will also bring about increased centralisation of that legal order. But that does not necessarily entail, as is usually

---

[22] H Kelsen, *General Theory of Law and State* trans A Wedberg (New York, Russell & Russell, 1961) 306. On the sphere of validity of norms see *ibid*, 42–44; *Principles of International Law* (n 10) 93–96.

[23] Kelsen, *General Theory of Law and* State, *ibid*, 308. This whole question of centralisation and decentralisation of orders is covered at 303–27.

understood and as some of Kelsen's writings may have given us to believe,[24] that we are moving towards the constitution of a 'world state'. It is not inevitable, however, that it should become centralised to the same extent as the nation states.

The International Organisation as a Comparatively Centralised Legal Order and its Relations with the State

The international organisation, like the state, is therefore a combination of a central legal order, the institutional order created by the treaty and of partial legal orders, those of states parties to the treaty. Each treaty thus creates a special international legal order relative to the general international legal order. But this international legal order is also a central legal order, with the legal orders of all the states and those of international organisations making up only partial legal orders. Naturally there are differences between all these 'comparatively centralised' legal orders. Two of these differences are examined here.

The first concerns the attribute of sovereignty which is attached to the state and to the state alone. Kelsen defines sovereignty differently from his predecessors: sovereignty attaches to the legal order with a territorial basis whose validity is founded in general international law. This can be expressed otherwise as 'the state [is] a community subjected only to international law'. This definition breaks completely with the myth of sovereignty as absolute and unconditional power and once again allows for the existence of international law as true law whose obligatory character matters for its subjects.

It follows from this that there is in the theory of groups of states a fundamental distinction between the *Staatenbund* (confederation) and the *Bundestaat* (federation). This distinction does not lie in the constitutive charter (constitution or treaty)[25] but in the fact that confederation is a grouping of states which is not itself a state in the

---

[24] See below, n 27.

[25] See also the fairly involved case of the Treaty of Unification between the Federal Republic of Germany and the German Democratic Republic concerning the establishment of German unity (Berlin, 31 August 1990—Federal Republic of Germany–German Democratic Republic—Treaty on the establishment of German Unity, 31 August 1990, *ILM* (1991) 457). Under this 'Treaty of Unification': 'Upon the accession of the German Democratic Republic to the Federal Republic of Germany in accordance with article 23 of the Basic Law taking effect on 3 October 1990 the Länder of the Federal Republic of Germany' (Art 1 of the Treaty of Unification). On the process of unification, see M Fromont, 'Les techniques juridiques utilisées pour l'unification de l'Allemagne' (1991) 8 *Revue Française de Droit Constitutionnel* 579. The author notes that 'this treaty is incontestably an

eye of international law, whereas a federation is a grouping of 'states' which is itself a state. In other words, from the instant a federation is formed, the states it groups vanish as states subject to international law and become partial legal orders which are founded in the constitution of the federation and not in general international law. The federal state alone has a basis in the international legal order, or, put differently, is in immediate contact with that order.[26]

A second difference arises from the very contrasted proportion of central norms and local norms in the state and in the international orders, be it the global international legal order or the legal order of international organisations. In the state, central norms make up the most part of the total legal order whereas in international orders it is local norms that are in the majority. Accordingly, the degree of centralisation of an order can be evaluated from the ratio of the number of central norms to the number of local norms.

That said, for Kelsen, the dynamics of centralisation/decentralisation begins within the state with the contractual order created by two persons by virtue of the law of the state. It continues in the organisation of the state, and then extends beyond the states in the constitution of higher centralised legal orders, international organisations and, beyond that, of the community of all states, the *civitas maxima*, the law of which is general international law.[27] This

---

international treaty . . . [which] has international effects since its coming into force has entailed the disappearance of one of the parties, the GDR, as an international subject. But in domestic law [it] is original in two ways: it is in part a constitutional text and in part a legislative and regulatory text' (at 583).

[26] Kelsen, *Principles of International Law* (n 10) 168–74.

[27] It is in his 1920 book on sovereignty that Kelsen develops at length his idea of international law as the law of a *civitas maxima*, expressly invoking Christian Wolf (in the Italian translation consulted: *IL problema della sovranità* (trans A Carrino, 1989) 355–402). However, it seems that Kelsen no longer used the expression *civitas maxima* after his Hague Lecture; see 'Les rapports de système' (n 12) 318–20, 331. He wrote in particular: 'Since the idea of the sovereignty of the national state has until now, rightly or wrongly, proved an obstacle to any attempt to organize the international order to create specialized organs, to develop, apply and execute international law, in a word to transform the international community, which is still hardly evolved to date, into a *civitas maxima*, in the full meaning of the word'. And Kelsen ended his lectures by writing: 'And it is this organization of the world into a universal state that should be the ultimate, though still distant goal, of all political endeavour', *ibid*, 331. I suggest that Kelsen abandoned the expression *civitas maxima* because these expressions can be used to designate any supreme legal order. But he suggests that the international legal order could also evolve towards a form of state in the strict sense of the term. But if we take it that by 'universal state' Kelsen meant simply a more developed and peace-loving international legal order, which does not imply the disappearance of nation states, it can be said that he never gave up this political ambition. See also below, n 41.

principle of centralisation of orders that Scelle preferred to call 'Federalism'[28] is, according to Kelsen, 'the fundamental principle of organization of the different legal communities . . . the law which allows them all to be arranged in a strictly continuous series . . .'[29] This point, though, calls for a clarification that seems to derive from Kelsen's theory of the state: there is necessarily a separation between the phenomenon of centralisation/decentralisation within the state and that found outside the state. Between a state and an international organisation, albeit a very 'centralised' one like the European Union, there is a difference of kind and not merely of degree, as argued above.[30]

This difference lies in the recognition or non-recognition of the statehood of an entity by international law. But how do we get from a group of states that is not a state to a group of states that is itself a state while its component parts lose this standing in international law? And conversely, how do we get from a federal state, for example, the USSR, to a group of sovereign states in international law, such as the Commonwealth of Independent States (CIS), say?

The events of recent years have corroborated a very old answer of international law doctrine: it is the transfer of competence in terms of defence and foreign affairs that is the main (although possibly not the only) point in the shift.[31] The state legal order is a coercive order, and it is necessary therefore the (federal) state formed from a group of states to be able to concentrate the military might given up to it by the member states.[32]

By contrast, the breakup of the Soviet Union and of Yugoslavia has shown that the emergence of new states follows closely on the breakup of the military monopoly of the former state. It further shows that the implementation of a foreign policy goes along with this breakup and manifests the birth of new subjects of international law.

---

[28] G Scelle, *Précis de droit des gens* (Paris, Sirey, 1938) (Reprint Dalloz, 2008) 187–287.

[29] H Kelsen, 'Aperçu d'une théorie générale de l'Etat' (1926) *Revue du Droit Public* 619. See also 'Les rapports de système' (n 12) 319–20.

[30] See text above at n 24.

[31] *Principles of International Law* (n 10) 168–74; see also the 2nd edn of *Principles of International Law* (revised and edited by RW Tucker) (New York, Holt, Rinehart and Winston, 1966) 263, fn 89; C Leben, 'A propos de la nature juridique des Communautés européennes' (1991) 14 *Droits* 61, 69–71.

[32] M Virally, *L'Organisation mondiale* (Paris, Armand Colin, 1972) 23.

The European Union as a Possible Horizon of International Law

Elsewhere I have inquired into the nature of the European Communities and concluded that whatever the very great originality of the Community legal order, it remained less than a state and still came under the theory of international organisation.[33] This point of view, which has been criticised as being overly marked by internationalist bias, has since then been confirmed at all tiers of the Community legal order. For the Court of Justice of the European Communities the clarification came in a case concerning Germany 'that the rules concerning the relations between the Community and its Member States are not the same as those uniting the Bund and the Länder'.[34]

For the courts of the Member States, and more particularly the constitutional courts which are primarily concerned with this question, the French Constitutional Council reiterated in its Maastricht ruling (9 April 1992) that nothing in the Constitution precluded France from concluding 'subject to reciprocity, international commitments with a view to participating in the creation or development of a permanent *international organization* endowed with legal personality and invested with the decision making power by the effect of transfer of competence consented by the Member States'.[35] And similarly, the German Constitutional Court specified in its ruling of 12 October 1993, concerning the constitutionality of the Maastrich Treaty, that 'European Union treaty creates . . . an association of States . . . and not a State formed by an European people' and that in any event 'the foundation of a "United States of Europe" comparable to the formation of the United States of America is not contemplated at the present time'.[36]

As for the states themselves, they reasserted at the European Council of Edinburgh on 12 December 1992 that the Union is constituted of 'independent sovereign States that have freely elected to

[33] Leben, 'A propos de la nature juridique des Communautés européennes'(n 31) 69–71 and below ch 9. For thoughts on the signification of the 'supranational' character of the community, see JH Weiler 'The Community System: The Dual Character of Supranationalism' (1981) 1 *Yearbook of European Law* 267.
[34] Case C-359/92 *Germany v Council* [1994] ECR I-3712, at 38.
[35] See the text of the decision in (1992) 3 *Revue Française de Droit Administratif* 403–408, point 13 (emphasis added); L Favoreu and P Gaïa, 'Les decisions du conseil constitutionnel relative au traité sur l'Union européenne' (1992) 11 *Revue Française de Droit Administratif* 389
[36] The text of the French decision in (1993) 3 *Revue Universelle des Droits de l'homme* 286, 290 (cols 1 and 2). The German text is in (1993) *EuGRZ* 429.

exercise some of their competences jointly pursuant to the treaties in force'.[37] But above all, the European Union, as established in the Maastricht Treaty marks, as everyone knows, a step backwards in Community integration because the Union has no legal personality proper and because the two 'pillars' of common foreign and security policy and of cooperation in the fields of justice and home affairs operate according to classical mechanisms of cooperation in international law and are not subject to the control of the European Courts.[38]

Coming on to the way the Community works, it can be said that the distinctive features of its operation almost all exist but in a far less developed and efficient state in the international legal order. This is the case of the direct applicability of conventional norms, the principle of which was recognised in the Advisory Opinion of the Permanent Court of International Justice in the *Jurisdiction of the Courts of Dantzig Case*. And what was at the time an exceptional occurrence, namely that '. . . the very object of an international agreement, according to the intention of the contracting Parties, may be the adoption by the Parties of some definite rules creating individuals rights and obligations and enforceable by the national courts' has now become something quite common.[39]

And the same is true of the primacy of the international law: it is just as much an 'existential condition' (in the well-known expression of Pescatore) of the existence of this order as of the Community order. In an international court, as in a Community court, a state cannot invoke domestic reasons to justify the non-performance of its obligations. Moreover, different national constitutions themselves provide for the primacy of international norms. This is the case of Article 55 of the French Constitution on the superiority, under certain circumstances, of treaties over legislation, even when enacted subsequently.[40]

---

[37] Documents d'actualité internationale (Paris, La documentation française, 1993) 48.

[38] On all these points see J Verhoeven, 'La notion "d'applicabilité directe" du droit international' (1980) *Revue Belge de Droit International* 187.

[39] *Case of the Jurisdiction of the Courts of Dantzig*, PCIJ Rep Series B No 15, 17–18 (1928). See also Verhoeven, *ibid*, 243.

[40] This principle has struggled for acceptance in French courts. The *French Cour de cassation* first confirmed it in its *decision Société des cafés Jacques Vabre* (24 May 1975); but the Conseil d'Etat supported this position, ie, the precedence of the treaty over subsequent legislation, only since the Nicolo decision of 20 October 1989. See M Long, P Weil, G Braibant, P Delvolvé and B Genevois, *Les Grands arrêts de la jurisprudence administrative* 17th edn (Paris, Dalloz, 1996) 656–67.

However, the existing potential in international law is only rarely realised as the effectiveness of the principles of direct applicability and primacy of such law are entirely at the mercy of state courts which usually give restrictive interpretations. The existence of the Court of Justice of the European Communities and the preliminary ruling procedure mean that national judges, on the contrary, exercise dual functions (*dédoublement fonctionnel*) making them at one and the same time judges of the national legal order and the Community legal order. As such, and because they are bound in law by the answer to the questions themselves put to the European Court, they will be led to set aside the national law, including statutes (the question is more problematic for constitutional laws) to apply Community law according to the centralised interpretation given by the Luxembourg Court.

The bottom line is that the Community legal order is a comparatively centralised legal order, less than a state order but more than that of any other international organisation. And when thinking about the future of international law, it is easy to imagine that it may advance through the multiplication of specialised legal order based on constituent treaties of international organisations which may in the long term tend to provide the international order with the institutional and normative advances that are part of the Community legal order today. This is a trend that is already observable in the context of human rights conventions, and primarily the European Convention, but also, as has already been noted above, in the context of a legal order established by the Marrakech Agreement creating the World Trade Organization.

In this way, Kelsen's *civitas maxima* begins to take recognisable shape. It is not a world state, as then there would be no international law but merely the domestic law of that state. However, it is possible to imagine that the *civitas maxima* might borrow a number of features from the Community legal order, an order in which states remain sovereign.[41]

---

[41] Do states really retain their sovereignty in the Community legal order? This question has been the subject of heated debate in France and the other countries of Europe. In an important work of doctrine, O Beaud, 'La souveraineté de l'État, le pouvoir constituant et le traité de Maastricht' (1993) 6 *Revue Française de Droit Administratif* 1045 (and see his *Théorie de la Fédération* 2nd edn (Paris, PUF, 2009)); the author argues that a state cannot give up its monetary sovereignty without ceasing to become a state worthy of the name (at 1053); that after the Maastricht Treaty states only retain pseudo-sovereignty (at 1058); that the European Union can no longer be characterised as an international organisation and that 'the process at work in

Changes in International Law: Internationalised State Contracts and the Status of Private Persons in the International Legal Order

The question of the status of individuals in international law is mostly addressed by examining international humanitarian and human rights law. The question is whether individuals have the capacity of (limited) subjects of international law. The most prudent response is to observe that private persons are increasingly the addressees of rights defined by international instruments, which makes them passive subjects of international law. Their capacity as active subjects is still exceptional. As Dupuy remarks:

> In order to be considered an active subject of a legal order an entity must of course first be invested by that order with clearly defined rights and obligations. But that is not enough. There must also be the possibility of acting directly through appropriate procedures to ensure effective observance of the exercise of the rights one enjoys. The capacity to act is the decisive criterion of legal personality.[42]

European construction leads to a loss of sovereignty . . .' (at 1066). Underpinning the entire paper is a rejection of the 'formalist' conception of the sovereignty and the assertion that 'sovereignty of state means fullness of power . . .' and that it consists in taking on any important political matter . . .'. It is just this material conception of sovereignty that Kelsen denounced as early as his 1920 work *Das problem der Souveränitat und die Theorie des Völkerrechts*. Such a conception runs counter to the tide of development of international law. As Professor Vedel remarked in 1954 during the controversy about ratification of the European Community Defence Treaty, such a conception means that virtually no treaty can be concluded without revising the Constitution which it necessarily affects (see G Vedel, 'Schengen et Maastricht' (1992) 2 *Revue Française de Droit Administratif* 173). Beyond the material conception of sovereignty as 'fullness of power', ie, *summa potestas,* which is not readily compatible with the existence of international law, and beyond the confusion between the ideas of economic independence (if there is any such thing) and legal sovereignty, the holders of this view have a political ambition, which is just as legitimate as the opposite conception, namely, to halt the development of the European Union in its path towards becoming a true federal state. It will be observed that since 1985, the French Constitutional Council has considered that an international commitment would be contrary to the Constitution if it affected the 'essential conditions of exercising national sovereignty (decision of 22 May 1985; see also B Genevois, 'Le traité sur l'Union européenne et la Constitution' (1992) 3 *Revue Française de Droit Administratif* 373).

[42] P-M Dupuy, *Droit international public* 3rd edn (Paris, Sirey, 1995); and see also the valuable analysis by Combacau of the international personality of subjects of domestic law in J Combacau and S Sur, *Droit international public* 3rd edn (Paris, Montchrestien, 1997) 307–18.

This same problem of the importance of the individual in international law will be addressed here but by examining the law of investment and what are termed state contracts. It will be shown that Kelsen's theory of international law accounts for phenomena that many hesitate to categorise as public international law.

Of the areas where the question of changes in international law has been raised in the second half of the twentieth century, that of contracts between states and private persons is probably one of the most controversial.[43] More specifically, this concerns not all the contracts between states and individuals, but only those characterised as state contracts and which for some commentators may be governed by public international law. Other scholars consider this to be impossible because of the nature of international law. They argue that it is strictly interstate law, the legal order of which cannot accommodate individuals.[44]

However, if we examine the points of fact, that is, contract practice and also the provisions contained in some international conventions, individuals do indeed appear in the international legal order, and not only in the connection with the question of human rights (a well-surveyed area) but in that of international investments. This situation which is unthinkable for some commentators, is hardly surprising however if we adopt Kelsen's view of international law.

[43] I cover this issue in detail in 'Retour sur la notion de contrat d'État et sur le droit applicable à celui-ci' in *L'évolution du droit international*. *Mélanges offerts à H. Thierry* (Paris, Pedone, 1998) 247–80 above ch 1 (and see Leben, 'La théorie du contrat d'Etat et l'évolution du droit international des investissements' (2003) 302 *Recueil des Cours de l'Académie de Droit International de La Haye* 201–387.

[44] To mention only a few names from a large selection of references: in favour of possible internationalisation of these contracts, see P Weil, 'Problèmes relatifs aux contrats passés entre un Etat et un particulier' (1969-III) 128 *Recueil des Cours de l'Académie de Droit International de La Haye* 94 and 'Droit international et contrat d'État' in *Mélanges offerts à Paul Reuter* (Paris, Pedone, 1981) 549, and likewise RB Lillich, 'The Law Governing Disputes under Economic Development Agreements: Reexamining in the Concept of Internationalization' in RB Lillich and CN Brower (eds), *International Arbitration in the 21st Century: Towards 'Judicialization' and Uniformity?* (New York, Transnational Publishers, 1994); P Weil, 'Problèmes relatifs aux contrats passés entre un Etat et un particulier', *ibid*, 61. Among the opponents of internationalisation, see F Rigaux, 'Des dieux et des héros—Réflexions sur une sentence arbitrale' (on the TOPCO award) (1978) *Revue Critique de Droit International Privé* 435 and similarly DW Bowett, 'State Contracts with Aliens: Contemporary Developments on Compensation for Termination or Breach' (1988) 59 *British Yearbook of International Law* 49, 51–52. For an all-round study see E Paasivirta, *Participation of State in International Contracts and Arbitral Disputes* (Helsinki, Lakimiesliiton Kustannus,1990).

The Notion of a State Contract

From that, arbitration awards concerning petroleum concessions in the 1950s and 1960s (*Abu Dhabi, Ruler of Qatar; Aramco; Sapphire* awards) and then in the 1970s and 1980s (*TOPCO; Liamco; BP; Aminoil*) and finally from the awards made in the context of the ICSID arbitration centre, it would appear that practice produces contracts which are not contract in national law nor international contracts as are concluded by private persons together. These contracts usually concern investment operations, but Mann, who coined the expression 'state contracts' in 1944, used the term for certain types of loan agreement in which the parties chose international law as a governing law.[45]

In any event, almost all observers agree that not all the contracts between a state and a private person are state contracts in the strict sense of the term. Yet they are hard pressed to provide a purely legal criterion to distinguish them from ordinary contracts concluded by states. For example, state contracts have been defined as 'economic development agreement', but authors have struggled to come up with an objective criterion to indicate from what point of view and under what circumstances an investment agreement (or loan agreement) could be so characterised.

Pierre Mayer seems to be the only commentator to have come up with a strictly legal definition of state contracts, allowing a distinction to be drawn between contracts between states and private persons on the one hand, and *state contracts* in the strict sense of the word on the other. The former are concluded *in the legal order of the state* and with a state as it appears in its legal order, that is, government administration, whereas the latter are concluded by the state as a subject of public international law *in a legal order that is external to it*. The recognition of state contracts *stricto sensu* involves purely legal criteria: existence of an arbitration clause, neutralisation of the normative power of the state by inclusion of stabilisation clauses to state law, if this is applicable, possible integration of the contract in the international treaty and, under certain circumstances, internationalisation of the governing law.[46]

---

[45] FA Mann, 'The Law Governing State Contracts' (1944) 21 *British Yearbook of International Law* 11 et seq text reprinted in *Studies in International Law* (Oxford, Clarendon Press, 1973) 179–210.

[46] P Mayer, 'La neutralisation du pouvoir normatif de l'État' (1986) *Journal du Droit International* 5, 29–39, and see below ch 8.

This genuine discovery of a new category of contracts between the state *as a subject of international law* with a private person (in practice a corporation) did not, however, lead Mayer to consider that the legal order in which this state contract was passed could be the legal order of public international law. Instead, he presents a renewed and, in my view, unconvincing version of the *contrat sans loi* theory, that is, a contract detached from every municipal or international law. His refusal to accept that state contracts in the strict sense can constitute a new category of legal instruments within international law is based on a fairly widespread conception that international law cannot accept individuals as active subjects and, incidentally (for other commentators) that international law cannot deal with certain types of legal relations apprehended by domestic law alone. These postulates were rejected by Kelsen in his earliest writings on international law.

The Possibility of Individuals to be Limited Subjects of International Law

The main argument of who objects to including state contracts in the legal order of public international law is a theoretical one. For Mayer, international law 'has as its sole object relations between constituents of that society: states and the legal entities they form' (international organisations).[47] Similarly, back in 1959, Sereni wrote, 'Each legal system serves the purpose of regulating the status and relations of social entities for which and among which it exists. An attempt at applying international law to private relations would be tantamount to seeking to apply matrimonial laws of France or England to relations between cats and dogs'.[48]

One could retort, of course, that state contracts are not 'private relations', but Sereni's cutting criticism was indeed aimed at discussions about the law governing petroleum concessions. We are confronted here with two irreconcilable conceptions of what international law should be and could be. On the one hand are commentators who consciously or unconsciously profess a dualist vision of relations between domestic law and international law. Thus, in his

[47] *Ibid*, 21.
[48] AP Sereni, 'International Economic Institutions and the Municipal Law of States' (1959-I) 96 *Recueil des Cours de l'Académie de Droit International de La Haye* 133, 210.

1923 lectures at The Hague, Triepel maintained that 'international public law governs relation between states and only between perfectly equal states. . . . The private person, from the point of view of a community of law uniting states as such, cannot be endowed with his own rights and duties, deriving from a legal system of *that* community'.[49]

When lecturing three years later on this same subject, Kelsen asserted on the contrary that the fact that international law applied immediately to states and only mediately to individuals '. . . is not inherent to international law [and] is not a necessary character of its norms . . .'.[50] The demonstration was made still more fully in the 1932 lectures with the same conclusion: 'International law has, as a general rule, states as its subjects, that is to say individuals in a mediate way [ie individuals whose action or inaction will be counted as actions or inactions of the state as a state can only act through individuals]—and exceptionally too individuals in the immediate way. *It is not contrary to the nature of international law that what is today an exception should one day become the rule*'.[51]

In the face of these two theories that are so opposed in their very basics, the legal scholar must observe facts to decide which conceptualisation provides the more accurate account of reality. It is clear for me that it is Kelsen's, for reasons I shall try to outline here.[52]

The starting point is what may be called the revolution of mixed or transnational arbitration proceedings, that is, between a state and a private company. This means of settling disputes, made the mechanism of diplomatic protection, which was for a long time the only means of internationalising a conflict between a foreign company and a host state, obsolete. Through transnational arbitration, any company which invests by contracting with a state knows that it has a legal instrument with which to bring the state before an arbitration panel, that is, independent of that state in order to have a dispute opposing it to that state settled directly. This is not the time nor place to go into the debate about the international character of ad

[49] H Triepel, 'Les rapports entre le droit interne et le droit international' (1923) 1 *Recueil des Cours de l'Académie de Droit International de La Haye* 77, 80 (emphasis in original).

[50] Kelsen, 'Les rapport de système' (n 12) 283–86, citation at 284.

[51] H Kelsen, 'Théorie générale du droit international public. Problèmes choisis' (1932) 42 *Recueil des Cours de l'Académie de Droit International de La Haye* 121, 141–72, citation at 170 (emphasis added).

[52] For more important developments see Leben (n 43).

hoc arbitration tribunals asserted in different awards (*Aramco*, *Topco*, *Liamco* and with some hesitation *Aminoil*) but rejected by some scholars.[53]

Doctrine does recognise, however, the international character of arbitration tribunals set up by an interstate agreement, as with the Iran–US Claims Tribunal on Iran–American disputes and, more especially, ICSID tribunals set up on the basis of the 1965 Washington Convention. This Convention was ratified in August 1997 by 129 countries (out of 142 signatory states) and consecrates the capacity for direct action of investors against host states. This capacity for action is further increased by the considerable development of treaties promoting and protecting investments concluded between capital-exporting states and host states. Such bilateral investment treaties (there are said to be more than 1300 at present [2676 in 2008]) commonly include clauses allowing for cases of alleged breach of obligations subscribed by the host state in the treaty to be brought before ICSID tribunal, even if there is no contractual tie between the state and the investor.

This possibility was confirmed in the case of *AAPL v Sri Lanka* (award of 27 June 1990) where, for the first time in the ICSID, arbitration proceedings were brought not on the basis of an arbitration clause or a compromise, but on the basis of an undertaking made in the treaty protecting investments between the states issuing and accepting the investment.[54] Such actions can only become more common in the future, if it is considered that in 1996 there were 350 bilateral treaties proposing this type of possibility to investors.[55] To this it must be added that certain multilateral treaties contain similar provisions. Thus, the NAFTA Treaty in Chapter 11, Section B: 'settlement of Disputes between between a Party and an Investor of another Party'[56] sets up a procedure giving investors the possibility

[53] Mayer holds that the international character of the arbitration tribunal depends on the law governing the arbitration clause; see Mayer, 'La neutralisation du pouvoir normatif de l'État' (n 46) 32. For Rigaux, on the contrary, only an arbitration court created by treaty can be characterized as international; see F Rigaux, 'Contrats d'État et arbitrage transnational' (1984) *Rivista di Diritto Internazionale* 489, 502.

[54] See (1991) *Fordham International Law Journal* 526–97 and E Gaillard, 'Chronique' (1992) *Journal du Droit International* 216. See also TL Brewer, 'International Investment Dispute Settlement Procedures: The Evolving Regime for Foreign Direct Investment' 'International Investment Dispute Settlement Procedures: The Evolving Regime for Foreign Direct Investment' (1995) 26 *Law and Policy in International Business* 633.

[55] E Gaillard, 'Chronique' (1996) *Journal du Droit International* 274.

[56] (1993) *ILM* 639.

of asking for an arbitration tribunal to be formed under the aegis of the Washington Convention or that of a supplementary mechanism proposed by the ICSID when there is a dispute between states that are not parties to the Convention. For the first time in 1997 two cases were submitted to the ICSID under this section of the NAFTA Treaty. Similar provisions are found in the Energy Charter Treaty,[57] opened for signature in December 1994, and in the Multilateral Agreement on Investment, the text of which should have been adopted in Spring 1998.[58]

Examination shows then that the mechanisms by which investors, private persons, can bring states before international arbitration tribunals are becoming common place. If we now turn to the law applicable to state contracts, a quick survey of a collection of petroleum contracts[59] shows that clauses referring to international law are not hard to find in recent agreements (1987–1995). Wording is frequently found that refers to the law of the country and 'to such rules of international law as may be applicable including rules and principles as have been applied by international tribunals' (Ghana 1988; Pakistan 1990; Nepal 1986; Bulgaria and Poland 1991).

In addition, the Washington Convention of 18 March 1965 creating the ICSID has brought about a revolution in disputes over state contracts by providing in article 42(1) the possibility, under certain circumstances, for public international law to apply. According to this article, 'The Tribunal shall decide a dispute in accordance with such rules of law as may be agreed by the parties'. But, in the absence of such agreement, the Tribunal shall apply the law of the Contracting State party to the dispute (including its rule on the conflict of laws) and such rules of international law as may be applicable'.

This is not the place for exegesis of this article, nor for describing ICSID case law as it applies to international law. However, it can be seen that there is a movement towards international law by several ICSID tribunals, such as the one presided over by Rosalyn Higgins in the case of *Amco Asia v Indonesia* (award of 31 May 1990). After analysing the meaning of 42(1), she stated: 'Thus international law

---

[57] See T Wälde, 'International Investment under the 1994 Energy Charter' (1995) 29 *Journal of World Trade* 5, 47–50.

[58] OECD, *Accord multilatéral sur l'investissement*. Texte consolidé, DAFE/MAI/NM (97)1 'Procedure entre un investisseur et un État' 61–68 (15 September 1997); OECD, *Towards Multilateral Investment Rule* (1996).

[59] The collection of *Basic Oil Laws & Concessions Contracts*, published by the Barrows Company of New York.

is fully applicable and to classify its role as "only" supplemental and corrective" seems a distinction without a difference. In any event, the Tribunal believes that its task to test every claim of law in this case first against Indonesian law, and then against international law'.[60]

If we turn now to the differences opposing an investor and the host state on the basis of a protection treaty alone, it can be seen that in the case of *AAPL v Sri Lanka*, the arbitrators decided, in view of the arguments between the parties, to consider that the provisions of the bilateral conventions were the main source of law in the case in point, given that the convention referred also to other sources of law such as general international law and other conventions.[61] For the NAFTA Treaty and provisions of the settlement of disputes between a party and an investor of another party, article 1131(1) provides that: 'A tribunal established under this Section shall decide the issue in dispute in accordance with this Agreement and applicable rules of international law'.[62]

In the Energy Charter Treaty, article 26(6) on governing law is worded in exactly the same way. As for the OECD Multilateral Agreement on Investment draft, it states that 'Issues in dispute [between an investor and a state] shall be decided in accordance with this Agreement, interpreted and applied in accordance with the applicable rules of international law'.[63]

After looking at these facts we can return to the difference between Triepel and Kelsen regarding the nature of international law and its capacity or incapacity to bestow rights and duties on individuals. Kelsen has already observed, in relation to the question of whether individuals can be direct subjects of international rights that 'individuals can have international rights only if there is an international court before which they can appear as plaintiffs'.[64] Such a situation came about after the First World War when the peace treaties pro-

---

[60] *Amco v Indonesia*, Resubmitted Case, award of 31 May 1990, *ICSID Reports* 1, 569, at 580 no 40. See also the highly controversial use made by the ICSID Tribunal in *SPP (ME) v Arab Republic of Egypt Case*, award of 20 May 1992, *ICSID Reports* 3, 189, Dissenting opinion, at 249–355.

[61] (1992) *Journal du Droit International* 217.

[62] (1993) *ILM* 645.

[63] OECD, *Accord multilatéral sur l'investissement* (n 58) 61–68, point 14 at 66 (English text at 64).

[64] Kelsen, *General Theory of Law* (n 22) 347 and in more detail, *Principles of International Law* (n 10) 124–48.

vided that the subjects of the allied powers could claims reparations in mixed arbitration tribunals.[65] But this situation, which was the exception after 1918, has now become commonplace and Kelsen emphasises in the *Pure Theory of Law* that 'the tendency of [contemporary] international law to lay down direct rules of obligation and authorisation of individuals must necessarily be reinforced to the same degree as it increasingly extends to subjects of areas that were previously governed by state law alone'.[66] In writing these lines, Kelsen was probably not thinking of investment law, but there is no escaping the fact that they apply perfectly to the development of this law. It is also worth recalling Kelsen's position expressed above[67] that it is possible to consider a subject of international law any *person capable of entering into dispute directly with another subject of international law as such and, possibly, of bringing that subject before an international court* (provided consent is given in one form or another). From these premises it can be understood how the change which has come about with state contracts means that the individual can be considered as a (limited) subject of international law. But if we look closely, it is in fact in the entire field of international investment law that individuals benefit increasingly, through bilateral or multilateral treaties, from the privilege of bringing actions against states directly, and thus obtain the same status as subjects of international law.

---

[65] *General Theory of Law, ibid*, see the examples at 347–48. On this point Lauterpacht shared Kelsen's opinions and they may both be considered as representatives of the Grotian tradition of international law. Thus, in the paper 'The Subjects of the Law of Nations' (1947) 63 *Law Quarterly Review* 438 and (1948) 64 *Law Quarterly Review* 97, Lauterparcht sets out to show that 'The doctrine that States are only subjects of international law is not an accurate statement of the actual legal position' (1947, at 439). He first shows that the individual can have procedural capacity in international law. There is no principle in international law, he comments, which 'prevents States, if they so wish, from securing to individuals . . . access to international courts and tribunals' (1947, at 451). He demonstrates this, just as Kelsen did, by the example of the courts provided for under arts 297 and 304(b)(2) of the Treaty of Versailles and of the corresponding provisions of the other peace treaties (at 452). He goes on to show that 'There is no rule of international law which precludes individuals . . . from acquiring directly rights under customary or conventional law . . .'(1948, at 112) and that 'Similar considerations apply the question of subjects of duties imposed by international law' in particular in the field of international criminal liability (1948, at 112–13).

[66] H Kelsen, *Pure Theory of Law* 2nd edn, trans M Knight (Berkeley, University of California Press, 1967) 327 (emphasis added).

[67] See text above at n 51.

Under these circumstances, there is no reason other than dogma for continuing to refuse to face up to the reality of modern international law, namely that by means totally different from those used in the field of human rights,[68] private persons have acquired in the legal institution of state contracts, and more generally in the field of investment law (limited) international legal personality by dint of their capacity to act directly against the state for the defence of their rights and to do so in international courts.

It can be seen once more that Kelsen's theoretical positions both anticipated the change in international law during the course of half a century and provided the theoretical framework within which to account for the current state of law as well as to offer a cautious glimpse of its future advances.

---

[68] The comparison between the two fields of investment law and human right is also made by G Burdeau, 'Nouvelles perspectives pour l'arbitrage dans le contentieux économique intéressant les États' (1995) *Revue de l'Arbitrage* 3, 16, and by Lillich, 'The Law Governing Disputes under Economic Development Agreements' (n 44) 67–68.

6

The Notion of *Civitas Maxima* in Kelsen's Work*

THOSE WHO HAVE worked on Kelsen's first course of lectures at the Hague Academy of International Law on the systemic relations between domestic law and public international law[1] may have been struck by the number of references it makes to the *civitas maxima*, a notion Kelsen borrowed openly from Christian Wolff, one of the masters of the school of the Law of Nature and Nations. They will probably also have been taken aback by the very emphatic way Kelsen ends his course, as he makes an appeal of sorts to '[t]ransform the international community, which is still hardly evolved to date, into a *civitas maxima* in the full meaning of the word'. Kelsen added as the final sentence of his course: 'And it is this organisation of the world into a universal state that should be the ultimate, though still distant goal, of all political endeavour'.[2]

The idealist aspect of this appeal, its moralising character even—since it all ends a paragraph 54 entitled 'The moral superiority of legal objectivism', which is nothing other than the moral superiority of pacifism over imperialism[3] intrigued me and I had long intended to try to look into what, to my mind, was this rather surprising aspect of Kelsen. Carlos Herrera gives me the opportunity to do so here; but I must say from the outset that in his own *Théorie juridique et politique chez Hans Kelsen*, Herrera provides significant information

---

* First published as 'La notion de *civitas maxima* chez Kelsen' in CM Herrera (ed), *Actualité de Kelsen en France* (Paris, LGDJ, 2001).

[1] H Kelsen, 'Les rapports de système entre le droit interne et le droit international public' (1926) 14 *Recueil des Cours de l'Académie de Droit International de La Haye* 231.

[2] Kelsen, 'Les rapports de système', *ibid*, 326.

[3] *Ibid*, 323, 325

about the philosophical and political background to Kelsen's conception of *civitas maxima*.[4] My own contribution, then, can be but a modest one. I shall try simply to present the way I have understood the conception of *civitas maxima* in Kelsen's works such as he uses it in his 1926 Hague course of lectures and above all in his first major work of international law, which dates from 1920, *Das Problem der Souveränität und die Theorie des Völkerrechts. Beitrag zu einer reinen Rechtslehrer.*[5]

I should add before beginning that although the notion of *civitas maxima* is very much present in that work—in which there is a whole chapter (chapter nine) on it—and the influence of Wolff is so strong that the book opens with a quotation from that philosopher and disciple of Leibniz (*Paradoxum hoc videbitur iis, qui nexum veritatum non prospiciunt et ex factis jura aestimant*),[6] unless I am mistaken, Kelsen made no further mention of *civitas maxima* or of Wolff in any of his later writings. That too intrigued me, and what I would like to lay before you now are the very provisional conclusions of a very brief enquiry.

So, in reading Kelsen's 1920 and 1926 writings, it seemed to me that his reference to Wolff and his idea of *civitas maxima* addressed three concerns: (1) founding the primacy of international law; (2) presenting a theory of legal orders for which there is no difference in kind between state legal orders and the international legal order; and (3) asserting the existence and unity of a universal legal order, the expression of humankind that will one day overcome its divisions in a pacified universal state.

---

[4] CM Herrera, *Théorie juridique et politique chez Hans Kelsen* (Paris, Kimé, 1997) 55ff, 242ff.

[5] H Kelsen, *Das Problem der Souveränität und die Theorie des Völkerrechts. Beitrag zu einer reinen Rechtslehrer* (Tübingen, Verlag von JCB Mohr (Paul Siebeck), 1920). I consulted the Italian translation by A Carrino, *Il problema della sovranità e la teoria del diritto internazionale. Contributo per una dottrina pura del diritto* (Milan, Giuffrè, 1989). I also benefited from a translation of ch IX of that work by G Carducci, for which I am grateful to him. References here are to the German work and its Italian translation.

[6] 'This may seem paradoxical to those who fail to see the connection between truths and who judge laws from facts'. *Prolégomènes du Jus Gentium Methodo Scientifica Perptractum* para 13 (Oxford, Classics of International Law, Carnegie Endowment, Clarendon Press, 1934) vol 1 Latin text, vol 2 English trans J Drake. Wolff's proposal, which he expects some to find paradoxical, is that in the *civitas maxima*, nations as collectivities are allowed to constrain individual nations that refuse to perform their obligations or that are remiss in such performance.

Civitas Maxima *and the Primacy Of International Law*

Kelsen asserts from the beginning of paragraph 53 ('Universal legal order and universal state') of his book on sovereignty that 'the philosopher [Wolff] is the first to have recognised and asserted the primacy of the international legal order in terms of a pure theory of law'.[7]

To understand this assertion, it should be recalled very briefly and schematically[8] that Wolff, very classically for the time, distinguishes between a natural law of nations that is 'quite unchanging; and no nation can free itself from the obligations arising from it' and a positive law of nations.[9] But the latter is itself subdivided into three: a customary law of nations, a conventional law of nations made up of the undertakings of states that enter into treaties and—and this is the most important point for us here—a 'voluntary law of nations'; an 'infelicitous term' as Kelsen observed,[10] for it seems to say something other than what Wolff meant by it.

This voluntary law of nations was initially the natural law of the 'great society' that states form among themselves. Wolff wrote:

One considers the different nations as so many free persons living in the state of nature and who are bound to fulfil, both towards themselves and towards others, the same duties as the law of nature imposes on individuals. It is therefore natural law that must serve as the rule to their conduct.[11]

The comparison between the state of nature that supposedly existed for individuals and the one supposedly existing for states goes back at least to Hobbes.[12] But while Hobbes draws from it an

---

[7] Kelsen, *Das Problem der Souveränität* (n 5) 249 German edn, 366 Italian translation.

[8] On Wolff's thought, see E Jouannet, *Emer de Vattel et l'émergence doctrinale du droit international classique* (Paris, Pedone, 1998) 86–104. My thanks to E Jouannet for sharing some of her knowledge of the school of the law of nature and nations in general and of Wolff and Vattel in particular. Also on Wolff, see L Olive, 'Christian Wolff' in A Pillet (ed), *Les fondateurs du droit international* (Paris, Giard & Brière, 1904) 447.

[9] See C Wolff, *Principes du droit de la nature et des gens*, edn summarised by JH Samuel Formey (Amsterdam, 1758) 3 vols reprinted in *Bibliothèque de philosophie politique et juridique* (Caen, 1988) vol 3, 258; Jouannet, *Emer de Vattel* (n 8) 86.

[10] Kelsen, *Das Problem der Souveränität* (n 5) 251 German edn, 369 Italian trans.

[11] Wolff, *Principes du droit de la nature et des gens* (n 9) vol 3, 257.

[12] 'But though there had never been anytime, wherein particular men were in a condition of war one against another; yet in all times, Kings and persons of sovereign authority, because of their independency, are in continual jealousies, and in the state of posture of gladiators; having their weapons pointing, and their eyes fixed on one another' *Léviathan*, (London, Cosimo Classics, 2009) 71.

explanation for the state of permanent war among nations, Wolff derives from it a category of law, the voluntary law of nations. This is the law necessary to maintain peace among nations that form among themselves a great city, a great republic, or a great state, depending on how one wants to translate the expression *civitas maxima*. Wolff writes:

> Nations, like individuals, are bound to act in concert and to join their forces to work for their common perfection. It is a social bond that nature itself has made between them and from which results a body that might be called the great city (*civitas maxima*). The members or citizens of this body are the various nations.[13]

There are at least two original features in this construction. First, the *civitas maxima* for Wolff is a hypothetical construction, a fiction. Further on, Wolff states: 'By continuing the same fiction, one discovers the origin of a universal empire, or of all the nations together . . .'.

Secondly, although it is derived from natural law, the law governing the *civitas maxima* is not the same as natural law. In any city, in any state, natural law combines with a civil law that is the positive law laid down by the city's lawgiver for its specific needs. The same is true of the society of states. Only, for this society, one must imagine a hypothetical legislator making laws that take account of the purpose, says Wolff:

> [T]he purpose for which nature itself has established the great city, in the same way as it has established society among men, with the result that nations are bound to consent to this law, and it is not for their free will to choose whether or not they wish to accept it.[14]

This leads to what Wolff calls the voluntary rights of nations that can be discovered by reason as the law allowing nations 'to act in concert and to join their forces to work for their common perfection'. This law *inter gentes* therefore has 'some relation to civil law [but at the same time] is not separate in all respects from natural law, nor does not follow it in all things'.[15]

---

[13] Wolff, *Principes du droit de la nature et des gens* (n 9) vol 3, 259.

[14] The *jus gentium volontarium* is a set of legal norms that must be deduced 'ex fine civitatis maximae, quam perinde ac societatem inter homines instituit ipas natura, ut in jus istud consentire debeant gentes, non vero libertati earum relictum sit, utrum consentire malint aut nolint'. Wolff, *Jus Gentium* (n 6) 6.

[15] Preface to *Institutions du droit de la nature et des gens*, p XLI, cited by Jouannet, *Emer de Vattel* (n 8) 97.

This law is said to be 'voluntary' since it is inconceivable that nations might not subscribe to it. In this way, for example, it must be considered this society of nations is strictly egalitarian since:

[T]here is among nations a perfect equality of duties and rights, because there is a perfect equality of nature. None among them is entitled to claim prerogatives, precedence or other advantages for itself. None of them has any right over the actions of any other; freedom belongs to all of them and the exercise of that freedom cannot be interfered with.[16]

This voluntary law of nations therefore essentially contains obligations requiring each state to respect the sovereignty of others and all the specific rules that follow from this general principle.

That, then, is a very brief outline of Wolff's construction. It must be asked why it held such sway over the Kelsen of the 1920s. I think there are four reasons, all of which relate to the idea of the superiority of international law, the law of a universal legal community.

Kelsen praises Wolff for having been the first person to recognise and assert the primacy of the international legal order over the specific legal orders of states. He adds:

The legal hypothesis that the norms of international law form a universal legal order above the partial legal orders of individual states, a legal order that apprehends all of them (in itself) is identified . . . with the hypothesis of a universal community that is above individual states, a community that apprehends (in itself) all states. This community being fundamentally of the same nature as the different states may be defined as a personification of the world or universal legal order, as a world or universal state, as the *civitas maxima*.[17]

The second reason is the hypothetical character of the *civitas maxima* in Wolff's writings. For it is very clear for Wolff that this city, the *civitas maxima* and its super lawgiver do not actually exist and would even be harmful to states if they were real. They are but fictions for rationally working out the contents of the voluntary law of nations. So for some commentators like Haggenmacher, the *civitas maxima* 'comes down to a scientific hypothesis, comparable to Kelsen's *Grundnorm*'.[18]

---

[16] Wolff, *Principes du droit de la nature et des gens* (n 9) vol 3, 258, para 2. However, Wolff characterises the perfect equality of nations among each other as 'necessary law of nations', which is a more 'felicitous' term, to pick up on Kelsen's expression (n 5).

[17] Kelsen, *Das Problem der Souveränität* (n 5) 249 German edn, 367 Italian trans.

[18] P Haggenmacher, 'La naissance du sujet de droit international' (1992) 16 *Droits* 12, fn 1. This interpretation is contested by Jouannet, *Emer de Vattel* (n 8) 100, fn 409.

In any event, in his book on sovereignty, Kelsen emphasised the 'contribution of genius' from Wolff, who was the first to understand 'the logical necessity to found all positive law on a legal hypothesis'[19] and who therefore understood also that 'international law, like any law, requires a higher community among all those who live pursuant to such law, a legal community above the free will of the various subjects (of law)'. And he added that 'Wolff first had recognised this is a postulate of international law'.[20]

Kelsen's infatuation with Wolff went so far as to absolve him of any sin of jusnaturalism! While the 'jusnaturalist' character of the foundation of international law in the German jurist-philosopher's presentation 'cannot and should not be denied', Kelsen added immediately that:

[I]nasmuch as this 'jusnaturalist' foundation is limited only, as a legal hypothesis, to making possible a legal order among coordinated subjects—a legal order that, filled with content and perfected by a positive regulation must be presupposed as sovereign—no particular order can be without such a jusnaturalist foundation . . . [and] it is not contradictory for Wolff to found positive international law on a legal community *quam instituit ipsa natura* . . .[21]

Perhaps this is what gave arguments to Kelsen's detractors, like Ross, who argued that the notion of fundamental hypothetical norm is but a hangover from natural law philosophy and that the author of the *Pure Theory of Law* was just a pseudo-positivist.[22] Others have distinguished in Kelsen a (criticised) material jusnaturalism and a (legitimate) formal jusnaturalism, similar, it seems to me, to what Kelsen discovered in Wolff.[23]

But the third reason Kelsen was attracted to Wolff's presentation of international law was precisely that, by starting from the legal

---

[19] Kelsen, *Das Problem der Souveränität* (n 5) 255 German edn, 375 Italian trans.

[20] *Ibid*, German edn, 374 Italian trans. In fact, this is a quote from Kaltenborn, approved by Kelsen, but who criticises him for not accepting the consequences of this conception, namely the elimination of the dogma of sovereignty.

[21] Kelsen, *ibid*, 252 German edn, 371 Italian trans.

[22] A Ross, 'Validity and the Conflict between Legal Positivism and Natural Law' in S Paulson and BL Paulson, *Normativity and Norms: Critical Perspectives on Kelsenian Themes* (Oxford, Clarendon Press, 1998) 160. See also the excerpt from a paper by Ross given in C Grzegorczyk, F Michaut and M Troper, *Le positivisme juridique* (Paris, LGDJ, 1992) 204.

[23] See the analyses by A Carrino, 'Le positivism critique de Kelsen: une fondation logico-formelle des normes' (1991) 20 *Cahiers de Philosophie Politique et Juridique* 79, 85.

hypothesis of the *civitas maxima*, it led to an assertion of the existence of 'a legal community in which the freedom of subjects (states) is limited by their fundamental legal equality'.[24] Thus, 'the *civitas maxima* characterises both the legal equality of subjects in that they are subjected to the same extent to a legal order and their condition as legally bound subjects'.[25]

Similarly Wolff wrote about the *civitas maxima* as already quoted:

By virtue of this necessary law of nations, there is among nations a perfect equality of duties and rights, because there is a perfect equality of nature. None among them is entitled to claim prerogatives, precedence or other advantages for itself. None of them has any right over the actions of any other; freedom belongs to all of them and the exercise of that freedom cannot be interfered with.[26]

The fourth reason, finally, is that the conception of the *civitas maxima* and of the voluntary law of nations arising from it is quite independent of any recognition by states. It has been seen that the *civitas maxima* was simply a necessary fiction to discover the rules derived from natural law and adapted to the characteristics of the society of states. States cannot be presumed not to have accepted these rules. Similarly, concluding his 1926 course and summarising his arguments, Kelsen writes that 'by eliminating the dogma of state sovereignty [a point we shall return to], it shall be established that there is a universal legal order, independently of any recognition and above the states, a *civitas maxima*'.[27]

Civitas Maxima and Kelsen's Conception of Legal Orders

The conception of international law as the law of a *civitas maxima* that Kelsen finds in Wolff means Kelsen can see in the eighteenth-century legal philosopher a precursor of his own conception of legal orders. Kelsen sees no divide between the state and its legal order. The state is nothing other than the personification of a legal order, such that one may speak indifferently of state or legal order. In that, there is something akin to Spinoza's *Deus sive natura*, a sort of *ordo juris sive civitas*. So once it is admitted that there is such a thing as

[24] Kelsen, *Das Problem der Souveränität* (n 5) 252 German edn, 370 Italian trans.
[25] *Ibid.*
[26] Wolff, *Principes du droit de la nature et des gens* (n 9) vol 3, 258, para 2.
[27] Kelsen, *Les rapports de système* (n 1) 326.

international law, which naturally Kelsen, like Wolff, does, that law is the law of a legal community that Wolff names the *civitas maxima* and that may, correctly, be termed the state by Kelsen, for 'any supreme legal order, even the most primitive of them in critical terms, may be called state'.[28]

And in his book on sovereignty already cited (above note 5), Kelsen underscores that the universal community 'being fundamentally of the same nature as the various states, may be defined as a personification of the world or universal legal order, as a world or universal state, as *civitas maxima*'.[29]

These assertions may in turn be compared with this passage from Wolff's *Principes du droit de la nature et des gens*:

> By continuing the same fiction [that is, that of the great city whose members . . . are the different nations], one discovers the origin of a universal empire, or of all the nations taken together, which is based on the universal right they have to settle the determination of the actions of each of them in particular, so as to contribute to the common salvation and to constrain even those who would like to elude it to comply with this obligation.[30]

The law of the *civitas maxima*, therefore, for Wolff, is far above the law of states, that is, far above the partial legal order, to use Kelsen's terms. The voluntary law of nations of this *civitas maxima* is,

> deduced from the purpose for which nature itself has established the great city, in the same way as it has established society among men, with the result that nations are bound to consent to this law, and it is not for their free will to chose whether or not they wish to accept it.[31]

If need be, Wolff contemplates even compelling those nations that might seek to elude it.[32]

This dependence of states in respect of international law implies, for Kelsen—and this is the important point for him—that sovereignty can be attributed only to international law, which alone is not dependent on any other law superior to it. Thus he writes:

---

[28] Kelsen, *Les rapports de système* (n 1) 319.

[29] Kelsen, *Das Problem der Souveränität* (n 5) 249 German edn, 367 Italian trans.

[30] Wolff, *Principes du droit de la nature et des gens* (n 9) vol 3, 259 para 6 and see (n 4).

[31] Wolff, *ibid*, para 2.

[32] See Wolff, *Jus Gentium* (n 6) para 13. However, as *civitas maxima* is only a fiction, it is hard to see how it could compel reluctant states. See Jouannet, *Emer de Vattel* (n 8) 96–100.

[I]f one thinks the essence of the legal order named 'state' consists . . . in its property of being the supreme, sovereign order; it is necessary then to apply this denomination . . . to the personification of the universal higher legal order, the only one that can henceforth be considered sovereign.[33]

Kelsen adds that 'This is nothing else than the legal meaning of Wolff's theory of *civitas maxima*'. And this point—that is, the transposition of the sovereignty of states to the universal legal order personified by the *civitas maxima*—is indeed capital since, as Kelsen was to emphasise in the first edition of his *Pure Theory of Law*, 'The theoretical dissolution of the dogma of sovereignty . . . is one of the most substantial achievements of the Pure Theory of Law'.[34] Indeed it is the whole question of the 1920 book on the problem of sovereignty and the theory of international law.

However, can we speak of state when personifying the international legal order in the same way we speak of state to personify national legal orders? Kelsen claims that, from the standpoint of legal science, this is quite legitimate. Thus, in his 1920 writings he specifies that legal knowledge 'can grasp the state only as a personification of the legal order, the exclusive object of legal science'.[35]

And that is the essential point that entitles us to call the personification of any legal order a 'state'. Admittedly it is always possible to reserve the name 'state' for a single category of legal orders, those 'that confer the application of sanctions to specialised organs'. That is acceptable terminology provided, Kelsen warns 'that one does not lose sight of the fact that between a primitive law, such as international law still is today, and a technically more developed legal order, that is characterised as state *stricto sensu*, there is a difference of degree and not of kind'.[36]

Kelsen, though, does not settle for asserting there is only a difference of degree between the state *stricto sensu* and the state *largo sensu* so to speak. He asserts that at the end of a development of international society, the state *largo sensu* may join ranks with the state *stricto sensu*. However, Kelsen's writings on this matter are not unequivocal.

---

[33] Kelsen, *Das Problem der Souveränität* (n 5) 259 German edn, 368 Italian trans.

[34] BL Paulson and S Paulson, *Kelsen, Introduction to the Problems of Legal Theory* (Oxford, Clarendon Press, 1992) trans of *Reine Rechtslehre* (Vienna, Franz Deuticke, 1934) 124.

[35] Kelsen, *Das Problem der Souveränität* (n 5) 259 German edn, 367 Italian trans.

[36] *Ibid*.

The World State: Cognitive Postulate or *State Stricto Sensu*?

While Kelsen abandoned, it seems, all reference to the *civitas maxima* and to Wolff after 1926, throughout his works he reasserted his belief in the possible advent of a world state.

His early writings (those of the 1920s) are very explicit. His 1926 course of lectures states in several places that 'there is nothing to stop a development that would make the international legal order, that is currently still very primitive, a perfect order of the international community, a true state [that is, *stricto sensu*]'.[37]

If we turn now to what Kelsen wrote in his advanced years, the following passage is to be found in the final edition of his *Pure Theory of Law*: 'as the ultimate goal of the legal development directed toward increasing centralization, appears the organizational unity of a universal legal community, that is, the emergence of a world state'.[38]

It would seem, then, that the *civitas maxima* could truly become a world state or, as Wolff put it, a 'universal empire'. But while for Wolff the 'universal empire' and the *civitas maxima* remained and were to remain fictions, Kelsen for his part seems to contemplate a historical evolution, which, through the centralisation of legal orders, would lead to the advent of a truly universal state.[39]

However, while Kelsen constantly and repeatedly took positions on the question of a 'world state', those positions were not entirely unambiguous. In his early thinking, the world state was merely the personification of the unity of the universal legal order. In his 1926 course, Kelsen noted that 'by eliminating the dogma of state sovereignty, it shall be established there is a universal legal order, independently of any recognition and above the states, a *civitas maxima*'.[40]

This universal legal order is apprehended by theory as the union of the state orders and the international order. From the standpoint of legal science, it allows us to conceive of a specific personification corresponding to this universal order.

In the second edition of his *Pure Theory*, Kelsen again asserts: 'so that the ultimate goal of the legal development directed toward

---

[37] Kelsen, *Les rapports de système* (n 1) 318 and see also 319.
[38] H Kelsen, *Pure Theory of Law* trans M Knight (Berkeley, University of California Press, 1967) 328.
[39] Herrera, *Théorie juridique et politique chez Hans Kelsen* (n 4) 58–61.
[40] Kelsen, *Les rapports de système* (n 1) 326.

increasing centralization, appears [to be] the organizational unity of a universal legal community, that is, the emergence of a world state'.[41]

However—and this is capital in Kelsen's thought—international law is not doomed to remain for ever at the same level of decentralisation and so of 'primitivism'. International law advances in its techniques, new subjects arise, such as interstate organisations but also individuals,[42] and courts are established, including at a universal level [and there is now an international criminal court alongside the existing International Court of Justice and the Tribunal For the Law of the Sea]. To which must be added the advance in the jurisdictionalisation in international organisations, the most striking example of which is the World Trade Organization.[43]

This type of transformation, Kelsen notes in the second edition of the *Pure Theory of Law*,

> has—in the last analysis—the tendency to blur the border line between international and national law, so that as the ultimate goal of the legal development directed toward increasing centralization, appears [to be] the organizational unity of a universal legal community, that is, the emergence of a world state.[44]

But is this truly a state *stricto sensu*? There is a certain ambiguity here that, it seems to me, has never been dissipated. For example, in his 1920 work on sovereignty, Kelsen is the voice-piece of scholars, particularly Oppenheim and Lasson, who oppose the idea of a universal state.[45] He quotes Lasson:

> A legal order having force of constraint would be a state, and the states that submit themselves to it are not states but subjects. In place and stead of the great number of states there would be then a universal state, which neither can nor should come to be. With it all freedom would vanish from the Earth and humankind would have nothing left apart from common rot and decomposition in the equal ruin of all.

---

[41] Kelsen, *Pure Theory of Law* (n 38) 328.

[42] From the beginning, Kelsen maintained that international law could lay down direct rules of obligation and authorisation for individuals. See Kelsen, *Les rapports de système* (n 1) 283–86; H Kelsen, 'Théorie générale du droit international public. Problèmes choisis' (1932) 42 *Recueil des Cours de l'Académie de Droit de la Haye* 141–72; Kelsen, *Pure Theory of Law* (n 38) 328.

[43] See H Ruiz-Fabri, 'Le règlement des différends dans le cadre de l'organisation mondiale du commerce' (1997) 3 *Journal du Droit International* 709.

[44] Kelsen, *Pure Theory of Law* (n 38) 328.

[45] Kelsen, *Das Problem der Souveränität* (n 5) 274 German edn, 401 Italian trans.

Kelsen's response is odd and oddly overblown even, since he says it is a matter of 'preventing a serious profanation of legal science [and] ensuring its purity and honour'.[46] He argues that,

the international legal order may also become an 'organised' community, a 'state' in the full meaning of the term, without in any way threatening its nature. It would not become in this way anything essentially different from what it already is, insofar as the idea of its primacy is shared.[47]

Is Kelsen speaking here of the state *stricto sensu*? One may wonder, for if so, I fail to see how we can escape Lasson's argument which perfectly describes the transition from several sovereign states to a single state, federal or otherwise, encompassing them and making them disappear. And should this phenomenon spread to all states, there would indeed be formed a universal state, *stricto sensu*, and the disappearance not just of the former states but also of international law itself, which can only be conceived of among sovereign states. In its place there would be nothing but the domestic law of the world state.

That is a terrifying prospect for the commentators he cites (Oppenheim and Lasson). However, it seems Kelsen sees it on the contrary as progress for humanity. In this 1926 course, he notes:

The legal unity of humanity, whose more or less arbitrary division into states is but provisional, the organisation of the world into a *civitas maxima*: such is the political kernel of the hypothesis of the primacy of international law; but such is at the same time the basic idea of pacifism as the antithesis of imperialism . . .[48]

And the entire passage ends with the sentence cited at the beginning of this chapter: 'And it is this organisation of the world into a universal state that should be the ultimate, though still distant goal, of all political endeavour'. Which echoes the passage from the second edition of the *Pure Theory of Law*: 'as the ultimate goal of the legal development directed toward increasing centralization, appears [to be] the organizational unity of a universal legal community, that is, the emergence of a world state'.[49]

---

[46] *Ibid*, 274 German edn, 402 Italian trans. It is likely that Kelsen ironises here on the emphatic style of German doctrine of his time and especially of Lasson, whom he had just quoted. I am grateful to Professor O Pfersmann for his explanations on this point.
[47] Kelsen, *Das Problem der Souveränität* (n 5) 274 German edn, 402 Italian trans.
[48] Kelsen, *Les rapports de système* (n 1) 325–26.
[49] Kelsen, *Pure Theory of Law* (n 38) 328.

From all these passages, I find it difficult to tell whether Kelsen meant by this expression what elsewhere he calls a state *stricto sensu*, or whether he is still referring to the personification of a world legal order, admittedly a more centralised—less 'primitive' one—than that known until now, but one that would not see the disappearance for all that of existing states, that is, states *stricto sensu*. It seems to me Herrera opts for the first hypothesis in his book.[50] Personally, I lean rather towards the second hypothesis. If we remember that, for Kelsen, states *stricto sensu* are themselves merely 'relatively centralised' legal orders within which the centralisation and decentralisation of norms is organised, it is not aberrant to think that—except in, say, a thousand years—the world state will be just the personalisation of a more centralised legal order, for example, something not too far removed from what the European Community was until the 1980s. Something, then, giving greater scope to an efficacious system of dispute settlement among states, as Kelsen continually advocated.[51]

Conclusion

Here are a few observations to conclude. Kelsen's abandoning of any reference to the *civitas maxima, expressis verbis*, and to Wolff may be explained by the criticism levelled at Kelsen by contemporary German doctrine.

For the world state, it would be interesting to sketch out a comparison between Kelsen and Kojève, who in his *Esquisse d'une phénoménologie du droit*,[52] develops a theory of international law as potential law in the process of its realisation. He too announces the advent of a universal society with the nature of a state *stricto sensu*. He concludes with the observation that 'We can say, then, that if public international law tends to actualise itself, it can do so only by becoming a *federal law*, that is, "public" *domestic* law, that is, the "constitutional" and "administrative" law of a federated state'.[53] And he goes on: 'law in act can be "public" only by not being "international" and "international" only by not being "public". International public law exists in act only as the domestic public law of a federated state'.[54]

[50] Herrera, *Théorie juridique et politique chez Hans Kelsen* (n 4) 56–61 and the reference to Scarpelli at 57, fn 1.
[51] See C Tournaye, *Kelsen et la sécurité collective* (Paris, LGDJ, 1995).
[52] A Kojève, *Esquisse d'une phénoménologie du droit* (Paris, Gallimard, 1981).
[53] *Ibid*, 389.
[54] *Ibid*, 389, fn 2.

In other words, as part of the historical development that, Kojève claims, will see the federation propagate to encompass the whole of humankind,[55] public international law 'tends to suppress itself insofar as being international'.[56] The comparison is tempting, but that must be for some other time.

---

[55] *Ibid*, 391.
[56] *Ibid*, 392.

7

International Courts in an Interstate Society*

THE FEW PAGES that follow about what may well be the most prized topic of twentieth-century international doctrine can present but some succinct thoughts on what I feel is the crux of the problem posed by the international judicial function: what should be the place of international courts as organs for applying and interpreting law among states?[1] It is a question here of examining international society in its primal 'nakedness', that is, in as much as it constitutes (and, despite the advances in institutionalisation in the twentieth century, it still does constitute) an anarchic order in which sovereign states are not subject to any Legislator, any Executive, or any Judiciary.[2] The courts in question will, therefore, be the two courts of universal vocation (the Permanent Court of International Justice (PCIJ) and the International Court of Justice ICJ)) and the interstate arbitration tribunals.[3]

The answer to this question has invariably fluctuated with time and commentators between radical scepticism verging on nihilism and sometimes disarmingly candid optimism. The 'temperature' of Western doctrine is currently approaching moderate scepticism, while doctrine closer to the Third World seems eager once again to take up the torch of international 'judicial activism' that had been

---

* First published as 'La jurisdiction internationale', (1989) 9 *Driot* 143.

[1] See Société Française pour le Droit International, *La juridiction internationale permanente* (Paris, Pedone, 1987); M Virally, 'Le champ opératoire du règlement judiciaire international' (1983) 2 *Revue Générale de Droit International Public* 281; J Verhoeven, 'A propos de la fonction de juger en droit international public' in P Gérard et al (eds), *Fonction de juger et pouvoir judiciaire. Transformations et déplacements* (Brussels, FUSL, 1983).

[2] H Bull, *The Anarchical Society. A Study of Order in World Politics* 2nd edn (New York, Columbia University Press, 1995).

[3] This paper was written at a time of crisis for the ICJ from which it emerged in the 1990s. The International Criminal Court did not exist at the time of writing.

defended by many European scholars when the Society of Nations was founded.[4] The argument here will not be part of the familiar exercise of situating the truth halfway between two extreme opinions. It will be maintained that the existence of international courts and tribunals is not a mere attempt to acclimatise, within a hostile legal system, a form of application and interpretation of the law that is specific to municipal systems. The existence of international courts and tribunals is on the contrary the telltale sign that interstate society constitutes a true legal order. But it is an anarchic order. The contribution of international courts and tribunals to the advancement of this legal order and to the development of international law can only be made under the highly restrictive conditions of a decentralised society. Anything more would involve overcoming anarchy, which is something that the international judiciary is unable to do.

The Decisive Criterion for the Existence of an International Legal Order

That there might genuinely be law in the relations among sovereign states, that is, something that looks sufficiently like what is found within state societies, is an idea that comes up against so many obstacles that many commentators have dismissed it. More especially, if, as Austin does, we view law as a system of commands matched with sanctions, the normative element governing interstate relations cannot be the normativity of law but something else that has to do with morality or mores. I have always felt this view was misguided. Anthropolgy, like legal theory, allows law to be thought of as something other than simply an injunction sanctioned by a sovereign.[5]

Law as a System of Justiciable Rules

People are often surprised at the importance international law writings ascribe to arbitration awards or decisions of the ICJ, which are both modest in number and restricted in their legal scope to the resolution of specific disputes between parties. Some have seen in

---

[4] Compare opinions expressed at the conference on *La juridiction internationale permanente* (n 1) with those of E McWhinney, *United Nations Law Making: Cultural and Ideological Relativism and International Law Making for an Era of Transition* (Paris, Unesco; New York, Holmes and Meier, 1984).

[5] C Leben, *Les sanctions privatives de droits ou de qualité dans les organisations internationales spécialisées* (Brussels, Bruylant, 1979) 35–69.

this an oddity of academics imbued with municipal law and used to granting pride of place to case law and commenting on it.[6] Yet it is evident that the thinly strewn decisions, rendered haphazardly depending on the good will of a few states and on a small number of issues, by courts and tribunals that together form no structured system, cannot yield any homogenous case law having comparable authority to that of municipal law. If, then, we doff our professorial spectacles and observe the real world of international relations as governments do as they go about their business, the function of international courts and tribunals, for some commentators, can only be assigned a minor role both as a means of settling disputes (one among others and the least used)[7] and as a privileged instrument for the affirmation and development of law.

It appears though to many observers that beyond the binding effect of a judgment on the parties that they have, the decisions of international courts exert considerable influence on the development of international law. The paradox of the disproportion between the activity of international courts, which is ever so slight, and the attention paid to it, and in practice not just by legal scholars but also by the actors in international society, can only be explained if we perceive the specific role played by courts in constituting a legal order. For this, we must discard the Austinian approach to law (even in Kelsen's more complex presentation of it) and analyse the phenomenon of law as a system of interpersonal relations that may, in the event of dispute, be the subject matter of a decision by a third party invested with special authority. It is this very special quality of rules of law in being *justiciable*, that is, of being at least potentially liable to be the subject matter of a judgement by a third party, that constitutes their legal character.

This thesis, systematically defended by Kantorowicz and Kojève, can also be associated with Hart's conception of the legal order as developed in *The Concept of Law*.[8] For Hart, any legal order is made up of the union of a set of 'primary' rules with a set of 'secondary'

---

[6] See L Condorelli, 'L'autorité de la décision des juridictions internationales permanentes' in *La juridiction internationale permanente* (n 1) 288.

[7] See the list in United Nations Charter art 33(1): negotiation, enquiry, mediation, conciliation, arbitration, judicial settlement, resort to regional agencies or arrangements, or other peaceful means of their own choice.

[8] H Kantorowicz, *The Definition of Law* (Cambridge, Cambridge University Press, 1958) 79; A Kojève, *Esquisse d'une phénoménologie du droit* (Paris, Gallimard, 1981); HLA Hart, *The Concept of Law* 5th edn (Oxford, Clarendon Press, 1970) 77ff; see also J Carbonnier, *Sociologie juridique* (Paris, Armand Colin, 1972) 135. For a particularly enlightening presentation of Hart's theory, see N Bobbio, 'Nouvelles réflexions sur les normes primaires et secondaires' in *Essais de théorie du droit* (Paris, LGDJ, 1998) 159.

rules. The first category of rules is made up of prescriptive rules requiring subjects of law to perform or to refrain from certain actions (prohibition of violence, observance of property or sovereignty and so forth). The second category contains not rules directed at subjects of law but rules that, within the system, govern the way that the primary rules may be created, abolished, altered, how they may be interpreted officially and how they may be enforced if need be. But it is not this ultimate constraint that constitutes the legal order, but the union alone of a set of primary rules with the secondary rules.

It is true that for the needs of his general demonstration Hart accepts that a set of primary rules could be considered as law independently of any secondary rules. It would be a purely 'static' and anarchic system governed by very slowly evolving customary rules.[9] It is doubtful, though, that such a system constitutes a true system of law, that there has ever been such a system and even more that international law, past or present, bears any likeness to this. If we follow Kantorowicz's analyses (taken up by Carbonnier), any system of law, however primitive, is necessarily the combination of a set of primary rules (customary or 'revealed') with at least one secondary rule, that commanding the interpretation of this law by the authorised third parties.

From this it ensues that 'pure anarchy'—that is a system where there might be primary rules but no secondary rule providing the *possibility* for an authorised third party to adjudicate on them—is simply not a system of law. It is a space where the 'natural law' of the strongest is deployed. The international legal order, however, may be characterised as a 'tempered' anarchic system insofar as it recognises, outside the mechanism of self-interpretation of law by its subjects themselves, the validity of *juridictio* by a third-party instance. In other words, while there may be a legal order without a Legislator (other than the subjects of law themselves), or an Executive (imposing itself on its subjects by force), there cannot be one without some form of Judiciary able to adjudicate on the interpretation of the primary rules and the settlement of disputes.[10]

One can better understand the paradox of the international judicial function: regardless of how demeaned it may be in the practice of international relations, it is its very existence that constitutes the

---

[9] Hart, *The Concept of Law* (n 8) 90.

[10] See N Bobbio, 'Kelsen et les sources du droit' (1982) *Archives de philosophie du droit* 141: 'The courts are not only a source of law . . . they are the necessary condition for there to be a legal order'.

legal character of international law. This is why the 'aura' Verhoeven considers somewhat exaggerated 'that continues to surround international justice' can only be explained if we are aware of the deep meaning of the 'ontological intimacy between judge and law'.[11]

International Law as a System of Minimally Justiciable Rules

International law, while it is true law, is nonetheless largely potential law as Kojève puts it.[12] The international legal order ensures but minimum enforceability of international relations corresponding to the characteristics of what is largely potential law.

Optional Courts and Mandatory Courts

Generally states very seldom resort to international justice. One of the fundamental reasons for this is the tremendous misgivings most states have about a form of dispute settlement that leaves decision-making to the final appreciation of a third party. This wariness is sometimes justified on theoretical grounds: unacceptable limitation of the state's sovereignty, impossibility of setting up a truly impartial court, or the injustice of existing international law. However, states generally do not raise objections of principle but prefer in practice an alternative pacific means of dispute settlement (see article 33 of the Charter) that is less constraining than international justice.

The reluctance of states to resort to international courts and tribunals continues even when they have concluded multilateral or bilateral treaties that include arbitration or jurisdiction clauses. The ICJ counts close to 240 treaties containing clauses referring to its jurisdiction.[13] And this figure would be higher still if one counted the instruments containing clauses referring to international arbitration. There is admittedly there—and this is capital—a real recognition of the justiciability of disputes that might arise from treaty-based relations. But in practice only a tiny minority of disputes are settled by applying these clauses.[14]

[11] Verhoeven, 'A propos de la fonction de juger' (n 1) 458.
[12] International law is in potential existence insofar as it excludes the possibility of an irresistible constraint from a third party over sovereign states. As potentially existing law, it must necessarily tend to come into being by seeking the means to make third party intervention irresistible (Kojève, *Esquisse* (n 8) 376).
[13] *ICJ Yearbook* 1986/1987, 99.
[14] See C Philip and JY de Cara, 'Nature et évolution de la juridiction internationale' in *La juridiction internationale permanente* (n 1) 26ff and Condorelli, 'L'autorité de la décision' (n 6) 284ff.

Guy de Lacharrière observed in 1983 that 'court control of the interpretation and application of international law show[ed] no progress and [was] even regressing'.[15] Perhaps we can be less pessimistic for matters submitted to international courts by special agreement (*compromis*) at least in certain areas such as the delimitation of maritime boundaries between states.[16] Conversely, there is no denying this regression when looking at the mechanism specifically devised to introduce a diluted form of mandatory court into the international legal order. This was the famous article 36(2) of the PCIJ/ICJ statute.

This allows a state to undertake in advance to recognise 'as compulsory *ipso facto* and without special agreement, in relation to any other state accepting the same obligation, the jurisdiction of the Court in all legal disputes . . .'. Accordingly, the state loses control over the opportuneness of resort to the Court and may be taken before it on the strength of a unilateral application.

We now know that this attempt to build a form of mandatory jurisdiction ended in failure on almost all fronts: failure because of the very limited number of states that accepted this jurisdiction (46 states in 1987 for 162 states parties to the Statute—compared with 40 out of 52 in 1939); failure because of the reservations accompanying many declarations of acceptance by states and so depriving the declaration of any real effect; failure because of the ill will shown by almost all states when implicated in an action before the Court. This ill will quite often leads the defendant state to refuse to appear in the Court, a tactic employed by countries as different as Albania (1949), Iceland (1974), France (1974), Iran (1980) and the United States (1986) to mention but a few examples.[17]

The withdrawal of the United States after the Court declared in 1984 that it had jurisidiction in *Military and Paramilitary Activities in and against Nicaragua* may mark a watershed in what has been called

---

[15] G de Lacharrière, *La politique juridique extérieure* (Paris, Economica, 1983) 175 (see the entire study of the international courts 135–76).

[16] Since 1983, the Court has examined matters as different as US military intervention in Nicaragua (1984) or the presence of the PLO representation at the UN (1988, with an advisory opinion requested by the General Assembly). Most matters, though, are about state borders (Burkina Faso/Mali 1986, El Salvador/Honduras 1986) and more especially maritime borders (see Denmark's action against Norway in August 1988). For a study of the considerable case law of the Court on the topic, see P Weil, *Perspectives du droit de la délimitation maritime* (Paris, Pedone, 1988).

[17] CA Colliard, 'La non-comparution' in *La juridiction internationale permanente* (n 1) 167; G Arangio-Ruiz, 'Notes on Non-appearance before the International Court of Justice' in *Etudes en l'honneur de R Ago* (Giuffrè, Milan, 1987) t 3, 3.

the 'agony of the clause'.[18] Since 1951, 11 states that had accepted the compulsory jurisdiction of the Court (either by the declaration of article 36(2) of the Statute or by article 35(5)) have ceased to accept it and the United Kingdom now remains the only permanent member of the Security Council to maintain its declaration of acceptance. Many reasons have been invoked in doctrine to explain this disaffection: the imprecise character of international law which fails to provide parties with the security and predictability required for the satisfactory operation of a court; the fact that international law lags behind the development of international society; the impossibility of forming a truly impartial court (the ICJ being judged sometimes too conservative and sometimes too open to new ideas).[19] The fact of the matter is, in the final analysis, almost all states refuse to abandon the tempered anarchy model governing international society. Consolidation of a compulsory court necessarily leads to a whole other mode, as shall be argued below.

Mandatory Judgment and Enforceable Judgment

Another aspect of the minimal justiciability of international law is the authority attaching to the decisions of international courts. No one denies they at least have binding effect on the parties. Article 59 of the Statute of the International Court of Justice states that 'The decision of the Court has no binding force except between the parties and in respect of that particular case'. The same is true too of any decision of an interstate arbitration tribunal. But it is clear that these decisions are not enforceable insofar as the Court or an international abritration tribunal have no recourse to any power that is able to compel a reluctant state to abide by these decisions although they are mandatory by law.

---

[18] J Verhoeven, 'Le droit, le juge et la violence. Les arrêts Nicaragua c/ Etats-Unis' (1987) *Revue Générale de Droit International Public* 1161, 1199–200.

[19] Absolute impartiality is an ideal and Litvinov was not entirely wrong in writing of an attempted seizure of the PCIJ against the USSR that 'only an angel could be impartial in the legal examination of Russian cases' (cited by Philip and de Cara, 'Nature et évolution' (n 14) 28). The accusation of partiality is also, under whatever skies, the commonest reflex of the losing party. See the violent charges by the United States against ICJ judges from a Warsaw Pact country after the decision on the jurisdiction in *Military and Paramilitary Activities in and against Nicaragua* (1984) (1985) *ILM* 248; PM Eisemann, 'L'arrêt de la CIJ du 26 nov. 1984 . . .' (1984) *Annuaire Français de Droit International* 372; and M Lachs, 'A Few Thoughts on the Independence of Judges of the International Court of Justice' (1987) 3 *Columbia Journal of Transnational Law* 593.

This powerlessness of international courts and tribunals largely contributes to the unflattering picture that domestic law practitioners and scholars have of international law. Like one nineteenth-century French author, they generally wonder: 'What is a judgement with no means of enforcement? A simple word of advice, invariably spurned by anyone whose interests it would rattle'.[20] Internationalists can hardly defend themselves by invoking the supposedly comparatively small number of instances of such outright scorn: given the modest number of disputes that are brought before international courts, any refusal to execute their decisions is a blow to the very principle of an international court function.

This is why various attempts have been made to remedy the weakness of international judicial decisions. The main attempt, universally, is by the United Nations Charter whose article 94(2) provides that, should a party fail to comply with an ICJ decision, the Security Council 'may, if it deems necessary, make recommendations or decide upon measures to be taken to give effect to the judgement'. Practice has shown that the Security Council had almost never contemplated going down this road even in the event of flagrant non-compliance.[21] In any case, these recommendations are subject to the veto of the permanent members and one of the rare attempts to implement article 94(2), further to the decision on the merits of 27 June 1986 on *Military and Paramilitary Activities in and against Nicaragua* failed because of the inglorious but logical veto of the United States.[22]

It should be underlined, though, that the organisational weaknesses of international society once again provide insight into the essential characteristic of a legal institution. While it is true that in domestic legal orders the essential function of courts is 'directed at the performance (or the mere threat) of a measure of constraint'[23],

[20] See Cass. 2 janv. 1849 (Gouvernement espagnol c/ Casaux), S, 1849. I. 81, quoting Henrion de Pansey, *De l'autorité judiciaire en France* (1810).
[21] See the commentary of art 94 by A Pillepich in J-P Cot and A Pellet, *La Charte des Nations Unies* (Paris, Economica, 1985) 1269.
[22] Votes on the draft resolution presented in July 1986 by the non-aligned countries were 11 for, three abstentions, and the United States against. A second draft resolution was voted down in similar circumstances in October 1986; see P Tavernier, 'L'année des Nations Unies' (1986) *Annuaire Français de Droit International* 515. There are also institutional mechanisms for applying pressure in regional organisations, eg, art 54 of the European Convention on Human Rights providing for the intervention of the Committee of Ministers of the Council of Europe, see *La juridicition internationale permanente* (n 1) 42 and 296.
[23] P Mayer, 'Droit international public et droit international privé sous l'angle de la notion de compétence' (1979) *Revue Critique de Droit International Privé* 561.

this performance of the constraint is not the essence of the Court's function. This essence is to be sought in the decision of an independent and impartial third party being mandatory on the parties even if it cannot be enforced as various examples show in domestic law too.[24]

Judicial Third Party and Political Third Party

Nowadays there is substantial justiciability of interstate relations by political entities such as the Security Council and other specialised bodies of the many international organisations. That has been one of the major developments of international society in the twentieth century. From the standpoint of the sociology of law, the idea has been defended that the legal phenomenon begins with the authorised intervention of a third party, even if the third party does not have the characteristics of the ideal type of a court, that is, independence and impartiality.[25]

It has also been argued that the intervention of a political third party in international society might be preferable to that of an international court. Whereas such a court is *bounded* by law, the political third party can correct the stringency of law by considerations of opportuneness that are better able to settle a dispute in depth.[26] This argument may not be wrong, provided it is properly understood: the political third party cannot be a court in the narrow sense of the word. If it does take the law into consideration, it is not because it is compelled to lay down the law, but because law is one factor among others in its mode of operation. And it is a mode of operation that is less important nowadays than in the post-war years, as shown especially by the ever small proportion of law in the Security Council's decision-making mechanism.[27]

---

[24] See the difficulties administrative tribunals have, in France or elsewhere, in forcing the administration to comply with their decisions. Enforcement of a court's decision may also fall foul of the various immunities provided for by law. There are yet other examples.

[25] See Kantorowicz, *The Definition of Law* (n 8) 74; Carbonnier, *Sociologie juridique* (n 8) 135.

[26] See Lacharrière, *La politique juridique extérieure* (n 15) 151ff.

[27] See R Higgins, 'The Place of International Law in the Settlement of Disputes in the Security Council' (1970) *American Journal of International Law* 1; MF Labouz, 'Commentaire de l'article 37 de la Charte des Nations Unies' in Cot and Pellet, *La Charte des Nations Unies* (n 21) 627.

International Courts and the Advancement of the International Legal Order

The role of any international court is to fully assume the function that a judge fulfils in any legal system: to ensure subjects are subordinated to the rules of the law. Its role, though, cannot be to reform international society in its anarchic structure that is willed by states. How can any decisive advancement of law be imagined under these circumstances?

Primacy of the Rule of Law and State Sovereignty

The judge is first of all the instrument by which the primacy of legal rules is directly asserted in respect of states. Admittedly it is not common to see 'crop out' in their doctrine the refusal on principle that they are as subjects *subjected* to international law. More often than not this provocation is pointless because of the self-interpretation of law that is the mark of anarchic society. But should this self-interpretation be disturbed by the intervention of international courts, arguments will arise that hark back to the repressed desire of states (or their rulers) not to be *sub lege* but to enjoy unbridled sovereignty. Courts, for their part, can only act in compliance with a rationale that maintains the rule of law.

Judicial Interpretation and Self-Interpretation of International Law

International courts are led to defend the juridicity of the international order where the state tends spontaneously to accentuate the anarchic aspects of that order to the point of complete anomia. This was seen from the first decision of the PCIJ (*SS Wimbledon*)[28] in which the Court opposed a conception of state sovereignty defended by German lawyers that would have made any treaty commitment by a state discretionary. It dismissed the conclusion that a treaty could be analysed as an abandonment of sovereignty, seeing in the right of entering into international engagements, on the contrary, an attribute of that sovereignty. The state was therefore under an obligation on which a court could adjudicate.

---

[28] *The SS Wimbledon* (Judgment) PCIJ Rep Series A No 1 (17 August 1923).

One area where opposing logics of state self-interpretation and judicial interpretation have most frequently come into conflict is that of the determination of the jurisdiction of the international judge. Thus, in the optional clause of compulsory jurisdiction subscribed in 1946 in favour of the ICJ, several states (including the United States and France) tried to maintain their freedom of interpretation by reserving the questions arising from national competence as they themselves defined them. The Court then chose to play for time while returning this type of reservation against those using it (*Certain Norwegian Loans*, 1957).[29]

But confrontation was inevitable when the Court fully applied article 36(6) of its statutes giving it control over its jurisdiction. Thus, in *Nuclear Tests*, the Court, having accepted to record the claims from Australia and New Zealand, and to order conservation measures, encountered a sharp reaction from France. France criticised the Court for disregarding the reservation excluding disputes relating to national defence and ceased to accept its mandatory jurisdiction.[30]

The problem arose acutely in the dispute between Nicaragua and the United States. The United States, having been unable to get the ICJ to find it had no jurisdiction in the 1984 decision, also withdrew its consent to compulsory jurisdiction. As the United States was traditionally a defender of the international court function, a violent polemic ensued among US jurists.[31] It is interesting that one of the main arguments raised by supporters of the US administration was that of an excess of power committed by the ICJ. Accordingly, Reisman argued: 'it is an affirmation and not a repudiation of law to reject a decision by a tribunal that had no jurisdiction to make such

---

[29] *Case of Certain Norwegian Loans* (Judgment) [1957] ICJ Rep 9 (6 July 1957); C Rousseau, *Droit international public* (Paris, Sirey, 1983) t 5, 457.

[30] See G de Lacharrière, 'Commentaires sur la position juridique de la France à l'égard de la licéité de ses expériences nucléaires' (1973) *Annuaire Français de Droit International* 235; *Nuclear Tests (Australia v France and New Zealand v France)* (Judgments) [1974] ICJ Rep 253, 457 (20 December 1974).

[31] See HW Briggs, '*Nicaragua v United States*: Jurisdiction and Admissibility' (1985) 79 *American Journal of International Law* 373; TM Franck, 'Icy Day at the ICJ' (1985) 79 *American Journal of International Law* 379; A D'Amato, 'Modifying US Acceptance of the Compulsory International Law' (1985) 79 *American Journal of International Law* 385; WM Reisman, 'Has the International Court exceeded its Jurisdiction?' (1986) 80 *American Journal of International Law* 128; GL Scott and CL Carr, 'The ICJ and Compulsory Jurisdiction: The Case for Closing the Clause' (1987) 81(1) *American Journal of International Law* 57; K Highet 'Evidence, the Court, and the Nicaragua Case' (1987) 81(1) *American Journal of International Law* 1.

a decision'.[32] This argument amounts to considering the state as the arbiter in the last resort of a question of jurisdiction raised before the international courts. The Court's decision, instead of being binding on the state, becomes an interpretation of the law co-existent with the state's contrasting self-interpretation (which is the only effective interpretation).[33] And so jursidiction is denied in the name of a purely anarchic conception of international law. Notice that the solution to the genuine and serious problem of excess of power of the court is sought, in any legal order, through reinforcing the judicial function and not through weakening it.

Legal Disputes and Political Disputes

There is another line of argument that states regularly resort to in order to remove some of their actions from legal judgment. Under an old doctrine dating back to Vattel, international law should recognise the distinction between legal and political disputes. Political disputes are supposedly disputes bearing on a matter of vital importance for a state or disputes that are but one aspect of a generalised conflict of interests among states or disputes for which there is purportedly no applicable legal rule either because of the incomplete character of international law or because of its rejection a priori by one of the parties.[34]

The wording of article 36(2) of the PCIJ/ICJ Statute is evoked in favour of this distinction as it institutes the optional clause of compulsory jurisdiction for 'all legal disputes' and the wording of article 36(3) of the Charter that provides that 'legal disputes should as a general rule be referred by the parties to the International Court of Justice'. Thus, only this type of dispute is supposedly justiciable, while political disputes allegedly are not. In several recent cases this line of argument has been raised by states in the ICJ or at least has been the implicit cause of their negative attitude towards the Court. This was the case of France in the *Case of Nuclear Tests* (1974), of

---

[32] Reisman, 'Has the International Court exceeded its jurisdiction?' *ibid*, 134.

[33] See the opinion of G Arangio-Ruiz, in *Société Française pour droit international* (n 1) 415.

[34] H Lauterpacht, 'La théorie des différends non justiciables en droit international' (1930) 34(4) *Recueil des Cours de l'Académie de Droit International de La Haye* 499; I Brownlie, 'The Justiciability of Disputes and Issues in International Relations' (1967) 42 *British Yearbook of International Law* 123; A Cassese, 'The Concept of Legal Dispute in the Jurisprudence of the International Court' in *Il processo internazionale: Studi in onore de G Morelli* (Milan, Giuffrè, 1975) 173.

Iran in the *Case of United States Diplomatic and Consular Staff in Teheran* (1979) and of the United States in the *Case of Military and Paramilitary Activities in and against Nicaragua* (1984 and 1986). It is not difficult to see what the consequences would be if international courts were to entertain the theory of political disputes. To dismiss the justiciability of certain relations would be to maintain that, for such relations, states can only have relations of pure anarchy among them, scarcely attenuated by the intervention of the political third party. But since states themselves (in the reservations imposed on acceptance of the jurisdiction of the ICJ or in arbitration conventions) define which relations are non-justiciable, it is in fact almost all of international relations that could little by little be called into question by a mechanism akin to Gresham's law in economics.

The theoretical proof, from the standpoint of international law, that such a distinction cannot be accepted, is given by Lauterpacht in his famous course at The Hague in 1930. The ICJ subsequently corroborated the scholarly proof by asserting twice that 'if the Court were, contrary to its settled jurisprudence, to adopt such a view, it would impose a far-reaching and unwarranted restriction upon the role of the Court in the peaceful solution of international disputes'.[35]

Is there any need, though, to point out that political disputes do indeed occur? Domestic courts encounter them and find they have no jurisdiction, referring the suit to the legislative or executive. But international courts, in their solitude, cannot admit such a category. This is not without danger for the juridsdictional function (increased tension, non-performed decision, enhanced distrust of the court) but the contrary attitude would certainly lead to the gradual demise of the function itself.

The Development of International Law

Some international law scholars in the 1920s thought that international courts might be a powerful way to reform international law so as to ensure peace and international justice. Various mechanisms were put in place to this end, the main one probably being that which attempted to set up an ersatz of a compulsory court in interstate society.

---

[35] *Case concerning United States diplomatic and consular staff in Tehran (United States of America v Iran)* [1980] ICJ Rep 19–20; *Case of military and paramilitary activities in and against Nicaragua* [1984] ICJ Rep 439; Verhoeven, 'Le droit, le juge et la violence' (n 18) 1183–94. However, see an implied criticism of Lauterpacht's arguments in C de Visscher, *Théories et réalités en droit international public* (Paris, Pedone, 1970) 91ff.

Although the hopes of the Wilson years were disappointed, and often tragically so, a doctrinal strand has survived to call for international courts and above all the ICJ to be more daring in the law-creating power that each judge in any legal system necessarily wields. The 'development' of international law by international courts is supposedly that much more desirable as its interventions are rare and the 'thirst for law' is not satisfied by any other instance of international society. In these conditions, the international court could perform what Condorelli calls a true function of legislative supply work.[36]

The idea is taken even further by commentators of the US 'realist' movement for whom judges must commit themselves to the defence of the fundamental values of the society in which they operate. The judge is not just a 'substitute legislator' but a co-legislator working to transform society.[37]

The dramatic weakness of such a doctrine transposed into international society is not just that it tends to substitute the judge (and any other type of politico-judicial third party—UN General Assembly, UN Secretary-General, International Law Commission, etc) for states in creating law, which is quite simply contrary to the realities of international society, but it attempts more profoundly to replace positivist processes (*mediocrely* positivist in their view) of application of the law by a sort of 'free discovery' of the law by judges.[38] But who stands to gain today in clouding the boundary between legislation and the application of law in interstate society? Unless, as in de Lacharrière's telling remark, we wish to add 'to the mass of states that distrust judges because they apply the law . . . the troop of those who fear them because they do not apply it'.[39]

The End of Anarchy

Any decisive advancement of law ultimately presupposes going beyond (or at least avoiding) the anarchic system. This can be seen nowadays in the success of the Community legal order and, in another way, in the emergency of a 'transnational' legal order.

It is well known how important the European Court of Justice (ECJ) in Luxembourg is. It is evidence that, in their mutual relations,

[36] See Condorelli, 'L'autorité de la décision' (n 6) 306ff.
[37] McWhinney, *United Nations Law Making* (n 4) 131ff and 274ff.
[38] On the *Freirechtslehre* theories see W Friedmann, *Théorie générale du droit* (Paris, LGDJ, 1965) 301.
[39] Lacharrière, *La politique juridique extérieure* (n 15) 175.

European states have emerged from anarchy by creating a Community where the legislative, executive and judical functions are carried out with a degree of effectiveness that could not be achieved in a tempered anarchy. Some observers remain sceptical about the change brought about relative to classical international courts. The ECJ no more than the ICJ has the wherewithal to enforce a decision against a state. EC Treaty article 171 states very prosaically that, should a state fail to fulfil any of its obligations, 'the State shall be required to take the necessary measures to comply with the judgement of the Court of Justice'.[40] This admittedly means that the European Community is not yet a federation. But the true upheaval is that a state in joining the Community accepts, with no possible way out, the compulsory jurisdiction of the Court. That is what constitutes the road from anarchy towards a *supranational* order. As for the enforcement of decisions, it is assured by the very existence of a social contract that the state would take the risk of breaking if it persisted in a hostile attitude towards the Court.

Another escape route from the international order is possible in a direction that could not even have been thought of forty years ago: that of a *transnational* legal order. This concerns for the time being just a very limited area of international law but there is no reason to think this area should not expand. It concerns disputes between investors and host states arising from breaches of contracts and nationalisation measures. This was, before the Second World War, one of the main sources of interstate claims through the intermediary of diplomatic protection.

For twenty years, it can be seen that most contemporary case law on the international law of nationalisation has been the work of *transnational* arbitration, that is, arbitration arranged between states and foreign private persons. The mechanism of diplomatic protection of claims has become extremely rare. To avoid the drawbacks of such hit-and-miss protection, investors now commonly have arbitration clauses written into contracts. The awards of transnational arbitration tribunals can then be directly recognised in domestic legal

---

[40] Since the Maastricht Treaty (art 228(2)) lump sum or penalty payments can be ordered against states that persistently fail to abide by the Court's decision. For the first cases see Case 387/97, *Commission v Greece*, (Judgment) [2000] ECR I-5047 (4 July 2000); Case 278/01, *Commission v Spain* (Judgment) [2003] ECR I-14141 (25 November 2003); Case 304/02, *Commission v France* (Judgment) [2005] ECR I-6263 (12 July 2005) and more recently: Case 121/07, *Commission v France* (Judgment) (9 December 2008); Case 109/08, *Commission v Greece* (Judgment) (4 June 2009).

orders (by the exequatur procedure) and enforced by those orders.[41]
It should be emphasised that this change has arisen from a reaction
by firms to the lack of effectiveness of international law. Firms must
still, to enjoy the full advantages of the state legal order, obtain a
change of domestic law as to immunities that states may enjoy. Such
a transformation is underway in the industrialised nations.[42]

What is striking about the two ways of overtaking or getting round
the international courts that have just been indicated is that they both
have as their reference, in the final analysis, the state model. This is
obvious for the Community legal order. But it is obvious too for the
'transnational order' whose effectiveness depends entirely on the
possible exequatur of arbitration awards with states.

Should we conclude with Kojève that public international law can
only exist potentially? Insofar as it does come into being, it disappears as international law and changes into domestic law.[43]

---

[41] For the particularly significant example of ICSID arbitration see A Giardina,
'L'exécution des sentences du centre international pour le règlement des différends'
(1982) 71 *Revue Critique de Droit International Privé* 273. On the growing importance
of the role of international law in the settlement of disputes between states and private
investors, see above, ch 1 and C Leben, 'La théorie du contrat d'Etat et l'évolution du
droit international des investissements' (2003) 302 *Recueil des Cours de l'Académie de
Droit International de La Haye* 197.

[42] See M Cosnard, *La soumission des Etats aux tribunaux internes face à la théorie des
immunités de l'Etat* (Paris, Pedone, 1996).

[43] Kojève, *Esquisse* (n 8) 392. Since this paper was written the establishment of the
WTO's Dispute Settlement Body has introduced a most important mandatory sys-
tem among its members that is reminiscent – *mutats mutandis* – of that of the
European Union.

8

The State within the Meaning of International Law and the State within the Meaning of Municipal Law (On the Theory of the Dual Personality of the State)*

I T IS NOT without some misgivings that I present, in these *Mélanges* dedicated to an eminent scholar of the Italian dualist (or pluralist) school of international law, a chapter inspired by what he characterised as the 'constitutional conception of international law'[1] and—to tell the whole truth—as Kelsenian-influenced

---

* First published as 'L'Etat au sens du droit international et l'Etat au sens du droit interne: à propos de la théorie de la double personnalité de l'Etat' in *Studi di diritto internazionale in onore di Gaetano Arangio-Ruiz* vol I (Naples, Editoriale Scientifica, 2004) 131.

[1] G Arangio-Ruiz, *L'Etat dans le sens du droit des gens et la notion de droit international* (Bologna, Cooperativa Libraria Universitaria, 1975) first published in (1975) *ÖZöRV* 3 and (1976) *ÖZöRV* 265. See especially the general presentation at 3–9. These ideas were first developed in what is probably one of the foundations of Arangio-Ruiz's view of international law, *Gli enti soggetti dell'ordinamento internazionale* (Milan, Giuffré, 1951). They are subsequently expounded several times and especially in the important appendix to his Hague lectures: G Arangio-Ruiz, 'The Normative Role of the General Assembly of the United Nations and the Declaration of Principles of Friendly Relations' (1972-III) *Recueil des Cours de l'Académie de Droit International de La Haye* 648 and taken up again, with modifications, in *The UN Declaration on Friendly Relations and the System of the Sources of International Law* (Alphen aan den Rijn, Sijthoff & Noordhoff, 1979) 199. Some of the main ideas in these writings are summarised in 'Le domaine réservé. L'Organisation internationale et le rapport entre droit international et droit interne' (1990) 225 *Recueil des Cours de l'Académie de Droit International de La Haye* 13, 434–79 and in 'On the Nature of the International Personality of the Holy See' (1996) *Revue Belge de Droit International* 354, especially 355–59. See also the references below in n 27. The expression 'constitutional conception of international law' pertains to conceptions by which universal human society is said to be 'a magnified version of a national society, within which

monism.[2] I have resolved myself to this by placing my trust in the benevolence of a major scholar for whom a doctrinal disagreement does not disqualify its author. I even feel encouraged in this insofar as, in working recently on the theory of the state, I have been led to re-read the important essay by the dedicatee of these lines on *L'Etat dans le sens du droit des gens et la notion du droit international* and to set it against the theoretical problems facing me.

Those problems related to 'state contracts' defined, as was done for the first time by Pierre Mayer, as contracts entered into between an individual and a state within the meaning of international law (or within the meaning of the law of nations, to use Arangio-Ruiz's terminology) as opposed to contracts in the domestic legal order entered into by the state-administration (that is the state within the meaning of domestic law) with a private natural or juristic person.[3] The former—state contracts in the specific sense of the term—can, I argue, be governed by international law and are even a new act of international law,[4] whereas the latter are municipal law contracts, for example, administrative contracts, for countries that recognise this type of law.

It can be seen that this analysis appeals to two notions of the state: the state in the sense of international law and the state in the sense of domestic law (the state-administration). But what is the nature of the

international law would approximately occupy the place—and perform the functions—occupied—respectively—performed in a national system by the constitution, preferably a federal constitution, or by constitutional law in general', *The UN Declaration on Friendly Relations, ibid*, 200. Scholars defending this conception are Arangio-Ruiz, Scelle, Kelsen, Verdross, Kunz and Guggenheim. See among others Arangio-Ruiz, 'Le domaine réservé', *ibid* 5, fn 2; *The UN Declaration on Friendly Relations, ibid*, 206ff.

[2] G Arangio-Ruiz's attitude to Kelsenian theory is complex. First, opposing Kelsen on essential points, he states 'As regards "collective" persons of municipal law in general, the State included, I stand with those who conceive of them in the legal terms proposed by Hans Kelsen . . .' (*L'Etat dans le sens du droit des gens* (n 1) 399). And again, even more decisively: 'I think the best results can be obtained in studying the relationship between international law and municipal law by taking account at one and the same time of *both* the essential ideas of Triepel and Anzilotti *and* of certain notions of the general theory of law from the *Reine Rechtslehre'*. *L'Etat dans le sens du droit des gens* (n 1) 405; see also 393, fn 376 and 395, para 102.

[3] On the distinction between state administration and the state within the meaning of international law, see above ch 4 and below, this ch, as well as P Mayer, 'La neutralisation du pouvoir normatif de l'Etat' (1986) *Journal du Droit International* 5 and especially 9–29, and see above ch 1.

[4] On this point I oppose Mayer, who considers that state contracts are not governed in the strict sense by any law and who presents a new version of the *contrat sans loi* theory. See above, ch 1.

two 'states' implied by the theory of state contracts? It is this matter of the possible duality of the state as a person, an issue Arangio-Ruiz has examined in detail, including in the aforementioned essay,[5] that I wish to take up again here, having addressed it in what now seems to me an unsatisfactory manner in an earlier study.[6]

We shall study first the theories that in one way or another take a dual approach to the state, whether perceiving in it two sides or seeing in it a real double personality. We shall then address Kelsenian theory, which repudiates any dual approach of this kind, to critically examine it.

The Two Sides or Double Personality of the State

The Two Sides of the State in Classical French and German Doctrines

Léon Duguit (1859–1928), in his *Traité de droit constitutionnel*, referred to an old theory that 'distinguishes two personalities in the state, the personality of the public authority and, on the other side, the patrimonial or fiscal personality'.[7] It seems it was Louis Michoud (1856–1916) who popularised the notion of the two sides of the state in France. In his 1895 article on the state responsibility, he claimed:

> Today we conceive of the state as a two-sided personality: it is in some respects a legal entity in private law performing acts to manage its property, dealing with individuals in contracts, engaging in certain industries, owning certain goods and subjected, in principle, in its acts to the rules of private law; it is in other respects a higher legal being with eminent rights to which no other individual can lay claim and which take their source in the right of sovereignty, or the right to command individuals and to be obeyed by them.[8]

In his epoch-making work on the theory of legal personality, Michoud returned to this idea on several occasions. He noted, to give just one example:

---

[5] Arangio-Ruiz, *L'Etat dans le sens du droit des gens* (n 1) 299–303 and 400ff, and see the works cited above in n 1 and below in n 27.

[6] See above, ch 4.

[7] L Duguit, *Traité de droit constitutionnel* vol I, 3rd edn (Paris, E de Boccard, 1927) 622–23 with reference to the corresponding German doctrine at 624.

[8] L Michoud, 'De la responsabilité de l'Etat à raison des fautes de ses agents' (1895) *Revue du Droit Public* 1, 2.

[T]he legal personality of the state offers two sides: as a legal person in public law, it exercises the rights pertaining to the idea of sovereignty and directs the services of general interest necessary to the community of which it is the legal representative; as a legal person in private law, it exercises the patrimonial rights which have in sum the same purpose as the former, which do not differ from them in the goal in view of which they are recognised, but solely in the way they exist.[9]

The theory of the double-sidedness of the state person is, in this version, a theory concerning the state as it appears in public and private municipal law.

Michoud, who discusses the possibility of divisions of the state other than the division into property-owning state/public authority state,[10] apparently misses the division arising from the distinction between municipal and international law. It is also a version in which there is no double personality of the state: the state has two sides, admittedly, but these do not constitute two persons.[11] Thus, he comments:

The state as public authority and the state as a legal person of private law are one and the same subject of law. If we separate them arbitrarily either by breaking up the state into two personalities or, what amounts to the same thing, by limiting the idea of personality to just one of its manifestations, that of private law, we shall be led to unacceptable consequences: we shall have to say, for instance, that the state as the public authority is not responsible for the acts of the state as a private person and vice versa; that the contract entered into by the one is *res inter alios acta* for the other; that *res judicata* in respect of the one is not in respect of the other.[12]

Michoud dismisses such consequences both because they entail 'inextricable difficulties' but also, and more profoundly, because

---

[9] L Michoud, *La théorie de la personnalité morale et son application au droit français* (Paris, LGDJ, 1906) (reprinted in 1998) t I, 114. In his paper on state responsibility (at 2) Michoud remarks of the double-sided personality that 'everyone, in France at least, now accepts this idea' but makes no reference to doctrine. And when he introduces this idea in his treatise, he refers only to his 1895 paper. See also J Dabin, *Doctrine générale de l'Etat* (Brussels, Bruylant, 1939) 108–11.

[10] Michoud, *La théorie de la personnalité morale* (n 9) 276ff.

[11] So this theory is not that meant by Arangio-Ruiz when he states: 'The distinction [between state persons] is supposedly one of *sides*, a separate legal personality being attached to each side. On the inside there is the personality-side of municipal law, on the outside the personality-side of international law . . .'. As we shall see, Arangio-Ruiz dismisses this doctrine. See Arangio-Ruiz, *L'Etat dans le sens du droit des gens* (n 1) 300.

[12] Michoud, *La théorie de la personnalité morale* (n 9) 271–72.

they run counter to the unity of the state person 'which is the legal embodiment of the Nation' and so, like it, indivisible.[13] He goes on:

It may be useful from some points of view to distinguish in the state the two sides of its personality . . . But we shall never achieve a satisfactory legal theory if we do not maintain the principle that all the state's acts must be considered as those of a single personality, which has just different organs and various manifestations.[14]

But while we know what it means from a legal point of view to have a double personality (whether we accept or reject it), it is hard to understand what is meant, other than metaphorically, by the two sides of a legal personality, and Duguit is not really wrong in seeing in it 'a vague turn of phrase' and in wondering how the sovereign will of the state 'shall show at one time its public authority side and at another time its private person side'.[15]

The theory of the two sides applies not only to the person of the state, but to sovereignty insofar as it is its necessary attribute. There is supposedly a domestic notion of sovereignty and an external notion that are just the two sides of the same sovereignty, which is a second version of the theory of the two sides of the state. As Carré de Malberg (1861–1935) states: 'Thus sovereignty has two sides. And yet one should not see two separate sovereignties in internal and external sovereignty'.[16] And similarly Mérignhac, to whom Carré de Malberg refers, comments:

If we take . . . the problem of sovereignty in public international law, we must . . . point out that this sovereignty does not change in character outside. It is

---

[13] Michoud, *ibid*, 271. Duguit contrasted the French doctrine of the state for which it is the nation that is the holder of sovereignty (see A Esmein, *Eléments de droit constitutionnel* 6th edn (Paris, Sirey, 1914) (reprinted in Editions Panthéon-Assas, 2001, 1) and the German school for which it is the state as such which is the holder (Duguit, *Traité de droit constitutionnel* (n 7) 618–19).

[14] Michoud, *La théorie de la personnalité morale* (n 9) 276.

[15] Duguit, *Traité de droit constitutionnel* (n 7) 624. For Duguit the state-person is a mere fiction. See, eg, L Duguit, *L'Etat, le droit objectif et la loi positive* (Paris, Fontemoing, 1901) 5–6. See also H Laski, 'La conception de l'Etat chez Léon Duguit' (1932) *Archives de Philosophie du Droit* 121.

[16] R Carré de Malberg, *Contribution à la théorie générale de l'Etat* (Paris, Sirey, 1920, reprint Paris, CNRS, 1969) 71, fn 26 and 35–51. See also H Bonfils and P Fauchille, *Manuel de droit international public* 6th edn (Paris, A Rousseau, 1911) 90: 'sovereignty is either internal and intranational or external and international'. And similarly J Combacau, 'Pas une puissance, une liberté: la souveraineté internationale de l'Etat' (1993) 67 *Pouvoirs* 49–50: 'sovereignty . . . includes two aspects in which classical publicist doctrine has clearly seen the two sides of *the same state object* . . .' (emphasis added). See also J Combacau and S Sur, *Droit international public* 5th edn (Paris, Montchrestien, 2001) 232–33.

still unique national sovereignty that is in question; just as we do not conceive of an internal state personality and an external state personality [but see the dualist doctrine below], we cannot likewise envisage a double sovereignty, given that sovereignty is but the qualifying term of personality.[17]

As for the meaning of each of the two sides, most scholars take it that sovereignty, in the internal sense, relates to some superiority of the state person over all its subjects whereas external sovereignty can mean only independence relative to other equal states in the eyes of international law and not being subjected to any other higher person.[18] In German doctrine, the theory has taken on a specific and important aspect in Jellinek. He defends the idea that there are two ways of understanding the state in theory: the sociological and the legal modes. Against the syncretism of methods of analysing the state as a phenomenon, he maintains that 'depending on the standpoint one takes, [there are] different notions of the same object, notions that must not contradict each other but that cannot be conflated without making a mistake of method'.[19]

---

[17] A Mérignhac, *Traité de droit public international* (Paris, LGDJ, 1905) 162–63. And Mérignhac refers to Jellinek for whom, he claims, external sovereignty is the necessary outward extension of supreme political power, 162, fn 2 citing *Gesetz und Verordnung* (Freiburg, Mohr JCB (P Siebeck) 1887) 197, which I was unable to consult. We can trace this back at least to GWF Hegel, *Principes de philosophie du droit*, translated and annotated by JF Kervégan (Paris, PUF, 1998). In his analyses Hegel distinguishes between 'inward sovereignty' and 'outward sovereignty': see para 278 and para 321ff.

[18] See Duguit, *Traité de droit constitutionnel* (n 7) 714–15, summarising majority French doctrine (which he opposes). For an outline of this doctrine see the references in n 17 and n 18 and F Despagnet, *Droit international public* (Paris, Larose, 1894) 80; L Le Fur, *Etat fédéral et conféderaton d'Etats* (Thesis, Paris, Marchal et Billard, 1896) reprinted by University Panthéon-Assas (Paris 2, 2000) 443–45; M Réglade, *La notion juridique de l'Etat en droit public interne et en droit international* in *La technique et les principes du droit public: études en l'honneur de Georges Scelle* (Paris, LGDJ, 1950) 507. For a more recent doctrine, see S Rials, 'La puissance étatique et le droit dans l'ordre international. Eléments d'une critique de la notion usuelle de "souveraineté externe"' (1987) *Archives de Philosophie du Droit* 189; JD Mouton, 'La notion d'Etat et le droit international public' (1993) 16 *Droits* 45; H Ascencio, 'Droit international public' in D Alland, *Droit fondamental* (Paris, PUF, 2000) 100; and for its general interest, J Verhoeven, 'L'Etat et l'ordre juridique international' (1978) *Revue Générale de Droit International Public* 749 and *Droit international public* (Brussels, Larcier, 2000) 125; Combacau, 'Pas une puissance, une liberté' (n 16); P-M Dupuy, *Droit international public* 5th edn (Paris, Dalloz, 2000) fn 32ff; P Daillier and A Pellet, *Droit international public* 6th edn (Paris, LGDJ, 1999) 274ff and 419ff.

[19] Quoted by Michoud, 'De la responsabilité de l'Etat' (n 8) 94 referring to *Allgemeine Staatslehre* 1st edn, 160–61 that I was unable to consult. See also *Allgemeine Staatslehre* 3rd edn (Berlin, Springer, 1919) 136–40 on the different ways of knowing the state and particularly the opposition between the historico-political mode and the legal mode of knowledge. There is an Italian translation: G Jellinek and VE Orlando,

This is a third version of the theory of two-sidedness: the state is both a legal construction and a social reality, and any theory of the state must allow for this duality.[20] Kelsen, who called this version the *Zwei-Seiten-Theorie*, decried it:

> There is no sociological concept of the State besides the juristic concept
> ... There is only a juristic concept of the State: the state as—centralized—legal order. The sociological concept of an actual pattern of behavior, oriented to the legal order, is not a concept of the State, it presupposes the concept of the State, which is a juristic concept.[21]

Kelsen set himself at length in his work on *Le concept sociologique et le concept juridique de l'Etat*, to studying and refuting the possibility of a double sociological/legal approach to the state and in particular to the *Zwei-Seiten-Theorie* as presented by Jellinek.[22] Thereafter, Kelsen extended his condemnation of any dual theory of the state to that defended by the Italian dualist school, characterising it too as *Zwei-Seiten-Theorie*.

La dottrina generale dello Stato (Rome, Società Editrice Libraria, 1921) 302–08. In French, see G Jellinek, *L'Etat moderne et son droit* (Paris, Fontemoing, 1904) t I, 12–13: 'The state should be examined in all its elements and studied under all its aspects. We thus find two special spheres corresponding to two essential points of view. The state appears as a social formation; it appears also as a legal formation. We are then led to distinguish a social doctrine of the state and a legal doctrine of the state or public law'. And also at 110 on the need to recognise 'the existence in science of two different points of view from which one can contemplate the state, the social point of view and the legal point of view'.

   [20] Duality of the same order can be found in Anzilotti and, on a different basis, in Scelle.

   [21] H Kelsen, *General Theory of Law and State* trans A Wedberg (New York, Russell & Russell, 1961) 188–89 where it is Max Weber's theory that is in question. Notice that Jellinek does not use the expression *Zwei-Seiten-Theorie*. He speaks of the various standpoints (*Standpunkte*) that allow access to knowledge of the nature of the state, Jellinek, *L'Etat moderne et son droit* (n 19) 110: 'These questions [of doctrine of the state] are only truly illuminated when it is recognised that there are two different standpoints in science from which to envisage the state: the social [sociological] standpoint and the legal standpoint'.

   [22] H Kelsen, *Der soziologische und der juristische Staatsbegriff* 2nd edn (Tübingen, Mohr, 1928) 105–32. There is an Italian translation: *Il concetto sociologico e il concetto giuridico dello Stato* trans A Carrino (Naples, Edizione Scientifiche Italiane, 1997). The author discussed, for sociology, is Kistiakowski, a student of Simmel's, 106–13; Jellinek, whom Kelsen tells us is from the legal standpoint the main representative of the *Zwei-Seiten-Theorie* is discussed at 114–32 (Italian trans 123–40). On Kelsen's attitude to the sociological approach to law, see C Eisenmann, 'Science du droit et sociologie dans la pensée de Kelsen' in *Méthode sociologique et droit* (colloque de Strasbourg 1956) (Paris, Dalloz, 1958) 59–73. On his relation with Max Weber's sociology, see Kelsen *Il concetto sociologico e il concetto giuridico dello Stato* 1928 (n 22), and Italian trans 164–78. See also N Bobbio, 'Max Weber e Hans Kelsen' (1981) 1 *Sociologia del diritto* 135–54.

The Double Personality of the State in Italian Internationalist Doctrine

The existence of two state persons follows from the basic principles of the dualist analysis of legal orders and of the theory of legal personality. Legal personality is indeed a creation of the law, that is of the legal order and has no meaning or existence other than relative to that order.[23] Consequently, if there is not a single order of law (as in Kelsenian monism) but two clearly distinct ones, the international legal order on the one hand and the national (or internal) orders on the other, it follows that there are two personalities named state: that of international law and that of municipal law.

In this way Anzilotti argues in his *Cours de droit international*: 'the term "State" signifying . . . the subject of a national legal order, determines a subject entirely different from the State as the subject of international law'. In particular, where national laws apply to foreign states (for example, if the foreign state acquires goods or enters into contracts), 'the word state designates a different legal subject from that to which the same word refers to in international law'. Legal science, adds Anzilotti, 'cannot not to see two different subjects where ordinary language seems to designate just one'.[24]

Such an analysis is common place in the Italian school. Ago, for example, asserts the need to:

> [C]learly separate the subjects of the two orders. This does not mean the latter cannot consider the same *de facto* entities respectively as their own subjects, which is most likely and which is borne out in fact. It means on the contrary that despite the *de facto* entities being the same, the two subjects created by the two orders and on their basis remain quite separate and it is in no way legitimate to conflate them.[25]

---

[23] That does not stop Ago from warning against the idea that legal persons are a simple creation of the law. Even if personality is a creation of law, that does not rule out, he says, there being an intrinsic structure, a real entity: R Ago, *Lezioni di diritto internazionale* (Milan, Giuffrè, 1943) 19–20.

[24] D Anzilotti, *Cours de droit international* trans Gidel (Paris, Sirey, 1920) (reprinted Université Panthéon-Assas (Paris 2), 1999) 53–54 and see also 405: [contrary to treaties] 'the law has in view ways of behaving of entities subject to the legislator's authority, including the state itself, the word 'state' then indicating a different subject from the state as subject of international law'.

[25] Ago, *Lezioni* (n 23) 50–51, para 13.

And similarly Perassi holds:

> [F]or a state, the personality of international law is a characterisation given to it by the international legal order and that does not pre-exist it. For the same reasons, one must dismiss the hypothesis that the international personality of a state can be considered necessarily as attached to its personality in internal law. Such an interpretation could be maintained if the two personalities are considered simply as two ends of a single personality, depending on a single legal order: but this cannot be maintained if the international order and the internal order of each state consider one another, as is right, as two different and so separate orders.[26]

In Arangio-Ruiz there is strenuous criticism of the theory of the duality of state persons. But this criticism is original in that it is not directed at reasserting the state as a single person, but on the contrary at recognising a radical schism between two entities of completely different natures: the state in the sense of domestic law and the state in the sense of international law.[27] Thus, in his essay already cited on *L'Etat dans le sens du droit des gens*, he vigorously criticises the Italian dualist doctrine, that of Anzilotti and his successors, on the double personality of the state.

He claims, for example:

> The distinction [between state persons] is supposedly a matter of *sides*, a separate legal personality being attached to each side. Internally there is supposed to be the personality-side of internal law, externally the personality-side of international law . . . In my view . . . this theory of two sides is to be retained neither internally nor externally.[28]

This distinction, which assimilates the two-sided theory to that of the double personality—which is not always so as we have seen—is dismissed because it fails to allow for the essential distinction between the nature of the internal entity, which is a true legal person, and that of the external entity, which is but a factual entity, a power.

---

[26] T Perassi, *Lezioni di diritto internazionale* (Padova, Cedam, 1952) 46–47, para 19.

[27] These ideas were defended by Arangio-Ruiz in his earliest writings. See *Rapporti contrattuali fra state ed organizzazione internazionale* (Modena, Società Tipografica Modenese, 1950); *Gli enti soggetti dell'ordinamento internazionale* (n 1), an excerpt from which on the theory of legal personality was published separately as *La persona giuridica come soggetto strumentale* (Milan, Giuffrè, 1952). See 'Diritto internazionale e personalità giuridica' in *Novissimo Digesto Italiano* vol XVIII and G Arangio-Ruiz, L Margherita and E Tau Arangio-Ruiz, 'Soggettività nel diritto internazionale in Digesto' *Discipline pubblicistiche* IV Edizione, vol XIV (Rome, UTET, 1999). See also the publications cited in n 1.

[28] Arangio-Ruiz, *L'Etat dans le sens du droit des gens* (n 1) 300–303 and 400.

This is one of the main points of the international law doctrine in Arangio-Ruiz: the completely distinct character of the international order compared with the internal order.[29] For the internal order, we are in the presence of a true legal order that directly conditions its subjects, private persons ('interindividual' character of law), the reality of which prevails over any other factual reality of the sociological or historical type. So, against certain doctrines that purport to analyse the state in internal law in anything other than legal terms, in terms of history (the state as a 'historical fact'), of organisation or of structure,[30] he maintains that '[t]here is no basis for asserting that the state's internal legal order as a whole consists in anything other than in relational rules *stricto sensu* and organisational rules'.[31]

He adopts, then, for the state in the sense of internal law, the Kelsenian analysis of legal persons in general and of the state person in particular, except that he claims to do so on the basis of an examination of positive law and not on the basis of logical considerations.[32]

Things are quite different for the state as an entity of international law. There is a difference of nature or of 'quality', to use one of his expressions, between domestic law and international law insofar as the latter cannot condition persons from inside, that is, if I understand rightly, that it cannot reach individual persons, in other words 'the human social base',[33] contrary to what Duguit and Scelle maintained.

The dedicatee of these lines therefore dismisses the 'constitutionalist' idea that between the internal legal orders and the international legal order there is but a difference of degree, as is the case between the legal order of a federal state and that of the federated states. If

---

[29] Arangio-Ruiz has explained his conception of international law at length in the writings cited (n 1 and n 27). To give just two specific references, see *L'Etat dans le sens du droit des gens* (n 1) 10–28 and 372 and see the appendix to *The UN Declaration on Friendly Relations* (n 1) 199ff.

[30] See S Romano on the 'impossibility of reducing the institution to norms', *L'ordre juridique* (Paris, Dalloz, 1975) 36–38, para 16.

[31] Arangio-Ruiz, *L'Etat dans le sens du droit des gens* (n 1), 276.

[32] Arangio-Ruiz, *ibid*, 399, fn 389.

[33] See Arangio-Ruiz, *ibid*, 25–26. International law is made up of a 'body of *sui generis* rules governing the co-existence of factual entities, that is not conditioned from the inside—especially in their interindividual component—by any legal order of human society'. That international law cannot reach individuals directly is marked too by the fact that it contains no rules aimed directly at individuals to tell them under what circumstances they are subjects of such or such a state.

that were so, he argues, the theorist could indeed reason on a unified universal community, of which international law would be the constitution. Such a community would comprise the international legal order and the municipal legal orders, and the relations between the two categories of order would be similar to those between the legal orders of federated states with those of the federation. That is the 'federal analogy' expounded by scholars like Bourquin, Verdross, Scelle, Kunz and Kelsen, or for earlier scholars, Vittoria and Suarez.[34] All of these authors, despite their great differences, would agree on defending a 'constitutionalist' theory of international law, that is, the idea that there is a universal human community whose subjects are or could be, in the final analysis, individuals. Still from this standpoint, states would be merely subdivisions of the universal human community (so many *provinciae totius orbis*).[35]

But, for Arangio-Ruiz, this 'universal community of public law' is a purely theoretical view and owes its success simply to its 'greater ideological appeal'.[36] States 'exist in a "space" devoid of rules of any interindividual public law that can be attached to the universal society of man'.[37] The beings existing in this space are not persons, in the sense of municipal law, but 'powers' (states in the sense of the law of nations—*im Sinne des Völkerrechts*—, the Holy See, governments in exile, insurrectional parties).[38] And the rules governing these powers are not those of 'universal human society' or of 'a universal legal order of mankind', in other words, rules of some interindividual law, but rules that 'exist and act only as a function of the interests and conflicts of interest among powers'.[39] In other words again, the international law of interstate relations belongs to a

---

[34] Arangio-Ruiz, *L'Etat dans le sens du droit des gens* (n 1) 5ff and Arangio-Ruiz, *The UN Declaration on Friendly Relations* (n 1) 201–16 and 221. For the rejection of the idea that international society could constitute a universal human community, see Arangio-Ruiz, *The UN Declaration on Friendly Relations* (n 1) 216–33. See also Arangio-Ruiz, 'Le domaine réservé' (n 1) 435–79.

[35] See Arangio-Ruiz, 'The Holy See' (n 1) 355. For a glimpse of Kelsen's use of the notion of *civitas maxima* in C Wolff, see above, ch 6.

[36] Arangio-Ruiz, 'The Holy See' (n 1) 356.

[37] Arangio-Ruiz, *L'Etat dans le sens du droit des gens* (n 1) 11–12.

[38] Arangio-Ruiz, *ibid*, 13.

[39] Arangio-Ruiz, *ibid*. Elsewhere Arangio-Ruiz emphasises: 'One cannot deny that some of the features of States *qua* international persons resemble . . . those of merely factual groups within national societies (including the most unlawful ones)'. And he himself specifies at another point of his manuscript that he is thinking of mafias ('criminal associations and other factual associations'). Arangio-Ruiz, *The UN Declaration on Friendly Relations* (n 1) 356–57.

wholly different kind of law from municipal law, interindividual law.[40] The consequence of this analysis for the question of the personality of the state is that:

> The true vindication—indispensable for explaining the nature and very existence of international law—is accomplished solely on condition of perceiving we are neither in the presence, purely and simply, of two *sides* of the same entity nor in the presence of two different *portions*—state and government—of this same entity. These are rather two separate entities in the sense that on the side of municipal law there is the state-government-legal order: on the side of the law of nations there is power. The two entities do not coincide either in a vertical sense (ie as to their *social basis*) nor in a horizontal sense (as to the addressees of their rules); neither in space nor in time.[41]

One could say there is an opposition, in this presentation, between a positivist analysis of municipal law, and of the state as a legal person of internal law and a contrasting realist analysis of international law, and of the state as a factual collective entity of that law. And indeed international law, because its social basis cannot be made up of individuals, because it cannot condition persons directly, cannot be analysed in the same legal terms as municipal law. It is part of a realist analysis that sees in states but 'real entities, that is sociological units' and not legal persons.[42]

Ultimately, the traditional dualist doctrine of the double personality of the state, or of two sides, is doomed because:

---

[40] Arango-Ruiz, *L'Etat dans le sens du droit des gens* (n 1) 11–12. See among the very many references that could be given: Arangio-Ruiz, *ibid*, 24–26. The distinction between municipal law and international law is not a question of degree because the rules of international law are '*sui generis* rules governing the co-existence of factual collective entities', whereas the rules of municpal law 'find their reason for being in relations among individuals'. In fact, interindividual law is not only national law, as there are 'precarious and embryonic formations of non-state interindividual law'. That could be the case of the *lex mercatoria*. All that leads to a new version of the dualist theory: 'In the place of the somewhat narrow-minded, late nineteenth-century dualism or pluralism I envisage a more specific and flexible dualism between two *species* of legal phenomena going on within universal human society. These two "species of law" correspond to interindividual law on one side and to law between states or governments as powers on the other side' (Arangio-Ruiz, *ibid*, 25).
[41] Arango-Ruiz, *ibid*, 301. The transition from 'interpower–international [to] interindividual' supposes 'a quality leap' (404). However, the author recognises 'one cannot hide . . . the difficulty of conceiving a separation between legal phenomena such as the interpower–international on the one hand and the interindividual on the other' (at 402). And on the idea that internal law and international law belong to two separate genres, see fn 189 and 399–402.
[42] Arango-Ruiz, *ibid*, 302.

By starting from a rudimentary notion of legal persons and of the state of municipal law, a notion that is a mixture of interindividual and collective, of legal and factual, it arrives at the notion of a person with two sides, at first sight fit for everything but that cannot disappoint anyone . . . this is a false notion as it fails to describe exactly either the person of the state or the international person.[43]

Conversely, the existence of two separate entities, a legal person of domestic law and a factual (or real) person in international law, is asserted radically by Arangio-Ruiz.

This is no place to attempt a critical discussion of these arguments, assuming I have the conceptual faculties to do so. We are in the presence of a carefully thought out doctrine, refined over more than fifty years and that has already answered all the objections levelled at it.

If I have evoked some of the objections here, it is to indicate my feeling about some or other point of the argument of the dedicatee of these lines, without nurturing the naive illusion that he has not already taken account of the criticism I raise.

One of Arangio-Ruiz's arguments is that international law does not govern states in the way municipal law governs ordinary legal persons. The proof of this is that international law does not frame the birth and death of these factual entities that are states. Admittedly there is an often quoted rule, namely that international law, in matters of the existence of states, takes account of effectiveness. But he claims that is a false rule, 'a tautological rule; that is purely and simply a non-rule'.[44] It is there just to legitimise governments that have their power simply because they hold power and to de-legitimise those that no longer have it for the simple reason that they have lost it.

This pseudo-rule has nothing normative about it, then, and it reflects only 'straightforward historical causality'. For the rule to have any real normative scope would involve, he tells us, showing:

[T]hat a state order as a whole so legitimized [by the pseudo-rule of effectivity] continues to be valid as a whole for the law of nations over some time—at least provisionally and transiently—notwithstanding the fact that as a whole it has ceased to be actually effective. One should prove in other words that it is not true that for international law the government or the corresponding legal system begins to exist when in fact it exists and vanishes as soon as it disappears in fact.[45]

[43] Arangio-Ruiz, *ibid*, 303.
[44] Arangio-Ruiz, *ibid*, 271.
[45] Arangio-Ruiz, *ibid*, 272.

Arangio-Ruiz asks, then, for an example of decoupling between the government of a state, that is, the power exercised over a territory and a population, and the legal system, that is, the state as a person with regard to the law of nations. It is clear that this can occur only in exceptional and borderline cases. It is possible, I feel, to find such an example in the situation of Germany after its capitulation in May 1945. At that date the entire German 'government', all that was connected closely or remotely with the power exercised over the German territory by the German authorities, had been completely annihilated and transferred to the organs of the allied powers occupying Germany. The situation may have been one of classical *debellatio*. In such a case, by ancient international law, the 'subjugated' state disappeared and was annexed by its conquerors. In 1945, this was a schema that was still defended by Kelsen.[46] But this is not all that happened. The allied powers declared (First Declaration of Berlin of 5 June 1945) that their occupation, and the fact that they were exercising supreme authority in Germany, did not have the effect of annexing the German state.

The allied position, if appraised from a strictly legal standpoint (without ignoring its political dimension) becomes significant from the moment one considers that it relates to a customary rule prohibiting any territorial modification by the use of force.

For that matter, it was this rule that was invoked against Germany at least from 1942 onwards in order to consider that the Reich's territorial acquisitions as from 1938—like the conquests of Albania and Ethiopia by Italy—were unlawful.[47] But a second rule must be

[46] See H Kelsen, 'The Legal Status of Germany according to the Declaration of Berlin' (1945) 39 *American Journal of International Law* 518–26, 519: 'The existence of an independent government is an essential element of a state in the eyes of international law. By abolishing the last Government of Germany the victorious powers have destroyed the existence of Germany as a sovereign state'. He maintains his analysis until the 2nd edn by R Tucker and W Holt of his *Principles of International Law* (New York, Holt, Rinehart and Winston, 1966) 75–77.

[47] See K Marek, *Identity and Continuity of States in Public International Law* 2nd edn (Geneva, Droz, 1960) 263–545 for an in-depth study of the cases of Austria after the Anschluss, of Czechoslovakia, Ethiopia, Albania, the Baltic States and Poland. See also R Yakemtchouk, 'Les Républiques baltes en droit international. Echec d'une annexion opérée en violation du droit international' (1991) *Annuaire Français de Droit International* 259–89. On the doctrine of non-recognition of unlawful situations see C Rousseau, *Droit international public, Les compétences*, (Paris, Sirey, 1977) t 3, 518–26 who notes that the Stimson doctrine 'represents an attempt to subject the formation of states to the principle of legality' at 519. Scholars diverge over whether there as a customary rule on this before 1939. Marek says yes but Verhoeven contests this (See *La reconnaissance internationale dans la pratique contemporaine* (Paris, Pedone, 1975) 277–310). In any event, it seems difficult to refuse to admit such a rule today

assumed, namely the prohibition of territorial changes by force also protects the aggressor state, which explains why the total military occupation of Germany and the disappearance of all German authority did not result in the disappearance of the German state. We have here, then, a general rule of international law, 'a wartime occupation, albeit lawful, must not lead to the disappearance of the occupied state', which asserts the continuance of a state even though the criterion of effective power might suggest it had ceased to be.[48]

Coming now to the dismissal of the 'federal analogy' for analysing the relations between international law and municipal law, we can understand Arangio-Ruiz's reservations. But all the features of the inadequacy of international law he notes may be interpreted either as making any analogy impossible, or on the contrary, as being a constituent part of the analogy. And indeed an analogy, that is, a resemblance, implies by definition the existence of differences for without them things would not be analogous but identical. Consequently, everything separating international law from federal law may be taken into account on the basis of the specific character-istics of international law, without that excluding an overall and nonetheless significant resemblance. I believe the attitude an author adopts in the face of such a choice (analogy or not) is a matter of per-sonal sensitivity: reality is ambiguous enough for it to be interpreted either way. And it is self-evident that 'ideological appeal' plays a decisive role as it is at heart a question of value. For my own part, I am reluctant to conceive of international law on the model of rela-tions among *mafiosi*, even if I well understand it may be conceived of in that way. But this analysis (in terms of factual powers) would be no more 'realistic' than a 'constitutionalist' analysis. It too would be a projection, on a complex reality, of a certain reading of things.[49]

on the basis of the United Nations Charter and of a customary rule born of practice. See also H Ruiz Fabri, 'Genèse et disparition de l'Etat à l'époque contemporaine' (1992) *Annuaire Français de Droit International* 153–78.

[48] On the condition of Germany after capitulation, see M Virally, *L'Administration internationale de l'Allemagne* (Paris, Pedone, 1948) 85–93. On the point that the rule prohibiting territorial change works in favour of the aggressor state too, see Ruiz Fabri, 'Genèse et disparition de l'Etat' (n 47) 156.

[49] We have an example of this type of reasoning in Kelsen's attitude to the theory of just war. This theory assumes that resort to war is not a decision left to the uncon-ditional freedom of the state, but is possible only as a sanction, that is, in the event of a prior breach of international law. Did twentieth-century international law contain a rule prohibiting war except in the case of *bellum justum*? Kelsen argued so very early on, but emphasising that his position was politically motivated: 'It is not a scientific, but a political decision which gives preference to the *bellum justum* theory . . . We

As for the issue of the double personality of the state, we have seen that for Arangio-Ruiz, the state within the meaning of international law, is not a legal person—in the sense understood within a domestic legal order—because of the great differences existing between these two entities. So, while the state of domestic law merges with the legal personality, according to the Kelsenian scheme of things, the state of international law is a factual collectivity, not conditioned from inside, that imposes its presence, its being there, if I may put it this way, on international law just as human beings impose theirs in domestic law. The latter is in its essence an interindividual law whereas the former is in its essence the law of relations among these factual powers that are states. And just as individuals are not created by domestic law but are realities that impose themselves on it, states are not created by international law but impose themselves on it.[50] But is it true that individuals impose their reality on domestic law? There is room for doubt. Admittedly all domestic law deals with human beings. But for a long time it dealt also with animals and even things.[51] Can it be said that these things 'imposed' their reality? Is it not rather the law that sometimes accepted and sometimes rejected them? As for the personality of human beings, of any human being, is this not a recent invention of certain legal orders over the last two or three centuries? For thousands of years the personality of human

choose this interpretation hoping to have recognised the beginning of a development of the future, and with the intention of strengthening as far as possible all the elements of the present day international law which tend to justify this interpretation, and promote the evolution we desire' *Law and Peace in International Relations: The Oliver Wendell Holmes Lectures*, (Cambridge, Harvard University Press, 1942) at 54–55. He maintained his position at the end of the Second World War as 'only this interpretation conceives of the international order as law' *General Theory of Law and State* (n 21) 341). In *Pure Theory of Law* trans M Knight (Berkeley, University of California Press, 1967) and depending on the changes observed in international society, he asserts that henceforth 'it is hardly possible, in other words, to deny the general validity of the *bellum iustum* principle' (at 322). *Mutatis mutandis* one could reason in this way about the factual nature or otherwise of states and so about the nature of international law, whether or not it is of the same ilk as municipal law.

    [50] '. . . the reality of the State—its constituency, its organisation, its very establishment, form and vicissitudes—escapes international law in such a measure as to prove that the current conception of States as juristic persons, let alone as organs of international law or legal subdivisions of the legal community of mankind, is a unwarranted, theoretical assumption.' Arangio-Ruiz, *The UN Declaration on Friendly Relations* (n 1) 217.
    [51] Kelsen notes that 'In Antiquity there was in Athens a special court whose function it was to condemn inanimate things, for instance a spear by which a man had been killed': Kelsen, *General Theory of Law and State* (n 21) 3, fn 1, with references. Legal anthropology could probably supply many other examples.

beings—slaves, serfs, untouchables, prisoners of war—simply failed to 'impose' itself. Humans beings are creations of law and not natural realities that impose themselves on it. Human beings are what the law (the legal order) wants them to be. This is so obvious it hardly needs restating. Admittedly, things are less artificial because individuals have a physical birth that owes nothing to the law whereas a legal entity is entirely a creation of the law and the result of interactions among physical persons or, if one prefers, the result of their legal intercourse.

Is that enough to consider that in domestic law there is a difference in kind between physical persons and juristic persons? I do not think so.

In the everyday life of law, it is not apparent that we are in the presence of two entities of completely and absolutely different natures. One might have thought so when legal entities first appeared. But evolution has shown that in all major legal systems juristic persons tend to be increasingly likened (even in criminal matters) to physical persons.[52]

And similarly, for states in the sense of international law, their factual power does not impose itself any more on international law than that of individuals in domestic law. Just as the personality of the latter may have been ignored for centuries and millennia, the personality of certain human groupings with all the characteristics to claim to be states in the sense of international law has been refused. It is worth recalling here what Verhoeven wrote about the state in international law:

No more than a state 'person' imposes itself does a state 'fact' imposes itself in international relationships. No more than there is, say, outside of law a 'marriage' fact separate from a 'living together' fact is there in itself a 'state' fact; the fact is that of a power, but it is in itself infinitely diversified without the state . . . being in any way able to claim the monopoly. The fact of power is not a 'state' fact other than by law and for law, and it is in this sense that the hold of law on the state is decisive, even if its birth escapes fundamentally from its prescriptions. That explains the basically legal, that is verbal, reality of the 'law of nations' state.[53]

---

[52] For French law, see the loi du 22 juillet 1992 and loi du 16 décembre 1992 reforming the Criminal Code and introducing criminal liability of legal entities for many offences. See G Stefani, G Levasseur and B Bouloc, *Droit pénal général* 16th edn (Paris, Dalloz, 1997) fn 309ff. See also Kelsen, *General Theory of Law and State* (n 21) 145 and n 55 below.

[53] J Verhoeven, 'L'Etat et l'ordre juridique international' (n 18) 749, 753.

It can be understood that states are not the only factual powers in international relations and Arangio-Ruiz draws our attention to the point that 'the term power is not synonymous with international person'.[54] Thus, mafias, multinational firms and big trade unions are powers but 'are not ordinarily part of the field of international law'. These entities 'remain outside of the sphere of international persons even if they sometimes come close to it'.[55] But what is it that explains that these powers are kept out and how they approach the international sphere? What is it that means that, however powerful they may be, multinational firms and mafia groups are never raised to the same status as states which are often weaker?[56] It is because states are personalities recognised by international law as legal entities of a certain kind, sovereign entities, and that the others are not.

In other words there are many factual powers in international relations but only one is accepted by international law to be its subject *par excellence.*

Arangio-Ruiz makes another distinction between juridical personality in the technical sense of the term and the capacity of the subject of law which he also terms personality but, it seems, in a weaker sense. Thus, for instance, he discusses the personality of the Holy See and concludes positively:

> [T]he Holy See enjoys an international personality . . . Just like any other sovereign body . . . the Roman Church is endowed with the rights and is subject to the obligations deriving from the rules of customary or conventional law applicable to the Church's diplomatic relations . . .[57]

The state, to take up the reasoning with him, is supposedly, then, a person of international law in the sense that, like other 'persons' (international organisations, the Holy See, etc) it is the holder of rights and subjected to obligations in the international legal order. It is allegedly then a subject of this order but not a juristic person in the sense that the state is a juristic person in the domestic legal order. The state, within the meaning of international law, is supposedly a

---

[54] Arangio-Ruiz, *L'Etat dans le sens du droit des gens* (n 1) 290.

[55] Arangio-Ruiz, *ibid*, 291.

[56] I am not happy with the concept of 'power' of which Arangio-Ruiz says it does not imply the existence of an international person, nor a military power, nor a power of control or constraint, but recognises ultimately that it is 'inevitably imprecise' noting that it is 'amenable to a general definition only approximately': Arangio-Ruiz, *L'Etat dans le sens du droit des gens* (n 1) 293–94.

[57] Arangio-Ruiz, 'The Holy See' (n 1) 364–65.

factual entity that imposes itself on this law and is not one of its creations. Can a distinction be made, though, between the capacity of subject of law and the capacity of legal person? Can one be a subject of law and, at the same time not be, in the eyes of the legal order, a person in the technical sense of the term? What is it to be a subject of law if not to be the recipient of rights and obligations; and what is it to have legal personality if not to be liable to benefit from rights and be subject to obligations in a given legal order?[58]

In other words, the fact that states, in international law are not persons similar in every way (assuming this analysis is accepted) to legal entities of domestic law has no bearing on the fact that they are indeed subjects of international law and therefore that they are juristic persons in the eyes of this law. It is only if one wants to scrutinise the *substratum* of these persons, their raw reality, that one can say they are very different persons from those in domestic law.[59] But the legal theory of persons need not consider the *substratum*.[60] Only the position in law

[58] See Anzilotti, *Cours de droit international* (n 24): 'being a person in a given legal order is equivalent to being the recipient of the norms composing that legal order . . . Personality therefore expresses a relation between an entity and a given legal order. Thus . . . there are no persons by nature' (at 122). On the analysis of notions of subject of law and of person, see the lengthy developments in Kelsen, *Pure Theory of Law* (n 49) 168–92. For Kelsen, the physical person 'is not a human being, but the personified unity of the legal norms that obligate or authorize one and the same human being. It is not a natural reality but a legal construction, created by the science of law—an auxiliary concept in the presentation of legally relevant facts. In this sense a physical person is a juristic person' (at 174). So there is no difference, from this standpoint, with legal entities. In both cases we are in the presence of 'a complex of legal obligations and rights whose totality is expressed figuratively in the concept of "person". "Person" is merely the personification of this totality' (at 173). Arangio-Ruiz, *L'Etat dans le sens du droit des gens* (n 1) explains, to the contrary, that 'in the domain of subjects of law, the only clear notion is that of physical person. It is a given and simple entity conditioned in its existence by nature alone' (at 293). I cannot accept this position. For a glimpse of the changes in legal thinking since Savigny, who considers that the notion of person, subject of law, coincides with that of the human being and that others subjects of law are just a pure fiction until Kelsen for whom any person is necessarily legal and has nothing to do with the physical person, as a biological and psychological concept, see SL Paulson, 'Hans Kelsen's Doctrine of Imputation' (2001) 14 *Ratio Juris* 47, 52–55.

[59] See, eg, Arangio-Ruiz, *The UN Declaration on Friendly Relations* (n 1) 244, fn 105: 'to assume States as institutions of the legal community of mankind . . . is to shut one's eyes to the crucial aspect of international organisation represented by "that sociological unity", so to speak, which is proper to each State and which proves hard to penetrate by external rules and so hard to condition by the operation of external bodies'.

[60] Which is why Ago's assertion (n 25) that legal persons are not just creations of law but also real entities, makes me uneasy. If it is a matter of saying that a legal entity is also a concrete structure with its directors, its members, its activities and so on, that goes without saying. But if it is to argue that before the creation of law there is already an 'intrinsic structure, a real entity', I fail to see quite what that means.

counts, that is, all that matters is whether these entities are depositories of rights and obligations in a given legal order. If the answer is affirmative, they are indeed legal persons of that order.[61]

To conclude on a general remark, Arangio-Ruiz dismisses what he calls the constitutional conception of international law, that is, the conception that international law is like the constitutional law of an international legal order of the same nature as the domestic legal order, for the reason that international law has no rules to say to individuals (physical persons) under what circumstances they are the subjects of such or such a state constituted pursuant to that law. Domestic law, on the contrary, invariably includes rules that can be invoked by persons concerning the legal conditions that must be observed by any group, recognised by the legal order, to be legally constituted. Thus, he asserts: 'When a State or government is established or modified, international law has nothing to say for or against that fact to the human community involved, either prior or subsequently to the fact'.[62] And we have seen that he dismisses the rule of effectiveness of power that is supposedly just the simple recognition of a state of fact.

However, the dedicatee of these lines admits there may be rules of conventional international law that have something to say in this domain (and he cites the Tobar, Wilson and Estrada doctrines). He even accepts there may be customary rules but insists that such rules remain within the sphere of interstate relations: they may create 'international subjective legal situations' but can only affect individuals and peoples in a purely factual and indirect way.[63] We reencounter here the dualist position that governs all of Arangio-Ruiz's analyses.

It is quite clear that for the time being there is no subjective right of individuals that they could rely on at international level to safeguard,

---

[61] I leave aside here the issue of whether the capacity of a subject of law requires procedural capacity too.

[62] Arangio-Ruiz, 'The Normative Role of the General Assembly of the United Nations and the Declaration of Principles of Friendly Relations' (n 1) 648 and Arangio-Ruiz, *The UN Declaration on Friendly Relations* (n 1) 218.

[63] See Arangio-Ruiz, *The UN Declaration on Friendly Relations* (n 1) 218–19: 'Treaty rules which make exception to the so-called ideological or political "indifference", or limit the so-called "freedom of organisation" prevailing at the level of general international law, simply do what rules of international law, treaty-based or customary, usually do with regard to the conduct of States concerning *any* subject matter; . . . It is arbitrary, in our opinion, to understand such rules—or the doctrines such as the Tobar, Wilson and Estrada doctrines—as rules affecting the constitution of the State or government in question *vis-à-vis the subjects of that State*'.

say, a right to uphold democracy. But the difference between dualist and monist doctrines on this matter is that the latter considers that even if this does not exist as of the present time, there is nothing in the nature of international law to prevent it being contemplated, whereas the former considers that, by its very nature, international law could never include such subjective rights in favour of individuals.[64]

And in addition, if international law had very detailed rules in this domain (of the same type as those governing the creation of a federated state in a federation), it would doubtless (already) be the municipal law of a world state and so would have disappeared as the law of nations. It does not follow from this that any concept of international law, and in particular that of legal person, is marked by such particularism that any analogy with the concept of domestic law is inappropriate because of the specific characteristics of the law of nations and its subjects. Any 'advancement' of this law would have been made impossible if at the beginning of the twentieth century, to take a not too remote starting point, people (states, courts, scholars) had insisted on its irreducible specificities. We would have been stuck with international law as analysed by Hegel. Ultimately, one fails to see why one should not extend a realistic interpretation to the domestic legal order and, vice versa, why one should not apply a positivist interpretation to the international legal order.

The Double Personality of the State: Kelsen's Analysis

The issue of the double personality of the state in Kelsenian doctrine seems capable of a very quick solution. On more than one occasion Kelsen condemned the *Zwei-Seiten-Theorie* quite trenchantly.[65] And

---

[64] But here again Arangio-Ruiz's position is more complex. He readily acknowledges (*The UN Declaration on Friendly Relations* (n 1) 218, fn 50) that nothing limits international law *ratione materiae* and that nothing prevents it from governing the internal conduct of states. And this is consistent insofar as his claimed dualism is not logical but, one might say, empirical dualism: it is examination of the realities of international life that governs, for him, the dualist diagnosis. It is not a question of being able to contradict him on this. Let us just note, as we have already done, that realities are sufficiently complex to lead people acting in good faith to very different conclusions.

[65] The terms are ambiguous here. Kelsen criticises Anzilotti for wanting to revive the *Zwei-Zeiten-Theorie*. It is clear, though, that although he uses the expression to designate a theory of the two-sidedness of the state, it bears no relation to Jellinek's theory, so characterised by Kelsen (*Der soziologische und der juristische Staatsbegriff* (n 22) 324). In addition, the Italian scholar does not defend a double-sided theory but a theory of the double personality of the state.

yet, a closer look reveals a curious ambiguity in the argument of the Viennese scholar and invites us to look again at the issue of double personality in the very context of a Kelsenian theory of the state.

Ambiguities in Kelsen

With regard to international law, it was over Anzilotti's doctrine that Kelsen returned to criticism he had made earlier in the domain of the general theory of the state and against Jellinek. In a 1936 article on 'La transformation du droit international en droit interne' Kelsen dismissed the 'overly famous theory of the double aspect or the double nature of the state, *Zwei-Seiten-Theorie*'.[66] If one maintains, he writes, both that the state has a double juridical personality (domestic and international) and that it is the same state, one must admit that the state has some substance independently of its juridical personality, which Kelsen rules out:

> [T]he state exists . . . for the theory of law, only as a subject of law (or as a legal order . . .). And if, in a legal theory, two distinct subjects of law are both characterised as states, they can only be two separate states. Eliminating the identity of the state as a subject of both the international legal order and the domestic legal order is, to tell the truth, merely an inevitable consequence of the dualist conception whereby international law and the domestic law of the state are two completely separate systems of norms that are isolated from one another. But this consequence, to which the dualist conception logically leads, brings out its very absurdity.[67]

Similarly again, in his *General Theory of Law and State*, Kelsen returns to this question:

> If, then, there were no unifying relation between international and national law, the State, in its former capacity, would have to be an entity totally separate from the State in its latter capacity. From the juristic point of view, there would then exist two different States under the same name, two Frances, two United States, and so on, a France of national law, and a France of international law, etc.[68]

[66] H Kelsen, 'La transformation du droit international en droit interne' (1936) *Revue Générale de Droit International Public* 5, 22, reprinted in C Leben (ed), *Kelsen: Ecrits français de droit international* (Paris, PUF, 2001) 175–214, 191. On Jellinek's position see above, n 19.

[67] Kelsen, 'La transformation du droit' (n 66) 23.

[68] Kelsen, *General Theory of Law and State* (n 21) 376–77. Arangio-Ruiz, 'The Holy See' (n 1) 358, fn 7 comes to Anzilotti's rescue. He observes that Kelsen read Anzilotti 'in the French translation of his course', a veiled criticism that applies to the present author too. He says Anzilotti was not thinking of there being two Frances, two

One could even imagine, he wrote, that these two Frances might contract with one another, all of which are consequences it is difficult to take seriously. Admittedly a state has both an international personality and a state personality but simply in the sense in which one says that a human being is both a moral subject, that is he is the addressee of moral norms, and a juridical subject as he is also the addressee of norms of law. The double personality theory seems therefore to be utterly condemned. However, one observes in Kelsen the existence of a triple definition of the state, examination of which may entail a reappraisal of his position on this issue.

The broadest Kelsenian definition is the one that apprehends the state as the personification of a legal order such that any legal order, even a decentralised legal order, *provided it is supreme*, may be called the state. There is, however, some hesitation in Kelsen as to the place to be reserved for this condition. In his work on sovereignty he claims:

[I]f one considers the essence of the legal order called 'state' consists . . . in the property of being the supreme, sovereign order, this denomination must then be used . . . for the personification of the universal higher legal order [that is, the international legal order] the only one that may henceforth be considered sovereign.[69]

However, he very commonly continues to refer to the legal orders of municipal law as states and accepts that the name of state be reserved for a legal order in which the main legislative, executive and judicial functions are centralised, that is, for states in the common sense of the term, without that calling into question his general conception of legal orders:

Should one wish to reserve the use of the word state to the case where the coercive order institutes specialised . . . organs, there is nothing to object to that. But one must realise that there is between this legal order and the

United States and so on but only two juridical personalities. Which is why Anzilotti was wrong, because, Arangio-Ruiz argues, one should indeed speak of two Frances, etc, and that '[f]ar from absurd, this distinction is quite well-founded upon the four sets of facts I just indicated and a number of further facts'.

69 H Kelsen, *Das Problem der Souveränität und die Theorie des Völkerrechts. Beitrag zu einer Reinen Rechtslehre* (Tübingen, Verlag von JCB Mohr (Paul Siebeck), 1920) 250; Italian translation by A Carrino, *Il problema della sovranità e la teoria del diritto internazionale. Contribto per una dottrina pura del diritto* (Milan, Giuffrè, 1989) 368; Kelsen, *Pure Theory of Law* (n 49): 'Only the international legal order, not the national legal order, is sovereign' (at 338). See also above, ch 6

primitive legal order but a difference of technical organisation and in no way a difference in kind.[70]

But alongside the doublet of the state-*supreme* legal order/state-centralised legal order, there stands another, with implications that raise difficult problems in Kelsen's theory itself. This is the distinction between the formal concept and the material concept of the state. This distinction is found as early as his *Allgemeine Staatslehre* of 1925 and subsists in his *General Theory of Law and State*.[71] It is reasserted with a slight change of terminology in the two editions of *Pure Theory of Law*. Thus, he writes in his 1926 article in French, which is directly inspired by his *Allgemeine Staatslehre* of 1925:

> If by state one understands the apparatus of state organs, public agents (paid from a central treasury, subject to disciplinary law) then one may say the state can, apart from jurisdiction, also develop an administrative

[70] H Kelsen, 'Aperçu d'une théorie générale de l'Etat' (1926) *Revue du droit public* 561, 575. Following the logic of this presentation, the word state designates both a supreme legal order and a relatively centralised legal order that is immediate to international law and whose material competence is not delimited by a basic treaty unlike international organisations. States in the traditional sense of the term can only be designated such in the second sense, whereas the international legal order is a state in the first sense of supreme legal order. See also Kelsen, *Pure Theory of Law* (n 49): 'Only the international legal order, not the national legal order, is sovereign. If national legal orders or the legal communities constituted by them, i.e. the states, are denoted as "sovereign", this merely means that they are subject only to the international legal order' (*völkerrechtsunmittelbar*) (at 338).

[71] See H Kelsen, *Allgemeine Staatslehre* (Vienna, Österreichische Staatsdruckerei, Nachdruck 1993) 238–40 and 275–76. There is a Spanish translation: *Teoria general del estado* (Barcelona, Madrid, Buenos Aires, Editorial Labor, 1934) 312–14 and 357–58. (I thank Professor Oriol Casanovas for obtaining this rare book.) See also, 'Aperçu d'une théorie générale de l'Etat' (n 70) 576ff and 631ff. Kelsen indicates in a fn (562) that this article summarises 'the main lines of a book I published recently as *Allgemeine Staatslhere* under the direction of Springer J., Berlin 1925'. See also *Théorie pure du droit* 1st edn, trans Thévenaz (Neuchâtel, Editions de la Baconnière, 1953 and 2nd reprint 1988) 172–74; *General Theory of Law and State* (n 21), 192 and *Pure Theory of Law* (n 49), 266 and 293. This is why it is surprising that M Troper, in his article on this dual defintion of the state in Kelsen writes that after publishing his *Allgemeine Staatslehre*, Kelsen 'tried . . . to minimise the importance of this concept'. See M Troper, 'Réflexions autour de la théorie kelsenienne de l'Etat' in *Pour une théorie juridique de l'Etat* (Paris, PUF, 1994) 143, 153, fn 11. Troper justifies his assessment by noting that Kelsen did not develop his notion of state in the narrow or material sense in the 2nd edn of his *Sociologische und Juristiche Staatsbegriff* (1st edn from 1922). But in the preface to this edn he advises that he introduced in his *Allgemeine Staatslehre* of 1925 alongside the formal concept of state a new, more restrictive, material concept and refers interested readers to that book. It should be observed that all Kelsen's works on the theory of law include a double definition of the state, a general or formal one and a restricted or material definition: the *Allgemeine Staatslehre* (1925), the *Théorie pure du droit* (1st edn 1934), the *General Theory of Law and State* (1945) and the 2nd edn of *Pure Theory of Law* (1960).

activity. In this way, in the face of the formal concept of the state, which comprises the whole system of law, the set of all legal facts, one obtains a narrower material concept that includes only certain rules, certain legal features just as alongside the formal notion of the state organ, there is a narrower material notion that comprises only the juridical acts performed by a certain category of individuals.

However, the formal and broad concept of the state or of the state organ must—this results from our explanations—be considered as the fundamental concept.[72]

There is, therefore, a narrow(er) notion of the state characterised as the material notion and a broad notion of the state characterised as the formal notion. The contrast between these two notions of the state is maintained *expressis verbis* in *General Theory of Law and State*.[73] Conversely, these two adjectives are abandoned in the two editions of *Pure Theory of Law* to be superseded by the contrast between narrow and broad notions of the state. Whereas the latter includes all individuals living in a territory, the former, the narrow notion, includes only 'the individuals having the capacity of civil servants of the state and them alone: it is the state as a bureaucratic machinery of officials, with the government at its head'.[74]

It goes without saying that the 'broad and narrow' notions of the state refer to the contrast between the 'formal and material' notions of the state. Kelsen has simply relinquished the two terms, for reasons that escape me. But at the same time, he gives a clearer presentation of what makes up the nature of the two states of which he speaks. In both cases these states are identified with legal orders: the total legal order for the state in the broad sense of the term and a partial legal order for the state in the narrow sense. Thus, he writes:

> The norms governing the conduct of these individuals [civil servants] by specifically imposing obligations of service and conferring specifically on them powers, prerogatives of function, form *within the total legal order that governs the conduct of all individuals living within its domain of territorial validity, a partial legal order from which result a partial collectivity* comprising the individuals having the capacity of officials of the state and them alone: it is the state as a bureaucratic apparatus of officials with the government at its head [emphasis added].[75]

[72] Kelsen, 'Aperçu d'une théorie générale de l'Etat' (n 70) 576.
[73] Kelsen, *General Theory of Law and State* (n 21) 193–95.
[74] Kelsen, *Pure Theory of Law* (n 49), 266 and 1st edn, 172–74.
[75] Kelsen, *Pure Theory of Law* (n 49) 266 and 293. And in the 1st edn (trans Thévenaz) Kelsen writes: 'We can therefore make a distinction between the state understood in the restricted sense of a set of organs fulfilling specific legal functions

Thus, the state in the broad sense is the personification of the unity of the total legal order, whereas the state in the narrow sense is the partial legal order grouping all of the substantial (or material) rules governing the working of the state machinery through the intermediary of individuals, that is, the organs in charge of the administrative function. That is the state in the material sense of the term.[76] This identification of the two notions of the state with the total and partial legal orders provides homogeneous definitions of the state. A (too) rapid reading of the 1926 article (and so of Kelsenian thinking in the *Allgemeine Staatslehre*) gives the impression of opposing a 'broad and formal legal concept of the state' to a narrow and material concept of political-sociological inspiration: the state as 'the apparatus of state organs' or 'what is usually named the administration'.[77] One has the impression of being faced with a notion of the state as the state apparatus of constraint, that is completely distinct from the general and formal notion of the state as a personification of the legal order.

In actual fact, the famous 'bureaucratic apparatus of officials' is not a set of 'material' offices and individuals but is nothing other than a partial legal order within the total legal order.[78] The two notions of state are perfectly homogeneous and correspond to two levels of personification of the legal orders: partial and total. And the two orders hang together as does a part relative to the whole.

All of this arises clearly from the second edition of the *Pure Theory of Law* but was not invented by it. This presentation is adumbrated as early as the 1926 article. Kelsen contrasts in this article the 'formal concept of the state which comprises the entire system of law, the set of all legal facts' with 'the narrower material concept that

and the state understood in the broad sense of total legal order. The said set of organs may then be considered a partial legal order, delimited more or less arbitrarily with the total legal order', 173–74.

[76] See also C Eisenmann's definition of 'the state in the narrow sense': it is a 'group of people that make up the governing apparatus of this social unit, of this political collectivity that is also called the state—and not of this collectivity itself in full in its total unity', 'Les fonctions de l'Etat' in *Encylopédie française*, t X, L'Etat (Paris, Société nouvelle de l'Encyclopédie française, 1964) 291, 292 (reprinted in *Ecrits de théorie du droit, de droit constitutionnel, et d'idées politiques*, Paris, Panthéon-Assas, 2002). Eisenmann observes that it is the state as public power, the state as governing apparatus. But he identifies this state with a 'group of people' whereas I identify it with the set of specific rules governing that group of people.

[77] Kelsen, 'Aperçu d'une théorie générale de l'Etat' (n 70) 576 and 631.

[78] Kelsen, *Pure Theory of Law* (n 49) 266 and 293 and Kelsen, *General Theory of Law and State* (n 21) 194.

comprises only certain rules, certain legal features'.[79] The 'totality of the system of law' is quite obviously the total legal order and although the characterisation of material concept does not refer expressly to another system or order comprising only 'certain legal features' that is indeed what it is, a system or partial order. And this is confirmed by the *General Theory of Law and State* where the state as 'the bureaucratic apparatus formed by the officials of the State' designates 'a partial legal order distinguished by a material criterion'.[80]

Kelsen's thought seems, therefore, to be quite continuous on this point. That does not mean it is perfectly clear, and especially as regards the unity or duality of state persons. The double definition of state in Kelsen is astonishing in more than one respect. We do not know, at first glance, why he thought it useful to supplement the broad or formal notion of state, which he repeats is the only fundamental one, by a narrower or 'material' notion. It seems that the narrow notion allows him to recover the state in municipal law, that of the constitutionalists and administrativists, but as far as I know he barely explains this point.

Troper sees in this distinction a symptom of the fact that Kelsen never managed to provide a firm and final solution to the question of the relations between state and law. Admittedly, the state as a legal order is conflated with law but not the state in the material or narrow sense. Yet it is this state in the narrow sense 'that coincides in reality with the concept of state in the traditional doctrine'. And it is also this state that is in question when one poses the question of control of the state's action, that is, the limitation of the state by norms with which it is not to be confused.[81]

Moreover—and above all, for what concerns us here—, does the duality of definitions of the state not refer to a duality of state persons and so to a Kelsenian version of the *Zwei-Seiten-Theorie*? The contrast between the state in the narrow sense and the state in the broad sense could easily cover the distinction between the state within the meaning of municipal law and state within the meaning of international law. However, there is never any question in Kelsen's theory of such duality. He does not speak of it in his major works on the state from the *Allgemeine Staatslehre* to the *Pure Theory of Law*.

[79] Kelsen, 'Aperçu d'une théorie générale de l'Etat' (n 70) 57. The equivalent passage is in *Allgemeine Staatslehre* (n 71) 275 and in the Spanish trans at 358.
[80] Kelsen, *General Theory of Law and State* (n 21) 194.
[81] Troper, 'Réflexions' (n 71) 157 and for the entire critical analysis, 153–59.

And when he does speak of it expressly, as in the 1936 article cited above, it is to object radically to the doctrine.

An overly respectful reading of the Viennese scholar would lead then to a duplicated negation of the theory of the double-sidedness of the state; a misreading the present author made in an earlier study.[82] And yet the question is right under our noses. For the state in the narrow sense of the term is the personification of the partial legal order that governs the conduct of officials, just as the state in the broad sense is the personification of the total legal order. We are indeed in the presence of two separate persons and it is surprising that Kelsen did not say as much himself, when, while speaking of personification of the partial legal order, he did not go so far as to present the state in the narrow sense as a juridical person in so many words. But, when he argues that the state in the narrow sense is 'the personification of the partial legal order' or that the attribution of the functions performed by officials to the state in the narrow sense 'means that they are related to the unity of the partial legal order',[83] it can only be a question of a person in the juridical sense of the term. And it is in exactly these terms that he presents the state in the broad sense *mutatis mutandis*.[84]

Notice, though, that Kelsen in the passage already cited from the *Pure Theory* endeavours to exclude implicitly any possible discrepancy between the state in the broad sense and the state in the narrow sense. He takes great care to explain that:

---

[82] See above, ch 4, fn 102 (at 116).
[83] Kelsen, *Pure Theory of Law* (n 49) 266.
[84] 'The juridical norm is the rule by virtue of which is imputed to the state, which as a subject of state acts is merely the personification of the legal order' ('Aperçu d'une théorie générale de l'Etat' (n 70) 572). See also the Kelsenian conception of person ('Aperçu d'une théorie générale de l'Etat' (n 70) 23, fn 55): 'any normative order regulating the behavior of individuals can be personified; any thus regulated behavior and any obligations to be fulfilled by this behavior or rights to be asserted may be referred to the unity of this order—they may be attributed to the thus constructed juristic person', *Pure Theory of Law* (n 49) 190. The use of the concept of imputation by Kelsen is currently the subject of criticism. Kelsen allegedly used this notion sometimes in a classical sense (that attribution of some action to a subject of law who was its author) and sometimes in a specific sense, derived from Kantian theory, and meaning 'the relation between the conditions to which a norm prescribes a conduct and the conduct prescribed' (Troper, 'Réflexions' (n 71) 157). See also the entry 'imputation' by the same author in AJ Arnaud, *Dictionnaire encyclopédique de théorie et de sociologie du droit* 2nd edn (Paris, LGDJ, 1993) and S Paulson, 'Hans Kelsen's Doctrine of Imputation' (n 58) 47. I was unable to take account of this at the time of writing.

The attribution of these functions [of individuals qualified as state officials] to the state [in the narrow sense] means the relation to the unity of this partial legal order. But by relating these functions to the unity of the partial legal order, they are at the same time related to the unity of the total legal order that includes this partial order. The attribution to the state in the narrower sense implies the attribution to the state in the wider sense.[85]

The result is that the state person, in the narrow sense, finds itself still absorbed in some sense by the state in the broad sense without there being need to think further about the relation between these two entities. Is this not, however, a sort of blind spot of Kelsenian theory of the state that refuses to consider the possibility of duality of the state person although it could follow from this theory itself?

The Double Personality of the State in a Normativist Conception of Legal Orders: A Proposal

It seems to me we can readily accept the duality of persons, in the very terms of the Kelsenian theory of the state. The state in the broad sense is the total legal order, that is, the state in the sense of international law. The state in the narrow sense is the state of municipal law, the personification of a partial legal order within the total legal order. How can this state, that is, this partial legal order, be designated more specifically? It was referred to earlier by the expressions 'municipal law state' or 'constitutionalists' state'. We can try to be more specific. Mayer, as said, adopted the expression 'state-administration' in contradistinction to the state within the meaning of international law[86] and I have used this terminology myself. But upon reflection it does not seem satisfactory.

When speaking of state-administration, one naturally thinks of the state in its function of executive power and more especially of the state as it is apprehended in France by administrative law. And this presentation can apparently claim to be Kelsen's since the definition of the state as 'bureaucratic machinery of officials with at its head the government' ends a whole development in the *Pure Theory of Law* on

[85] And if they are related to the unity of the legal order, one cannot stop at the unity of the partial legal order but will continue until the unity of the total legal order is achieved. See *Pure Theory of Law* (n 49), 266.

[86] See above, n 3. Mayer notes that the two notions of state are designated by different expressions in English: 'state' for the state within the meaning of international law and 'government' for the state-administration. For a different viewpoint on the relations between the state in municipal law, government and international state person, see Arangio-Ruiz, *L'Etat dans le sens du droit des gens* (n 1) 296–99.

the 'administration'.[87] But if one reads the passage in question carefully, one realises that the notion of government does not account for what Kelsen means. He writes, as already seen, that:

> The norms regulating the behavior of these individuals by imposing specific official obligations upon them and bestowing specific competences on them constitute, within the total legal order that regulates the behavior of all individuals within its territorial sphere of validity, a partial legal order that constitutes only the partial community of officials: the state as a bureaucratic machinery, headed by the government.[88]

Ultimately, careful reading shows that this partial legal order is nothing other than the set of norms which both put in place the state organs[89] and regulate their operation by attributing to them power and prerogative but also duties.

This presentation can be accounted for more clearly, I feel, by resorting to Hart's theory of legal orders.[90] Hart considers that in principle a (non-primitive) legal order is the combination of primary norms governing the conduct of subjects of law and of secondary norms pertaining to the creation, modification and application of primary norms (norms relative to other norms).[91]

My suggestion is that the partial legal order Kelsen speaks of, or the government suggested by Mayer, is nothing other in fact than the legal order formed by the secondary norms alone 'the secondary

---

[87] Kelsen, *Pure Theory of Law* (n 49) 262–67.

[88] *Ibid*, 266.

[89] All the organs of state, whether administrative, judicial or legislative, that exercise their attributions in the name of the state. This is why the expression 'bureaucratic machinery of officials' does not seem fitting to me as it could suggest that the courts and Parliament are not organs of the state; and, in addition, the government is not at their head. On the theory of organs in Kelsen, see *Pure Theory of Law* (n 49) 150–57. Kelsen shows that any individual carrying out acts for which he is authorised by the state legal order is just as much an organ of that state as the parliament or the courts. But he agrees that that is not a common presentation. Very generally the legal acts carried out by individuals authorised for the purpose are not considered state acts and the individuals supposedly act as private persons (at 156). One speaks of state organs only for individuals designated to legislate or to apply the law as judges or officials of an administration (but see 155 where Kelsen curiously cites only the legislator or the courts).

[90] Readers might be troubled by recourse to Hart's theory of legal orders in an analysis greatly influenced by Kelsenian analysis. Syncretism is frowned upon, and rightly so in general. But if one considers legal theories not as ideologies whose purity must be safeguarded, but as attempts at scientific or objective treatment of legal phenomena, there is no reason why one should not combine elements of one theory with elements of another so long as it provides a better account of the facts and does not lead to a contradictory whole.

[91] See HLA Hart, *The Concept of Law* 2nd edn (Oxford, Oxford University Press, 1997) 91. And see the presentation of it by N Bobbio, 'Nouvelles réflexions sur les normes primaires et secondaires' in *Essais de théorie du droit* (Paris, LGDJ, 1998) 159.

norms state' (SNS). In other words, this SNS is the personalisation of the partial legal order formed by the secondary norms and it appears to be what is usually called the state within the meaning of municipal law. Not the government, insofar as this expression could suggest it was a question of the state as administration in the narrowest sense of the term ('the offices') whereas it is all of the organs ensuring the creation of legislative and regulatory norms, the modifications of those norms, their application by the administration and by the courts independently of the executive.[92]

This partial legal order may rightly be termed 'state' as it represents the 'power' or 'state power' that makes up most of the definition of the state. And when one says that a state is a power exercised over a territory and a population, what one means by power is the whole of the constraints, rights and competences put in place by the secondary norms and that allow the 'dominating activity of the state' (as Carré de Malberg has it) as it is exercised through legislation, regulations and decisions of the administration and the courts.[93]

It is partial compared with the total legal order formed by the state that includes all of the primary and secondary norms.[94] It is not the only partial order within the total legal order. Other partial legal orders co-exist, as for example the legal order of local councils, or the partial legal orders formed by juridical persons (associations and

---

[92] It would be interesting, in further research, to see how Hart's theory of secondary norms squares with the classical theory of functions of the state in French publicist doctrine. Carré de Malberg defines the functions of the state as 'the various activities of the state as they constitute separate manifestations and varied modes of exercise of state power' or 'the various forms in which the dominant activity of the state is manifested' (Carré de Malberg, *Contribution à la théorie générale de l'Etat* (n 16) t I, at 259). Eisenmann, 'Les fonctions de l'Etat' (n 76) specifies: 'the state exercises a function that consists in creating rules of law, another function that consists in laying down decisions that concern either an individual or a given situation, another that consists in materially carrying out these rules or these decisions' (at 292). Thus, 'trialist' theories of the functions of the state distinguish three main functions of the state: legislative, administrative and judicial (297–300, with the discussion of the theories of Jellinek and Duguit). We are not far from Hart's scheme of secondary rules. Other scholars, like Kelsen and less clearly Carré de Malberg, consider there are actually just two main functions ('dualist' functions), legislative and executive, the latter covering both administration and justice (see the discussion of this doctrine by Eisenmann, 'Les fonctions de l'Etat' (n 76) 295–96).

[93] Carré de Malberg, *Contribution à la théorie générale de l'Etat* (n 16) t I, 259, fn 1.

[94] Remember that Eisenmann, 'Les fonctions de l'Etat' (n 76) defines the state machinery of public power as 'the group of people that constitute the governing apparatus of this social unit, this political collectivity that is also called state—*and not the collectivity itself, in full, in its total unity*' (at 292, emphasis added). This is a distinction that covers that presented here of the state as total legal order and the state as SNS legal order.

clubs), that is, all specific legal collectivities created pursuant to the law of the state, as the total legal order that encompasses them all. But can it be considered that the set of secondary norms constitutes an order? Yes, if it is remembered that what makes a set of norms an 'order' or 'system' is the possibility of relating each norm ultimately to one and the same fundamental hypothetical norm.[95] This is indeed the case of all of the secondary norms that form the constitution of the state, in a material and broad sense, that is, the set of norms determining the organs and procedures for creating and applying primary norms.[96] These norms form a hierarchical structure culminating in the Constitution in the formal sense and this in turn finds its valid basis in the hypothetical fundamental norm that 'one must conduct oneself as the Constitution prescribes'.

The relationship between the two 'state' persons is a relationship of a set to a subset, or of the partial legal order to the total legal order. This indicates how the personalisation of these orders comes about. A legal order cannot be a person in its own eyes but only in another's eyes. Precisely, the state in the narrow sense is a person in the eyes of the total legal order in which it is included, whereas the state in the broad sense (the total legal order) is in the eyes of the international legal order in which it is itself included. It is in this international legal order that we find the norm of positive law that underpins the validity of the state legal orders on the principle of the effectiveness of power exercised over a territory and a population.

As for the international legal order itself, it is not, to my mind, personalised. One can only say it is a legal order whose validity and unity rely on the fundamental hypothetical norm of international law that 'establishes custom among states as the law-creating fact'.[97]

---

[95] Kelsen, 'Aperçu d'une théorie générale de l'Etat' (n 70) 582: 'A set of rules constitutes a relatively independent order when the validity can be related to one and the same norm, that we shall call the fundamental norm or rule of that order'. On the notion of legal order, see C Leben, 'De quelques doctrines de l'ordre juridique' (2001) 33 *Droits* 19–39.

[96] 'The constitution . . . in the material sense, is . . . the set of rules relating to the organisation [of a] state, that is, to the designation of the people who exercise power, to their competencies and to their mutual relations': M Troper, 'Droit constitutionnel' in F Hamon and M Troper, *Droit constitutionnel* 28th edn (Paris, LGDJ, 2003) 18.

[97] Kelsen, *Pure Theory of Law* (n 49) 216. Admittedly, Kelsen readily argues that one can speak of state for 'any supreme legal order be it even the most primitive' and that the universal community 'having fundamentally the same nature as the various states, may be defined as a personification of the world legal order, as a world or universal state, as a *civitas maxima*' (*Il problema de la sovranità e la teoria del diritto internazionale. Contributo per une dottrina pura del diritto*, Milan, Giuffrè, trans A Carrino, at 376). But there is no supreme legal order in whose eyes the world state could be a

It is understandable too how the narrow concept of state presupposes the broad concept, as Kelsen writes,[98] for the legal order constituted by secondary norms has no existence of its own outside the total legal order and its primary norms, which can also be put as follows: the set of organs of power instituted by secondary norms exist only as organs of a power governing certain individuals in a certain territory. And indeed, while one can imagine, at a push, a very primitive legal order composed solely of primary rules,[99] one cannot conceive of a legal order, *in actu*, composed solely of secondary rules.[100]

Can it be said, as has been suggested, that the SNS (or government) can represent, as an organ that is itself not admitted to the capacity of subject of international law (as it cannot act in its own name), the state subject of international law in the latter's relations with other subjects of international law? This presentation does not seem satisfactory to me. The SNS as a person does not act as an organ for the state as a subject of international law. The SNS is not an organ but a legal sub-order whose organs are necessarily those of the state as a total legal order and a subject of international law. And the complex of organs put in place by the secondary norms constitutes the power (over a territory and a population, or in a certain sphere of spatial, personal and temporal validity, as Kelsen would put it) which is the very condition for the existence of the state in the eyes of international law. But an organ is not to be confused with the entity of which it is the organ.

So it is the organs put in place by the secondary norms that act for the state as a subject of international law and not the SNS, which itself is not the organ of the state as a total legal order.

person in law, which is why the personification of the international legal order as a world state seems abusive to me.

[98] See Kelsen, 'Aperçu d'une théorie générale de l'Etat' (n 70) 582.

[99] Hart, *The Concept of Law* (n 91) 213–37 examines the hypothesis of a legal order including only primary rules, by studying international law. However, international law very certainly has secondary rules, particularly rules for the production of law by custom and treaties, and it can even be doubted that there can be a legal order made up solely of primary rules. It seems that any legal order includes norms about the application of law by other organs. Thus, Bobbio, 'Nouvelles Réflexions' (n 91) 172 considers that the transition from a primitive social system, that he does not characterise as a legal order, to a (true) legal order is made first by the institution of a judge, and secondly only by the institution of a legislator.

[100] That the legal order formed by secondary norms does not exist in itself outside the total legal order fits in with Kelsen's assertion that '[t]his material concept of the State is a secondary concept, presupposing the formal concept' (*General Theory of Law and State* (n 21) 194).

Moreover, what is true of the total legal order, namely that it identifies with the state in the broad sense (or in the formal sense, that is, the state as a subject of international law) is true also for the state in the narrow sense, which identifies with the partial legal order. In both instances, what is denied, in this theoretical presentation, is the duality of law and state. And just as there is no *substratum* 'state' separate from the total legal order, there is no pre-existing *substratum* of organs constituting the substance of the state in the narrow sense.

The organs exist only because they are put in place by the partial legal order, and this is personalised in the notion of state in the narrow sense or SNS.

On this issue of the dualism of state and law one may consider that the solution suggested by Troper for the state in the broad sense applies equally for the state in the narrow sense. Troper observes that while it is difficult to understand how the state, which is confused with the legal order, can be limited by that same order, conversely one 'can perfectly well speak of the definition and limitation by law of the action of state organs, because those organs, taken *ut singuli*, are not confused with law. The competences of each resulting from the authorisation conferred on them by the legal order . . .'.[101] The same goes for the relations between the state as a partial legal order and its organs.

We can at last return to certain criticisms levelled at the theory of the double personality of the state. We have seen that Kelsen dismisses the possibility, from the viewpoint of the theory of law that 'two different subjects of law can both be characterised as state'.[102] But he himself presents two concepts of the state that refer in fact to two legal orders, that is, if one applies to the one the same personalisation operation as to the other, to two states: the state of the total legal order, in other words the state within the meaning of international law and the state as partial legal order or the state within the meaning of domestic law and, for us, the SNS.

Does this amount to a dualist conception of the relations of international law and domestic law? There would be nothing scandalous about it and we would be in excellent company. But it is not so. And for a reason already seen and set out by Kelsen himself: namely, that everything that is attributed to the partial legal order, the state in the narrow sense, is related *ipso facto* to the total legal order, that is to the

---

[101] Troper, 'Réflexions' (n 71) 154.
[102] See above ch 4, fn 102 (at 116).

state in the broad sense. This can be seen in the example, which was the starting point of our research, of the contract entered into between a firm and the state. If it is a contract governed by domestic law, like any administrative agreement in France, the contract is made between the 'administration', that is, in our presentation the SNS and the firm. This agreement is located within the total legal order, that is, of the state in the broad sense, and the validity of the contractual legal tie between the firm and the SNS can be related, ultimately, to the fundamental norm of the legal order requiring that all subjects of law act as the Constitution requires. In addition, the undertaking of the SNS (state in the narrow sense) is obviously binding on the organs by which this state is engaged and which are at the same time the organs of the state in the broad sense.

Conversely, when it is the state in the broad sense, the state of international law, that enters into the contract, the contract is situated outside the total legal order of the state, in a space that for me is that of international law. In this case, the validity of the contractual legal tie between the firm and the state total legal order/state within the meaning of international law is related ultimately to the fundamental norm of international law governing the mandatory character of custom. And in addition, any undertaking by the state in the broad sense, in the sphere of internal law, compels the organs by which the state has entered into the agreement and that are at the same time the organs of the state in the narrow sense.

It can be seen that, under both assumptions, the risk evoked by Michoud, that the contract entered into by the one (the state in the broad sense or in the narrow sense) is *res inter alios acta* for the other, is non existent.

This also allows us to answer the criticism that 'the State (in international law) would have to be an entity totally separate from the State (in national law)'.[103] This is not so. The SNS is part of the total legal order just like the other infra-state partial legal orders and all of the primary norms. There is here no separate *substratum* from the legal order but the break-down of *one and the same legal order* into sub-sets that are both separate and organically linked so that everything that is attributed to the one is attributed to the other.

Could one, as Kelsen suggests,[104] finish up with this chimerical figure of a contract that is entered into between the two state persons? In

---

[103] This was the criticism Kelsen levelled at proponents of the pluralist (dualist) interpretation of legal orders. See *General Theory of Law and State* (n 21) 376.
[104] Kelsen, *ibid.*

no manner, for the total legal order, the state in the sense of international law, acts, as said, through the intermediary of the same complex of organs as the state in the narrow sense. So there can be no contract between these two persons that would suppose that these organs enter into an agreement between the two entities that act through their intermission. Now, the organs are not the 'representatives' of these entities. It is their (the organs') will that is attributed to the state entity in the broad sense or the state entity in the narrow sense, and that will cannot be split so as to allow a contract between them and themselves.

This presentation refers to two personalised entities and not to 'two portions' of the same entity, according to the conception dismissed by Arangio-Ruiz of two entities representing 'two different portions'. And in addition, they are two personalities of the same nature (legal order) whatever the differences of degree existing between the legal order of domestic law and the international legal order. This presentation does not fall foul of Duguit's criticism of the distinction between the patrimonial state/juristic person in private law and the state as public power, namely that it was irreconcilable with the unity of the state.[105] But here the unity of the state is not brought into question any more by the recognition of the partial legal order of the SNS than it is by the existence of partial legal orders of local councils or of various 'corporations'.

These are a few reflections arising from the reading of the very rich writings of Arangio-Ruiz. They are set out here in the provisional form that they are in and bearing in mind that, as concerns them, being criticised is not, as Max Weber observed, an inevitability of scientific research but on the contrary its very purpose.

---

[105] Duguit, *Traité de droit constitutionnel* (n 7) 623.

Part III

European Union Law:
International Law Surpassed or
International Law Advancing?

9

On the Legal Nature of the European Communities*

FOR NEARLY 20 YEARS now it has commonly been said that there is nothing more to say about the legal nature of the European Communities.[1] The main arguments were set out in the 1960s and analysed in depth in Constantinesco's *Compétences et pouvoirs dans les Communautés européennes: contribution à l'étude de la nature juridique des Communautés*.[2] The genre has survived, even if the analyses of the nature of the European Communities are nowadays more readily institutional or politicist.[3] Conversely, analyses relying on the legal theory of the state have become rare. That, though, is the perspective taken up here.

It is frequently written of the European Communities, that it is a potential federation. And there is no shortage of arguments in support of this characterisation (existence of 'supranational' organs, its own normative powers, direct application of Community norms, autonomous legal order, 'primacy' of that legal order, role of the European Court of Justice, election of the European Parliament by

---

* First published as 'A propos de la nature juridique des Communautés européennes' (1991) 14 *Droits* 61.

[1] I have conserved the two terms *European Communities/European Community* as used in the early 1990s.

[2] V Constantinesco, *Compétences et pouvoirs dans les Communautés européennes: contribution à l'étude de la nature juridique des Communautés* (Paris, LGDJ, 1974).

[3] See JL Quermonne, 'Existe-t-il un modèle politique européen?' (1990) (April) *Revue Française de Science Politique* 192. For legal approaches later than Constantinesco's, see P Dagtoglou, 'La nature juridique de la Communauté européenne' in Communatés européenes, Commission, *Trente ans de droit communautaire* (Luxembourg, Office des Publications des Communautés européennes, 1982) 35; J Weiler 'The Community System: The Dual Character of Supranationalism' (1981) 1 *Yearbook of European Law* 267; ML Jones, 'The Legal Nature of the European Community: A Jurisprudential Analysis using HLA Hart's Model of Law and a Legal System' (1984) *Cornell International Law Journal* 1. See also the major work by O Beaud, *Théorie de la Fédération* 1st edn (Paris, PUF, 2007) that sets out ideas that are largely contrary to those expounded here.

direct universal suffrage, and so on). At the same time, it is seen that states are resisting the process of 'actualisation' of a federation and emphasis is placed on a more 'confederal' organ, the European Council. For the future, there is speculation about the confrontation between the federal vocation of the Communities—incontestably willed by the 'founding fathers'—and the reluctance of states to transfer any further shares of their sovereignty.

Others say of the European Communities that their legal nature cannot be analysed in terms of a federation, or in terms of a confederation, or even in terms of an international organisation: that it is a *sui generis* institution or, as Quermonne wrote recently, taking up Jacques Delors' expression, 'an unidentified political object'.[4]

I would like to defend a different argument here. There is no question, of course, of denying the originality of the European Communities and the immense progress in legal techniques engendered by their constitution and their working. But it is a matter of seeing whether this 'unidentified' object might not be recognised if proper lighting were shone on it, in other words if it were conceptualised in a suitable legal way. There is no cause for amazement if this conceptualisation borrows the gist of its argument from Kelsen.

Understanding the *legal nature* of the European Communities means associating two pairs of concepts: the 'centralisation/decentralisation' pairing, which are concepts that apply to any legal order, with the 'legal order/state legal order' pair that is used to differentiate the concept of state from the general concept of legal order. One of the sources of confusion prevalent in the legal analysis of the European Communities is that the federal features that can be discerned in the Community construction are connected up with the features of a federal *statelike* legal order. But the European Community is not a state. It is true, though, that the relations that are established between the Community and the states making it up fall within the domain of federal techniques, provided federal techniques are understood as *centralisation* techniques that may be implemented in a legal order.

Centralisation/Decentralisation of a Legal Order

Kelsen's interpretation of federalism needs to be recalled here because, while celebrated among international law scholars, it remains

---

⁴ Quermonne, 'Un modèle politique européen?' (n 3) 196.

unfamiliar to a wider audience. However, just one aspect of it shall be contemplated, the 'static' (as opposed to the 'dynamic') analysis of the federalist phenomenon, for that is all that is needed for present purposes.[5]

The Kelsenian Interpretation of Federalism

The very simple idea that can be taken as the starting point is that any legal order (state or non-state) is composed of two categories of norms: 'central' norms valid for the whole territory over which the legal order extends and 'local' norms or 'partial' norms whose 'territorial sphere of validity' is a part of the territory only. Any legal order involves such a combination of norms. A wholly 'centralised' legal order, with no 'local' norms is theoretically conceivable but is impossible to implement in practice. Conversely, a wholly decentralised legal order, with no central norm, is inconceivable, for a legal order must have at least one central norm ensuring the unity of the territory that otherwise could not be recognised as the territory of a single legal order.[6] In this way the two 'poles' of the range of variation of the centralisation/decentralisation function of a legal order are excluded from the possibilities. However, within that domain, the function may take any value, that is, the degree of centralisation or decentralisation of an order may vary along a continuous scale. For example, reasoning from the state legal order, there is no difference in kind between the various forms of organisation of the state; whether a unitary state (French style), a state with extensive regional autonomy (Italian or Spanish style) or a federal state (like Switzerland, West Germany or the United States). There is always a combination between a central legal order whose norms are valid for the whole territory and partial legal orders whose norms have a territorially limited sphere of validity. So the state, for Kelsen, is merely a 'relatively

---

[5] Kelsen's interpretation of federalism in its static (opposition of a central legal order to local legal orders based on the criterion of territorial validity of norms) and dynamic (centralisation or decentralisation of orders based on the way norms are created and enforced) aspects is set out in H Kelsen, *General Theory of Law and State* (Cambridge, MA, Harvard University Press, 1949) 303–27, and in his 'Aperçu d'une théorie générale de l'Etat' (1926) *Revue de Droit Public* 608–19. The static aspect alone is set out in his *Pure Theory of Law* trans M Knight (Berkeley, University of California Press, 1967) 313–17. On the different interpretations of federalism, see C Rousseau, *Droit international public* vol 2 (Paris, Sirey, 1974) 138–213 and G Scelle, *Précis de droit des gens* (Paris, Sirey, 1932–34) (reprinted CNRS 1984) 187–287.

[6] Kelsen, *General Theory of Law and State* (n 5) 306.

centralised' legal order.[7] And likewise, beyond the state legal order, any form of grouping of states is characterised by the constitution of a central legal order that is the order in which the norms applying to the entire territory of the grouped states are valid; an order that co-exists with the partial legal order of each of the states. Again, then, we are dealing with 'relatively centralised' legal orders. From this standpoint, it goes without saying that the end purpose of the grouping is of little matter: whether it is a grouping for political and defensive purposes that in the nineteenth century, was called a confederation of states, or an economic or technical grouping that in the twentieth century is more readily called an international organisation.

Admittedly there are differences among all these 'relatively centralised' legal orders: in states, the central norms make up a very large proportion of the total legal order (comprising the central legal order and the partial legal orders), whereas in international orders it is local norms that predominate. The degree of centralisation of an order can be gauged from the ratio of the number of central norms to the number of local norms. It can also be observed that some sectors of normative activity (defence, currency, taxation, citizenship, etc) are generally reserved to the central order in a state, whereas they are maintained at a decentralised level in an international legal order, that may be called a confederation or an international organisation. But ultimately these are invariably legal orders where decentralisation (and conversely centralisation) is of varying degrees and that, for Kelsen, is 'the fundamental organising principle of the various legal communities . . . the law that allows them all to be arranged in a strictly continuous series . . .'.[8]

The Community legal order can now be tackled by showing it is an international legal order that is the subject of a novel and important centralisation process, but without losing its international character and so without acquiring the character of a state order.

The European Community: A Relatively Centralised International Legal Order

First it must reasserted, however shocking it may be, that in legal terms the Communities are run-of-the-mill international organisations.

---

[7] For a development of Kelsenian presentation of this subject see C Eisenmann, *Centralisation et décentralisation, esquisse d'une théorie générale* (Paris, LGDJ, 1948).

[8] Kelsen, 'Aperçu d'une théorie générale de l'Etat' (n 5) 619. There is a break point when moving from the non-state order to the state order (see below, this ch, at the end of the section on the primacy of Community law).

There has been a lot of gloss on the European Court of Justice's assertion in *Van Gend en Loos* (1963) that 'the European Economic Community constitutes a new legal order of international law . . .'. Even more emphasis has been laid on the fact that the Court, from as far back as *Costa v Enel* (1964), no longer characterised this new legal order as being 'of international law' and refused to see in the Community treaties any 'ordinary international treaties'.[9] Yet there is no escaping the alternative: either relations among Community Member States are no longer governed at all by international law and we are in a federal state, with the relations among the constituent entities being governed by domestic law and ultimately by a constitution, which no one can argue of the Communities; or relations among Member States are indeed governed by the treaties that set up the Communities and, whatever the peculiarities of those treaties and the peculiarities of their interpretation by the Luxembourg Court, they remain plainly within the international legal sphere.[10]

The Community is indeed, then, an autonomous legal order (as any order created by treaty is autonomous) and an international order, as it is grounded in international treaties. As for the fact that the Community legal order is 'integrated' into the legal system of its Member States (see *Costa v Enel*), this can be understood in the light of the theory of centralisation/decentralisation of legal orders. This is the relation between the central (Community) legal order, whose norms are valid for the whole territory of the Community, and the partial legal orders of the Member States, whose norms are valid each for their own territory. What makes the Community highly original, however, as an international order, is the exceptional extent of the centralisation process going on within it.

The Importance of Central Norms

This centralisation process is perceived first of all in the importance being taken on by the Community central norms compared with the Member States' 'local' norms. Admittedly this is not the situation of a

---

[9] Case 6/64, *Flaminio Costa v Enel* [1964] ECR 585.

[10] This is how the use of counter measures or the implementation of *exceptio non adimpleti contractus*, generally admitted by international law are rejected by the ECJ because the treaty establishes a new legal order (Case 90/63 and 91/63 *Commission EEC v Luxembourg and Belgium* (ECJ 13 November 1964) Rec. 1964, 1220). But the same is true for other international organisations, though to a lesser extent, see M Sørensen, 'Autonomous Legal Orders: Some Considerations relating to a System Analysis of International Organisations in the World Legal Order' (1983) *International Comparative Law Quarterly* 559.

federal state where the central norms surpass the local norms, or at least represent a mass of comparable size. Within the Community legal order, the norms whose territorial sphere of application is the Community as a whole remain a minority (whatever some might say), even if directives are added to the treaties and regulations. Directives must, in principle, be implemented by domestic law and so should count as 'local' law, except that established ECJ case law considers this type of norm as 'central'.[11] In any event, the ratio of central norms to local (state) norms undergoes a considerable quantitative increase if compared to the ratio in any other international organisation, in other words in any other special international legal order.[12] This is where the now all too familiar complaint about 'democratic deficit' stems from. For, whatever corrections are attempted, the Community remains constructed on the ground plan of the international organisation. In this model it is the council of states alone that has central normative power and takes its decisions unanimously, most of the time. Things are obviously more complex in the Community where the Commission and the European Parliament are variously involved in this normative power and where the Council can now takes decisions on a majority basis. Be that as it may, as in any ordinary international organisation, it is the organ that brings the states together that has inherited most of the central norm creating power, even when the unprecedented importance of that power entails a degree of centralisation of the Community legal order that is crying out, politically, to be re-balanced along the lines to be found in the federal state: sharing of central normative power between a council of states and a chamber of the people, constitution of a central executive organ answerable to the chamber and released from its ambiguous relation with the council of states (in the instant case the Council of Ministers or the European Council).[13]

The Existence of a Court to Rule on the Apportionment of Jurisdiction between the Central Order and the Local Orders

The Community treaties do not include, as federal constitutions do, whole sectors (defence, currency, justice, education, and so on)

---

[11] See P Manin, 'L'invocabilité des directives. Quelques interrogations' (1990) *Revue Trimestrielle de Droit Européen* 669.

[12] See B Oppetit, 'L'eurocratie ou le mythe du législateur suprême' (1990) *Recueil Dalloz-Sirey, chronique* XIII, 22 mars 1990.

[13] On the institutional threesome—Commission, Council, European Parliament—see MF Labouz, *Le système communautaire européen* (Paris, Berger-Levrault, 1988) 188–212.

attributed to the central legal order. What is attributed to this order and its organs is a series of 'actions to be taken and functions to be fulfilled' in the economic sector to achieve the Common Market, establish various common policies, complete the Single European Market and even subsequently economic and monetary union, etc. This, as Isaac observes, has resulted in 'a tangle of state and Community competencies'[14] that it is very exacting to present plainly. And yet, from the standpoint adopted here, this is still a legal order in which there coexist central norms whose territorial domain of application is the Community (or more or less so) and 'local' norms that are valid only in the territory of Member States. One of the great novelties, however, is the inclusion among the Community organs (or 'institutions') of a Court of Justice which is able to oversee the apportionment of competencies between the central order and the partial orders and whose action is so much more decisive because this apportionment does not arise clearly from the founding treaties. As in other similar instances, the apportionment is in part controlled and in part produced by the ECJ's activity, in a sense that is not detrimental, to say the least, to the central legal order. The Luxembourg Court therefore plays a capital part in the process of reinforcing this order. It is reminiscent in this regard of the role played by constitutional courts in federal states over the apportioning of competencies between the federation and the Member States. The analogy arises from the centralisation process underway within the Community; the differences, which are important, arise from the fact that the Community is not yet a federal state in any shape or form.

The Direct Applicability of Community Law

A further remarkable feature of the centralisation of the Community order is that the subjects of the order are not just the states but the individuals within the states. This is not an innovation in the technique of international law, since, even without citing such flagrant cases as that of the order created by the European Convention on Human Rights, it can be recalled that the Permanent Court of International Justice (PCIJ) in its celebrated advisory opinion of 3 March 1928 in *Jurisdiction of the Courts of Danzig* had accepted in general terms that 'the very object of an international agreement, according to the intention of the contracting Parties, may be the

---

[14] Isaac, *Droit communautaire général* (n 9) 36. See also JP Jacqué, 'La communautarisation des politiques nationales' (1989) 48 *Pouvoirs* (Europe 1993) 29.

adoption by the Parties of some definite rules creating individual rights and obligations and enforceable by the national courts'.[15] Such an agreement, therefore, creates a special international legal order whose subjects are both the contracting states and their nationals. This hypothesis is realised in a quite special way in the case of the Community order, above all if the treaty is examined through the spectacles of the Luxembourg Court. The upshot is that the norms of the central legal order, under certain circumstances laid down by the treaties and by case law, produce a direct effect in the partial legal orders, those of the states and are implemented as central norms by the state courts. These courts are, therefore, in a position where they operate twofold as organs, sometimes of the central order, sometimes of the partial legal order of their states. This is a quite classical situation in relations between a centralised order and decentralised orders. It is only a mark of 'federalism' if what is meant by that is the phenomenon of centralisation of legal orders.[16] So the very fact that a good proportion of Community norms is directly applicable does not mean that it is henceforth impossible to analyse the Community order as an international order, even if the scope of the centralisation of norms that it experiences is unprecedented *for an order of this type*.[17] This is all the more so because direct applicability goes along with the principle of primacy of the Community legal order and will contribute to making it more effective than anything encountered elsewhere.

The Primacy of Community Law

Pescatore wrote that the primacy of the Community order over the national orders was an 'existential condition' of the definition of that order.[18] But the same is true of the primacy of international law over

---

[15] *Jurisdiction of the Courts of Danzig* (Advisory Opinion) PCIJ Rep Series B No 15 (3 March 1928) 17–18.

[16] For an echo of Kelsen's analysis of federalism see C Kakouris, 'La relation de l'ordre juridique communautaire avec les ordres juridiques des Etats membres. (Quelques réflexions parfois peu conformistes)' in F Catoporti, C Ehlermann, J Frowein (eds), *Du droit international au droit de l'intégration. Liber Amicorum Pierre Pescatore* (Baden-Baden, Nomos Verlagsgesellschaft, 1987) 319.

[17] See J Verhoeven, 'La notion d'"applicabilité directe" du droit international' (1980) *Revue Belge de Droit International* 237. For Community law see Isaac, *Droit communautaire général* (n 9) 156–66; B de Witte, 'Retour à Costa. La primauté du droit communautaire à la lumière du droit international' (1984) *Revue Belge de Droit International* 425.

[18] Cited in Isaac, *Droit communuataire général* (n 9) 169.

state laws if the Kelsenian conception of the relations among these orders is adopted. However, the primacy of international law does not entail, in this conception, its actual superiority. A norm of domestic law that is contrary to a norm of international law remains valid as there is generally no procedure for annulling the unlawful norm.[19] However, in a federal state, the primacy of the central order goes along with its superiority insofar as such annulment procedures (or equivalent procedures) do exist. The position of the Community order is similar on this point again to the federal order. The combination of the principle of direct applicability with that of primacy leads, here again, to the real pre-eminence of the central order. It is not a matter of actually annulling the norms of state orders, otherwise we would already be within the context of a federal state order. But the Community order already has both a court authorised to rule on the violation of its norms, the European Court of Justice, and a procedure, that of Article 177/EEC (150/EAEC, 41/ECSC) allowing (and in some instances compelling) state courts to refer to the Luxembourg Court on a possible contradiction between the (local) state norm and the (central) Community norm. This preliminary ruling procedure is all the more often raised when the individuals on the receiving end of a large number of norms of primary or derived Community law are authorised to rely on them in national courts because the direct applicability of these norms is recognised.

Now, we know what consequence the European Court of Justice (ECJ) has derived from the combination of these factors (some of which it created itself): if annulment is not possible, the Court has clearly asserted that all national authorities should refuse to apply 'a national rule recognized as incompatible with the treaty'.[20] More especially, as regards the national court which is also an organ of the (central) Community order responsible, in the context of its jurisdiction, for applying the Community's norms, it is under an obligation to ensure their full effect, leaving as necessary unapplied, by its own authority, any provision that is contrary to national legislation, even later legislation, without having to ask or wait for such legislation to be removed by legislative means or by any other constitutional proceeding.[21] It ensures that if the organs for applying law in the Member States comply with this case law of the European

---

[19] See Kelsen, *Pure Theory of Law* (n 5) 332.
[20] Case 48/71, *Commission EEC v Italy* [1972] ECR 529.
[21] Case 34/67, *Firma Gebrüder Lück v Hauptzollamt Köln-Rheinau* [1968] ECR 359 at 370.

Court, any breach of Community law that is recognised as directly applicable by the European Court must lead to paralysis of the contrary national rule without it actually being annulled. But the consequences of the decision of the United States Supreme Court recognising the non-constitutional character of laws are no different: the law is not annulled, but it is no longer enforced subsequently by any legal authority. So one can validly speak, under this assumption, of the primacy of the Community legal order and of the pre-eminence of many of its norms over those of the partial state orders, which is a capital step forward in the centralisation of an international legal order.

However, article 177 organises a collaboration between the ECJ and the national courts and not hierarchical subordination that would compel them to bend to this very radical interpretation of the primacy of Community law given by the Court of Justice. In practice, the national courts, in particular the courts of last instance and the constitutional courts, retain their freedom in respect of the Luxembourg Court. This is yet further evidence that the centralisation of the Community international order has not crossed the line to centralisation that constitutes a state federal order. Other obvious evidence is that there is no means of constraint to sanction a state's refusal to bend to a decision of the ECJ, especially a decision recognising the unlawfulness of its legislation in respect of Community law. The position of President Eisenhower sending troops to Little Rock in 1959 to enforce the *Brown* decision of the Supreme Court (1954), which had recognised the unconstitutional character of racial segregation in schools and had laid down the principle of integration, is obviously unimaginable in the context of the European Community. This suggests that the centralisation of a legal order is not, in fact, a continuous process that could unfold in a gradual way. Insofar as the non-state legal order changes into a state, there must be a break point for the transition from quantitative to qualitative change, from international order to internal order.

The International Legal Order/The State Legal Order

Both the supporters and the opponents of European construction reason in terms of becoming caught up in a system: admittedly the European Communities do not form a federal state. The very people who advocated one knew it could not come about at the outset. But the economically-oriented organisations put in place should end up, because of the importance and the complexity of the competences delegated to them by states, smoothly and even without there being any real awareness of it, at a federal state. Such a pattern implies that there can be a seamless transition from an international legal order that is the subject of substantial centralisation to a genuine federal state. But not all centralisation leads to the birth of a state. This pre-supposes minimum legal conditions that are very far from being met, even in the most ambitious scenarios for the Community.

Of the Birth of the State

In the theory of centralisation of legal orders, it is easy enough to determine the point beyond which we move out of the international order and into a state structure. In an international order, states that are collated in a single collectivity remain subjects of international law and the basis of validity of their legal order lies directly in the general international legal order. On the contrary, states that are members of a federal state are no longer sovereign within the meaning of international law. Although members of such a federation are commonly called 'states' they differ in their legal nature from states that are the subjects of international law and in practice are of the same ilk as regions, provinces, communes, all units that are forms of decentralisation of a state and so subjects of that state and not of international law.[22] But this answer merely moves the difficulty a little further on: at what point can it be said that states that have moved together by treaty, that have created a new organisation in this way, a central legal order, to which they have delegated a number of competences, have lost their sovereignty in respect of international law and become the component parts of a new state? It is clear that if the states hand over all their competences, the situation will come about. But short of that point, can any limit be laid down? Does this take into account the number of powers handed over, the way they are handed over (temporary delegation, permanent transfer) or the nature of the competences transferred (some implying the disappearance of sovereignty, others not)? The answer to these questions is less certain than the general theoretical answer.

However, this is a starting point from which one may try to deduce others. Since the question is about the creation of a new state, from a

[22] Similarly see H Thierry, J Combacau, S Sur and C Vallée, *Droit international public* 5th edn (Paris, Montchrestien, 1986) 216.

grouping of collectivities, it necessarily follows that it is a coercive legal order and first in respect of the entities joined together. Concretely, as Virally writes, 'the federal state must gather within its hands the military might the member states have relinquished in its favour . . .'.[23] So the transfer of the states' powers in the realm of defence is a decisive feature in forming a new body. The federal state alone having the defence forces (police forces may be divided up between the central order and the decentralised orders) as the means to ensure the ultimate efficacy of the legal order (see the example of de-segregation of US schools in the late 1950s).[24] In an international legal order, though, the central order never has its own military forces. In the most extreme case states may delegate their troops to the central order (United Nations forces, NATO 'integrated' forces). In the event of conflict within this international order (international organisation, confederation), it is necessarily troops of some states that will fight the troops of other states. The conflict will be an international one. In a federal state, on the contrary, only the central order has force immediately to hand. Any conflict with its constituent entities is, in the eyes of international law, an internal conflict, a civil war or a revolution (see the break-up of Yugoslavia in the 1990s).

In addition to the transfer of competence for defence, it is very generally considered that the handover of competence for the conducting of foreign relations entails the disappearance of sovereignty within the meaning of international law. The two phenomena may be related by observing that the control of armed forces is closely related to the conduct of foreign policy. It is true, however, that this assertion seems less sure than that concerning defence: one of the examples given by classical doctrine of international law to prove the phenomenon—the disappearance of the international personality of the protected state because of the transfer of conduct of its foreign policy to the protector state—was not unanimously accepted even in the days when the institution of the protectorate existed and has been fervently dismissed since because it reeks of colonialism.[25]

Moreover, it is commonly observed that, in the workings of several federal states, the constituent entities retain certain capacities to conclude treaties. But apart from historical situations (the German Empire between 1871 and 1918, or the USSR's largely fictitious

---

[23] M Virally, *L'Organisation mondiale* (Paris, Armand Colin, 1972) 23.
[24] The forces of a federal state may prove powerless, of course. It is the state's existence that is then at stake, as recent events show.
[25] See Rousseau, *Droit international public* (n 5) 276–86.

federation), the position of federal states in this field is very clearly different from that of any other international groupings.[26] Any constitution of a federal state entails a major *capitis diminutio* as to treaty-making capacity (and so to conduct foreign policy) of the grouped entities. Whether it is considered, as in dualist doctrine, that this capacity is strictly dependent on the limits laid down by the federal constitution, or whether it is argued, in line with monist doctrine, that it is international law that must set these limits, as it is international law that defines the legal subjects entitled to make treaties,[27] the outcome is virtually the same. The birth of a federal state is recognised by the decisive transfer it implies of competence in the area of foreign policy: the federal state has, in this domain, a general competence, while the constituent entities have but residual and limited competences.

Can one go further and grasp other aspects in the process of centralisation of an international legal order that lead this order to cross the 'state line'? This is the place to mention the possibility of changing the nature of the constituent act underpinning the grouping of states. For an international organisation, that act will be a treaty. For a federal state, it will usually be a constitution. But there are federations that result from the conclusion of one or more treaties (the German Empire in 1870). In this instance, the constitution of the federation is the purpose of the treaty by which theretofore independent states unite to form a new federal state. This transition from an international act to an act of internal law occurs, for Eisenmann, 'whenever the treaty provides that its clauses on the organisation of the collectivity that it creates may be revised by a procedure of internal legislation, of constitutional revision, that is by a majority rule and no longer by a unanimous rule'. In this event, the clauses on the organisation of the grouped collectivity 'although originally rules of international law' are changed into rules of state law through the fact of the way they are to be subsequently modified. The 'mode of historical establishment in the past no longer counts: the treaty

---

[26] See Rousseau, *ibid*, 78–80. Reuter studies this issue so astutely that one might cite his entire contribution: P Reuter, 'Confédération et fédération—Vetera et Nova' in *Mélanges offerts à Charles Rousseau* (Paris, Pedone, 1974) 199; see also E Zoller, 'La conclusion et la mise en œuvre des traités dans les Etats fédérés' (1990) *Revue International de Droit Comparé* 737.

[27] See the discussion on this within the International Law Commission in 1965 when preparing the future Vienna Convention on the Law of Treaties (1965) 1 *Annuaire de la CDI*, 265–75, and its presentation in Reuter, 'Confédration et fédération' (n 26) 208–18.

[becomes] the constitution'.[28] There do not seem to be any other equally decisive factors entailing the crossing of the state threshold. In particular, the formation of an economic and monetary union among states does not imply this as a consequence, as shown, among others, by the old-established union between Belgium and Luxembourg. Admittedly, the attribution of real legislative powers to an Assembly elected by universal suffrage would, incontestably, be a mark of the existence of a federal state. But in this case we would be well over the threshold indeed! Some straightforward conclusions can now be drawn about the legal nature of the Community.

Of the Legal Nature of the Community and its Future Development

That the Community is a *sui generis* organisation, an unprecedented 'supranational' organisation or an 'integrational organisation' is probably true, provided the Community is clearly ranked among international organisations, that is special international legal orders. In a typology of organisations, there is nothing to prevent the difference being marked among organisations established by the treaties of Paris and Rome and others, quite the contrary.[29] But if the typology concerns all legal orders, including states, and if the problem is one of federalism, then it must be repeated that (a) the Community is not an unknown legal object but simply a set of international organisations established by treaties; (b) if federalism is conceived of in international society as the constitution of centralised legal orders alongside the general international legal order, then federalism begins with the most modest and powerless of international organisations and continues in an unbroken graduation with regional or universal, political or technical organisations that all have a central legal order and more or less extensive competencies in respect of the states that set them up; (c) this central legal order and these competencies may, by reaching a certain level, entail the disappearance of the quality of state of the constituent entities and the birth of a new federal (or unitary, no matter) state; (d) on this continuum, there is

---

[28] C Eisenmann, *Cours de droit administratif* (Paris, LGDJ, 1982) t 1 429; L Le Fur, *Etat fédéral et confédération d'Etats* (Thesis, Paris, Marchal et Billard, 1896) reprinted by University Panthéon-Assas (Paris 2, 2000) 540–89 reviews learned discussions in France and Germany at the time on the possible formation of a federal state by treaty.

[29] See Virally, 'La notion de fonction dans la théorie de l'organisation' (n 2) 277.

an excluded middle between groupings of states that in the eyes of international law are not states and groupings that are states.

Quite clearly then the Community falls very far short of the statehood, and even if projects currently under discussion were to be accomplished, it would still not meet the mark. Economic and monetary union does not have this effect. Political union will improve cooperation among Member States for greater coordination of foreign policies, without endowing the Community as such with competence in this area, even less with exclusive competence. As for suggestions made here and there about defence, it would be a question of starting from the Western European Union allowing Europe 'to set up a *sui generis* armed force' for M Dumas (French foreign minister) but 'without relinquishing national armies for all that'.[30] In any event, then, the Community Member States intend to remain sovereign. And they shall remain so as long as they watch over what forms the basis of the state for international law.

This, by the same token, suggests an answer to the question raised in France by the decision of the *Conseil constitutionnel* on 29–30 December 1976 (European Assembly). The Conseil drew a distinction between *transfers* of sovereignty, prohibited by the Constitution, and *limitations* on sovereignty 'required for the organisation of defence and peace', expressly authorised (subject to reciprocity) by the preamble of the 1946 Constitution (confirmed in 1958). The distinction, as presented by the Conseil, is hard to defend, for any international organisation, any centralisation, presupposes a transfer of sovereignty and the European Court repeated this many times with regard to the Community. But, in the spirit of the 1976 decision, which was, if I understand rightly, the defence of 'observance of national sovereignty', the following distinction might be proposed: the *transfer-limitation* of sovereignty by which a state consents to the centralisation of a variable number of its competences for the benefit of an institutional structure in the international order, as opposed to the *transfer-abandonment* of sovereignty by which a state accepts centralisation of such a degree that it vanished as a state in the eyes of international law leaving a new state collectivity in its place. It is probable, as concerns the Community, that such a transfer-abandonment presupposes the still far-off birth of this new psycho-sociological reality of a European nation, conserving Europe's old nations at the same time as it transcends them.

---

[30] See *Le Monde* (12 March 1991).

10

A Federation of Nation States or a Federal State?*

I T IS RARE for a major politician's thoughts to turn away from the immediate and pressing problems of his position in order to consider basic problems whose solutions cannot be immediate. When it does happen, the analysis brings out the capacity for long-term thinking, that is, the capacity to have a genuine vision of the future. This is just what makes the speech given by German Foreign Minister Joschka Fischer at the Humboldt University in Berlin, on 12 May 2000, so interesting.

We do not wish to pick up all the elements of this very rich analysis here, but to focus solely on the problems in the theory of the state that are at the core of Fischer's thinking. And just as he deliberately expresses himself in the long term, taking care to stress that these are only personal thoughts and that 'no-one need be afraid of these ideas' (at 8 of the English version), we shall devote ourselves to theoretical thinking 'beyond the Intergovernmental Conference' as he, once again, specifies.

Wishing to summarise the question that the minister asks both himself and his Union partners, one might put it like this: how can the Community institutions be made simpler, more transparent, more effective, more democratic, more welcoming to candidates, more effective with thirty countries, rather than fifteen, while enabling progress along the path of integration and maintaining the nation-states intact? This is a problem that looks rather like squaring the circle.

For Fischer, the solution is fairly simple: to move from the present state of the Union, which he, as we shall see, very rightly analyses as

---

* First Published in C Joerges, Y Meny, JHH Weiler, *What Kind of Constitution For What Kind of Polity? Responses to Joschka Fischer*, (Robert Schuman Center for Advanced Studies, European University Institute, The Jean Monnet Chair, Harvard Law School, 2000).

that of a confederation, to a higher stage which he calls a federation, whose features we shall have to examine. However, before doing so, it would be a good idea to clarify the source of the bulk of the Community's (or the Union's) dysfunctions.

The Reasons for Community Europe's Dysfunctions

These reasons, we feel, lie in the twofold logic which presided over the functioning of the three Communities from the outset. On the one hand, these Communities, each founded by a treaty, constitute international organisations in the classical sense of the term in public international law. The logic governing such organisations is an intergovernmental, or better-stated, inter-state, logic. It means that it is the sovereign states that are the masters of the game and that there is no point in talking about democracy without such institutions, since the only legitimacy that counts is that of the states and their sovereign equality.

Yet, simultaneously parallel to this logic, there is another one at work in the Communities: a logic of integration, or, if you wish, a supranational logic. This is expressed in: (1) the institution of the Commission; (2) the possibility given to the Community authorities (Commission and Council) to create derived law that may, in the case of the Regulation, have full direct effect; (3) the creation of a Court of Justice, which, through its case law, has extended the possibility for all of the derived law to have direct effect, by asserting the primacy of Community law over the whole of national law. To this should be added the existence of a parliament elected by direct universal suffrage, whose powers have been enhanced by the various treaties that have come along to revise the original ones.

The result, as the Community construction has evolved, has been great confusion about determining who holds ultimate power in the Community: the Council, ie, the state organ; the Commission, the supranational organ; the European Parliament; or the Court of Justice itself? The breakdown of powers between the states and the Community is another area of confusion that has ever been present as it has never been clearly defined but simply left up to the case law of the European Court of Justice (ECJ), namely a body that has actually been given the mission of defending the Community's supranational character.

Hence the accusations of opacity of decisions and of democratic deficit made to the institutions, to mention only these reproaches. It will, at this point, be noted that the reproach related to the democratic deficit implies that the Community (and beyond it, the Union) is regarded as something different from a mere international organisation. The United Nations, for instance, have never been reproached with suffering from a democratic deficit. They may have been accused of the obsolete composition, in some eyes, of the Security Council, but never to our knowledge have they been subject to criticisms about democracy, the separation of powers, or the rule of law. The UN functions on the logic of an international organisation, viz, the interstate logic.

But if, by contrast, democratic deficit is talked of in the case of the Union, it is necessarily in relation to Union citizens. It supposes that the ultimate basis of the legitimacy of the institution being talked of is the people, the people of the Union, the people who are, in democratic theory, sovereign, taking decisions either by themselves or through their representatives and controlling the executive. But the supremacy of the democratic logic over the inter-state logic is not organised by the treaties, which at least in their initial version, give supremacy to the body, the Council, which represents the inter-state logic. And the more the Community construction advances, in other words, the more the elements of integration progress, the more the distortion between the two logics accumulates, to the point of becoming insupportable. This is what Fischer clearly sees when he says that 'A tension has emerged between the communitarisation of economy and currency on the one hand, and the lack of political and democratic structures on the other . . . (at 6).'

The simple solution—in logical terms, although by no means in political terms—to these problems would be to set up a federal state, which would allow the antagonism between these two logics to be transcended and to set up the democratic institutions and a state based on rule of law: a parliament endowed with genuine legislative powers, a responsible executive, independent and impartial judicial institutions, with everything being based on a constitution which includes a human rights charter. But it is just this simple solution that the German minister refrains from invoking, since he knows that merely mentioning it would raise such hostility among some EU states as practically to prohibit debate.

That is why he imagines another solution, which he calls a federation rather than a federal state (*Föderation*, not *Bundesstaat*). What this solution consists of and whether it is theoretically well-founded and practically achievable is what we shall now attempt to consider.

Federation and the Constitutional Theory of the State

When studying groupings of states, and the European Union is undoubtedly a grouping, classical constitutional theory knows only two possible types: the confederation of states and the federal state. Can there be a third type, a federation but not a federal state, as Fischer's speech seems to suggest?

Confederation of States and Federal State

As from the end of the nineteenth century, German (Laband and Jellinek) and French constitutionalists, starting from Le Fur's thesis that inspired the ideas of Esmein, Hauriou, Duguit and Carré de Malberg, formulated a clear legal distinction between two great formulas for groupings of states: confederations and federations.[1] The confederation of states does not constitute a new state but just an association of sovereign states (*Staatenbund*), while the federal state (*Bundesstaat*) is, as its name indicates, both *Staat* and *Bund*, state and federation. As Le Fur writes: 'The federal state, in virtue of being a state, has sovereignty' (at 590), whereas 'the confederation of states is only an association of sovereign states [and] does not itself possess sovereignty, nor, consequently, the character of a state' (at 498).

In the twentieth century, Kelsen, while incorporating his theory of federalism into a more general theory of the centralisation and decentralisation of legal orders,[2] confirms the distinction between the federation of states, which is a grouping of states, not itself a state, but a 'purely international union of states . . . on the model of the League of Nations', and the federal state which is, as its name indicates, a state within the meaning of international law. The members of the federation are, in contrast, collectivities that are no longer states within the meaning of international law. This is because their foundation is to be found in the constitution of the federal state, and

---

[1] See, L Le Fur, *Etat fédéral et confédération d'Etats* (Thesis, Paris, Marchal et Billard, 1896) reprinted by University Panthéon-Assas (Paris 2, 2000) with a foreword by Charles Leben for a general study on the question, see O Beaud, *Théorie de la Fédération* (Paris, Presses universitaires de France, 2009).

[2] For a tentative analysis of the European Community in the context of Kelsen's theory, see C Leben above ch 9, 257.

not directly in the international legal order.[3] Consequently, Fischer is quite right to call the present Union a confederation. But what exactly does he mean by a federation?

The Federation (J Fischer) or Federation of Nation States (J Delors)

There is evidence of the fact that the choice of the term 'federation' raised a problem for Fischer. In the Chevènement–Fischer dialogue that appeared in *Le Monde* on 21 June 2000 (at 15–17), the French Minister of the Interior said, in connection with the European Union, that 'It is neither a federation nor a confederation. It is something that has never been described anywhere, and does not even resemble the Holy Roman Empire of the German Nation'. Fischer clarifies as follows: 'We sought a neutral word in German instead of, and in place of, federation. Translated into French or English, it still remains federation; so we resigned ourselves. We have to accept the fact that federation is the word that best suits'.[4]

It is easy to see why the word federation embarrassed the German minister: in ordinary language, just as in the language of constitutionalists, 'federation' immediately evokes the 'federal state,' and this is what has to be avoided, even at the cost of a polemical vocabulary which is absent from the rest of his speech at the Humboldt University. Thus, he says:

> Only if European integration takes the nation-states along with it into such a Federation, only if their institutions are not devalued or even made to disappear, will such a project, in spite of all the difficulties, be workable. In other words, the existing concept of a federal European state replacing the old nation-states and their democracies as the new sovereign power reveals itself to be an artificial construct which ignores the established realities in Europe (at 9–10, my emphasis).

But, at first sight, the solution Fischer offers to the Community's problem looks enormously like a federal state. Thus, again (at 9) he writes that for all the problems of enlargement of the Union 'There is a very simple answer: the transition from a Union of states to full

---

[3] H Kelsen, *General Theory of Law and State*, (New York, Russell & Russell, 1961) 303–27.

[4] *Le Monde* (21 June 2000) 17. On the comparison, curious if nothing else, between the Union and the Holy Roman Empire of the German Nation, see *Le Monde* (21 June 2000) 16.

parliamentarisation as a European Federation . . ... And this means nothing less than a European Parliament and a European government which really do exercise legislative and executive power within the federation. This federation will have to be based on a constituent treaty'. If it is added that this European Parliament is to have two chambers, one to represent the Europe of nation-states (a 'senate' on the American or German model, at 10), with a European government able to be formed from the national governments (at 10) or else opting for the direct election of a president with 'far-reaching executive powers', distinct from the Commission, which would become a mere administrative body,[5] one may legitimately ask what would really separate this federation, which, like Jacques Delors, he calls a 'federation of nation-states' (at 13), from a classical federal state.

This point is a capital one politically, as his French colleague H Vedrine showed in his 'reply to Joschka Fischer' published in Le Monde on 11-12 June 2000, by dotting the i's as follows:

> The core of the ideas is the concept of federation and of federation of nation states. Does this, at the end of the day, amount to one and the same thing, classical federalism? In that case, we are moving towards an impasse.

Everything in the constitutional model presented by the German minister, thus depends on the survival of the nation-states. They would not disappear as in a federal state, or rather, taking up what might be a slip of the pen, not disappear 'complètement[6]'. It is one thing to affirm the co-existence of the federation and the nation-states, but quite another to present a convincing picture of it. But we have seen that, in this federation, there is to be a European Parliament made up of two chambers and endowed with legislative powers, a European government (perhaps under the aegis of a President of the Union) to act as an executive, and also a 'constituent treaty which lays down what is to be regulated at European level and what still has to be regulated at national level' (p 11).

But instead of what the Minister rightly calls 'inductive communitarianism', there will be 'clear definition of the competences of the

---

[5] This is the solution he prefers: see his declaration before the European Parliament's Committee on Constitutional Affairs Le Monde (8 July 2000) and International Herald Tribune on 7 July 2000. But the idea has been rejected by Chancellor Schröder, who calls it a 'perfect illusion': Le Monde (18 July 2000) 3.

[6] Translator's note see quotation above – in the French version; neither the English nor German original contain this adverb.

Union and the nation states respectively in a European constituent treaty, with core sovereignties and matters which absolutely have to be regulated at European level being the domain of the federation, whereas everything else – the least essential bits, let us not forget – would remain the responsibility of the nation-states (p 11).

To know what this 'finalised federation' (p11) might look like, one can again go to the description Fischer gives of the federation that might be set up among the Member States belonging to the 'centre of gravity' that are resolved to go forward without waiting for all EU states to be ready to do so. Here is how the Minister sees the action of the states belonging to the centre of gravity.

Without dwelling on the feasibility of this sort of federation within the Union, one should note that the 'militant' aspect of this federation, that might be called 'interior' *and would still, in principle, fail to be a federal state*, is, after all, hard to reconcile with a constitutional model in which the nation-states conserve their sovereignties: the federation speaks with a single voice on as large a number of questions as possible, and has a strong parliament and a directly elected president.

But this interior federation foreshadows the European Federation which is the last stage of European integration (at 15). Can one, in these circumstances, be satisfied with the assertion that:

> . . . All this will not mean the abolition of the nation-state. Because even for the finalised Federation, the nation-state, with its cultural and democratic traditions, will be irreplaceable in ensuring the legitimation of a union of citizens and states that is wholly accepted by the people (at 11).

Or again:

> The completion of European integration can only be successfully conceived if it is done on the basis of a division of sovereignty between Europe and the nation-state. So what must one understand by the term 'division of sovereignty'? As I said, Europe will not emerge in a political vacuum, and so a further fact in our European reality is, therefore, the different national political cultures and their democratic publics, additionally separated by linguistic boundaries (at 10).

Sovereignty and Nation States

It seems that one of the difficulties attaching to the current debate is the confusion between a legal notion, that of sovereignty, and a historical, political or even philosophical notion, that of the nation-state.

Sovereignty

As it is not possible to go into the complex discussions about the notion of sovereignty here, we shall content ourselves with a few remarks. Among the various ideas that this notion can cover, we shall take two. Regarding a state, in the sphere of public international law, we call sovereign a state that is not legally dependent upon another state, or as Kelsen says, a state that has its foundation directly in the international legal order and not in the constitution of another state.[7] This is why the Member States of a federation are not sovereign within the meaning of international law, while those that are part of a confederation are.

In the domestic legal system, we call sovereign the real or fictitious entity that possesses the *summa potestas* on which the whole legality/legitimacy of the order depends. Thus, we say that, in such a state, it is the people or the nation that are sovereign.

Coming back to international law, the problem raised by groupings of states is that of either 'limitations' or 'transfers' of 'sovereignty' or 'powers' that most constitutions authorise in favour of what may generally be termed as international organisations. Thus, in France, the Constitutional Council, after distinguishing 'limitations' of sovereignty (permitted) from 'transfers' of sovereignty (unconstitutional, and possibly requiring amendment of the constitution) currently distinguishes the notion of treaties (or treaty provisions) on the basis of whether they infringe 'the essential conditions for the exercise of national sovereignty', or not.[8]

It will, however, be noted that, to date, whenever the Council has encountered such provisions, in the Maastricht and Amsterdam treaties for instance, what has followed is not a refusal by France to ratify the treaties, but a revision of the French constitution. The conclusion must be drawn that these provisions, while infringing 'the essential conditions for exercising national sovereignty', did not do so to such a degree that the French authorities genuinely feared for France's sovereignty.

One can, however, well imagine a state which transfers all its powers to an international organisation (a grouping of states) losing its sovereignty in the eyes of international law. Where, then, is the break-

[7] See Kelsen, *General Theory of Law and State* (supra n 3)303.
[8] To speak as the French Conseil Constitutionnel, *Traités européens*, DC 19 nov 2004 in L Favoreu and L Philip, *Les grandes décisions du Counseil Constitutionnel* 15th edn (Paris, Dalloz, 2009) 751§22.

ing point? The reply of classical international theory is that the transfer of the powers to conduct external relations and national defence by a state bring a disappearance of sovereignty within the meaning of international law.[9] To this, some would add, though in my view wrongly, the transfer of monetary powers.[10]

It will be noted that in order to highlight the 'truly historic turnaround' made by the European Union, Fischer notes in his speech that, 'In Maastricht, one of the three essential sovereign rights of the modern nation-state-currency, internal security and external security-was, for the first time, transferred to the sole responsibility of a European institution' at. 5). This does not entirely fit the criteria set forth, but comes close. Yet, as long as the Member States ultimately remain masters of their defence and foreign policies, which is still the case in the present Union, they retain their sovereignty. If the states were truly to transfer their powers in these areas, ie, their right to decide their policy in the last instance by themselves, then there would be loss of sovereignty.

Likewise, were the federation to endow itself with a parliament that possessed true legislative powers in major areas, but without supervision of either the 'government' of the federation or the national parliaments, this would undoubtedly mark the creation of a federal state. Let us note that it is on this point that Fischer's proposals appear not just weakest, but also least consistent. For all his desire to 'sell' the idea of a federation which leaves the nation-states with their sovereignty, he proposes a most peculiar solution for the chamber representing the European Union's citizens. This chamber, he writes (at 10) would be 'for elected members who are also members of their national parliaments', which would avoid any 'clash between national parliaments and the European Parliament'.

But what does this mean? Would the European parliamentarians be the faithful image of the party divisions of national parliaments? Ought they to be elected by them on the representative system, so as to reconstitute a sort of French, German, British etc, mini-parliament at the level of the European Parliament? Ought they to

---

[9] The point was quite well seen by President Jacques Chirac in his speech to the Bundestag on 27 June 2000: 'Neither you nor we are envisaging the creation of a European super-state that would replace our nation-states and mark the end of their existence as *actors in international life*' (*Le Monde*, 28 June 2000) 16.

[10] Leben, see above ch 9, 270. For a long time, there has been economic and monetary union between Belgium and Luxembourg without the consequence of ending the sovereignty of either state.

resign in the event of new national elections or changes in their national majority? Would they be prisoners of a binding mandate and could they be recalled by the national parliaments were they perchance to express through their vote convictions that differed from those of their constituents? This is a strange way of advancing the cause of European integration.

One last word on the idea of a 'European Constitution,' a recurrent idea taken up again by President Jacques Chirac in his speech to the Bundestag on 27 June 2000.[11] I do not wish to discuss whether such a 'constitution' is desirable in order to enable clearer and simpler distribution of powers, better participation by citizens and an enhancement of democracy within the Union here. I should merely like to recall that the word 'constitution' does not in itself refer to any institutional structure. Thus, the treaties setting up certain international organisations are called 'constitutions'. This is, for instance, the case for the treaty setting up the International Labour Organization ('the Constitution of the ILO').

It is, nonetheless, true that the normative pyramid of a state is crowned by what is ordinarily called a constitution. In the case of a federal state, this constitution may find its origin in one or more treaties. In this case, the constitution of the federation is the object of the treaty whereby the hitherto independent states combine to create a new federal state. The treaty of political union concluded by the two German States on 31 August 1990 for their reunification is a recent example of such a case.[12] In what circumstances does the transition from an international act to one of domestic law come about?

Eisenmann has explained this clearly. The transformation happens 'because the treaty provides that its clauses on the organisation of the collectivity that it sets up can be amended by a procedure of domestic legislation, of constitutional revision, ie, by a majority, no longer unanimity, rule'. For in this case the clauses on the organisation of the group collectivity, 'though originally rules of international law' become transformed into rules of state law because of the way

---

[11] Printed in *Le Monde* (28 June 2000) 16–17. See also the joint proposal by D Cohn-Bendit and F Bayrou presented on 13 June in Strasbourg *Le Monde* (14 June 2000).

[12] See M Fromont, 'Les techniques juridiques utilises foun l'unification de l'Allemagne', *Revue Française de Droit Constitutionnel* (1991) 579 and the other articles in this issue of the *Revue Française de Droit Constitutionnel* on the theme of 'Germany's reunification and constitution'.

they may be amended. The way they were historically established no longer counts: the treaty becomes a constitution.[13]

Nation States

If we now come to look at the concept of the nation-state, which nobody wants to 'abolish,' there is, I feel, ambiguity that confuses the discussion. It should be noted that the term nation-state hardly appears, if we are not wrong, in works and treatises of theory of the state or of constitutional law, at least those we have been able to consult. It can be sought in vain, for instance, in Kelsen's *Pure Theory of Law* or *General Theory of Law and State*. These works contain long studies on federal states, unitary states, decentralised or centralised states, but nothing about nation-states. In his *Contribution à la théorie générale de l'Etat* (Contribution to the General Theory of the State) Carré de Malberg devotes his consideration to the idea of the union of state and nation. He wishes, thereby, to reject the positions that the nation is the original subject of sovereignty and that it gave rise to the state, to which it is prior. For this eminent constitutionalist, instead, 'The state is not a legal subject that arises in the face of the nation and opposes it: as long as it is accepted that the powers of a state nature belong to the nation, it must also be admitted that there is an identity between the nation and the state, in the sense that the latter can be only the personification of the former'.[14]

But I do not believe that it is this debate, which turns around a very specific conception of national sovereignty among French constitutionalists, that the defenders of the idea of the nation-state are thinking of. They are seeking more to defend the durability of a collectivity founded in, and by, history that expresses a cultural *cum* religious, linguistic and political heritage, and, ultimately, a 'will to live together' (Renan) of a very special quality.

Need this will to live together necessarily imply that the collectivity through which the nation is expressed be a sovereign state within the meaning of international law?[15] This is undoubtedly what the

---

[13] See C Eisenmann, *Cours de droit administrative*, (Paris, LGDJ, 1982) Vol 1, 425 and Le Fur above n 1, 540–89 for the debates on this question in French and German legal theory at the end of the 19th century.

[14] See R Carré de Malberg, *Contribution à la théorie générale de l'Etat* (Paris, Sirey, 1920, reprint, Paris, CNRS, 1969) 12–13.

[15] This is the idea defended by President Jacques Chirac in his speech to the Bundestag: 'Our nations are the source of our identities and our roots. The diversity of their political, cultural and linguistic traditions is one of the strengths of the Union.

'sovereignists' think, to the point that during the debates on the ratification of the Maastricht Treaty, one could hear politicians declare that even a large majority in a referendum could not make sovereign France disappear, since it does not belong to a single generation. Each has received it from its forebears and has the duty to pass it on, still just as sovereign, to its children.

This is an entirely respectable political opinion which does not, in my view, imply that the cultural, religious, linguistic and political heritage, coupled with the very special quality of the 'will to live together', necessarily have to be expressed through a sovereign state rather than through a federated state within a larger federal state. Is it conceivable that the French, Italian, British, German, Irish etc, 'genius' would be unable to express itself in a federated state? Are our nations not sufficiently ancient to justify this hypothesis? Thus, when Fischer stresses that in the final (European) federation, 'the nation-state, with its cultural and democratic traditions, will be irreplaceable in ensuring the legitimation of a union of citizens and states that is wholly accepted by the people' (at 11) this does not, to my mind, mean that all this is possible only if the nation-states retain their sovereignty within the meaning of international law, as in that case, I do not see how the European federation and the nation-states (still meaning sovereign states) can be reconciled.

The European Federation: Squaring the Circle

So, we come back to the original question: how can the Community institutions be made simpler, more transparent, more effective, more democratic, more welcoming to candidates and more effective with 30 rather than 15 countries, while continuing to permit progress along the path of integration and maintaining the nation-states intact? Some recent scholarship, inspired by Schmitt's ideas on the 'federative pact' and brilliantly represented in France by Beaud, thinks these seemingly irreconcilable elements can be reconciled. Thus, Beaud writes:[16]

For times to come, the nations will remain the foremost reference for our peoples. Contemplating their extinction would be . . . absurd . . .'. (*Le Monde*, 21 June 2000). 'But who says the creation of a federal state entails the extinction of national identities? What we see in federal states (US, Germany, Switzerland), whose federated states have less ancient and less rich personalities than the Union's nations, does not necessarily lead to this conclusion'.

[16] O Beaud, 'La notion de pacte—fédératif. Contribution a une théorie constitutionnelle de la Fédération' in H Mohnhaupt, JF Kervégan (eds) *Liberté sociale et contrat dans l'historie du droit et de la philosophie* (Frankfurt, Klostermann, 1997) 269. See

The special feature of this theory of the federative pact is that creation of the federation does not make the nature of the Member States that have concluded it as political unit(s) disappear. In other words, there is no merger of the political units constituting a larger whole, ie, no absorption of the Member States into the federation. From this viewpoint, this theory of the federation differs from the ordinary law of moral personality; in private law, the created collective person makes a screen between its founders and its bodies, and one might say that the latter replace the former. In contrast, in this public-law conception of the federation, the authors of the pact, the subjects of constituent power, continue to exist.

One can readily see the political relevance of such a construction, which might, as if by magic, immediately dispel all the contradictions that analysts of the European Union stumble over: much more than an international organisation, ie, a confederation (with which it shares its creation through a treaty and maintenance of Member States' sovereignties) even though it be less than a federal state (but for how long if increasingly numerous powers are transferred to it?), the Union baptised a federation in Schmitt's sense, might simultaneously be as powerful and effective as a federal state while strictly maintaining the personality and sovereignty of its constituent parts.

I must confess to being very sceptical as to this sort of Hegelian transcendence of opposites and the emergence of a new synthesis. I do not see how a 'new animal' involving all the legal and political advantages of the federal state can be slipped into the theory of the state while still conserving the full sovereignty of the 'nation-states'. But I can very well understand politicians seeking, whether from sincere belief or from calculation, to acclimatise the idea that this sort of result could be reached. If the construction of the Community in Europe has such a price, we should be willing to pay it. After all, the 'academic' analyses are too uncertain to be able to rule out entirely the new synthesis defended by the scholarship which has just been summarised.

Nonetheless, despite everything, I hold to Spinoza's old idea that the essence of the circle is irremediably different from that of the squares, and that *tertium non datur*.

---

also, C Schmitt, *Théorie de la constitution* (Paris, Presses universitaires de France, 1993) 507–40. It would be interesting to know how far Joschka Fischer (or his advisors) have been influenced by these ideas of Schmitt's.

11

Is there a European Approach to Human Rights?*

... inalienable political rights of all men by virtue of birth would have appeared to all ages [before the eighteenth century in Europe] a contradiction in terms.

H Arendt, *On Revolution* (Penguin, 1963, 1965) 45

Introduction

A T FIRST SIGHT the question takes us by surprise, so closely linked in our minds are human rights with the universal, and not the particular. Certain quotations concerning the universal dimension of human rights spring to mind immediately: 'All men are born equally free and independent' (Virginia Declaration of Rights, June 1776); or 'all men are created equal, . . . they are endowed by their Creator with certain unalienable Rights' (Declaration of Independence of the Untied States of America, July 1776); 'Men are born free and equal in rights', and this is a 'sacred and inalienable right' (France, 1789).[1] And all those texts reach their apogee, as it were, in Article 1 of the *Universal* Declaration of Human Rights: '*All human beings* are born free and equal in dignity and rights'[2] and this time, moreover, the man/human being ambiguity is swept aside.

* First published in P Alston (ed), *The EU and Human Rights* (Oxford, Oxford University Press, 1999).

[1] For the complete text of these various declarations of human rights, see S Rials, *La Déclaration des droits de l'homme et du citoyen* (Paris, Pluriel, 1988). On a topic close to that under discussion here, see R-J Dupuy, 'Les droits de l'homme, valeur européenne ou valeur universelle?' *Communication de l'Académie des sciences morales et politiques* 414–28 (18 December 1989).

[2] Universal Declaration of Human Rights, adopted by UNGA Res 217A (III) (1948). In United Nations, *A Compilation of International Instruments* (New York, 1994) Pt 1, 1.

At the Second United Nations Conference on Human Rights in Vienna in June 1993, when several Third World countries were leading an attack on what they regarded as the Western values expressed in the 1948 Declaration, the Programme of Action finally adopted on 25 June reaffirmed in its first paragraph that 'the universal nature of these rights and freedoms is beyond question', and in paragraph 5 that 'All human rights are universal, indivisible and interdependent and interrelated', that 'it is the duty of States, regardless of their political, economic and cultural systems, to promote and protect all human rights and fundamental freedoms', even though the text also states that it is essential to bear in mind 'the significance of national and regional particularities and various historical, cultural and religious backgrounds'.[3]

In the same spirit, the Secretary-General of the United Nations wrote in a message marking the inauguration of the year commemorating the fiftieth anniversary of that Declaration that 'Human rights are the foundation of human existence and co-existence. Universal, indivisible and interdependent, they are what defines our humanity. They embody the principles which are the sacred cornerstone of human dignity'. And the Secretary-General went on: 'Human rights derive their strength from their universality, thanks to which no frontier, barrier or enemy can stand in their path'.[4]

On reflection, however, and without the slightest intention of challenging the aspiration to universality which is characteristic of human rights philosophy, the question asked does raise certain doubts: is not the historical basis of all the declarations cited above to be found in the intellectual development of Europe? Are not all those declarations the heirs of European Enlightenment, from Locke to Rousseau and Kant? So it is very natural that, in the context of relations between countries of the old world, Article 49 (ex Article O) of the Treaty on European Union, as amended by the Treaty of Amsterdam of 2 October 1997, makes the admission of any new European State to the Union subject to the condition that it 'respects the principles set out in Article 6 (*ex* Article F(1))'.

---

[3] *Vienna Declaration and Programme of Action*, A/CONF. 157/24 (1993). On the Vienna Conference, see P Tavernier, 'L'ONU et l'affirmation de l'universalité des droits de l'homme' (1997) 31 *Revue Trimestrielle des Droits de l'Homme* 79 and M Delmas-Marty, *Pour un droit commun* (Paris, Seuil, 1994) 266–71.

[4] Message of 10 December 1997, reproduced in (1997) 27 *Bulletin de l'Association Française pour les Nations Unies* 33.

Article 6(1) states that 'The Union is founded on the principles of liberty, democracy, respect for human rights and fundamental freedoms, and the rule of law, principles which are common to the Member States'.[5]

The Treaty on European Union does not, however, merely require its own members to respect those fundamental freedoms. As we shall see, the Union is going to extend and organise systematically a policy of encouraging and defending democracy, human rights and fundamental freedoms, and the rule of law which the European Economic Community initiated when it introduced into the Lomé III (1985) and Lomé IV Conventions provisions concerning respect for human dignity and human rights.

We are no longer, therefore, dealing with principles which only the members of the European 'club' are supposed to respect, but with principles which are projected onto the relations of this 'club' with any other non-member country since they are considered to be universally valid. And the same applies, with differences of detail, to the policy of defending human rights conducted at international level by the United States, principally since the Carter presidency.[6] As a result, the question raised, which has perhaps been understood and approached at the outset as a question on Europe as such, *applies to the West* as a whole. We are dealing with a Europe whose intellectual development in the sphere of human rights has taken place in the United States and Australia, and even Latin America. In the circumstances, the question before us concerns the (real or illusory)

---

[5] P Wachsmann, 'Les droits de l'homme [dans le traité d'Amsterdam]' (1997) 4 *Revue Trimestrielle de Droit Européen* 883, 894ff. The text of the Treaty of Amsterdam, and also the consolidated versions of the TEU and the EC Treaty, are reproduced in the same issue of the *Revue Trimestrielle de Droit Européen* at 929–1102.

[6] See O Schacter, 'Les aspects juridiques de la politique américaine des droits de l'homme (1977) 23 *Annuaire Français de Droit International* 53–74. In a speech given to the General Assembly of the United Nations, President Carter declared that 'no member of the United Nations can claim that ill treatment of its citizens is its affair alone. Nor can any member avoid its responsibility where cases of torture or unjustified loss of liberty in any region of the world are concerned'. This policy has been criticised on numerous occasions because of unilateral measures taken by the United States in cases of serious violations of human rights. But the principle that 'every State has an interest in the protection of human rights' and may adopt 'diplomatic, economic and other measures authorized by international law' in respect of the state responsible for those violations was accepted by the Institute of International Law at its session in Santiago de Compostela. See (1990) 63(II) *Annuaire de l'Institut de Droit International* 338. And see C Rucz, 'Les mesures unilatérales de protection des droits de l'homme devant l'Institut de droit international' (1992) 38 *Annuaire Français de Droit International* 579.

universal nature of human rights as they have appeared and developed in Europe and the West.

This brings us to a twofold extension of the question: extension of the European Union to Europe in general (or at least Western Europe), and then extension of Europe to the Western world. Such extension is essential, because how, in the general considerations of the Academy of European Law, can we ignore the charge of ethnocentrism, even of neo-colonialism, levelled by certain authors and certain countries against the European/Western concept of human rights?

However, the question can just as easily be understood in a more restrictive sense: is there a specifically European approach within those Western countries which all claim European descent? An approach which is specifically European by comparison with that of, for example, America? But here too it should be made clear what we mean by 'a European approach'. It would be neither desirable nor even feasible to confine it to the practice of the European Union. It is clear that the European Convention on Human Rights must be taken into account, given in particular the great influence it has on the decisions of the Court of Justice of the European Communities and the reference to the Rome Convention in Article F(2) of the Maastricht Treaty, confirmed by the Treaty of Amsterdam.[7] It seems, however, equally imperative to take into consideration the constitutional provisions of the European States and the mechanisms therein for the protection of human rights, and also the decision reached by national courts, insofar as certain specifically European features may be identified in this field.[8]

The West and the Rest: Europe and the Question of the Universality of Human Rights

The expression 'the west and the rest' is borrowed from an article by Kishore Mahbubani (former Singapore Assistant Secretary of State

[7] See Wachsmann, 'Les droits de l'homme' (n 5) 883–902.

[8] Accordingly, it has become possible, in connection with the growing convergence between the decisions of European constitutional courts and those of the courts in Strasbourg and Luxembourg, to speak of progress towards a 'European constitutional law'. See the special edn devoted to this topic in (1995) 7 *Revue Universelle des Droit de l'Homme*. See also M de Salvia, 'L'élaboration d'un "ius commune" des droits de l'homme et des libertés fondamentales dans la perspective de l'unité européenne: l'œuvre accompli par la Commission et la Cour européennes des droits de l'homme' in F Matscher and H Petzold (eds), *Protection des droits de l'homme: la dimension européenne. Mélanges en l'honneur de Gérard J. Wiarda* (Cologne, C Heymann, 1988) 555–63. See also Delmas-Marty, *Pour un droit commun* (n 3) 223–53.

for Foreign Affairs).[9] It expresses the revolt of certain Asian or Islamic countries against what they consider to be a manifestation of the old European/Western imperialism in respect of the rest of the world, demonstrating once again an arrogant disregard for any tradition or culture other than those of Europe.

That Europe in this instance stands for the West, because it is from Europe that the West was born, can plainly be seen in this extract published in *le Monde* of 15 March 1989 by Mohammed Akoun, Professor of the History of Islamic Thought at the Sorbonne, at the time of the polemic arising out of Ayatollah Khomeini's *fatwa* condemning the writer Salman Rushdie to death. It shows that the author, in formulating his criticisms, speaks indiscriminately of Europe and the West. In particular, addressing the intellectuals who had come to Rushdie's defence, he wrote:

> You cannot expect all cultures to follow the path traced for two centuries by France and Europe! To take that line would mean requiring other cultures to lock themselves into '*the one western model*' of historical development, intellectual and artistic achievement. It would mean a repetition of the colonial ideology which legitimised the subjugation of other peoples and cultures by the export of *a civilisation created in Europe* . . . Western thought shows that it is incapable of development outside the *historical models set up in Europe and backed up by the technological West.*

A little further on, the author adds:

> The perception of human rights in a western philosophy reduced to nothing more than bare positivist and historicist rationalism increases the misunderstanding with Islam, which conceives of these human rights in the wider context of God's law (emphasis added).[10]

In that text, as in others which could be quoted from the mouths of persons with political authority in Asian countries, there is both a challenge to what is seen as the ethnocentric short-sightedness of Europe/the West[11] and an implied declaration that there can be other

---

[9] K Mahbubani, 'The Dangers of Decadence. What the Rest can Teach the West' (1993) 72 *Foreign Affairs* 10–14. The article appeared in response to a study by S Huntingdon, 'The Clash of Civilizations?' (1993) 72 *Foreign Affairs* 22–49. It will be noted that, like Saudi Arabia, Singapore had not by 1995 ratified any convention on human rights involving an international review body. On the challenge which is sometimes called 'Asianism' in human rights; see the comments of M Bettati, *Le droit d'ingérence. Mutation de l'ordre international* (Paris, O Jacob, 1996) 31–34.

[10] Quoted by P Wachsmann, *Les droits de l'homme* 2nd edn (Paris, Dalloz, 1995) 43.

[11] A very striking symbol of the 'European–Western' coupling in the field of human rights is to be found in the pairing of René Cassin and Eleanor Roosevelt, the principal draftsman of the Universal Declaration and the chairwoman of the drafting committee.

approaches, other models of human rights, which are the product of other cultures and which take account of the specific fundamental features of those cultures (or civilisations). European/Western consciousness encounters a serious problem here as to the legitimacy of promoting and extending a model of human rights which it knows full well is the product of its own history.

The European Model of Human Rights: A Concrete Universal

Notwithstanding the protestations of Cassin, who announced in his lecture at The Hague that the Universal Declaration, 'not being subject to any particular doctrine not that of natural and absolute rights, nor the individualism of the eighteenth century, nor Marxist dialectic, is imbued with what is common to all these doctrines, namely the affirmation of the unity of the human family',[12] it is not difficult to show, as has been done on many occasions, how the invention of human rights, which was to lead to the publication of the Universal Declaration, is linked to the political, religious, and philosophical history of Europe and even of certain European countries. The appearance of a form of the state in which traditional political relations, favouring political authority over subjects, are turned on their heads thenceforth to favour the protection of citizens against the power or the rulers marks the passage to a new era. This new era, the earliest origins of which are to be found in the combining of the Graeco-Roman philosophical tradition with the Judeo-Christian religious tradition, was heralded by the philosophy of the Enlightenment, itself anticipated by the 'Glorious English Revolution' of 1689, and was to be proclaimed most solemnly in the declarations of independence of

---

[12] R Cassin, 'La Déclaration universelle et la mise en œuvre des droits de l'homme' (1951) 79(II) *Recueil des Cours de l'Académie de Droit International de La Haye* 209. It will be recalled that the first para of the preamble to the Declaration states: '[w]hereas recognition of the inherent dignity and of the equal and inalienable rights of all members of the human family is the foundation of freedom, justice and peace in the world'. The Universal Declaration was adopted by 48 votes for, non against, but with eight abstentions (Belarus, Czechoslovakia, Poland, Saudi Arabia, Ukraine, South Africa, USSR and Yugoslavia). Two states were absent—Honduras and Yemen. According to the delegate from the USSR, the rights set forth could only be a matter for 'formal democracy', and the result would necessarily be to encourage interference in the internal affairs of states. The Saudi Arabian representative justified his abstention more specifically on the ground that he could not accept Art 16 (the right to marry without any limitation due to race, nationality and religion) or Art 18, which sets out the freedom to change religion. See Rials, *La Déclaration des droits de l'homme et du citoyen* (n 1) 285–87.

the colonies, and then the United States of America and also in the Declaration of the Rights of Man and the Citizen of 1789. In the new European/Western state, protection of human rights is based on an individualist vision of society, defending the paramountcy of human beings as persons, which is considered the cardinal value, all of which finds expression in the creation of, first, a liberal and then a democratic state in the service of its citizens. As Bobbio has written in one of his many texts on this subject, the change in the eighteenth century from perceiving society as something organic to perceiving it in contractual terms constitutes a genuine 'Copernican revolution' in political thought, 'since, the relationship between the individual and society being overthrown, society is no longer a fact of nature existing whatever individuals intend, but rather an artificial body created by individuals in their image and pattern, in order to satisfy their interests and needs for the broadest exercise of their rights'.[13]

This revolution took place at a specific moment in history and in specific places. When, for example, the subject of human rights was no longer merely dealt with in philosophical works such as Locke's second 'Treatise of Government' (1690),[14] but became a declaration of faith justifying rebellion against tyranny and the creation of an independent political body. Thus, in the declaration of the rights of the State of Virginia (June 1776), a short introduction states: 'Declaration of the rights which must belong to us, now and for posterity, and which must be regarded as the foundation and basis of government', and then announces in Article 1: 'All men are born equal and independent: they have certain essential and natural rights of which they can by no contract deprive their posterity: such as the right to life and liberty, with the means to acquire and possess property, to pursue and attain happiness and safety'.[15]

In his commentary on this declaration, Bobbio writes:

[w]e must acknowledge that at that moment a new form of political regime was born, by which I mean something radically 'unprecedented', a form

---

[13] N Bobbio, *Libéralisme et démocratie* (Paris, Cerf, 1985) 20–21.

[14] J Locke, *Two Treatises of Government* (London, Thomas Hollis, A Millar et al, 1764). Of the many quotations which could be selected from the second treatise ('Essay on the origin, limits and true ends of civil government' §137) I offer this: 'Absolute arbitrary power, or governing without settled standing laws, can neither of them consist with the ends of society and government, which men would not quit the freedom of the state of nature for, and tie themselves up under, were it not preserve their lives, liberties and fortunes, and by stated rules of right and property to secure their peace and quiet.' (para 137, 214).

[15] Text in Rials, *La Déclaration des droits de l'homme et du citoyen* (n 1) 495.

of political regime which is neither merely the rule of law as opposed to that of men, a form of government earlier praised by Aristotle, but which is at the same time the rule of men and of law, of men who make laws and of laws which find their limits in existing rights which those same laws may not infringe: in a word, the liberal State which leads, by internal development and without loss of continuity, to the democratic State.[16]

The unprecedented phenomenon which appeared at that time and which was to be given further backing by the events of 1789 in France was, as Hannah Arendt writes in the sentence which serves as epigraph to our text, 'inalienable rights for all, by virtue or their birth' or, as Fichte radically expresses it, 'The opportunity [for anyone at all] to acquire rights'.[17] Those rights are first, in what is subsequently recognised as the liberal tradition of human rights, those maintained by the individual against any power liable to infringe those 'natural' rights: power of the state, of the Church, of economic might, even of science and technology.[18]

[16] N Bobbio, *L'età dei diritti* (Torino, Einaudi 1992) 260.

[17] The exact quotation is: 'This alone constitutes the true right of man which falls to him as a man: [namely] the possibility of acquiring rights': J Fichte, *Fondement du droit naturel* (Paris, Vrin, 1984) Annex II, para 22, 394. This does not mean that the sudden appearance of a human rights ideology between the 17th and 18th centuries happened *ex nihilo*. I argue to the contrary (see text to n 30 below) that this sudden appearance was the culmination of a long history which began on the one hand with religious consciousness and the declaration in Genesis that man, every man and every woman (at the time of his creation Adam is both) is created in the image of God, and, on the other hand, with philosophical awareness and the Greek heritage. This history continues with the first, then the second, scholasticism, to issue forth in the 17th century in the school of the law of nature and peoples. Statements can therefore be found in the past, and not only that of the West, which can be translated into the language of human rights. This does not in any way lessen the unprecedentedness of human rights philosophy as it took shape in Europe and America in the 18th century.

[18] See, eg, the Universal Declaration on the Human Genome and Human Rights, adopted unanimously by the General Conference of UNESCO on 11 November 1997. Art 1 declares that the human genome is the heritage of humanity, and Art 2(2)(a) states that 'Everyone has a right to respect for their dignity and for their rights regardless of their genetic characteristics'. Similarly, in the Council of Europe Convention for the protection of Human Rights and Human Dignity with regard to the Application of Biology and Medicine, Art 1 provides that: 'The Parties to this Convention shall protect human beings in their dignity and identity and shall guarantee every person, without discrimination, respect for his integrity and his other rights and freedoms with regard to the applications of medicine'. In a different field, but one not far removed, the objective of French Law of 29 July 1994, introduced into the Civil Code at Arts 16 to 16-9, is to ensure that the human body is respected. Art 16 states: 'The law shall guarantee the primacy of the person, prohibit any injury to its dignity and ensure that human beings are respected from the moment their life begins'. Art 16-1 continues: 'Everyone shall be entitled to have his body treated with respect. The human body shall be inviolable. The human body, its parts and products may not be the subject of any right of property'.

Side by side with this liberal tradition, however, and first appearing in the early texts of the French Revolution, we see the assertion of what are later to be called 'social rights',[19] an expression of the socialist tradition of human rights which came to supplement the liberal tradition in Europe.[20] Thus, the first French constitution of 3 September 1791 states in the first Title headed 'Fundamental Provisions Guaranteed by the Constitution' that 'A general system of *public assistance* shall be established and organised, to bring up abandoned children, comfort the poor when they are sick, and provide work for the able-bodied poor who have been unable to find any'. And the following paragraph further states: 'Public Education shall be established and organised, common to all citizens, free as regards the elements of education indispensable for all men'. These 'second-generation' rights are again asserted, with more force and style, in the Montagnard Constitution of 24 June 1793, which includes them in its new Declaration of the Rights of Man and the Citizen. Article 21 declares: 'Public assistance is a sacred duty. Society owes its unhappy citizens the means of subsistence, whether by finding them work or by ensuring that those who are unable to work have sufficient to live on'. Article 22 adds: 'Education is a requirement for all. Society must with all its power promote the progress of public reason, and put education within the reach of all citizens'.

These two great categories of rights, which are still intertwined in the Universal Declaration of 1948 (Articles 22 to 28), were later to form the subject-matter of two separate treaties: the International Covenant on Civil and Political Rights (ICCPR) and the International Covenant on Economic, Social and Cultural Rights (ICESCR).[21] It is, however, clear how far a large part of their content is already present in the great founding texts of the American and French revolutions. Does this deep-rootedness in history mean that doubt is cast on the universal character of the European/Western doctrine of human rights or, conversely, that this doctrine represents the only possible

[19] On the opposition between 'freedoms' and 'social rights', see J Rivero, *Les libertés publiques* vol 1, *Les droits de l'homme* (Paris, PUF, 1997) 97–101; L Ferry and A Renaut, 'Droits-libertés et droits-créances' (1985) 2 *Droits* 75–84.

[20] Bobbio, *L'età dei diritti* (n 16) 262 considers that there are three main currents in the European political tradition which have ended up by converging on the question of human rights: liberalism, socialism and social Christianity.

[21] International Covenants on Economic, Social and Cultural Rights and Civil and Political Rights adopted by GA Res 2200 A (XXI) (1996), in *International Instruments* (n 2) 8, 20.

path which all the civilisations of the world must necessarily follow? It seems to me that the answer to both questions must be 'No'.[22]

As Imbert (Director of Human Rights at the Council of Europe) has so perfectly expressed it, 'for anybody, humanity is accessible only through his own particular culture. In this there is a priori no contradiction with the requirement of the universality of human rights.'[23] This is the idea which I myself have tried to express by using the Hegelian concept of 'the concrete universal'.[24] Even so, though, the path taken by the particular culture still actually has to lead man to universality.

It is Possible to Conceive of the Universal and Human Rights Starting from Other Traditions

In support of this argument, three points must be developed: (1) contrary to the large-hearted declarations of the Secretary-General of the United Nations or of the Conference of Vienna of 1993, quoted above, it is not all acknowledged human rights, even within Europe/the West, that have universal scope; (2) in theory it is possible to follow paths to the universal other than those followed by

---

[22] On the question of the universality of human rights, see the collection of articles in the first issue of the *Revue Universelle des Droits de l'Homme* (1989) 1–34, with contributions from Badinter, Badjaoui, Cassese, Imbert and Kodjo. See also, *L'Universalité du droit international des droits de l'homme dans un monde pluraliste*, symposium organised by the Council of Europe (1990); J D'hommaux, 'De l'universalité du droit international des droits de l'homme: du *pactum ferendum* au *pactum latum*' (1989) *Annuaire Français de Droit International* 399–423. Also recommended is the short but excellent analysis by Wachsmann, *Les droits de l'homme* (n 10) 35–49; see also Y Madiot, *Considérations sur les droits et devoirs de l'homme* (Bruxelles, Bruylant, 1998) 23–109 (for a natural law and yet evolutionist approach to human rights) and Delmas-Marty, *Pour un droit commun* (n 3) 254–81; in English see C Cerna, 'Universality of Human Rights and Cultural Diversity: Implementation of Human Rights in Different Socio-Cultural Contexts' (1994) 16 *Human Rights Quarterly* 740; M Perry, 'Are Human Rights Universal? The Relativist Challenge and Related Matters' (1997) 19 *Human Rights Quarterly* 461. See also the comments of Bettati, *Le droit d'ingérence* (n 9) 31–34.

[23] PH Imbert, 'L'apparente simplicité des droits de l'homme, réflexions sur les différents aspects de l'universalité des droits de l'homme' (1989) 1 *Revue Universelle des Droit de l'Homme* 24.

[24] The concept of the concrete universal is developed in *The Science of Logic* which is, beyond a doubt, one of the most difficult works in the history of philosophy. I do not claim to use it in a sense entirely in conformity with Hegelian philosophy. I simply mean that there is no such thing as a universal value arrived at by pure abstraction, irrespective of actual social and doctrinal history. This use of the concept of the concrete universal seems to me to be an approximation of Hegel's highly complex arguments. For an initial approach see S Auroux (ed), *Les notions philosophiques* (Paris, PUF, Folio, 1990) ii, 2679, 'Universel concret'.

Europe. However, those paths necessarily cross those of Europe/the West at some point; (3) the fact that the idea of the universal first saw light in a certain society at a certain time in certain circumstances in no way detracts from the truth of that idea as universal. It does not descend from some heavenly abstraction, but is the result of the labours of men engaged in their time, its ideology and problems. The universal necessarily emerges from the particular and concrete, just as human freedom is the freedom which each person achieves in his own particular situation.

The Universal and the Particular in Human Rights

Human rights as expressed in Europe or the United States do not spring in their entirety from the universal, that is, from principles that may be expressed in universal terms. There are accidents of history on both sides of the ocean and as between European countries themselves. To give just one example, few Europeans would be willing to accept Article II of the American Bill of Rights (1789–91) which states that 'the right of the people to keep and bear Arms, shall not be infringed'. Similarly, speaking of the European Convention on Human Rights, de Salvia points out that: 'The rights enshrined in the Convention are those of a man defined by his triple identity: national identity; European identity, and universal identity . . . There is, therefore room beside a *ius commune* for a *ius proprium* of fundamental rights particular to each State'.[25]

If, then, these particular features exist within the Western arena itself, it is in no way inconceivable that a non-Western society, from the starting point of its own history and its own civilisation, may formulate human rights which in part belong to the category of rights which we may call universal, but in part arise out of the particular features of the society and regions in which that society is located. There is no contradiction to be found in the juxtaposition of a European convention of human rights with an American convention or an African charter.[26]

---

[25] De Salvia, 'L'élaboration d'un "ius commune" des droits de l'homme' (n 8) 556.

[26] On these texts, see F Sudre, *Droit international et européen des droits de l'homme* 3rd edn (Paris, PUF, 1997) 98–105. It is, however, noteworthy that the author has reservations about the Universal Islamic Declaration of Human Rights (106–108) because of the priority given to the principles of Sharia law over all binding rules of international law.

Nevertheless, while it is unarguable that there exists a *ius proprium* of human rights, it is equally unarguable that there exists a universal *ius commune*. This finds expression where both the universal and the regional conventions on human rights set out, in comparable terms, the rights called sacrosanct from which no derogation is permitted. For an example, see Article 15(2) of the European Convention which classes in this category: the right to life (save lawful acts of war), the prohibition of torture and of inhuman and degrading treatment or punishment, the prohibition of slavery and servitude, the principle of the legality of punishment. But the double jeopardy rule in Protocol 7 of the European Convention and the provisions set out in the ICCPR (ratified by all the European states parties to the Rome Convention), which allow no derogations, as well as those corresponding to the case envisaged by Article 15(2) of the Rome Convention (Article 11 prohibits imprisonment for debt, Article 16 enshrines the right to recognition of legal personality, Article 18 enshrines the right to freedom of thought, conscience and religion) must also be taken into consideration.[27]

These are what is known as the nucleus of human rights, which hold good everywhere for everyone and which could, from the point of view of international law, be considered to form part at least of customary international law and, perhaps, even of a *ius cogens* for humanity.[28] Nevertheless, it must be acknowledged that there exists, beyond the first layer of rights, including those mentioned above, a second, and even third or fourth layer which are not unanimously agreed on, or are at least very differently interpreted: the right of people to self-determination, permanent sovereignty over natural

---

[27] Sudre, *ibid*, 152–56; G Cohen-Jonathan, *Aspects européens des droits fondamentaux* (Paris, Montchrestien, 1996) 92; Wachsmann, *Les droits de l'homme* (n 10) 55–62; Henkin considers that the rights listed in the first 21 articles of the Universal Declaration are rights 'to be enjoyed by all human beings universally' in 'General Course on Public International Law' (1989-IV) 216 *Recueil des Cours de l'Académie de Droit International de La Haye* 230.

[28] For a discussion of this question, see JF Flauss, 'La protection des droits de l'homme et les sources du droit international' in SFDI conference, *La protection des droits de l'homme et l'évolution du droit international* (Strasbourg, 29–31 May 1997) (Paris, Pedone, 1998) 28ff (typed report). See also what Delmas-Marty, *Pour un droit commun* (n 3) 271–78 calls 'elemental humanity'. To understand that this elemental humanity concerns every human being, it is sufficient, as Bettati has frequently remarked, 'to put oneself on the side of the victims: one would search in vain for any difference between a man tortured in Europe and one tortured elsewhere in the world, or between a woman raped in Europe and one raped elsewhere in the world, or between a child enslaved in Europe and one enslaved elsewhere in the world'.

resources, the right to development, the right to a healthy environment and so on.[29]

The European Universal and its Relations with other Civilisations

It seems to me to be beyond doubt that the path towards the universal may be found in any civilisation. The crux, however, is to discover how, in a given culture, it is possible to progress towards this conception of the universal. As regards European history, it has been remarked that it was the fusion over centuries of the Graeco-Roman philosophical tradition and the Judeo-Christian religious tradition that produced this result.[30] It is not a priori inconceivable that the same movement might occur independently in another civilisation. In practice, nevertheless, we find that it is when other world civilisations were brought into contact with European/Western culture, a contact which in general they did not desire, that they were induced to undertake the labour of self-examination which is the beginning of the journey towards the universal, and towards the ability to conceive of the rights of every human being.

Sometimes this meeting of civilisations occurred peaceably, as for instance when the Greek philosophical tradition was absorbed by the philosophers of the Islamic world such as Al Farabi, ibn Bajja, ibn Sina (Avicenna) and ibn Rochd (Averroes), who were themselves to fertilise Jewish and Christian thought in the twelfth to fourteenth centuries. The joining of intellectual positions which then took place meant that everyone, from the starting-point of his own religious tradition and his grasp of Greek philosophy, could reach out beyond his own particular circumstances to a mode of expressing thoughts

---

[29] Compare the lists given in the special edn of the (1989) (1–2) *Revue Universelle des Droit de l'Homme* by Badinter, 3; Bedjaoui, 9; Cassese, 17–18; and Imbert, 25.

[30] For a historical summary of the formation of the theory of human rights, see H Lauterpacht, *International Law and Human Rights* (London, Stevens, 1950) 73–141. In that work, the great British jurist adopts an undeservedly severe position vis-à-vis the Universal Declaration of Human Rights. In particular, he criticises the omission of any action whereby individuals can enforce those rights against states: 'there are, in these matters, no rights of the individual except as a counterpart and a product of the duties of the State. There are no rights unless accompanied by remedies' (420–21). But it is for the two Covenants to provide *remedies*, even if they may still be regarded as insufficient. For a historical study of all these declarations of rights, reference may also be made to C Faure, *Ce que déclarer des droits veut dire: histoires* (Paris, PUF, 1997).

comprehensible and meaningful to all.[31] At that time, obviously, the problems were not of human rights, but rather of theological and metaphysical matters. Nonetheless, what was taking shape was a form of universalism. This encounter was short-lived, in particular because philosophical thought was rejected by an Islam turning in on itself.

The circumstances were quite different when, in the nineteenth and twentieth centuries, Islam, like every Asian and African culture, met Europe. Most often, this meant an involuntary and forced encounter with a West which perceived itself as a part of history and thought in terms of rationalism and recognition of the value of the individual. This meeting necessarily produced adverse effects on traditional societies which, in their turn, found themselves pitched headlong into history, however hard they resisted. And entering history initially leads to the devaluation of tradition, as we can see in the history even of Europe and in that of the peoples touched by European culture.

The world becomes disenchanted, to use Max Weber's well-known expression; the old values are challenged and sifted by Western rationality.[32] The result may be a reflex withdrawal and the expulsion of the carriers of Western 'contamination'. This was the case, for example, when Japan shut itself off in the seventeenth century from the European presence. It is also the case where, from approximately the thirteenth century onwards, Islamic philosophical thought was repressed or where, in our days, Western values are rejected in the name of a return to the most intolerant traditional values to be found in various corners of the world.

It may, nevertheless, be thought that contamination by the 'ethnocentric' (European) idea of universality[33] is incurable, given the very action of those peoples and civilisations in turning the claim of the universal back on its inventors. For what is the basis for denouncing colonialism, racism or under-development, if it is not the morality of universality?[34] But this cannot long remain a weapon to be

---

[31] Without entertaining any naïve belief in some Edenic Andalucia, it is interesting to read *Le Colloque de Cordoue. Ibn Rochd, Maïmonide, Saint Thomas ou la filiation entre foi et raison* (Paris, Climats, Association freudienne international, 1994).

[32] For a study of Max Weber based entirely on the idea of 'modernity as disenchantment', see P Bouretz, *Les promesses du monde. Philosophie de Max Weber* (Paris, Gallimard, 1996).

[33] See E Weil, 'Du droit naturel' in *Essais et conférences* (Paris, Plon, 1970) 175, 191.

[34] Dupuy, 'Les droits de l'homme' (n 1) 423 remarks that the European social and cultural system ' has . . . disseminated throughout every continent, as Europe itself

used only externally. Sooner or later, this weapon will be seized by individuals who will then turn it against their own authorities.

As noted, for example, by the philosopher and Sinologist, François Jullien, in an interview published in *le Monde* of 19 September 1997: 'Most often we waver between a naïve universalism (as if the concept of law had always existed everywhere) and a lazy relativism (as though human rights were not valid for the Chinese, whereas experience shows us that ever since they discovered that concept, they have found it harder and harder to do without it'). In other words, today the process whereby societies join the stream of history and begin to protect individuals and their rights is under way throughout the entire world. This does not, however, mean that the roads to be travelled by each culture in that process must in every respect resemble those travelled in the West, as alleged by Akoun in the text quoted above. It is clear that for deeply 'holistic' societies, to adopt an expression used by Dumont, in which the relationship between the community and individuals is different from that in Europe (Dumont was thinking particularly of India), the paths will be different.[35]

Those differences cannot, however, serve as camouflage for regimes which quite simply deny all human rights (see the supposedly socialist conception of human rights argued in 1936 by Vichinsky, the Moscow public prosecutor of evil memory and the representative of the USSR to the UN at the time of the Universal

---

spread by means of colonialism and imperialism, the values of argument. Thus, French school teachers taught the peoples overseas a political philosophy which they were to use against the colonial power'.

[35] Dumont opposes individualism to the holism of traditional societies. He writes that in those societies 'the emphasis is placed on society as a whole, as collective man; the ideal is defined through the organization of society for the purposes of its own ends (and not those of individual happiness); order and hierarchy are paramount, each individual must contribute in his station to the social order and justice consists of adapting social functions to suit society as a whole' in *Homo hierarchicus. Le système des castes et ses implications* (Paris, Gallimard, 1966) 23. For another example of the integration of the individual in society, see J Matringe, *Tradition et modernité dans la charte africaine des droits de l'homme* (Bruxelles, Nemesis, Bruylant, 1996). It is noteworthy that Rawls, in his essay *Le droit des gens* (Paris, Esprit, 1996), maintains that the most fundamental rights, which in his view are 'the right to life and security, to personal property, and the elements of the rule of law and also the right to a certain [sic] freedom of conscience and association, together with the right to emigrate' (at 75) can equally well be accepted by traditions which conceive of the individual 'not, in the first place, as citizens possessing citizens' rights, but rather principally as members of groups: communities, associations or corporations'. For him the human rights referred to above can be protected 'in a well-ordered hierarchical State . . .'. This hierarchical state cannot but remind us of Dumont's description of holistic societies. On Marxist holism, see below, n 56.

Declaration in 1948). Nor can they be used to classify as illegitimate any criticism of one Asian regime or another under the pretext of cultural differences. It is an essential feature of every political system which truly cares for human rights that it accepts it must live under the critical gaze of its own citizens and of the rest of the world, however uncomfortable such a situation may be.[36]

If those conditions are satisfied, there is no contradiction in positing the existence of 'concrete universals' other than those of Europe/the West, any more than there is a contradiction in demonstrating that within that block there are differences, sometimes far-reaching ones, as to the definition of some of the most fundamental rights of human beings.[37] This argument has been objected to because of its optimism that all great civilisations can make their own way towards the universal. Some of them, perhaps, bar such a path. And this claim refers, pretty often, to Islam. Undoubtedly there are those among us who place their stake on the richness of the great cultures which can all, in our opinion, draw on their traditions for the resources which will enable them to chart their passage to the universal in human rights and democracy.

We are not alone in this sentiment. In a recent interview in *le Monde*, Salman Rushdie, who knows better than anyone what fundamentalism and fanaticism mean, responded with the following question to the question put to him: 'Does Islam necessarily give rise to that (ie, religious fanaticism and fundamentalism)? Is it possible

---

[36] For an insight into the reasoning of a politician from the Asian continent with regard to human rights, see Bilhari Kausikan (South-East Asia Director in the Singapore Ministry of Foreign Affairs), 'Asia's different standard' (Fall 1993) *Foreign Policy* 24–41, and the reply given by Aryeh Neier, former director of Human Rights Watch, 'Asia's unacceptable standard', *ibid*, 42–51. It is interesting to note Kausikan's remark that '[f]or the first time since the Universal Declaration was adopted in 1948, countries not steeped in the Judeo-Christian and natural law traditions are in the first rank' (at 32). Although he does not deny the nucleus of human rights, the author denounces the overly individualistic view of human rights in the West and suspects the West of targeting the cultural characteristics which gave a lead to the economic success of the countries of South-East Asia. For a discussion of the challenge to cultural relativism, see also above, n 22. In the *International Herald Tribune* (10 April 1998) may be found an article by one of the correspondents of *The Times* in Hong Kong, denouncing the hypocrisy of invoking 'Asian values': J Mirsky, 'What are "Asian Values"? A Justification for Repression'. See also Bettati, *Le droit d'ingérence* (n 9) 31–34.

[37] The reader may be referred to the special edn of the review *Esprit*, 'L'universel au risque du culturalisme' (December 1992), for the quest for a universalism that, without yielding to total relativism, still takes into consideration what in the cultural experience of each of us is unique and empowering for all humankind. See in particular the articles 'Les deux universalismes' by M Walzer, 102ff and P Hassner, 'Vers un universalisme pluriel?' 114ff.

to imagine an Islam corrected and amended, an Islam, in short, compatible with human rights?' To which the writer gave a positive reply, on the basis partly of his own experience of Islam in India 'which, because it was a minority religion, had nothing to do with the State and remained a matter of conscience' and partly on the basis of the existence in the twelfth century of a rationalist tendency which 'destroy[ed] the bases of fundamentalism and confer[red] legitimacy on debate as to interpretation, commentary, democracy in a way'. He adds 'these trends have of course always been those of a minority. But at least they have existed! A precious lesson . . . in politics as well as in theology'.[38]

But who can say how much more time will be needed before those civilisations join Europe/the West in recognising the universal values of the fundamental rights of human beings? Not too long, I should say, in the light of history. First of all, it is noteworthy that a number of countries belonging to non-European cultures have here and now ratified the two United Nations Covenants. This at the least goes to show that the values promoted therein are not rejected at first sight as completely pernicious.[39] The observance of those rights, in everyday practice, by some of these countries is perhaps less than satisfactory, to use a euphemism. The power of principles may, however, compel recognition over the course of years, as we saw with the Helsinki Final Act.[40] The fact that in 1975, the USSR and the popular democracies accepted the third package of human rights gave rise to committees for the verification of compliance with those rights which were intended to exert pressure on their governments to abide by the principles they had themselves proclaimed.[41]

[38] *Le Monde*, 10 June 1998, 13.

[39] As of 31 December 1995 the United Nations Covenant on Civil and Political Rights was ratified by 132 states and the Covenant on Economic, Social and Cultural Rights by 133.

[40] Helsinki Final Act, adopted at the Conference on Security and Co-operation in Europe, Helsinki, 1 August 1975, reprinted in (1975) 14 *ILM* 1292.

[41] The Declaration on the Principles Governing the Mutual Relations of the Participating States, the famous Decalogue states that: 'The participating States shall respect human rights and fundamental freedoms, including freedom of thought, conscience, religion or conviction. They shall promote and encourage the effective exercise of freedoms and civil, political, economic, social and cultural rights and others which all arise out of the dignity inherent in human beings and which are essential to their free and complete blossoming/development'. See E Decaux, *Que sais-je? La Conférence sur la sécurité et la coopération en Europe* (CSCE) (Paris, Presses Universitaires de France, 1992) 90. People were to take seriously the rights thus proclaimed and contribute to the political and ideological upheavals of the 1990s in all the countries of the Soviet bloc.

The Universal and the Eternal: The Birth of Universal Human Rights in and through History

The criticisms most frequently directed at the philosophy of human rights derive from the facts that the concept is of such recent provenance that the catalogue of rights has been significantly altered over time (Locke, for example, would probably not have subscribed to several of the articles of the Universal Declaration) and that there has always been disagreement on the scope of that catalogue (as indeed there is at the end of the twentieth century). How can it be maintained, in those circumstances, that those rights existed before the proper law which they act to limit? Or, in other words, how can it be envisaged that human rights constitute a universal and eternal superior law?

In actual fact, from our point of view, it is unnecessary to posit a genuine natural law 'over and above' positive law. Thus, to quote the Declaration of 1789, while liberty is one of the natural and inalienable rights of man (Article 2), the limits of the enjoyment of that liberty may be determined only by law (Article 4).[42]

Yet those human rights are said to change over periods of time and there were times when slavery was 'natural', just as the use of torture was in criminal trials in the Middle Ages and even later. And undoubtedly it would be possible to demonstrate that each of the most fundamental rights of our time had been unknown or denied at one time or another in the past or in one country or another (for example, the practice of 'exposing' babies in Rome).[43] This argument will worry only those with a naïve natural law vision of a sempiternal unchanging law. Or possibly, those who cling to the views of the seventeenth and eighteenth century philosophers (Hobbes, Spinoza, Rousseau) who believed that human rights sprang from the rights possessed by an individual marooned in nature.[44]

---

[42] In his introduction to No 2 of the review *Droits* devoted to human rights, Rials notes clearly the 'change of natural into positive law' marked by the Declaration of 1789. So, while Art 2 proclaims the 'natural and inalienable rights of man', most of the other arts 'charge the legislature with the task of establishing the bounds within which those rights are to be exercised': 'Généalogie des droits de l'homme' (1985) 2 *Droits* 11.

[43] P Girard, *Manuel élémentaire de droit romain* (Paris, Dalloz, 1978) 131. The *pater familias* can expose children, 'that is to say, abandon them, if he does not want to be responsible for them, as he can abandon slaves, animals, inanimate objects'. The author notes that 'the custom of exposing children is common to Romans, Greeks, Germans and Hindus'. Exposure is not directly an act of infanticide, but death is its highly probable result.

[44] Weil, *Essais et conférences* (n 33) 194.

Nevertheless, Man is a political animal conceivable only in civil society and not in some imaginary state of nature. For societies emerging from subjection to a non-historical tradition and entering history, the idea of universality, and thus of rights valid not just for the citizens of such and such a city but for all human beings, arises from the development of the city. Values are a product of history and their universal application is discovered by those who, in their awareness of their historical position, are seeking rules which may, as the philosopher Eric Weil says, 'be acknowledged *meaningful by all who ponder the question of universal meaning*' (emphasis added).[45] Even so, people must still ask this crucial question, and it is here that the meeting with Europe/the West is crucial, insofar as that is the first culture to have taken its part in history and to have begun the search for universal meaning.[46]

Consequently it is the gradual development of human consciousness which makes it possible to imagine that some rights may be of recent origin and yet express values which are potentially universal. Slavery, torture, the indiscriminate massacre of whole populations have not always been abominations. They have become so recently, and universally, and quite rightly those who do not accept that could be considered to be barbarians. As the philosopher Misrahi puts its, 'the individual [who holds the rights] is simultaneously a universal foundation and a slow historical discovery'.[47]

The progress of conscience also makes it possible to understand that even if the American declarations that followed Independence and the Declaration of the Rights of Man and the Citizen applied, in

[45] Weil, *ibid*, 187. See G Vedel, 'Les droits de l'homme: quels droits? quel homme?' in M Bettati (ed), *Humanité et droit international. Mélanges René-Jean Dupuy* (Paris, Pedone, 1991) 349–62, who shows how 'human rights are an intangible but not an immutable inheritance' (at 354) and that 'it is possible to envisage at one and the same time that human rights are everlasting and that they evolve' (at 355).

[46] See the overly catastrophic tenor of the article by the author of *The Clash of Civilization and the Remaking of World Order*, S Huntingdon, 'The West, Unique, not Universal' (1996) 75 *Foreign Affairs* 28.

[47] R Misrahi, *Qu'est-ce que l'éthique?* (Paris, Armand Colin, 1997) 239. See also Madiot, *Considérations sur les droits et devoirs de l'homme* (n 22) 32–34, who, after demonstrating that human nature 'develops gradually, throughout the progress of history', writes: 'A right becomes natural when it is possible to consider, at a given moment of historical progress, that it . . . has acquired such a value that to challenge it is now impossible. That value is conferred on it by the broadest recognition under internal laws (constitutions and statutes) and under international conventions or by a claim to which no reasoned argument is opposed. It is the setting up of a ratchet mechanism to prevent any backward movement (though plainly it cannot prevent attacks on such a right)'.

their authors' minds, to only part of humankind, the male white part, the seeds of universalism which they contained were, much later but necessarily, to blossom in a (truly) universal Declaration of the rights of every human being.

Europe and the West: The European (Properly Speaking) Dimension of Human Rights

If I am now to reflect on the specifically European approach to human rights within Western countries, it seems to me that I must give a historical perspective on the way in which European countries have tackled this question. If we can consider, as we saw in the first part, that Europe is the birthplace of the theory of human rights, we cannot overlook the fact that this theory remained long disregarded in its homeland. It is only very recently, since 1945 and even since 1970, that protection of human rights has become an essential element in the legal systems of Western European countries and in the relations between those countries and non-European countries. Knowing what obstacles Europe has had to overcome will make us better able to evaluate the difficulties encountered by non-European nations in setting up a system for the protection of human rights.

Birth, Disappearance and Rebirth of Human Rights in Europe

In her essay on *Les droits de l'homme et le droit naturel*, Barret-Kriegel stressed the fact that the fruits of the 1789 Declaration of Rights were belated, in comparison with the rights proclaimed in the American Bill of Rights of 1789–91.[48] There will be a time and place to qualify that statement (see below at 310). However, the fact remains that it is only since 1945 that the philosophy of human rights and its translation into law have known their present success.

The Enforced Hibernation of the Philosophy of Human Rights in Europe

There was in fact a very slow 'dissemination' of the 1789 Declaration in France and Europe, principally in the face of criticism from three

[48] B Barret-Kriegel, *Les droits de l'homme et le droit naturel* (Paris, PUF, 1989) 19ff. For an overview of how the protection of rights developed in the United States, see L Henkin, 'Les droits européens dans la constitution américaine' (1993) 45(2) *Revue Internationale de Droit Comparé* 429–38.

points of view: conservative, positivist-Utilitarian and Marxist.[49] We have no space in which to dwell on conservative criticism of human rights, such as that of Burke or de Maistre (even though those two authors start from different premises), since it forms part of a more general rejection of the achievements of the French Revolution.[50] I must, however, observe that the philosophical trends which adopted those achievements in whole or in part, and the modern development of political societies, contribute to the eclipse of a general theory of human rights.

Such a consequence resulted, first of all, from the rejection in the nineteenth century of the doctrine of natural law which had given rise to the declarations of rights. It is true that the Declaration of the Rights of Man and the Citizen carried in both its actual title and its contents the seeds of future progress. While 'men are born free and equal in rights' (Article 1) and 'the aim of every political association is the preservation of the natural and inalienable rights of man' (Article 2), it is for the law to establish the limits to every man's liberty (Article 4) and to establish all the safeguards for the rights set out in Articles 4 to 17. And since the law 'is the expression of the general will' (Article 6), it can do no wrong. Only a seditionmonger putting his own selfish interests above the general interest would rise up against the law in the name of pre-existing rights.[51]

Starting from those premises, there was to arise in France and, no doubt, in other European countries, the system known as *l'Etat légal*, that is, the state governed by the rule of law in which individuals are protected against abuses of power and infringements of their rights and freedoms attributable to acts of the Executive but not against

[49] See G Peces-Barba Martinez, *Curso de derechos fundamentales. Teoria general* (Madrid, Perolibros, 1995) 69–98.

[50] Just as radically, Villey pours scorn on the whole Modernist legal tradition from the 17th century onwards which, disregarding the Aristotelian and Thomist definition of law, invented the delusion of individualism, false equality and in addition a whole multitude of pseudo human rights good for nothing but gulling the credulous. It is not surprising that Villey, a Catholic writer in the Thomist tradition, finishes his diatribe against human rights by joining in a Marxist critique in *La Question Juive*, and even pretends to support the logic of the Marquis de Sade, in *Français encore un effort si vous voulez être Républicains*, which demanded, in the name of the rights of man, the freedom to indulge all passions, including incest, adultery and other amusements. See M Villey, *Le droit et les droits de l'homme* (Paris, Puf, 1990) 152 (for the reference to Marx) and 'Correspondance' in the special edn of the review (1985) 2 *Droits* 44 for the reference to Sade.

[51] On the inevitable absorption of the features of natural law in the 1789 Declaration by positive law, see P Wachsmann, 'Naturalisme et volontarisme dans la Déclaration des droits de l'homme de 1789' (1985) 2 *Droits* 13–22.

those committed by the Legislature itself. The very idea would have seemed laughable to a man in the Third French Republic, even though on numerous occasions one group or another would denounce the adoption of 'unjust' laws running counter to the rights of man. Parliamentary sovereignty, together with the dominant ideology of legal positivism, could conceive of and organise nothing beyond the defence of 'public liberties', as defined by statute and within the limits laid down by those statutes. While the 1789 Declaration still retained its prestige, it was of little effect in legal terms, except perhaps in the Conseil d'Etat's working out of the theory of the general principles of law.[52]

A similar result, but from different philosophical bases, was to follow in England from the Utilitarian philosophy of Bentham, and this too for a long period took on all the characteristics of a dominant philosophy.[53] On the question of natural and inalienable rights, Bentham never gave an inch: as soon as American independence was declared in 1776, he expressed his decided opinion that such a doctrine was contradictory, unintelligible and dangerous. Even after he was convinced of the advantages of democratic government, he continued to argue that a right which had not been created in and by a system of positive law was a contradiction in terms, as if one should speak of cold that is hot or of resplendent darkness (from which we may see that Bentham had no feeling for poetry).[54] In the end, the result to which Utilitarianism was leading was not so far removed, on this point of human rights, from positivism and the Continental theory of a centralised system of law. The corrections which John Stuart Mill wished to make to his teacher's ideas apparently met with no success.[55]

With regard to the third critique, the most famous and undoubtedly the most influential is that put forward in 1843 by Marx in his study *On the Jewish Question*, which is highly debatable in several

---

[52] See B Janneau, *Les principes généraux du droit dans la jurisprudence administrative* (Paris, Sirey, 1954); R Odent, *Contentieux administratif* (Paris, Les cours de droit, 1970–71) 166: 'confining ourselves to the present position of the Conseil d'Etat on this point, it would seem that most of the principles enshrined in the 1789 Declaration of the Rights of Man and the Citizen . . . must be considered to be general principles of law . . .'.

[53] See HLA Hart, 'Utilitarianism and Natural Rights' in *Essays in Jurisprudence and Philosophy* (Oxford, Clarendon Press, 1983) 181–97.

[54] Hart, *ibid*, 185.

[55] See HLA Hart, 'Natural Rights: Bentham and John Stuart Mill' in *Essays on Bentham, Jurisprudence and Political Theory* (Oxford, Clarendon Press, 1982) 79–104.

respects. In it, he denounces not only the 1789, but also the 1793 Declaration as the manifestation of bourgeois egoism hiding behind an ideology falsely claimed to be universal.[56] That is the source of all the diatribes launched by regimes declaring themselves to be Marxist (or Leninist) against formal bourgeois freedoms as opposed to real human rights to which only socialist states give effect. History would reveal the bloody tragedy spawned by that philosophy, so lending a prophetic note to the first sentence of the 1789 Declaration: 'whereas the sole causes of public misfortune and the corruption of governments are ignorance of or disregard or contempt for the rights of man'.[57]

I must, however, add here that it was not only in Europe that human rights sank out of sight after their solemn announcement in the eighteenth century and their enforced hibernation in the nineteenth century until the middle of the twentieth century. We find a similar phenomenon, albeit with differences of detail, in the United

[56] Marx writes, eg: 'Let us state first of all that "rights of man", as distinct from "citizens' rights", are nothing but the rights of a member of bourgeois society, that is to say, of selfish man, of man isolated from his fellow man and from his community': *La question juive* (Paris, 10/18, 1968) 37 and more generally at 34–35. Even in this piece of Marx's juvenilia we can perceive his proposed 'holistic' conception of socialist human rights: those rights should not divide a man from his community. This is repeated with the greatest precision in the doctrine of the 20th century socialist bloc countries in which, as Dupuy points out, 'man is . . . taken as integrated within his group', and all freedoms are subordinate to the construction of the new society (n 1) 420. On the Marxist critiques of human rights, see L Ferry and A Renaut, *Philosophie politique* (Paris, PUF, 1985) iii, 124–29 and Peces-Barba Martinez, *Curso de derechos fundamentales* (n 49) 95–98. It is noteworthy that the virulent opposition of an author such as Althusser, who so deeply influenced the 1960s generation in France, to even the Marxist 'ideology' of human rights contributed to setting back until after the 1970s any recognition of the value of the battle for human rights, so far as a part of the French intelligentsia was concerned. See Althusser, *Pour Marx* (Paris, Maspero, 1963) 227–58.

[57] Other important authors have contributed to the systematic devaluation of the doctrine of human rights in Europe: thus Nietzsche writes: '[w]e who acknowledge no fatherland . . . We preserve nothing; no return to the past; we are not "liberals", we do not labour for "progress", we do not have to block our ears so as not to hear the sirens of the future in the market-place singing the tune of "equal rights", the song of "free society" and "no more masters and slaves" none of which we find attractive': F Nietzsche, *The Joyful Wisdom* (New York, The Macmillan Cy, 1924) 343, para 377. Further on in this text, Nietzsche makes an appeal for danger, adventure, war and the reintroduction of slavery 'if necessary'. While we may not impute vile thoughts to Nietzsche, it is clear that the author of *Beyond Good and Evil*, who exerted considerable influence on European thought, was hardly a militant supporter of the rights of 'every human being', to put it mildly, and some of his writings lay themselves open to loathsome interpretations. For a study of other authors, see Ferry and Renaut, *Philosophie politique* (n 56) 109–29 and Peces-Barba Martinez, *Curso de derechos fundamentales* (n 49) 69–98 ('*Las negaciones totales del concepto [de derechos humanos]*').

States as well. In that country, it was only very slowly that the wealth of possibilities contained in the declarations of independence and the first ten amendments to the Constitution in 1791 became reality.

The chief distinction, in terms of human rights, between the United States and the old continent lies in the recognition by the Supreme Court in *Marbury v Madison*[58] that it was open to every judge to ascertain whether any given text, even a law voted by Congress, was compatible with superior law. From then on, the rights of Man, as set forth in the amendments to the Constitution, were an integral part of the law proper and their breach could be penalised by any court and, at last instance, by the Supreme Court. While I cannot undertake an examination of the case law of the Supreme Court concerning human rights, I shall nevertheless mention these facts with which we are all familiar: when the introduction to the 1787 Constitution speaks of 'promoting the common weal and ensuring the benefits of freedom for ourselves and our descendants', they naturally mean the welfare and freedom of men, and even more specifically, of white men.[59] In other words, slavery existing in much of the Federation was not affected by that pronouncement any more than by the words of the Declaration of Independence which proclaim that '[we] hold these truths to be self-evident, that all men are created equal, that they are endowed by their Creator with certain unalienable rights, that among these are Life, Liberty and the pursuit of Happiness'.

That irreconcilable contradiction between the theory and the reality of slavery was to lead to the war of secession. The war did not, however, put an end to the problem since, in its judgment in *Plessey v Ferguson*,[60] the Supreme Court granted the Southern States recognition of the constitutionality of their segregationalist laws (equal but separate).[61] It was not until the 1954 judgment in *Brown v Board of*

---

[58] *Marbury v Madison* 5 US 137 (1803).

[59] It was not until 1808 that the Constitution gave Congress the right to forbid traffic in slaves: see Henkin 'Les droits européens dans la constitution américaine' (n 48) 433. We may also recall the *Dred Scott* case in which in 1857 the Supreme Court declared that a black slave was a citizen neither of the United States nor of his state of origin and the he had no capacity to bring legal actions: *Dred Scott v Stanford*, 60 US 393 (1857).

[60] *Plessey v Ferguson* 163 US 539 (1896).

[61] The historian HC Allen notes: 'At the beginning of the 20th century the position of blacks was scarcely better than, and sometimes even as bad as at the time of the Black Codes . . . the 14th and 15th amendments remained a dead letter in the South'. Even before the 1896 judgment, another judgment of the Supreme Court, given on 15 October 1883, cited in *Civil Rights Cases* (109 US 3 (1893)), had essentially deprived

Education of Topeka,[62] that a Supreme Court, presided over by Earl Warren, engaged in a systematic policy of defending civil rights. So, finally, as in Europe, though for different reasons, it is only in the second half of the twentieth century that we can see the potential of the theory of human rights being fully realised.[63]

Barbarity in Europe and the Renewal of the Philosophy and Positive Law of Human Rights

It is true that concern for human rights had not disappeared from people's consciences, as demonstrated by the (belated) abolition of slavery in France (1848) and in other countries, leading up to the international conventions of 1890 and 1926. Similarly, after 1918, under the ægis of the League of Nations or the International Labour Organization (ILO), various conventions were adopted concerning the prohibition of traffic in women and children, the protection of decent working conditions or the protection of minorities.[64]

It was, however, the fall of part of Europe (countries of outstanding culture) into the barbarity of Nazism and Fascism, which were based on the absolute and total denial of the doctrine of human rights, which brought about a complete change in European thinking on this subject.[65] I shall not dwell in this chapter on the pivotal role played by the Rome Convention of 1950, or on the dissemination of the principles of that convention and of the case law of the

the 14th and 15th Amendments of any effect in combating discriminatory practices. See *Les Etats-Unis* (Verviers, Marabout- Universite, 1967) i, 220; D Borstin, *Histoire des Américains* (Paris, Laffont, 1991) 1493–95.

[62] *Brown v Board of Education of Topeka* 347 US 483 (1954).

[63] On the dismantling of discriminatory legislation after *Brown*, see Borstin, *Histoire des Américains* (n 61) 1507–10. On the question of 'affirmative action' and the judgment of the Supreme Court of July 1978, *Allan Bakke v Regents of the University of California*, 438 US 407 (1978) and J Belz, 'Equal Protection and Affirmative Action' in DJ Bodenhammer and JW Ely, *The Bill of Rights in Modern America. After 200 Years* (Bloomington, Indiana University Press, 1993) 155–73.

[64] For a general view of the international conventions adopted before and after 1945, see F Capotorti, 'Human Rights: The Hard Road towards Universality' in RS MacDonald and D Johnston, *The Structure and Process of International Law* (Leiden, Nijhoff, 1983) 977–1000.

[65] See the beginning of the press conference given by Cassin on 8 July 1947: 'The last war was essentially the "Human Rights" War, inflicted on peoples by those who espoused a monstrous racist doctrine, and waged simultaneously against man and the community of men, with unprecedented systematic cruelty'. The full text of the speech is given in Faure, *Ce que déclarer des droits veut dire* (n 30) 297–301.

Court at Strasbourg throughout the legal orders both of the individual states and of the European Union.[66]

I would merely point out that one of the principal changes brought about in Europe after 1945 was due to the adoption by most states (with the notable exception of the United Kingdom) of the Kelsenian system of review of the constitutionality of laws (also called 'the European model' as opposed to the American model).[67] As a result of this, European countries changed their systems from an '*Etat légal*'[68] to an '*Etat de droit*',[69] in which the Legislature itself can be sanctioned by a constitutional court for failure to observe the constitutional laws including (and above all) those safeguarding human rights. In France, as is well known, the *Conseil constitutionnel* was to incorporate the 1789 Declaration into the corpus of constitutional law, respect for which it enforces, thus as a Supreme Charter of human rights giving that text its full effect for the first time.[70]

Certain Features of the European Concept of Human Rights

Source of European Ius Commune

If I am to attempt to distinguish the specific features of the European conception of human rights, I must begin by identifying the sources likely to provide a list of the rights which are common to Europe, as opposed to the *ius proprium* of one state or another (for example, the extension of the protection of the right to life to the embryo in

---

[66] See G Cohen-Jonathan, *La convention européenne des droits de l'homme* (Aix, Presses universitaires d'Aix-Marseille, 1989); and by the same author, *Aspects européens des droits fondamentaux* (n 27). See also F Sudre (ed), *Le droit français et la convention européenne des droits de l'homme* (Montpellier, Engel, 1994); L Sermet, *L'incidence de la convention européenne des droits de l'homme sur le contentieux administratif français* (Paris, Economica, 1996); J-P Jacqué, 'Communatué européenne et convention européenne des droits de l'homme' in *L'Europe et le droit. Mélanges en hommage à Jean Boulouis* (Paris, Dalloz, 1991) 325–40.

[67] See H Kelsen, 'Le contrôle de la constituionalité des lois. Une étude comparative des constitutions autrichienne et américaine' (1990) 1 *Revue Française de Droit Constitutionnel* 17–30.

[68] Translator's note: that is to say, a state in which individuals and the executive are subject to the rule of law, but the legislature is sovereign and acts with impunity.

[69] Translator's note: or '*Rechtsstaat*', a civil law system in which all persons and organs of government are answerable to the law.

[70] See the decisions on freedom of association (16 July 1971), automatic taxation (27 December 1973) and nationalisation laws (16 January and 11 February 1982) in L Favoreu and L Philip, *Les grandes décisions du Conseil constitutionnel* (Paris, Sirey, 1991) 237ff, 269ff and 470ff.

Ireland). It is clear that the first of these sources is the European Convention on Human Rights, which was specifically intended by its authors to be an instrument in the unification of Europe in the realm of the maintenance and further realisation of human rights and fundamental freedoms.[71] I scarcely need stress the importance of that treaty and the protocols supplementing it, or refer to the role played by the European Court of Human Rights in Strasbourg, especially since 1974. It has become of even greater importance with the accession of several Central and Eastern European counties to the Rome Convention, although it is still too early to tell whether this is actually an opportunity to extend the protection of human rights to the entire continent of Europe or rather a watering-down of the Convention, owing to the fact that the eastern and western states are so heterogeneous.[72]

In any event, the European Convention, which was intended by its authors to be the first embodiment in actual law of the Universal Declaration, established a system for monitoring compliance with its provisions that is to this day unequalled, either at the regional level (although some interesting progress is to be found in the American convention on human rights signed on 22 November 1969),[73] or to the universal. It may be considered *a prime characteristic of the European approach* that, in certain conditions which I need not specify, it affords persons claiming to have had their rights infringed by the states which are parties to the Convention, an effective individual right of action before an international court with the power of review. In the end, a judgment given by a court and possessing binding authority can rule that such a right has been infringed and may possibly afford the plaintiff just satisfaction.[74]

---

[71] The third recital in the preamble to the Convention of Rome: 'Considering that the aim of the Council of Europe is the achievement of greater unity between its Members and that one of the methods by which that aim is to be pursued is the maintenance and further realization of human rights and fundamental freedoms'.

[72] The workload of the Strasbourg Court remained modest until 1973 (17 judgments delivered between 1959 and 1973, as against 448 between 1974 and 1993). See Cohen-Jonathan *La convention européenne des droits de l'homme* (n 66) 233 and Faure *Ce que déclarer des droits veut dire* (n 30) 226ff, who also lists the Central and Eastern European States which have signed the Convention, with the date of ratification for those which have already done so. As at 29 February 1996, those which had both signed and ratified were Bulgaria, Hungary, Lithuania, Poland, Romania, Russia, Slovakia and Slovenia. Those which had signed but not yet ratified were Estonia, Macedonia, Moldavia and Ukraine.

[73] See Sudre, *Droit international et européen des droits de l'homme* (n 26) 98–101.

[74] See Art 50 ECHR and Cohen-Jonathan, *La convention européenne des droits de l'homme* (n 66) 212–16.

The search for European conception of human rights cannot, however, be confined solely to consideration of the Rome Convention. We must take into account the way in which the matter of human rights has been raised within the European Community, both because the law in Luxembourg and the law in Strasbourg significantly influence one another[75] and because it is the Community, in its international relations, which applies pressure to non-member countries to make them undertake to observe certain fundamental rights.

Turning to the first point, that is the development within the Community, through the case law of the Court of Justice of the European Communities, of a policy of defending human rights which, as we known had no legal basis in the original treaties, we find that the Court has had recourse to two methods to achieve its ends. First, it has elevated *the constitutional traditions common to the Member States* concerning the protection of fundamental rights to the Community level by transforming them into general principles of Community law.[76] The classic formulation of this policy may be found in, inter alia, the judgment in *Wachauf*, in which the Court stated:

> The court has consistently held, in particular in its judgment of 13 December 1979 in Case 44/79, *Hauer v Land Rheinland-Pfalz* [1979] ECR 3727, that fundamental rights form an integral part of the general principles of the law, the observance of which is ensured by the Court. In safeguarding those rights, the Court has to look to the constitutional traditions common to the Member States, so that measures which are incompatible with the fundamental rights recognized by the constitutions of those States may not find acceptance in the Community.[77]

On the other hand, in seeking relevant general principles, the Court of Justice also turns to the European Convention on Human Rights, which has been ratified by all the Member States and conse-

---

[75] These cross-influences have been further strengthened by the Amsterdam Treaty since certain of the provisions of the TEU are henceforth subject to review by the ECJ to the extent that some authors have even spoken of the 'perverse effect of the complex Amsterdam construction'. See Wachsmann, 'Les droits de l'homme' (n 5) 893.

[76] This, however, does pose some awkward problems for national constitutional courts. See *Protection constitutionnelle et protection internationale des droits de l'homme. Concurrence ou complémentarité?* IXth Conference of European Constitutional Courts vol 2 (Paris, May 1993). See also J-P Puissochet, 'La Cour de justice et les principes généraux du droit' in Union *des avocats européens, La protection juridictionnelle des droits dans le système communautaire* (Brussels, Bruylant, 1997) 1–19.

[77] Case 5/88, *Wachauf v Germany* [1989] ECR 2609.

quently 'is of particular significance'.[78] Thus, as the Court declared in *Rutili*,[79] with regard to the powers of the immigration authorities and the reservation relating to public policy,

> [the] limitations placed on the powers of Member States in respect of control of aliens are a specific manifestation of the more general principle, enshrined in Articles 8, 9, 10 and 11 of the Convention for the Protection of Human Rights and Fundamental Freedoms.

Finally, Article 6(2) (*ex* Article F(2)) of the consolidated version of the Treaty on European Union repeats and confirms the Court's two sources of inspiration, declaring that:

> The Union shall respect fundamental rights, as guaranteed by the European Convention for the Protection of Human Rights and Fundamental Freedoms, signed in Rome on 4 November 1950 and as they result from the constitutional traditions common to the Member States, as general principles of Community law'.[80]

European *Ius Commune* in Cooperation Agreements

The second point of interest concerns the provisions relating to human rights which must be respected by the Member States of the Union and those which the Community seeks to include in its development cooperation agreements and its economic and co-operation agreements with non-member countries.[81]

As we have already seen, respect for the principles set out in Article 6 (*ex* Article F(1)—the principles of liberty, democracy, respect for human rights and fundamental freedoms and the rule of law—is henceforth an express condition for the accession of new Member States to the Union. It is, therefore, a condition to be satisfied not merely at the time of accession but also permanently, since the Council, meeting in the composition of the heads of state

---

[78] See Joined Cases 46/87 and 227/88, *Hoechst v Commission* [1989] ECR 2919. On that whole question, see J-P Jacqué, 'La Constitution de la Communauté européenne' (1995) *Revue Universelle des Droit de l'Homme* 407 and 'Communauté européenne et convention européenne des droits de l'homme' (n 66) 327ff.

[79] Case 36/75, *Rutili* [1975] ECR 1219.

[80] For this whole question, see Wachsmann, 'Les droits de l'homme' (n 5) 883–903, who emphasises the fact that 'human rights have thoroughly permeated the Community legal system' at 897.

[81] See the Luxembourg European Council's Declaration on Human Rights, June 1991 *Bull. EC* 6–1991, at Annex V, 17; *Commission Communication on the inclusion of respect for democratic principles and human rights in agreements between the Community and third countries*, COM(95) 216 final.

or government, 'may determine the existence of a serious and persistent breach by a Member State of principles mentioned in Article 6(1)' (Article 7 (*ex* Article F.1)). In that case, 'the Council, acting by a qualified majority, may decide to suspend certain of the rights deriving from the application of this Treaty to the Member States in question'.

These provisions are, it has been observed, similar to those laid down by the Council of Europe. Membership of the Council of Europe is open to a state only if it 'accepts the principles of the rule of law and of the enjoyment by all persons within its jurisdiction of human rights and fundamental freedoms' (Article 3 of the Statute of the Council of Europe, as referred to in Article 5). Moreover, 'a Member State of the Council of Europe which has seriously violated Article 3 of the Statute may be suspended from its rights of representation and requested by the Committee of Ministers to withdraw from the Council'.[82]

Returning to the European Community, the Treaty on European Union does not merely call on its own members to respect those fundamental rights, it makes that respect one of the conditions of both its policy of economic cooperation with non-member countries and of its common foreign and security policy.

As regards cooperation policy, in the second half of the 1980s the Community began to introduce clauses on respect for human rights into its agreements with non-member countries and, in particular, in the Lomé Conventions, notwithstanding the great reluctance of its ACP partners. Thus, a common declaration concerning Article 4, annexed to the text of Lomé III, stated that human dignity is an 'inalienable right and constitutes an essential objective in the achievement of the legitimate aspirations of individuals or of peoples'. There is an even greater emphasis in the Fourth Lomé Convention (1989) which calls respect for human rights 'a basic factor of real development'.

Article 5 then states that:

> Respect for human rights, democratic principles and the rule of law, which underpins relations between the ACP States and the Community and all provisions of the Convention, and governs the domestic and international policies of the Contracting Parties, shall constitute an essential element of this Convention.

[82] The procedure under Art. 8 of the Statute of the Council of Europe has only once been set in motion, against Greece under the Colonels. See Wachsmann, 'Les droits de l'homme' (n 5) 894–97.

And since this concerns an essential element of the convention, Article 366 bis declares, pursuant to the ordinary law of treaties (Article 60 of the Vienna Convention), that where there is failure to fulfil those obligations and refusal to consult, 'the Party which invoked the failure to fulfil an obligation may take appropriate steps, including, where necessary, the partial or full suspension of application of this Convention to the party concerned'.[83]

Subsequently the Community went on to make systematic reference to respect for human rights, first in its association agreements with Central European countries (1991 to 1992) and then in other economic cooperation agreements. The Treaty on the European Community confirms that policy, stating in Article 177 (*ex* Article 130U) that 'Community policy in this area [the sphere of development co-operation] shall contribute to the general object of developing and consolidating democracy and the rule of law, and to that of respecting human rights and fundamental freedoms'.

Furthermore, in a communication of May 1995, the Commission analysed the various wordings of those 'democracy and human rights' clauses in previous agreements and proposed that henceforth association agreements and economic and cooperation agreements should contain a standard provision as follows:

(a) in the provisions of the agreement:
a clause stipulating that 'the relations between the Community and the countries concerned and all the provisions of the agreement in question are based upon respect for the democratic principles and human rights which govern domestic and international policy both in the Community and in the country concerned and which constitutes an essential element of the agreement.

(b) in the preamble
references in general to respect for human rights and democratic values; references to universal and/or local instruments common to the two parties; in specific cases, an express suspension clause or a general non-performance clause may also be proposed.[84]

---

[83] For the text of the Fourth Lomé Convention, see [1991] OJ L229/3, and the Agreement amending the fourth ACP-EC Convention of Lomé signed in Mauritius on 4 November 1995 ([1998] OJ L156/3) and also *Le Courrier-ACP*, No 120 (March–April 1990). See also J Kranz, 'Lomé, le dialogue de l'homme' (1998) *Revue Trimestrielle de Droit Européen*, 451.

[84] See COM(95) 216 final.

It can therefore be seen that, just as a Member State which seriously and persistently breaches its human rights obligations may have its rights suspended, so a state bound by an economic agreement with the Community (Lomé Convention, association agreements, etc) may be penalised, by means of suspension of the Treaty, for breach of those undertakings relating to human rights and democracy 'which constitute an essential element of the agreement'.[85]

I must add that, apart from development cooperation, Article J.1 of the Maastricht Treaty, now Article 11 of the consolidated version of the Treaty on European Union, states that it is one of the objectives of (in this case) the Union's common foreign and security policy 'to develop and consolidate democracy and the rule of law, and respect for human rights and fundamental freedoms' (fifth paragraph of Article 11(1)).

European *Ius Commune* and Universal *Ius Commune*

I have above contrasted the *ius proprium* of one state with the *ius commune* of Europe. I must now mention the relations which, in this sphere of human rights, connect the individual, the local and the universal, concentrating my argument on the European situation but it being understood that other examples would be equally valid.[86]

The legal provisions adopted by European states concerning human rights may be divided into two parts. One set of provisions expresses the *ius proprium* of each state, which is not to be found at Community level. I have already cited the constitutional protection of the embryo in Ireland; we may also think of the various methods

---

[85] For a general consideration of this question and a distinctly critical assessment of this type of clause, see J Verhoeven, 'La Communauté européenne et la sanction internationale de la démocratie et des droits de l'homme' (1997) *Annuaire Français de Droit International* 799–809. The author concludes his study with the following remarks: 'Under the misleading guise of reciprocity, the Community is creating power for itself the exercise of which could be particularly wrongful since no provision is made for recourse to some arbitrator or third party in the case of dispute as to the lawfulness of the "appropriate steps" taken in response to the alleged breach of "democratic principles". To be troubled by this is not to disregard the fundamental importance attaching to certain rules, or to doubt the good intentions of the Community. On the contrary, the use of wrongful means to the end of respecting democracy is prohibited by democracy itself'. What I find dubious is the equal application of the same rules to all states in the same situation with regard to human rights and respect for democracy. Some lines of La Fontaine spring to mind: '*selon que vous serez puissants ou misérables*', etc (depending on whether you are mighty or wretched).

[86] See N Valticos, 'Nations, états, régions et communauté universelle: niveaux et étapes de la protection des droits de l'homme' in M Bettati (ed), *Humanité et droit international. Mélanges René-Jean Dupuy* (n 45) 339–48.

by which religious freedom is taken into consideration, depending on whether it is a secular country such as France, or a country such as the United Kingdom, etc. The other set gives expression to values which are common to the countries of Europe and therefore falls within the ambit of European *ius commune*. I would point out here that one of the means used by the Court of Justice in Luxembourg to elucidate that common law is to extract it from the constitutional tradition common to the Member States (see the text to n 76 above).

However, European *ius commune* itself may be divided into two: on the one hand, provisions specific to Europe (for example, those deriving from the secular character of the state itself, even if it is not secular on the French model) and, on the other, provisions forming part of a universal *ius commune*. The clearest illustration of this is the European Convention on Human Rights which is intended to represent the transposition into positive law of 'a common standard of achievement for all peoples' heralded by the Universal Declaration of 1948.

Thus each level, whether state, regional, or universal, contains an element of *ius proprium* characteristic of its level and an element of *ius commune* from the upper level. So when considering the question of the European approach to human rights, we have to distinguish the part of European law which is the expression at European level of universal rights from the part which is specific to Europe and constitutes its *ius proprium*.

If we now inquire what this universal *ius commune* of Europe, and more particularly the European Union, may consist of, we will first encounter those provisions for the protection of human rights and fundamental freedoms with which Europe requires non-member countries to comply (see the text to note 85). Indeed it is inconceivable that Europe should demand compliance with its *ius proprium* in the narrow sense, rather it is the *ius universale* contained in the *ius proprium* which must be observed.

In this regard it will be observed that the Community does not call for respect only for human rights and fundamental freedoms, but for a wider whole which also includes respect for democracy and the rule of law. By implication, this means that protection of human rights can be guaranteed only under constitutional arrangements similar in kind to those of the Member States of the Union, since the Union 'is founded on the principles of liberty, democracy, respect for human rights and fundamental freedoms, and the rule of law, principles which are common to the Member States (Article 6(1) of the Treaty of Union, *ex* Article F(1)).

The ultimate, ambitious aim of the Community foreign policy is therefore to promote the European constitutional model, which alone is considered capable of guaranteeing protection of human rights and fundamental freedoms. It might appear that such an intention is unconscionable and justifies the vituperation of those in the Third World who denounce the neo-colonialism of European (and American) human rights policy. However, I must observe that the links between democracy/rule of law/human rights and fundamental freedoms are not or are no longer a special feature of European *ius proprium*. Thus, in the Vienna Declaration and Action Programme, Article 8 states:

> Democracy, development and respect for human rights and fundamental freedoms are interdependent and mutually reinforcing. Democracy is based on the freely expressed will of the people to determine their own political, economic, social and cultural systems and on their full participation in all aspect of their lives.

Article 9 goes on to state that 'The World Conference on Human Rights reaffirms that least advanced countries committed to the process of democratization and economic reforms . . . should be supported by the international community'.

There is a reference to the rule of law in the ninth recital in the preamble, which emphasises the need to 'promote and encourage respect for human rights and fundamental freedoms for all . . . and also democracy, justice, equality, the rule of law, pluralism, etc'.[87]

We can see, therefore, that the triad of human rights/democracy, rule of law, which is not to be found either in the Universal Declaration (but see Article 21(3) on the will of the people as the basis of the authority of government) or in the Covenants, makes an appearance at international level, without any doubt on account of the actions of European states (but also of the countries of North America).[88] Furthermore, this 'activism' has only been made pos-

---

[87] It will, however, be observed that at a recent regional summit meeting in Entebbe, in which Eritrea, Ethiopia, Kenya, Tanzania, Congo-Kinshasa, Rwanda, Zimbabwe and the Organization of African Unity took part, the participants signed the 'Entebbe Declaration', in which they undertook to 'pursue a dialogue on the democratic process, recognizing that there is no defined/definite model of democratic institutions'. President Clinton, who had been invited to that regional summit meeting, also declared that 'there is no one model for the functioning of a democracy', *Le Monde* (1 April 1998).

[88] For American policy in the Carter era, see above, n 6. President Clinton has in part adopted a policy of international action in favour of democracy and human rights (with the same gaps as European policy, especially *vis-à-vis* the People's Republic of

sible by the collapse of the Soviet bloc and the peculiar conception of democracy promulgated by that bloc. This is clear to see in the documents adopted by the Conference on Security and Cooperation in Europe after 1989, such as the Copenhagen Document of 29 June 1990 or the Charter of Paris for a New Europe, of 21 November 1990, both of which also refer to the triad of 'human rights, democracy and the rule of law'.[89]

It may, therefore, be considered that what was once only one of the requirements of the European concept of human rights is at present being transformed into a universal concept. This does not, however, imply that third countries are aligning themselves completely on the European model, as we can see if we subject the distinctive features of that model to closer scrutiny.

Jacqué felt impelled to describe the characteristics of what was to be a kind of 'Constitution of the European Community'; that is to say, the introduction by the European institutions (legislative bodies and the Court of Justice of the European Communities through its decisions) of a body of provisions concerning the fundamental values of the Union, its structural principles and the principles governing the relations between the Community and the Member States.[90]

Among the sources used by Jacqué to establish the fundamental values of the European constitution, he cites the document on European identity adopted by the Conference of Heads of State and of Government in Copenhagen on 14 December 1973. According to that document, the Heads of State and Government there present:

> Desiring to ensure that the legal, political and moral values to which they are attached are respected, and anxious to conserve the rich variety of their national cultures, sharing the same conception of life, based on the desire to build a society conceived and created in the service of men, . . . intend to safeguard the principles of representative democracy, the rule of law and social justice, the aim of economic progress and respect for human rights, which are the fundamental constituents of a European identity.[91]

China). At the regional summit meeting of African countries in Entebbe on 31 March 1998, the 'Entebbe Declaration' (n 87) invites the participating states to work towards democracy, liberalization of the economy and respect for human rights, so as to avoid the recurrence of genocide in that area after Rwanda. As regards democracy, the States undertake to continue a dialogue on the democratic process, recognising that there is no definitive model for democratic institutions'. See *Le Monde* (1 April 1998).

[89] See Decaux *La Conférence sur la sécurité et la coopération en Europe* (n 41) 94–96; Sudre, *Droit international et européen des droits de l'homme* (n 26) 97–98.

[90] Jacqué, 'La Constitution de la Communauté européenne' (n 78) 397–423.

[91] Jacqué, 'La Constitution de la Communauté européenne' (n 78) 406.

Jacqué goes on to show that the case law of the Court of Justice confirms the five fundamental values set out in that text which form a sort of European constitution, namely: (a) respect for the principle according to which the Community legal order constitutes a 'Community governed by the rule of law'; (b) respect for fundamental rights; (c) the democratic principle; (d) the protection of social justice; and (e) the protection of cultural pluralism.[92]

It is striking how closely that list matches the list of provisions inserted in the Community's economic agreements. The 'Community governed by the rule of law' corresponds to the 'rule of law', and respect for fundamental rights and democracy (representative democracy according to the text of 1973) is to be found in both lists. On the other hand, there is no missionary zeal at the international level to propagate the protection of social justice and cultural pluralism, which rightfully belongs to the domain of the Constitution of Europe. It may well be thought that views on the last two points differ so much that in this sphere there may be a European *ius proprium* which does not, at least for the time being, lend itself to a process of universalisation.

If we turn now to this European *ius proprium* (which is at the same time the *ius commune* of the European States) and compare it with the *ius proprium* of the United States (in order to compare two bodies of legislation of equivalent importance), our starting point may specifically be the greater attention paid in Europe to social matters. It is true that (Western) Europe shares with the United States the conviction that, between freedom and equality, priority must be given to freedom as formulated by Rawls in his *Theory of Justice*, positing in the first place that 'Each person is to have an equal right to the most extensive total system of equal basic liberties compatible with a similar system of liberty for all'.[93]

Europe, however, which bears the stamp of social democracy, and France in any event (but Germany too, with its own vision of a social market economy), places greater emphasis than does the United States on the need for the state to take action to implement second-generation human rights, the celebrated 'social rights'. America, by contrast, is characterised by deep suspicion of state intervention.

---

[92] *Ibid*, 406–12.

[93] J Rawls, *A Theory of Justice* (Oxford, Oxford University Press, 1971). Rawls gives a list of the most important basic freedoms: 'political liberty (the right to vote and to be eligible for public office) together with freedom of speech and assembly; liberty of conscience and freedom of thought; freedom of the person [which includes] freedom from arbitrary arrest and seizure as defined by the concept of the rule of law. These liberties are all required to be equal by the first principle'.

Arendt previously contrasted the American 'political revolution' with French 'social revolution'. Habermas, explaining the different sources of inspiration for 1776 and 1789, writes: 'Then [1776], it was a matter of giving free rein to the spontaneous forces of self-governance in keeping with natural law, whereas now [1789] the objective is to impose, in the teeth of a depraved society and corrupted human nature, a coherent whole based on natural law'.[94] Notwithstanding the effects of 'globalisation', those two consciousnesses remain on either side of the Atlantic. Furthermore, it is noteworthy that Rawls' second principle (the principle of difference and equality of opportunity) is closer to social-democratic philosophy than to Reaganite liberalism.

A second feature of the European approach seems to me to be the awareness, arising out of the tragic history of the 1930s and 1940s, of the need actively to defend human rights against the enemies of humanity. This raises an important question of substance formulated during the French Revolution by Saint Just: what freedom must the enemies of freedom be allowed? Confronting that question, the United States displays great liberalism (the almost supreme right to free speech), which finds expression in the first reservation included in the ratification (in June 1992) of the International Covenant on Civil and Political Rights (ICCPR), which states: 'Article 20 [prohibiting war propaganda and any appeal to racial or religious hatred] shall neither authorize nor require the United States to adopt laws or other measures liable to restrict the freedom of speech and association protected by the Constitution and the laws of the United States'.

Europe, on the other hand, adopts a much more restrictive position arising from its historical experience. This is expressed in Article 17 of the European Convention: 'Nothing in this Convention may be interpreted as implying for any State, group or person any right to engage in any activity or perform any act aimed at the destruction of any of the rights or freedoms set forth herein or at their limitation to a greater extent than is provided for in the Convention'. That is also the tenor of the provisions of the German Basic Law on the protection of the Constitution.[95]

[94] J Habermas, *Théorie et pratique* (Paris, Payot, 1975) 129.

[95] Art 18 of the Basic Law of 23 May 1949: 'Any person who abuses the freedom of expression of opinions . . . in order to challenge the liberal and democratic constitutional order shall lose those fundamental rights. That loss, and its extent, shall be declared by the Federal Constitutional Court'. See S Rials and D Baranger, *Que sais-je? Textes constitutionnels étrangers* (Paris, Presses Universitaires de France, 1995) 50.

The Europe/United States comparison can be taken further, following the American reservations made to the ratification of the ICCPR. Under the second reservation, 'the United States reserve the right, subject to the limitations imposed by their constitution, to pronounce the death penalty against any person (other than a pregnant woman) duly found guilty under the laws in force or future laws permitting the imposition of the death penalty, including its imposition for crimes committed by persons aged less than 18.' We know that, by contrast, the countries of Europe have not merely acceded to the Sixth Protocol to the European Convention, abolishing the death penalty in peace time, but have also made abolition a condition of membership of the Council of Europe. It will astonish no one that this American reservation raised objections from several European states, such as Denmark, Finland, Norway and Sweden. The same countries have also objected to American reservations concerning 'cruel, inhuman or degrading treatment or punishment' which are to be interpreted in accordance with the amendments to the American constitution.

Objections have also been raised to some of the declarations of interpretation made by the United States, particularly the first, in which that country considers that exceptions to the prohibition on distinctions based on race, colour, sex, language, religion, or political opinion, etc are 'permissible where they are at least reasonably connected to a legitimate objective of public interest'. This interpretation, considered by some to be in fact a reservation, is of course used to take account of *affirmative action* policy. More generally, however, it demonstrates the tendency in the United States to think of society in terms of groups which may lawfully receive special treatment, subject to the review of the Supreme Court, if their situation is particular. This applies as much to minorities, whether ethnic, sexual or linguistic, as it does to the status of women or elderly persons, etc. In general, the consensus in Europe is to refuse any classification of citizens, which explains the unease experienced by several European states (including France) faced with any text concerning the protection of minorities—except of course minorities in other countries.[96]

[96] The Conciliation Committee of the European Conference for Peace in Yugoslavia considered that 'respect for the fundamental rights of human beings and the rights of peoples and minorities' was part of the 'overriding rules of general international law which . . . are imperative for all parties to the succession (ie, former Yugoslavia)'. See (1992) *Revue Générale de Droit International Public* 264–66. However, as regards this matter within Western European countries, we note the

The contrast between European and American attitudes to policies for minorities leads me to qualify the claim set out above, concerning European countries' greater sensibility to social questions. We may well consider that certain actions undertaken, and undertaken in an authoritarian manner, in the United States, in order to break the vicious circle of poverty and of communities trapped in the margins of society, such as bussing or affirmative action, would be hard to imagine in Europe, or at least in France. When I say this, I am not unaware of the contradictions and perverse effects to which those practices give rise.

Conclusion

In the end, is there a European approach to human rights? Without doubt, European practice is distinguished simultaneously by the pioneering role played by Europe in this sphere, which it continues to play, the fairly homogenous nature of European countries, and the close relations of those countries within the European Union and the Council of Europe, to which might be added, with regard to the countries of Eastern Europe, the Organization for Security and Co-operation in Europe, in the expectation that some of those states will in the end join the Union.

In comparison with the protective systems with characteristically 'holistic' features, that stress personal duties as well as rights, such as the African Charter or, to a lesser extent, the American Declaration of Human Rights and Duties, the European approach has preserved the stamp of eighteenth-century revolutionary individualism. But unlike its counterpart which struck independent root on the other side of the Atlantic in the same period, Europe, with variations according to country, has never rejected continued action by the state, that is to say the government; while government is admittedly the body against which rights have to be protected, it is also the representative of the will of the people and as such must guarantee that rights and fundamental freedoms are in fact protected.

Beside the technical details concerning one subject area or another, this protection is intended to defend the dignity of a human

adoption of a European Charter on regional or minority languages: (1993) *Revue Générale de Droit International Public* 411 and of a framework convention of the Council of Europe for the protection of national minorities, of 10 November 1994; See Sudre, *Droit international et européen des droits de l'hommeBelgian Linguistics Case (No 2)*, ECHR (1968) Series A, No 6; Cohen-Jonathan, La convention européenne des droits de l'homme (n 66) 518–20.

being, and thus of humanity itself, a term which is a good expression of the twofold dimension of this value: the human in man but also human kind which must, still and forever, be protected from the scourges of tyranny and oppression which, to quote the Preamble to the Universal Declaration, 'have resulted in barbarous acts which have outraged the conscience of humankind'. What is most outrageous, however, is that, 50 years after the Declaration, the 'barbarous acts' and 'untold sorrow' spoken of by the Charter of the United Nations belong, not to our world's vanished past, but to its unhappy present.

Index